Inquiring Organizations:
Moving from Knowledge Management to Wisdom

James F. Courtney
University of Central Florida, USA

John D. Haynes
University of Central Florida, USA

David B. Paradice
Florida State University, USA

IDEA GROUP PUBLISHING
Hershey • London • Melbourne • Singapore

Acquisitions Editor:	Renée Davies
Development Editor:	Kristin Roth
Senior Managing Editor:	Amanda Appicello
Managing Editor:	Jennifer Neidig
Copy Editor:	April Schmidt
Typesetter:	Marko Primorac
Cover Design:	Lisa Tosheff
Printed at:	Integrated Book Technology

Published in the United States of America by
    Idea Group Publishing (an imprint of Idea Group Inc.)
    701 E. Chocolate Avenue, Suite 200
    Hershey PA 17033
    Tel: 717-533-8845
    Fax: 717-533-8661
    E-mail: cust@idea-group.com
    Web site: http://www.idea-group.com

and in the United Kingdom by
    Idea Group Publishing (an imprint of Idea Group Inc.)
    3 Henrietta Street
    Covent Garden
    London WC2E 8LU
    Tel: 44 20 7240 0856
    Fax: 44 20 7379 3313
    Web site: http://www.eurospan.co.uk

Library of Congress Cataloging-in-Publication Data

Inquiring organizations : moving from knowledge management to wisdom / James Courtney, John Haynes and David Paradice, Editors.
    p. cm.
  Includes bibliographical references and index.
  ISBN 1-59140-309-X (hc) -- ISBN 1-59140-310-3 (sc) -- ISBN 1-59140-311-1 (ebook)
  1. Organizational learning. 2. Knowledge management. 3. Knowledge, Theory of. I. Courtney, James F. (James Forrest), 1944- II. Haynes, John D. (John Digby), 1948- III. Paradice, David B.
  HD58.82.I534 2005
  658.4'038'01--dc22

                      2004023591

British Cataloguing in Publication Data
A Cataloguing in Publication record for this book is available from the British Library.

Inquiring Organizations: Moving from Knowledge Management to Wisdom

Table of Contents

Section I: Foundations of Knowledge Media

Chapter I
Dianne J. Hall, Auburn University, USA
David Croasdell, University of Nevada - Reno, USA

Chapter II
Bongsug Chae, Kansas State University, USA
James F. Courtney, University of Central Florida, USA
John D. Haynes, University of Central Florida, USA

Chapter III
Alice Kienholz, Calgary, Canada

Chapter IV
Ahmed Y. Mahfouz, Texas A&M University, USA
David B. Paradice, Florida State University, USA

Foreword

A Dedication to C. West Churchman

It is appropriate that this volume is dedicated in the memory of C. West Churchman who passed away March 21, 2004. He spent his adult life pursuing the questions the present authors raise. His concern for wisdom and knowledge is part of a pragmatic tradition stemming back to William James. James observed that the world we live in and in which we must make our way is enormously complex, nuanced, varied, and continuously changing. In more modern words, our universe is indeterminate, interactive, and interrelated. Alfred North Whitehead, who took his inspiration from James, sums it up: reality itself is ultimately a dynamic process.

Whitehead observed that James discovered a "great truth" when he argued that every finite set of premises is based on notions that are beyond our direct purview. James concluded that morality was an essential component of the universe but that it could not be reduced to simple notions such as "the good" and "the right." Reality for him was just too all encompassing. Those of us who make decisions and act in this world live in a restless uncertain world in which we are forced to make assumptions and then act on them. Consequently, we must have a "will to believe."

Coping with a restless world requires a restless system for creating knowledge and understanding. Edgar A. Singer, one of James's last and most prized students at Harvard, took on as his life's project the development of an epistemology adequate for dealing with the world to which James introduced him. Churchman, whose intellectual thrusts probed deeply into logic and statistics under the tutorage of the renowned logician, Henry Bradford Smith, was captivated by Singer's project. As a student and then a colleague of Singer's at the University of Pennsylvania, he realized that in order to secure improvement in the human condition—a lifelong quest for Churchman—James's worldview and Singer's methodological approach offered the best possibility of success. *The Design of Inquiring Systems* is the culmination of his efforts to bring the project to fruition. The authors of this book seek to push the project further.

The two of us had the rare opportunity and privilege of studying with West as he was embarking on *The Design of Inquiring Systems.* Weekly we met in his sixth floor Barrows Hall office on the U.C. Berkeley campus. The view from his study stretched across the often foggy San Francisco Bay to the Golden Gate and beyond. This served as a background metaphor for the universe as we discussed—nay, actively debated—the works of the great philosophers whose ideas were the grist for his evolving mill of inquiry. Our challenge was clear. We were not pursuing the academic philosophical question "What did the thinker actually say and mean?" Rather, we were probing the texts asking "What insights and guidance can we glean from each thinker's ideas for contemporary inquiry systems?" Churchman's hope was that later inquirers would continue to ask this question and use their answers to develop practical systems, systems that produce wisdom and knowledge for solving society's pressing yet ever changing problems. The present authors are responding to that call.

The papers in this volume are a welcome addition to the literature on information systems. Indeed, they are a radical departure from the vast majority of previous efforts.

They are especially welcome because they take up the challenge of designing systems that are founded on different underlying modes of inquiry, Singerian and Churhmanian Inquiry Systems.

To say that Singerian and Churchmanian systems are underrepresented is putting it kindly. They are virtually nonexistent.

Singer and Churchman are concerned primarily with wisdom, not information. Now, it is certainly not the case that Singer and Churchman have a monopoly on truth or wisdom. Far from it. Rather, they have an important take—a profound insight—on them.

Most inquiries whether in science, the humanities, or everyday life start with certain givens, that is, fundamental taken-for-granted assumptions. These assumptions generally rest in the background where they rarely are raised up to the surface and challenged. In principle, every problem solver starts with the same accepted set of givens.

In contrast, Singer and Churchman are interested in the role of assumptions in the formulation of complex problems. In complex problems, different stakeholders almost never formulate the same issue in the same way. In a word, different stakeholders start with different takens, that is, fundamentally different assumptions about the nature of the world. We do not begin complex inquires with the same starting, or even ending, assumptions.

Singer and Churchman point out that our background assumptions function as moral imperatives. In effect, different disciplines argue, "If you want to be a good member in standing of our club, then you *ought* to look at the world in the ways that we do." While not ordinarily regarded as moral injunctions, they are nonetheless. Just ask those who challenge or violate a profession's or a discipline's ways of looking at the world.

We know of no information system currently in existence that regards our fundamental assumptions as moral takens. For this reason, we do not believe that at the present time we have anything even approaching a *true* information system, but the papers in this volume are a welcome start for they sense the problem even if the goal still eludes us.

Churchman ends his book with a question: "What kind of a world must it be in which inquiry becomes possible?" The question still stands, but readers of this book will be nudged a little closer to an answer.

Richard O. Mason

Carr P. Collins Distinguished Professor, Cox School of Business

Director, Maguire Center for Ethics and Public Responsibility

Southern Methodist University, Dallas, Texas, USA

Ian I. Mitroff

The Harold Quinton Distinguished Professor of Business Policy

The Marshall School of Business

Professor of Journalism, Associate Director

Center for Strategic Public Relations, The Annenberg School for Communication

University of Southern California, Los Angeles, California, USA

President, Comprehensive Crisis Management, Manhattan Beach, CA, USA

Preface

Mason and Mitroff brought Churchman's (1971) inquiring systems into the mainstream of information systems research with their landmark article in *Management Science* in 1973. Yet, today they write in this volume: "To say that Singerian and Churchmanian systems are underrepresented is putting it kindly. They are virtually nonexistent." This book hopes to take at least modest steps toward remedying that deficiency.

Some steps in this direction began with a paper entitled "Inquiring Organizations" presented in the first Philosophical Foundations of IS (PFIS) mini-track at the Americas Conference on Information Systems in 1996 (Courtney, Croasdell & Paradice, 1996). Inquiring organizations are learning organizations that generate knowledge based on one or more of Churchman's inquiring systems. The basic concepts were refined, extended, and presented at a workshop on philosophical aspects of information systems at Wollongong University in Australia in 1998. This paper was published in the *Australian Journal of Information Systems* later that year (Courtney, Croasdell & Paradice, 1998) and republished in the electronic journal *Foundations of Information Systems* also in 1998 (http://www.bauer.uh.edu/parks/fis/fis.htm). These concepts were also extended to knowledge management (Malhotra, 1997), decision support systems (Courtney, 2001), and Perspectival Thinking (Haynes, 2000).

In this book, we emphasize ethical organizational behavior and make a move toward the explication of organizational wisdom (although Chauncey Bell's chapter eloquently disputes organizational wisdom as a possibility). As Churchman (1982) put it in *Thought and Wisdom*, "wisdom is thought combined with a concern for ethics" (p. 9).

Inquiring Systems, Organizations, and IT Support

Churchman defines five inquiring systems based on the epistemologies of Leibniz, Locke, Kant, Hegel and Singer. The five inquirers and organizations and information systems based on them are described briefly below. For a more complete discussion, see the papers cited in the foregoing paragraph. Features of each inquirer and organi-

Table 1. Summary of Inquiring Systems

	Leibniz	Locke	Kant	Hegel	Singer
Input	None	Elementary observations	Some empirical	Some empirical	Units and standards
Given	Built-in axioms	Built-in labels (properties)	Space-time framework Theories	Theories	System of measurement
Process	Formal logic Sentence generator	Assign labels to inputs Communication	Construct models from theories Interpret data Choose best model	Construct theses, antithesis Dialectic	Strategy of agreement Sweeping-in
Output	Fact nets Tautologies Contingent truths	Taxonomy	Fact Nets	Synthesis	New standard Exoteric knowledge Simplistic optimism
Guarantor	Internal consistency	Consensus	Fit between data and model	Objective Observer	Replicability Hegelian over-observer

zation are summarized in Tables 1 and 2, respectively, and supporting information technologies are summarized in Table 3.

The Leibnizian Inquirer

A Leibnizian inquirer is a closed system with a set of built-in elementary axioms that are used along with formal logic to deductively generate more general fact nets or tautologies. The fact nets are created by identifying hypotheses with each new hypothesis being tested to ensure that it could be derived from, and is consistent with, the basic axioms. Once so verified, the hypothesis becomes a new fact within the system. The guarantor of the system is the formal logic used to derive new knowledge and is reflected in the internal consistency and comprehensiveness of the generated facts.

An organizational application of the Leibnizian approach may be observed when the policies, goals, ideas of purpose, and core values, established by the organization's designers, serve as Leibnizian axioms. *Truth* is determined in a procedural manner with a focus on structural or procedural concerns and with error detection and correction being a direct consequence of comparing inputs with the accepted axioms of the system (i.e., organization). The organization's basic theorems, so defined, must be mutually consistent, lending themselves to rote memorization and direct application. Furthermore, new ideas, plans, and visions, (i.e., hypotheses) developed within the organization must be compatible with the existing policies, goals, and core values of the organization. As creative tension is exercised to bring the organization closer to its vision, this test of consistency must be continuously reviewed. Military organizations exhibit these properties.

Despite being closed systems, Leibnizian organizations are still capable of learning by using formal logic to create knowledge. Many expert systems operate with a static set of rules. Interrogation of the system results in suggested course(s) of action for problem resolution. Unlike a database, an expert system can draw upon its rule base to make inferences. Some of these systems learn by updating the knowledge base as new situations are encountered.

The Lockean Inquirer

Inquiring systems based on Lockean reasoning are experimental and consensual. Empirical information, gathered from external observations, is used inductively to build a representation of the world. Elementary observations form the input to the Lockean inquirer, which has a basic set of labels (or properties) that it assigns to the inputs. The Lockean system is also capable of observing its own process by means of reflection and backwards tracing of labels to the most elementary labels. Agreement on the labels by the Lockean community is the guarantor of the system. A community of Lockean inquirers learns by observing the world, sharing observations, categorizing new knowledge into existing labels, and creating a consensus about what has been observed.

The Lockean organization's culture or subculture (a Lockean community) determines the nature of learning and the way in which it occurs. Equivocality refers to the multiple, varied, and conflicting interpretations about an organizational situation. The Lockean inquirer attempts to reduce equivocality by building consensus among team members. Agreement by Lockean communities helps to establish new direction, agreement, and organizational knowledge.

The Lockean organization is able to support both adaptive and generative learning. Lockean systems are open to outside influences and have no built-in preconceptions of the world. These characteristics enhance the firm's generative learning by fostering new ways of looking at the world and preventing rigid adherence to existing standards and ideas. By accepting observational inputs without a biased view, the Lockean organization may see more clearly not only how events occur but also the systems that control the events. This is critical information to facilitate generative learning. The Lockean system, with its ability to observe its own process and trace back any label to the most elementary set of labels, supports this need.

Several technologies have been developed to support consensus building among team members. Information technologies that aid Lockean decision makers include Group Support Systems (GSS), Computer-Supported Cooperative Work (CSCW), the World Wide Web, Computer Networks, and Distributed Databases. These technologies provide mechanisms to bring decision makers together, giving them access to information online to support the decision making process. Some of these systems allow anonymous participation to encourage nonbiased and unencumbered input.

The Kantian Inquirer

The Kantian system is a mixture of the Leibnizian and Lockean approaches in the sense that it contains both theoretical and empirical components. The empirical component is capable of receiving inputs, so the system is open. It generates hypotheses on the

Table 2. Properties of Learning Associated with Churchmanian Inquiry

	Leibniz	Locke	Kant	Hegel	Singer
System	Closed	Open	Open/Closed	Open	Open
Learning Style	Behavioral Single loop	Consensual Generative	Cognitive Generative	Generative Double loop	Generative Double loop
Learning Mechanism	Simple error detection and correction	Reduction of equivocality	Knowledge scan Model matching	Synthesis by objective mediator	Trial and error Agreement and partition
Learning Level	Low	High	Multilevel	High	Multilevel
Learning Framework	Procedural	Strategic Architectural	Procedural Architectural	Architectural	Procedural Strategic
Learning Source	Syntactic	Pragmatic	Pragmatic Semantic	Semantic	Syntactic Pragmatic
Learning Orientation	Normative	Developmental Capability	Developmental Capability	Developmental	Developmental
Developmental Orientation	Apprentice	Specialist Generalist	Specialist Generalist	Renowned	Renowned

basis of inputs received. A clock and kinematic system are used to record the time and space of inputs received.

Perhaps the most unique feature of Kantian systems is that the theoretical component allows an input to be subjected to different interpretations. This occurs because the Kantian theoretical component is comfortable with alternative models of the world (alternative worldviews). Representations and interpretations are based on an *a priori* model of the world, often containing causal connections maintained in models. Translations from one *a priori* view of the world to another are possible, allowing multiple interpretations of the world to be accommodated. The theoretical component contains a model building constituent, which constructs Leibnizian fact nets. It tests the alternatives by determining the best fit for the data, and the guarantor in this approach is the degree of model/data agreement. The use of alternative models permits, for example, one piece of economic data to be interpreted differently by different econometric models (e.g., competing models proposed by different political parties). Additionally, an executive routine turns the Kantian models on and off and can examine their outputs in terms of the degree of satisfaction with their interpretations. Thus, if a model is not producing satisfactory results, it can be turned off, while those which are more successful proceed.

Kantian inquiry acknowledges that inputs received from various knowledge sources may have different interpretations. The Kantian organization is able to use explicit knowledge and implicit knowledge (i.e., hunches, intuition, experience, insights) to consider the many interpretations of inputs. Incoming knowledge is compared to organizational memory allowing the inquirer to consider ways to create and incorporate new knowledge. By considering associations between extant knowledge and new information, the Kantian inquirer establishes new worldviews.

An application of the Kantian approach can be seen in market testing of new advertising campaigns. Different advertisements exploiting different types of cues are often tested to determine which advertising approach generates the best response. Each advertisement alternative provides a different model to be evaluated. Ultimately, one advertisement (or perhaps a few) is selected for general use based on responses from the test subjects. Simultaneously, the company represented in the advertisements and the marketing agency producing the advertisements has an opportunity to learn about the product market. The chapter by Mafouz and Paradice in this volume provides an example of a Kantian retail organization.

Kantian inquiry may be viewed as a method for interpreting inputs to provide direction. In organizations, middle management is responsible for interpreting inputs from upper management and providing direction for lower level organizational members. Middle managers use the resources at their disposal to determine how best to fit tasks into the ongoing operations of the organization. Executive Information Systems, Decision Support Systems, and Group Support Systems that employ organizational models and knowledge sources (e.g., data warehouse, corporate databases, etc.) illustrate ways in which Kantian inquiry could manifest itself in learning organizations. Corporate Intranets and news groups are a rich resource for comparing current issues with past decisions. Paradice's (1987) SmartSLIM system is an application of the Kantian approach.

The Hegelian Inquirer

Hegelian systems function on the premise that greater enlightenment results from the conflict of ideas. The Hegelian dialectic is comprised of three major players. The first player begins the dialectic with a strong conviction about a fundamental thesis. This player or subject, besides holding a strong belief in the thesis, constructs a view of the world in such a way that information, when interpreted through this worldview, maximizes support for the thesis. The second player is an observer of the first subject. The observer generates an opposing conviction to the original thesis. In fact, the observer is "passionately dedicated to destruction of the first subject's conviction" (Churchman, 1971, p. 173). The final player in the Hegelian dialectic is a "bigger" mind and an opposition to the conflict between the thesis and the antithesis. This bigger mind synthesizes a new (larger) view of the world which absorbs the thesis/antithesis conflict. Synthesis generated by the objective bigger mind acts as guarantor of the system. Objectivity is based on a kind of interconnection of observers (Churchman, 1971, p. 149). They promise that "the movement from thesis-antithesis to synthesis is a soaring to greater heights, to self-awareness, more completeness, betterment, progress" (Churchman, 1971, p. 186).

Hegelian organizations rely upon the dialectic to resolve diametrically opposing viewpoints, the thesis and antithesis. In the Hegelian component of an inquiring organization, arbitration is used to evaluate and synthesize contributions from opposing viewpoints resulting in a larger mind which absorbs the thesis/antithesis conflict. Knowledge gained through Hegelian inquiry may result in an entirely new strategic direction for a given organization, as Mason (1969) has shown in his work on dialectical planning systems. Labor negotiations and an adversarial court system, when undertaken in good faith by both parties, provide an example of a strict interpretation of the Hegelian approach.

Hegelian inquiry in organizations has little structure or formal mechanisms to guide it. Group support systems that include negotiating and arbitration elements assist organizations in Hegelian inquiry. Conklin and Begeman (1988) designed gIBIS (graphic Issue Based Information Systems) to facilitate argumentative dialog among stakeholders in order to help them understand the specific elements of each other's proposals. Mason (1969) demonstrates strategic planning as another example of Hegelian inquiry within organizations. Hodges's (1991) Dialectron system can manage the dialog necessary to generate synthesis between problem domains incorporating thesis and antithesis by characterizing the dialectic as two parallel disputations.

The Singerian Inquirer

Two basic premises guide Singerian inquiry (Churchman, 1971, pp. 189-191). The first premise establishes a system of measures that specifies steps to be followed in resolving disagreements among members of a community. Measures can be transformed and compared where appropriate. The measure of performance is the degree to which differences among group member's opinions can be resolved by the measuring system. A key feature of the measuring system is its ability to replicate its results to ensure consistency.

Table 3. Summary of IT Support of Inquiring Organizations

	Leibniz	Locke	Kant	Hegel	Singer
Input	None	Goals, decisions, standards, policies, and procedures	Knowledge Sources Organizational Memory	Mission Statement	Units, Standards
Given	Standards operating procedures Rule base	Organizational history Organizational structure and culture	Tacit & explicit knowledge Working theories	Opposing Views	System of Measures
Process	Cause and effect analysis Inference	Negotiation Communication Consensus building	Knowledge scanning Association building	Arbitration	Sweeping-in variables to overcome inconsistency
Output	Simple error detection and correction Suggested course of action	Equivocality reduction	Integrated, timely knowledge	Conflict resolution Enlarged perspective New strategic direction	New measures Exoteric knowledge
IT Support	Expert systems	WWW Database GSS Networking	WWW Knowledge and model bases EIS, GSS, DSS	GSS Dialectron	Expert systems WWW Objects

The second principle guiding Singerian inquiry is the strategy of agreement (p. 199). Disagreement may occur for various reasons, including the different training and background of observers and inadequate explanatory models. When models fail to explain a phenomenon, new variables and laws are "swept in" to provide guidance and overcome inconsistencies. Yet, disagreement is encouraged in Singerian inquiry. It is through disagreement that worldviews come to be improved. Complacency is avoided by continuously challenging system knowledge.

The Singerian model is thus teleological, yet places great emphasis on ethical behavior. Furthermore, Singerian organizations seek the creation of exoteric (common) knowledge, as opposed to the esoteric knowledge created by the other systems. The papers in this volume place special emphasis on ethical behavior and its relationship to wisdom.

The Singerian organization has the purpose of creating exoteric knowledge for choosing the right means for one's end. Knowledge must be connected to measurable improvements. Measures of performance are judged not only by organizational standards but also by what is good for all of society. A company has to know the kind of value it intends to provide and to whom. Knowledge is generated to be useful for all. In this regard, Singerian organizations model contemporary management trends where employees are empowered to contribute in the decision-making process. Working environments stress cooperation with fuzzy boundaries where teamwork and common goals are primary driving forces. Anyone may act as designer and decision maker.

Applications of Singerian inquiry are evident in standards making bodies, such as IEEE, ISO, and open-source software systems like Linux and Apache. Finally, Singerian organizations keep one eye turned to the needs of society to measure what is possible against what is good for humankind.

Systems and organizations that use metrics practice Singerian inquiry. Accounting systems are perhaps the *sine qua non* of measurement, as every enterprise must have one. However, accounting systems measure only the financial health of the firm. To understand and explain the organization fully, it is necessary to sweep in variables from a wide variety of sources both inside and outside organizational boundaries. Managers in a Singerian organization should develop measurement standards, continuously compare organizational performance to those standards, and modify models of performance as is required to achieve the standards.

Numerous examples of metrics exist in information technology. Telecommunications standards, reuse libraries, code generators, objects, and software metrics all incorporate standards and systems of measurement. The metrics and standards are constantly evolving due to the rapid pace of emerging and improving technologies. Organizations who become complacent can lose in a competitive marketplace. Other organizational elements that fit a model of Singerian inquiry include training offices and marketing departments. Training provides a forum for creating and measuring knowledge necessary for workplace activities. Marketing departments assign and evaluate sales quotas used to measure the success of organizational members. Richardson, Courtney & Paradice (2001) provide two detailed examples of Singerian organizations.

The Internet and World Wide Web serve as resource and dissemination agents for Singerian inquiry. During the sweeping-in process, inquirers are able to use the Web to gather and assimilate information that helps refine variables and reduce inconsistencies in the system of measurement. Once defined, new measures and standards can be posted to the Web and distributed to all interested parties. In this way, the exoteric knowledge goes forward to be useful "for all men in all societies" (Churchman, 1971, p. 200).

Organization of the Book

The book is organized into 16 chapters within four sections. In Section 1, Chapter I by Hall and Croasdell describe each of Churchman's inquirers as a process and how each can be perceived as an organizational form. By combining the forms suited to each inquirer, they show how an integrated organizational form founded on the inquirers can support an entire inquiring organization. Furthermore, they show how this form may be used to facilitate organizational learning and the creation and management of knowledge.

In Chapter II, Chae, Courtney, and Haynes demonstrate how Hegelian inquiring systems may be applied to "wicked" problem situations and knowledge work and how Hegelian inquiring organizations are well suited for the discontinuous environments of the new world of business. This chapter is based upon a multiple perspective pluralistic approach.

In Chapter III by Kienholz, Singerian Inquiring Organizations are further developed as the most appropriate type of inquiring organization for moving from knowledge management to wisdom by elaborating on the original knowledge management concepts and framework proposed by Croasdell, Courtney, and Paradice (1998). Finally in Chapter IV, Mafouz and Paradice discuss the Kantian inquiring system and apply it to an organization in the retail industry—Walmart.

 In Section 2, Chapter V by Lichtenstein, Parker, and Cybulski argues that the real promise of organizational communication technologies may lie in their potential to facilitate participative discourse between knowledge workers at all levels in distributed locations and time zones. Their chapter presents a case study of a Singerian Inquiring Organization which illustrates how a fluid dynamic community of employees can use e-mail to build knowledge, learn, make decisions, and enhance wisdom through a cycle of knowledge combination (divergence) and knowledge qualification (convergence).

Chapter VI by Hall and Guo examines the issue of technological support for inquiring organizations and suggests that the complexity of these organizations is best supported by agent technology. Accordingly, a multiagent system to support inquiring organizations is introduced.

In Chapter VII, Murray, Case, and Gardiner observe that many modern organizations have attempted to create knowledge by using technologies such as Data Mining and Knowledge Discovery in Databases (KDD). Although quite powerful, these technologies depend heavily on the skill and insights of the analyst. They propose that the role of the analyst in the application of these technologies is poorly understood. To advance our understanding in this regard, they dedicate the first part of this chapter to describing the KDD process and relate it to the five philosophical perspectives of organizational knowledge acquisition, as originally discussed by Churchman (1971). In the second part of the chapter, they draw parallels between the process of knowledge acquisition via KDD with the concept of information foraging (Pirolli & Card, 1999).

Lastly for Section 2, Chapter VIII by Lundin and Vendelø examines one of the oldest themes in information systems research: the relationship between developers and users of information systems. They suggest that the problematic developer-user dynamic can be addressed by introducing an inquiring practice approach to information systems development. Consequently, this chapter conceptualizes a new way of understanding information systems development through the lenses of inquiring practice, Socratic dialogue, and the uncovering of exformation.

Chapter IX in Section 3 by Mason defines epistemological myopia as a kind of near-sightedness that limits what and how the organization knows and how it learns. For the underlying theme of the organization as an inquiring system, he draws from four distinct areas of study and develops ways of overcoming myopia: systems theory, organizational knowledge and learning, the organization as a learning community and community of practice, and linguistic relativity. The potential solutions to epistemological myopia include deliberate nurturing of cultural diversity, the institutionalization of Singerian approaches to inquiry, and the fostering of managed risk in experiments that do not guarantee success.

In Chapter X, Haynes articulates that Tacit Knowing critically contributes to the sustainable growth and future direction of an organization through its connection with (1) intuition (2) holism, and (3) ethics. As an example of Tacit Knowing, particularly in terms of ethics and intuition, a sixth Inquiring System is proposed, namely, a Heideggerian Inquiring Organization.

In Chapter XI, Fielden argues that mindfulness is an essential quality of integrated wisdom within inquiring organizations. A holistic, rather than a scientific, view of knowledge is adopted. The discussion is also underpinned by a pragmatic approach that incorporates rational, emotional, psychological, and spiritual perspectives. She provides a plan for developing mindfulness within organizations, which is described including consideration of multilayered development and ordered, unordered, and disordered organizational arenas.

For Chapter XII, Bell explores the ways that wisdom and wise action appear in the work of organizations and asks how systems can be designed to support that. Building on Churchman's thought experiment with five philosophers about how to improve the design of systems, the author asks and brings fresh answers to the questions, "What is wisdom?" and "What is wisdom in organizations?"

Finally in Chapter XIII, Wickramasinghe considers knowledge a compound construct, exhibiting many manifestations of the phenomenon of duality such as subjectivity and objectivity as well as having tacit and explicit forms. Her thesis is that a full appreciation of the phenomenon of duality is necessary to enable inquiring organizations to reach the state of wisdom and enlightenment.

In Section 4, Hermeneutics, Transformations, and Abstractions, Chapter XIV by Dickey and Paradice uses cultural hermeneutics as a lens for understanding philosophies of inquiry in distributed work groups. The authors suggest that philosophies of inquiry can be ascertained through hermeneutic analysis of written texts created by distributed workers using computer-mediated communication systems.

In Chapter XV, Warne, Hasan, and Ali examine social learning at the Australian Defence Organisation (ADO). They identify factors that enable knowledge generation and transfer in organizations and contribute to the creation of an organizational culture that supports continuous learning. The chapter concludes with a description and suggested application of the Cynefin Model which offers a pragmatic and conceptual alternative to the orthodoxy of scientific management.

Finally in Chapter XVI, Kilov and Sack show how crucial aspects of organizational knowledge and organizational inquiry can be exactified using a relatively small number of abstract concepts common to various areas of human endeavor such as (exact) philosophy, business management, science, and technology. Exactification is achieved, first and foremost, by creating and using ontologies—business and organizational domain models with precisely defined semantics.

In summary, we believe that the chapters offered in this book constitute considerable coverage of the issues that underlie and parameters that extend Inquiring Organizations as inspired by C. West Churchman's work. It is our fervent hope that these 16 chapters provide a sufficiently broad theoretical foundation and, consequently, a solid enough *springboard* for future researchers and practitioners to pursue and to develop in their own *local colors*.

James F. Courtney, Orlando, Florida, USA

John D. Haynes, Orlando, Florida, USA

David B. Paradice, Tallahassee, Florida, USA

June 1, 2004

References

Churchman, C. W. (1971). *The design of inquiring systems: Basic concepts of systems and organization.* Basic Books.

Churchman, C. W. (1982). *Thought and wisdom.* Intersystems Publishers.

Conklin, J., & Begeman, M. L. (1988). gIBIS: A hypertext tool for exploratory policy discussion. *ACM Transactions on Office Information Systems, 6*(4), 303-331.

Courtney, J. F. (2001). Decision making and knowledge management in inquiring organizations: Toward a new decision-making paradigm for DSS. *Decision Support Systems, 31*(1), 17-38.

Courtney, J. F., Croasdell, D. T., & Paradice, D. B. (1996, August). Inquiring organizations. *Proceedings of the Americas Conference on Information Systems* (pp. 443-445). Phoenix, Arizona.

Courtney, J. F., Croasdell, D. T., & Paradice, D. B. (1998). Inquiring organizations. *Australian Journal of Information Systems, 6*(1), 3-15. Reprinted in *Foundations of Information Systems: Towards a Philosophy of Information Technology.* Retrieved September 1, 2004, from *http://www.mis.fsu.edu/philosophy/pfis/*

Haynes, J. D. (2000). *Perspectival thinking: For inquiring organisations.* New Zealand: ThisOne and Company.

Hodges, W. S. (1991). *Dialectron: A prototypical dialectic engine for the support of strategic planning and strategic decision making.* Unpublished doctoral dissertation, Texas A&M University.

Malhotra, Y. (1997). Knowledge management in inquiring organizations. *Proceedings of the Third Americas Conference on Information Systems*, 293-295.

Mason, R. O. (1969). A dialectical approach to strategic planning. *Management Science, 15,* B403-B414.

Mason, R. O. & Mitroff, I. I. (1973). A program for research in management information systems. *Management Science, 19*(5), 475-485.

Paradice, D. B., & Courtney, J. F. (1987). Causal and non-causal relationships and dynamic model construction in a managerial advisory system. *Special Issue of the Journal of Management Information Systems on Knowledge-Based Decision Support Systems, 3*(4), 19-53.

Richardson, S. M., Courtney, J. F., & Paradice, D. B. (2001). An assessment of the Singerian approach to organizational learning: Cases from academia and the utility industry. *Special Issue of Information Systems Frontiers on Philosophical Reasoning in Information Systems Research, 3*(1), 49-62.

Acknowledgments

First and foremost, the editors would like to acknowledge C. West Churchman to whom this book is dedicated. Indeed, without his lifelong effort to understand whether human beings have the wisdom to improve the human condition in a self-fulfilling and ethical way, this book would never have come into being. His many publications in that regard, particularly *Challenge to Reason, The Systems Approach and Its Enemies, Thought and Wisdom,* and most importantly, *The Design of Inquiring Systems,* have inspired us, the authors represented in this volume, and many others to explore Churchman's vital and enduring question.

We are also indebted to Richard Mason and Ian Mitroff for their inspirational Forward for this book. As Churchman's students, they have been the primary carriers of the inquiring systems torch for over 30 years. We hope that their comments will spark continuing interest in serious scholarly investigation into ethical and moral ways that humans can improve life on the planet for all living things.

We wish to thank all of the authors for their insights and excellent contributions to this book and to thank all who participated in the reviewing process. We believe that, in every case, the original chapters were improved significantly as a result of thoughtful, reflective, and constructive suggestions from the reviewers.

Special thanks also go to the publishing team at Idea Group Inc., in particular to Michele Rossi and Jan Travers, who continuously prodded us via e-mail and telephone to keep the project on schedule. Thanks also to Jennifer Sundstrom, who was responsible for preparing the marketing materials for the book and to Mehdi Khosrow-Pour, whose enthusiasm for this project ultimately led to the successful development of this volume.

In closing, we sincerely hope that the work represented in this book provides a step forward toward inspiring others to help foster and reflect upon a world in which inquiry, as an ongoing and unfolding process, in the tradition established by Churchman and extended into *Inquiring Organizations,* becomes possible.

James F. Courtney, Orlando, Florida, USA

John D. Haynes, Orlando, Florida, USA

David B. Paradice, Tallahassee, Florida, USA

June 1, 2004

Section I:

Foundations of Knowledge Media

Chapter I

Inquiring Organizations:
An Organizational Form Perspective

Dianne J. Hall
Auburn University, USA

David Croasdell
University of Nevada - Reno, USA

Abstract

This chapter describes each of Churchman's inquirers as a process and how each can be perceived as an organizational form. By combining the forms suited to each inquirer, we show how an integrated organizational form founded on the inquirers can support an entire inquiring organization and how this form may be used to facilitate organizational learning and the creation and management of knowledge. We have laid the foundation of organizational form perspective for researchers and believe this foundation will enable researchers to investigate organizational learning, knowledge management, and communication processes within the complexity of inquiring organizations.

Introduction

In order to manage knowledge and operate successfully in today's information intensive business environments, various organizational forms have emerged. The form that an organization takes has consequences for communication and dissemination of information and thereby the ability to engage in organizational learning. Some of these forms compress knowledge at the root level of the organization, while others facilitate the search for useful knowledge within the organization. Still other forms are capable of supporting organizational members in their quest to synthesize knowledge from diverse sources. By recognizing the importance of knowledge, organizations shift from industry-based strategy to the resource-based theory of the firm (Burns & Stalker, 1961). This strategy depicts a firm as being solely responsible for its own deeds and, therefore, performance. When a firm reconfirms that knowledge management and core competencies are at the heart of organizational performance, they also recognize the need to further develop core competencies and to create and manage knowledge. Organizations striving to move toward a learning orientation but maintain flexibility in the face of complexity may do well to consider the practices of inquiring organizations.

Combining contingency theory, the work of Lawrence and Lorsch (1967), and the definition of an inquiring organization, we maintain that:

1.   Both inquiry and organizational form are critical to a given context or environment.

2.   These contexts or environments differ throughout an organization and its units.

3.   They may change abruptly.

4.   An organization is most effective when applying different inquiry processes and different organizational forms as appropriate for the task at hand.

We therefore assert an inquiring organization as a complex structure of multiple organizational forms working together for the benefit of the organization. This chapter describes how each inquirer is a process built as an organizational form and how the forms, when integrated, provide support for the entire inquiring organization.

The following sections discuss inquiring organizations, organizational learning, organizational form, and the effect form can have on the learning environment of an organization. The inquiring systems described by Churchman (1971) and later framed and modeled as inquiring organizations and knowledge systems (Courtney, Croasdell & Paradice, 1998; Hall & Paradice, 2003; Hall, Paradice & Courtney, 2003) are described in the context of knowledge creation and its management, which provides the foundation for organizational learning and decision-making. Practices of individual archetypical forms are then integrated to present a holistic view of inquiring organizations incorporating multiple perspectives.

Conceptual Foundations of Inquiring Organizations

An inquiring organization (Courtney et al., 1998) is a learning-oriented organization that strives to include both creation and management of knowledge in its cache of core competencies. Churchman's (1971) discourse of knowledge creation and inquiring systems forms the philosophical foundations of an inquiring organization. The view-points of selected Western philosophers (Leibniz, Locke, Kant, Hegel, and Singer) are particularly suited to knowledge creation and knowledge management. The methods of inquiry serve to differentiate inquiring organizations from other learning organizations. Each of the inquirers discussed by Churchman (1971) has specific strengths that allow it to operate efficiently in specific contexts; together the inquirers have the ability to handle the complexity and the chaotic environment in which many modern organizations operate. Each of the inquirers is suited to a particular organizational form. For instance, the Leibnizian inquirer is suited to a hierarchical form where knowledge is pushed throughout the organization. Lockean inquiry is more suited to a network form where information is pulled into the network; knowledge is created specifically for that network's context.

Inquirers in the Churchmanian tradition embody different organizational forms from mechanistic (Leibnizian) to adhocracy (Singerian), but integration allows these forms to work together (homeostasis) to survive against the elements and, in doing so, support the characteristics of an inquiring organization. By considering inquiring organizations from both holistic and stratified perspectives, we provide additional perspectives for considering the utilization of inquiry in organizational decision-making.

Organizational Learning

To understand how Churchman's (1971) inquirers can be used to support organizational inquiry, it is useful to have a fundamental understanding of organizational learning and relevant mechanisms that assist the learning process. This section presents organizational learning concepts and organizational substructures that foster and enhance creativity, innovation, and learning.

Corporate epistemology is the theory of how and why organizations know (von Krogh, 1998). Learning is not focused on attaining a *right knowledge* but at least three coexisting pieces of knowledge: syntactic knowledge, pragmatic knowledge, and semantic knowledge. Syntactic knowledge pertains to grammar or structure. Pragmatic knowledge relates to the situated context within which learning takes place. Semantic knowledge refers to the meaning of words and symbols. The contest between different elements of knowledge continuously increases the complexity of total knowledge conveyed (von Krogh, 1998).

An organization's knowledge comes in part from the organization's employees. "Individuals have private knowledge that can be a basis for organizational knowledge. ... Knowledge of the organization is shared knowledge among organizational members" (von Krogh, 1998, p. 59). Individuals have private knowledge that can be an advantage for organizations and knowledge from various sources contributes to meaning (White, 1990). Ultimately, knowledge is the assimilation and utilization of some kind of integrated learning system to support *actionable learning* (Nevis, DiBella & Gould, 1995). Creation and maintenance of a corporate knowledge base allows core competencies to be developed and shared, further allowing actions that result in incremental or transformational change. One can see that there is a reciprocal relationship between knowledge management and organizational learning and that both must receive attention if the organization is to move toward inquiry.

Learning facilitates behavior change that leads to improved performance (Fiol & Lyles, 1985; Garvin, 1993; Senge, 1990). Learning occurs by improving actions through better knowledge and understanding (Fiol & Lyles, 1985), encoding inferences from history into routines that guide behavior (Levitt & March, 1988), and developing insights, knowledge, and associations between past actions, the effectiveness of those actions, and future actions (Fiol & Lyles, 1985). Discovery and affirmation (DiBella, 1995) may encourage learners to employ trial and error experimentation or search mechanisms to gain new knowledge. However, Mayhew (1992) maintains structure and organization are necessary for effective learning. Walsh and Ungson (1991) maintain that cultivating and expressly maintaining memory increases learning.

White (1990) emphasizes that knowledge from various sources contributes to meaning. Learning is considered to be low-level when a given set of rules is followed producing consequences for a particular behavior (Argyris & Schön, 1996). It is a result of repetition and routines and involves association building. Single-loop learning maintains central features or sets of rules. Learning at low levels is restricted to simple error detection and correction. High-level learning is more consistent with double-loop learning in that its purpose is to adjust rules and norms. The desired consequence is the development of frames of reference and interpretive schemes of cognitive frameworks. High-level learning develops an understanding of causation. Multilevel learning mixes elements of low-level and high-level learning. Multilevel learning occurs when frequently used procedures and specific rules are utilized to develop competency and understanding (Levitt & March, 1988). Multilevel learning produces increasing returns to experience via the persistent use of procedures or technologies; however, multilevel learning is susceptible to competency traps whereby superior procedures are ignored once an inferior procedure or technology is learned and used repeatedly. Abstract learning focuses on the learning process itself, thus enhancing the effects of multilevel learning, consistent with triple-loop learning.

Organizational learning is the development of new knowledge and insights that have the potential to influence behavior (Fiol & Lyles, 1985; Huber, 1991; Slater & Narver, 1995). Shanks and Olson (1995) describe a framework for organizational learning that produces results at three levels: procedural, which engenders continuous incremental improvement; architectural, which attempts to change how work is done; and strategic, which represents change in or reinvention of the business. When members of an organization share associations, cognitive systems, and memories, organizational learning is taking place. Organizational learning relies on individuals and groups as agents for knowledge transfer. Over time, what is learned is built into the structure, culture, and memory of the organization. Lessons (knowledge) remain within the organization even though individuals may change. Shanks and Olson (1995) theorize that organizational learning improves performance, enhances value, and creates new beginnings. They argue that well-designed learning programs improve mental models, facilitate effective analysis, forge commitment, and open senses to the real world.

Another view considers developmental learning as movement from rote memorization to understanding of concepts, integration of ideas, and synthesis of new ideas. A capability perspective posits that there is no one best way for organizations to learn (DiBella & Nevis, 1998). According to this perspective, learning processes are embedded in organizational structure and culture. As new models are presented to the system, it considers where they fit and revises its worldview accordingly. It is this learning perspective that exemplifies the inquiring organization and triple-loop learning and for which a comprehensive flexible organizational form is paramount.

Organizational Form

In a discussion of traditional organizational form, one must consider the environment in which the organization or organizational unit operates, the complexity of its tasks, its size, and its operational strategy. Complexity (height and width of the organization), standardization, and decision-making location are based on the factors that determine structure type. Rarely can one organization be represented in any one fashion. Indeed, contingency theory and the work of Lawrence and Lorsch (1967) indicate that an organization must be aware of its environment and its task and must structure itself and its units appropriately.

Organizations struggling to find ways to manage knowledge in turbulent environments could consider organizational structure and form as a means to create and manage organizational knowledge. Organizational units can and should develop different forms according to their needs, but integration of all forms is crucial to maintenance of the organization. In considering how and where inquiring organizations use various methods of inquiry, it is useful to consider a variety of organizational forms.

An organization's structure is largely determined by the variety of its environment (Mintzberg, 1992). Both environmental complexity and pace of change determine environmental variety. Mintzberg identifies four types of organizational form, which are associated with four combinations of complexity and change. Simple and stable organizations are considered *Machine Bureaucracies* with standardized work processes and outputs. Typically, technocrats standardize procedures and outputs. More complex organizations that are relatively stable with regard to change are considered *Professional Organizations*. These organizations are characterized by standardized skills and norms. Professionals rely on roles and skills learned from years of schooling and indoctrination to coordinate their work. A *divisional bureaucracy* is a combination of machine bureaucracies, each of which has a particular task such as production of a specific product. As with the first two forms, this form is also suited to relatively stable environments. Organizations that are more dynamic take the form of *Entrepreneurial Startups* or *Adhocracies.* The more simple form of entrepreneurship is characterized by direct supervision where managers directly supervise the work of subordinates. Adhocracies are more complex and require mutual adjustment of ad hoc teams. Teams of professionals from the operating core, support staff, and technostructure rely on informal *mutual adjustment* to coordinate their efforts. In administrative adhocracies, low-level operations maybe totally automated.

Other classical thought on the systematic body of knowledge of organizational structure distinguishes between three types of organizations: line organizations, functional organizations, and line-staff organizations. Line organizations are characterized by a hierarchy and divisions based on control and direction. Functional organizations are based on the idea that the main division of production should be determined by a systematic analysis of the work to be done. In this organizational form, workers are subjected to matrix management practices whereby they receive orders from a group of supervisors--each responsible for a specific function. Line-staff organizations are a middle ground between line organizations and functional organizations. They provide a means of utilizing special skills while maintaining a hierarchy of line authority. In this form, functional departments work through a line supervisor.

Burns and Stalker (1961) classify organizations as either mechanistic or organic systems. Mechanistic organizations are characterized by "a rigid breakdown into functional specializations, precise delineation of duties, responsibilities and powers and a well-developed command hierarchy through which information filters up and down and decisions and instructions flow down" (Burns & Stalker, 1961, p. 23). This form is most appropriate for stable organizations. Organic systems are more adaptable. Jobs that lose formal definition and communication up and down the hierarchy are more in the nature of consultation. The form flattens hierarchies and empowers organizational members through more permissive and participative management practices. Inherent in either type of organizational form is the span of control produced by the organizational structure. Mechanistic organizations have a narrow view that is more inclined to consider individuals, groups, or functional units. Organic organizations use a broad perspective that considers the organization as a whole.

The organizational form and relevant dimensions described above help set the stage for considering inquiring organizations as complex structures of different organizational forms. The next sections provide descriptions of each of the five Churchmanian archetypes in the language of organizational form and organizational metaphor (Morgan, 1997).

The Leibnizian Form

The Leibnizian inquirer is the most basic of the inquirers and provides the inquiring organization with its initial set of facts and axioms that comprise the foundation of organizational memory. This inquirer is considered a closed system; that is, it functions within a limited set of relationships. Learning that is attributed to the Leibnizian inquirer is primarily based in the theory of autopoiesis which is the ability to self-perpetuate and produce through a series of relationships in a closed, stable environment. Organizations or organizational units that exist in an environment of stability and routine do well to adopt the Leibnizian inquirer as their organizational form.

This inquirer, with its basis in accuracy and deduction, epitomizes the metaphor of an organization as a machine (Morgan, 1997). The Leibnizian inquirer is founded on formal rules and heuristics regarding interpretation of information based only on what it knows (its fact net and axioms); the mechanistic organization is autocratic, formal, and hierarchical. To be efficient, these organizational forms must be able to rely on a network of formalized rules and heuristics; innovation is not a reasonable task in this environment. Decision-making and learning exist in the highest levels of a mechanistic organization (a bureaucracy may be slightly more decentralized but is still represented as having hierarchical control); this promotes the reliability, predictability, and replicability needed in this environment. Problem structure is important in this system; highly structured problems with few unknown variables are required.

An organizational environment that is task-based and routinized fits within this form. For instance, the fast food industry has virtually mastered the art of routine assembly and consistent product. Little, if any, learning needs to take place at the bottom levels within the hierarchy. A new fry cook is able to function almost immediately simply by following the well-articulated systematic instructions that are set forth by the organization. No assimilation of information or transfer of tacit knowledge is required. Contrast that with a chef's apprentice, who learns by watching the master chef at work and by experimenting with recipes. While some rules may exist, most of what makes a master chef an expert is the ability to function without rules to create new dishes.

The structured Leibnizian environment requires adherence to rules and regulations; learning within the organization is a push rather than pull process. Learning occurs at the top of the organization and is pushed downward throughout the organization by processes such as demonstration workshops. Because of the explicit nature of information being passed downward throughout the organization, teaching is not generally a necessary means of information dissemination; the printed rules and handbooks of the organization serve the function well.

However, when information that is more precise or knowledge is required, particularly process knowledge, there are extant learning technologies available to facilitate it. For instance, expert knowledge systems perpetuate experiential knowledge in an explicit form through the organization. Likewise, computer-based training (CBT), Web-based learning, and virtual classrooms all serve the purpose of providing structured learning in a mechanistic environment.

Like all organizational forms, even this most basic (and perhaps oldest) form has both strengths and weaknesses. Its strengths are its ability to focus on reliability and replication. Growing organizational memory through expanding fact nets based on axioms serves to provide the organization with reliable accurate memory on which to function. However, this form fails to recognize the importance of changes in the external environment; failure to do so leads to difficulty in adapting as well as an attitude that the environment simply exists and is nonconsequential. This type of environment can also be difficult to maintain when the human *cogs* become noncompliant or when individual goals become stronger than organizational goals. Further, this form is most efficient in a stable environment.

While the Leibnizian form can be effective in stable environments, less stable environments require forms that are more open to the environment and are more socially aware. Organizations viewed as *culture* represent organizational forms that are more suited to a social environment but still seek relative environmental stability (Morgan, 1997). The Lockean archetype is appropriate for the organization as culture metaphor.

The Lockean Form

The Lockean inquirer is a well-suited system for a relatively stable but highly social environment. This inquirer is founded on principles of agreement embedded in classification of observations. The Lockean inquirer's members share a common belief and vision, culminating in shared mental models of the organization's environment, tasks, and strategies. Learning is a group effort and does not occur without consensus. Thus, relationships and communication are integral facets of this inquirer.

This organizational form is built around the pattern of development of the beliefs, practices, and rituals of everyday organizational life. As a culture, an organization immerses its members into a society of self-perpetuated myths and legends, encouraging each member to mold into the culture in a way that promotes shared mental models and organizational visions. Often the rituals that lead to a synthesis of mind are not visible to those outside the organization; they may take place as formalized rituals (team-building weekend retreats) or informal indoctrination (storytelling). The passing on and perpetuation of the culture, however, is critical to forming the shared mental models that allow the Lockean culture-based organization to be efficient. Sharing a worldview and reaching consensus are requirements for this form. As such, both problem structure and size are important considerations for determining when this form is appropriate. Organizations or organizational units that are small are better able to provide the collaborative atmosphere that is necessary; problems that are relatively structured, affected by their environment, and for which a consensus may be reached are necessary.

For example, the retail industry must remain in constant contact with its environment to sense when trends and fads are entering or exiting the marketplace. Although the basic organizational goal remains unchanged (that is, sales), the items to be sold, and the environment in which they are sold, may change. The rules and heuristics that are effective in a mechanistic organizational form fail to work because, although they may serve as guidelines, each salesperson must interpret the environment (an individual customer) and react accordingly. Thus, hard and fast rules are inappropriate. However, consensus must be met as to how, for instance, the salesperson will address the customer (consistency) or what level of help to offer and at what point. Different cultures may exist throughout one store. For instance, there is likely to be a different type of salesperson and environment for high-end merchandise (appliances) than in a department that has more frequent inventory turnover (casual wear).

The learning here is then both a push process (guidelines) and an assimilation process (the collective observation of senior sales personnel). Rather than demonstrate the techniques, formal teaching is likely to involve storytelling by top producers, combined with tried and true heuristics generated by those experts to react to specific situations, such as an irate customer. The new salesperson will strive to assimilate actions and processes that are observed to have favorable outcomes for senior sales personnel. This pull process is encouraged through the informal indoctrination process and by extrinsic motivation factors such as commission percentages.

Extant technologies to facilitate the type of learning that exists in a culturally-based organization may include the same as those for the mechanistic organization if the information is pushed and explicit. However, they would generally take the form of a more collaborative style that supports the collaborative nature of this organizational form. Learning networks and systems that exemplify group work are particularly appropriate.

Learning networks are structures that allow organizations to establish guidance in a way that emphasizes both the organization's need for employee instruction and the employee's desires for personal development. The theory combines social constructivism with the network perspective on organization (van der Krogt, 1998) to provide structure to the process of using existing organizational knowledge, combined with naturally occurring social interaction and communication to facilitate organizational learning irrespective of organizational culture or structure.

Learning networks often develop spontaneously and tend to be task or context oriented. Trainers facilitate learning by perpetuating the culture that guides the learning process. Whether the trainers are informal members of the network or formal organizational trainers depends on the organizational structure. In an organization that emphasizes culture, the trainer would most likely be an individual with informal authority and respect as well as a long-standing member of the organization.

The organization as a culture has benefits over the organization as a machine. For instance, it is tied to the environment and therefore more adaptable. Although still somewhat tied to stability and structure, the organization is more able to react to environmental changes. Unlike the mechanistic metaphor, the organization as a culture fully understands the social process of organizing as cocreation of both the organization and of the environment. Adaptability is enhanced through attention to symbolic references. In the Lockean organizational form, symbolic references are myths and legends that become classified observations enabling culture to be perpetuated and newcomers to be quickly indoctrinated. Lastly, this organizational form understands that change must be precipitated by a change in culture for it to be successful.

Like other organizational forms, the Lockean form has shortcomings. Culture in and of itself is difficult to discern and may be an integration of subcultures—some conducive to the organization and others subversive. Because of the importance of cultural artifacts, this form is sometimes reduced (very mechanistically) to the artifacts themselves rather than the process through which they were developed. For example, if employees do not read a book of narratives about the organization, the culture may fail to perpetuate. However, when those same narratives are passed down from old-timers to newcomers they generate the loyalty, shared models, and collaborative environment in which the Lockean inquirer thrives.

Both the Leibnizian (machine) and the Lockean (culture) inquirers are simple forms and independent of each other as described by Churchman (1971). Environments that are more complex require an organizational form that can recognize the need for rational and accurate information while remaining flexible and open to stimulus from the environment. Kantian inquiry provides such a form.

The Kantian Form

The Kantian inquirer is designed to incorporate both multiple perspectives and facts to determine models that are appropriate for the situation. Using Leibnizian fact nets to support its data analysis, this inquirer performs modeling techniques to detect causal connections between perspectives. After a model is chosen as being most appropriate for the particular context through a process known as best-fit analysis, the Kantian inquirer performs an analysis to determine whether that model continues to produce satisfying results; when a model fails to satisfy, it is removed from consideration. Learning in this inquirer is a combination of theoretical and empirical analysis. This form is most suitable in environments where there is some structure and some ability to formally analyze data but where a clear solution may not be evident or possible.

The Kantian inquirer incorporates multiple perspectives and an analytic process to create knowledge; it is sensitive to the environment and attempts to apply the best-fit answer to a problem. An organizational metaphor that supports these endeavors is that of the organization as an organism (Morgan, 1997). This form is frequently considered the antithesis of the mechanistic organization because it emphasizes environmental input and because it adapts readily to changes. Because of its fluidity, this form may contain temporary and informal structures (such as adhocracies) or more defined structures that can be disassembled and reassembled as necessary (such as a matrix). It should also be noted that this form is an overarching one—fluidity can also be seen in the political and brain metaphors discussed subsequently.

The organism organizational form must be able to maintain several levels of complexity, understand relationships between structure, specialization, and integration and apply this relationship knowledge to redirect the form as needed. These practices form the foundations of contingency theory and of Churchman's (1971) Kantian inquirer. The inquirer contains levels of complexity (fact nets, best-fit analyzer, and executor), has the ability to act analytically (structural) as well as theoretically (integration), and recognizes various perspectives (specialization). This approach supports an evolutionary (i.e., organic) perspective because its intent is to find the best way to fit the model to the data and carry out necessary actions.

This form depends on communication, organizational memory, and an understanding of culture to perform its modeling duties. It is still dependent on the stability of rules and regulations but is able to apply those to moderately uncertain situations. It is best suited for environments of moderate instability and problems of high-to-moderate structure. Organizations representing many perspectives (disciplines or organizational units) function well with this form. An organizational unit charged with new product decisions provides one example. Here, as in the cultural organization, learning takes place within the unit, but unlike the cultural organization, consensus is not a requirement. This organism believes in survival of the fittest—that is, following models with the best fit to the data.

Learning that occurs here is disseminated through the organization via the group members--the nature of the knowledge will affect whether formal or informal teaching applies. Learning may take place in the explicit form (a change in a process, for instance) that would likely be disseminated through a push process as well as being represented in the organization's memory (fact net). A new goal, mission, or cultural change may be disseminated less formally through narrative indoctrination.

Growth of organizational memory may be enhanced in this organizational form by the use of a system designed to discover and distribute information, particularly from the external environment. Organizational memory may then be used within the organization to facilitate knowledge creation and decision making. An example of a system designed to perform these duties on some level is Knowledge Cache (Elofson & Konsynski, 1991). The system can automatically assimilate the area specialist's knowledge and organize it by classes or categories (this feature also fits the cultural organizational form). Based in agent technology, the system uses machine-learning algorithms and models input by experts to analyze incoming information and add information and/or models to organizational memory. Another example of a similar technology is living design memory (Terveen, Selfridge & Long, 1995), originally designed to facilitate the software design domain.

The benefits of the organism organizational form include its sensitivity to the environment, flexibility, its focus on relationships, and its support for organizational development through contingency theory and the best fit between itself and its environment. When an organization has emphasis in these areas, it is better able to react quickly and effectively to changes. There are also, of course, weaknesses in this form. The very form itself is fragile when compared to a mechanistic form; while a biological organism is tangible, an organization is not and its social construction makes it even less distinct and difficult to interpret. It is also somewhat misleading to maintain that the organization reacts to its environment—in a true sense it enacts it (Weick, 1979) and thus has some control over it.

The flexibility and sensitivity of the organization as an organism make it a functional organizational form metaphor for organizations with moderate structure and in a moderately stable environment. However, many organizations find themselves embroiled in conflict and power struggles, both internally and externally. A different form is necessary when these elements are present. Fluid and flexible like the organism metaphor, the organization as a political system metaphor provides the support for organizational strife.

The Hegelian Form

The Hegelian inquirer is one of the most complex of Churchman's (1971) inquirers. At its foundation are opposing Leibnizian fact nets that contain the thesis and antithesis perspectives of the question under consideration. Each of these perspectives is examined for its underlying assumptions; these are then paired (one from each side) and examined together by the over-observer. As each pair is examined, the assumption with the most applicability to the situation at hand is synthesized into a new perspective that draws on the strength of each of the underlying perspectives. Communication is critical in this form where learning occurs during the synthesis process and a greater understanding of the context is obtained.

This dialectic is useful in organizations or organizational units where conflict is frequent and the environment is complex and uncertain, perhaps *wicked* (Rittel & Webber, 1973). Because conflict is not only present but is essential to the critical reflection of the synthesis process, this organizational form is reflected in the organization as a political system metaphor (Morgan, 1997). In this form, conflict, power, and the interests of stakeholders surface; these opposing forces are what ultimately holds the system in place and what affords the Hegelian inquirer with its win-win synthesis process. Political organizational forms acknowledge the importance of information and decision-making; they strive to keep communication channels open for both information flow and decision-making input. While similar to an organism in that informal structure and teams may be prevalent, the political organization is based in conflict and power rather than consensus.

Because of the emphasis on communication, political organizations may manifest themselves as more modern organizational structures, such as hubs or adhocracies. Hubs are organizational forms in which each member has a valued opinion (thesis or antithesis) and participates in the decision-making process. An adhocracy is an informal form with little structure where the creative abrasion of the Hegelian process is used to support innovation and other creative processes. For example, an organization in a high-risk industry, or one in a fledgling industry, will be served by the creative processes of an adhocracy. As the organization moves forward, or positions itself more solidly within the industry, other forms may be required along with, or instead of, such informal structures.

Learning in political organizations is the outcome of the dialectic. Lessons are disseminated throughout the form itself by communication among the members. Little formal teaching or observing is required because members of these organizations are active in the learning process; an exception would be when this form interacts with other forms at which point the teaching process would be in place according to the receiving form (for instance, formal workshops for the mechanistic form).

With its basis in conflict and negotiation, an appropriate extant technology to support this organizational form is Issue-Based Information Systems (IBIS) (Kunz & Rittel, 1970). This framework has been used in many negotiation support systems that can facilitate and formalize dialectic dialogue among members. Facilitators such as hypermedia knowledge bases and cognitive mapping tools help each side visualize the perspective of the other, thus enhancing the ability to synthesize opposing arguments into a stronger agreed-on premise.

While there are benefits to the organization as a political system, there are obvious drawbacks. Politics and conflict, when not controlled, may go beyond creative abrasion and lead to destructive abrasion. The Hegelian inquirer's over-observer is a check in this system to help prevent this. Political systems are also known to give rise to subversive counter groups; political power is often seen in groups without formal authoritative power. Still, the benefits are many in a well-structured and maintained political organization. Such a form allows members to clearly understand that all organizational behaviors, including goals, processes, form, and even technology adoption, are based on member interests. This allows us to better understand and prepare for the case where an organization may espouse culture and missions but act in a very different way. Lastly, like the organism metaphor, the organization as a political system metaphor illustrates that an organization is socially created and is constantly in a power struggle with itself for both form and function.

The four organizational forms discussed above have advantages and disadvantages; each is particularly suited to a given set of problems, environments, industries, and organizational life cycles. Some organizations, however, find themselves in need of a higher level of accuracy in information processing and modeling of perspectives and alternatives. Support for these more complex attributes can be found in the organization as a brain metaphor, which is epitomized by the Singerian inquirer.

The Singerian Form

The Singerian inquirer is the most complicated of Churchman's (1971) inquirers. Its primary purpose is to seek out inconsistencies throughout the organization and resolve the inconsistencies through a process of measuring, partitioning, and refining. During this process, the Singerian inquirer *sweeps in* variables and perspectives from as many stakeholders as possible, sometimes using the other inquirers for support. When there are no problems to be solved, the Singerian inquirer challenges the status quo and again enters the measurement process. A subcomponent of the inquirer reruns the models associated with the measurement process to ensure replication throughout the system. The learning associated with this inquirer is complex in both breadth and depth and is designed to enlarge the *natural image* with multiple perspectives, partitions, and refinements that allow an organization and its members to engage in a wider variety of innovative and creative tasks. This inquirer is appropriate for all environments but is most appropriate for tumulus environments where fast, efficient action is required and little experience with the problem context has been attained.

This inquirer is well represented by the brain metaphor (Morgan, 1997). Like the brain, this inquirer is complex and specialized, is capable of considering multiple perspectives, requires continuous communication and feedback, and depends on information processing and memory. An organization as a brain relies not only on the above characteristics but also on the ability to fragment processes and tasks to make them more manageable. In the Singerian inquirer, this fragmentation process is known as partitioning. By partitioning (or fragmenting) a problem context, an organization can make sense of the situation (Weick, 1979) by sorting the problem into what is known and what is unknown. The Singerian inquirer can then process the unknown further (refinement), generating cycles of disagreement and agreement until the problem is fully investigated and understood from all sides. This structure requires one that is fairly flat and decentralized to promote communication and feedback at all levels and across all units. It is the multidivision flow of information, both upward and downward, that allows the critical disagreement component to arise and, ultimately, for the agreement cycle to take place.

There are many organizations in today's environment that would benefit from the use of the characteristics of this organizational form. An organization with its main emphasis in knowledge creation, such as consulting, would benefit from the learning style of the organization as a brain as it is multilevel (Courtney et al., 1998; Hall et al., 2003) and highly complex, both features necessary for wicked problem contexts. An established traditional organization with a mechanistic structure would likely not find this inquirer as beneficial as would an organization on the brink of a new frontier, such as the effects of deregulation. The utility industry provides an example of an industry which faces uncertainty and complexity and for which the Singerian inquirer is appropriate (Richardson, Courtney & Paradice, 2001).

In such an environment, decision makers must be cognizant of the effect of service provision on the many different stakeholders within the extended service chain. These stakeholders become critical during the learning process; each has a unique viewpoint from which to view incoming information, and each will have their own needs and goals. In the utilities example, a consumer will desire low-cost yet dependable electricity; the provider may tolerate more service interruptions than the consumer may. A household consumer may tolerate more service interruptions than a consumer such as a hospital may. All of these perspectives must be taken into consideration and a balance struck as knowledge is created and processes defined. Created knowledge must be disseminated throughout the entire environment rather than just throughout the organization and its alliances. In the example, learning must be pushed downward toward the consumer to educate them on a new form of energy, a new process, or energy conservation measures.

The Singerian organizational form produces knowledge on all levels and therefore all of the aforementioned learning approaches may be appropriate. It is most likely that this organizational form would be best supported by an approach that is Web-based to allow for virtual information gathering and learning because of its need to include a wide range of individual stakeholders in the information gathering and dissemination process. Of particular importance to this organizational form and its acceptance of multiple perspectives is the concept of communities of practice.

A community of practice is a group of people who are "bound together by shared expertise and passion for a joint enterprise" (p.139), informal in nature, and deeply involved in sharing experience and knowledge in an attempt to create new problem-solving approaches (Wenger & Snyder, 2000). These communities can span organizational unit boundaries and through their combined knowledge and access to individuals with unique knowledge, can solve problems quickly and effectively. An organizational member may be a participant in several such communities, and many communities may be operating in a single organization, facilitating learning at different levels and incorporating different communication channels and media. This organization of communities is at the heart of the Singerian inquirer, which embraces multiple perspectives.

Genres of organizational communication vary both throughout and between communities of practice. Persons involved in consistent communication with each other develop patterns of behavior that all members of the involved organizational process understand

Figure 1. Flow of Knowledge between Communities of Practice, Learning Networks, and Organizational Support Structures

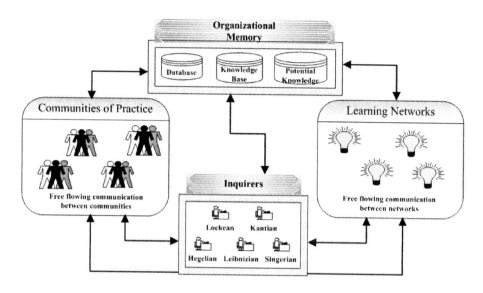

(Orlikowski & Yates, 1994), enabling the members to work effectively through the refinement and measurement tasks of the Singerian inquirer.

Because these communities, and particularly individual members, may overlap in their interests and group culture, an accurate and dynamic organizational memory is important. As contributions from communities of practice are stored in organizational memory, other organizational components, such as knowledge discovery components, may develop relationships between the new information and existing information that will be beneficial to another possibly unrelated community, thereby facilitating organizational learning.

The organization as a brain is one of the strongest metaphors to support cognition and learning. The structure of this type of organization leads to less formalization and centralization, which in turn creates communication and feedback opportunities. It, along with the other inquirers, may be integrated to support the inquiring organizations as an organizational form. Figure 1 demonstrates a possible implementation of a learning system dependent on Churchman's (1971) inquirers and organizational memory, which utilizes learning networks and communities of practice to facilitate organizational learning. In this figure, the inquirers are an integral support element of the overall system. Organizational memory is socially constructed from the interaction of the inquirers with (in this case) communities of practice and learning networks. For example, a formal learning network may use organizational memory to facilitate understanding of particular concepts and may turn to the Lockean inquirer for support in classifying information. A community of practice consisting of product development engineers may also interact with organizational memory to determine potential for product development (as well as past failures) and may turn to the Kantian inquirer for help in modeling those potential products to determine the one with the best opportunity for success.

Churchman's (1971) inquiring system on which an inquiring organization is based allows for multiple structures as has been described in the preceding sections. Borrowing from Bennis (1966) and Mintzberg (1979), we assign the inquirers to an organizational structure as shown in Table 1 which summarizes the preceding discussion. As indicated in the prior discussion, bureaucratic forms are marked by hierarchical authority among numerous offices and by fixed procedures. Such forms may use administrative systems in which the need or inclination to follow rigid or complex procedures impedes effective action. Mechanistic bureaucracies are the most rigid form. Professional bureaucracies are more closely aligned with the line-staff form of organizational structure presented at the beginning of the chapter.

While the Leibnizian, Lockean, and Kantian inquirers may be represented by different structures, the Hegelian and Singerian inquirers share the most informal structure. Waterman (1993) describes an adhocracy as any form of organization that cuts across normal bureaucratic lines to capture opportunities, solve problems, and get results. Hegelian and Singerian inquirers share this informal structure. Characterized by an adhocracy, these organizational forms facilitate free-flowing collaborations that can shift the balances of power. This form is appropriate for their turbulent environment.

Integration

The preceding sections have described characteristics of each of the five Churchmanian archetypes and their potential influence on a specific organizational form. Organizations and organizational units have been examined from a singular perspective. This section examines each organizational form and its capacity to be integrated with other forms in

Table 1. Organizational Structure of Churchman's (1971) Inquirers

Inquirer (metaphor)	Structure	Characteristics
Leibnizian (machine)	Mechanistic Bureaucracy	Formal routine tasks, stable environment, centralized high-level decision-making
Lockean (culture)	Divisional Bureaucracy	Formal routine tasks, stable environment, semiautonomous
Kantian (organism)	Professional Bureaucracy	Moderately formal and complicated tasks, moderately stable environment, more autonomy in decision-making
Hegelian (political system), Singerian (brain)	Adhocracy and Entrepreneurial Startup	Informal and often temporary complicated tasks, turbulent environment, decision-making primarily rests with the team

a single organization. The use of metaphors is appropriate when trying to understand the characteristics of a specific inquirer. To move toward integration, however, it is necessary to gravitate toward a more traditional organizational form discussion.

Task, environment, and decision-making strategy are important to determining an appropriate organizational form for any unit, but this is particularly true in the inquiring organization. Because the focus of the inquiring organization is learning and the accompanying decision-making, care must be taken to structure each organizational unit in a way that provides appropriate structure for the task and environment but does not limit learning potential. To understand how an inquiring organization can integrate multiple structures based on the inquirers, it is first necessary to understand how, from a schematic viewpoint, each of the inquirers may be procedurally integrated.

Like the forms in Table 1, inquirers are on a continuum from simple (Leibnizian) to complex (Singerian). Thus, an inquiring organization must be represented by a form that incorporates all levels but contains at its core organizational memory that is continuously updated, cleaned, and expanded by the inquiring process. The Kantian and Hegelian inquirers rely on the Leibnizian inquirer to generate organizational memory from which they process information in accordance with newly received environmental triggers. The Lockean and Singerian inquirers also add directly to organizational memory.

Figure 2 shows the conceptualization of an inquiring organization procedural integration and its relationship to organizational memory. When a trigger is received from the environment, the inquiring organization's first action is to determine the characteristics of the trigger. If the incoming information is structured or at most moderately unstructured but relevant to a stable or moderately unstable environment, it is passed through to the bureaucratic units. If the information is not structured or is from a complex environment, it is passed to the adhocratic units. From there, a determination is made whether a specialized unit should be called (Lockean, Kantian, or Hegelian). These specialized units may be in the form of permanent structures or temporary ones depending on the need.

For instance, if the problem concerns inventory control on a shop floor, it will be passed to an unspecialized mechanistic form (Leibnizian). If, on the other hand, the problem is complex and has potential for conflict (such as annual contract negotiations), a temporary unit (Hegelian) are assembled for the specific purpose of working through the problem. Generally, bureaucracies are permanent to semipermanent structures, whereas adhocracies may be temporary and flexible.

Carrying the above discussion further, it is instructive to consider some specific examples in order to fully consider the affect of the inquiry archetypes on organizational form and the potential for integrating the perspectives. The coordination of knowledge creation within the bounds of decision-making is likely the most common situation for an inquiring organization; however, as described in the discussion that refers to Figure 1, some knowledge creation may be ongoing without specific problem/decision context triggers (i.e., the Singerian and Leibnizian forms). When an organization is considering a problem, or when a decision is required, organizations not only rely on existing organizational memory to guide them, but an inquiring organization adds to that organizational memory as it goes through the process and learns.

Figure 2. Procedure Integration for an Inquiring Organization

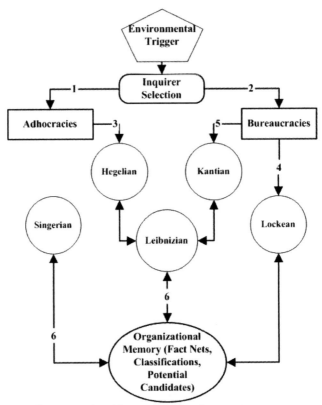

1. **Unstructured problem, turbulent environment**
2. **Structured to moderately structured problem, stable to moderately stable environment**
3. **Specialized adhocracy - potential for conflict**
4. **Specialized bureaucracy - potential for consensus**
5. **Specialized bureaucracy - moderately unstructured but analyzable**
6. **Do not require a trigger to be active**

Manufacturing firms provide an example that illustrates the existence of varying organizational forms in inquiring organizations. Factory floor workers following standard operating procedures and highly routinized tasks are representative of the Leibnizian form. Team members working together to analyze and reengineer business processes to improve efficiencies and productivity represent the Lockean form. Matching product development and production to market needs and developing strategy to meet consumer needs requires model fits typified by the Kantian form of inquiry. Labor talks and negotiated contracts are representative functions of the Hegelian form. Finally, organizational metrics that are used to inform productivity measures, assign performance bonuses, or modify existing practices would be typical of the Singerian inquirer. New knowledge from these processes (for instance, new consumer needs strategy or new productivity measures) are added to organizational memory.

Another organizational form that can be considered is the academic community that exists in higher education. Each form of organizational inquiry exists within the community. Staff members within a given area function at the Leibnizian level using formal mechanisms and routines. The academic work environment is typically stable and a relatively few administrators carry out centralized high-level decision making. Researchers working together through the process of publication are functioning in Lockean communities; committee and service commitments are also Lockean in nature. Kantian forms of inquiry are active when decisions such as budgeting or admissions standards are considered. These tasks are moderately formal and more complicated in nature and typically include more autonomy in the decision-making process. Hegelian forms of inquiry may exist between students and faculty and between faculty and the board of trustees. The tenure and promotion process would be typical of Singerian inquiry with the emphasis of measuring outputs by the number and quality of publications, student evaluation metrics, and quantified contributions to the referent discipline. Individuals go through a process of refining *research* to a specific number of publications, journal quality, contribution matrices, and so forth. These measures may vary by department. The newly created knowledge that arises from this decision-scenario may consist of new journal rankings, new productivity measures, and new ratios of service to research. Again, these are added to organizational memory.

Summary

Technology is limited and controlled by objectives, but technology itself limits and controls the organization and its behaviors. The use of information technology to enhance organizational forms molded from the philosophy of organizational inquiry can assist decision makers in analyzing business environments in order to take action based on a given set of inputs. In this chapter, we have articulated an approach for considering knowledge organizations through the focal lens of Churchman's (1971) philosophical inquirers. We have considered both functional and holistic forms of organizational structure and practice. Integrating perspectives illustrate how organizations practice multiple methods to enhance business processes. Considering how their organization can use the forms described may assist managers as they recast themselves and their organization or unit in the spirit of an inquiring organization.

References

Argyris, C., & Schön, D. A. (1996). *Organizational learning II*. Reading, MA: Addison-Wesley.

Bennis, W. G. (1966). *Changing organizations*. New York: McGraw-Hill.

Burns, T., & Stalker, G. M. (1961). *Management of innovation*. London: Tavistock.

Churchman, C. W. (1971). *The design of inquiring systems: Basic concepts of systems and organizations*. New York: Basic Books.

Courtney, J. F., Croasdell, D. T., & Paradice, D. B. (1998). Inquiring organizations. *Australian Journal of Information Systems, 6*(1), 3-15.

DiBella, A. J. (1995). Developing learning organizations: A matter of perspective. *Academy of Management Journal, Special Issue Best Papers Proceedings 1995*, 287-291.

DiBella, A. J., & Nevis, E. C. (1998). *How organizations learn: An integrated strategy for building learning capability*. San Francisco: Jossey-Bass.

Elofson, G., & Konsynski, B. (1991). Delegation technologies: Environmental scanning with intelligent agents. *Journal of Management Information Systems, 8*(1), 37-62.

Fiol, C. M., & Lyles, M. (1985). Organizational learning. *Academy of Management Review, 10*(4), 803-813.

Garvin, D. (1993). Building a learning organization. *Harvard Business Review, 71*(4), 78-91.

Hall, D. J., & Paradice, D. B. (2005). Philosophical foundations for a learning-oriented knowledge management system for decision support. *Decision Support Systems 39*(3), 445-461.

Hall, D. J., Paradice, D. B., & Courtney, J. F. (2003). Building a theoretical foundation for a learning-oriented knowledge management system. *Journal of Information Technology Theory and Application (JITTA), 5*(2), 63-89.

Huber, G. P. (1991). Organizational learning: The contributing processes and the literatures. *Organization Science, 2*(1), 88-115.

Kunz, W., & Rittel, H. (July, 1970). *Issues as elements of information systems* (Working Paper No. 131). University of California, Berkeley.

Lawrence, P. R., & Lorsch, J. W. (1967). Environmental demands and organizational states. In *Organization and environment: Managing differentiation and integration*. Boston: Harvard Business School.

Levitt, B., & March, J. G. (1988). Organizational learning. *Annual Review of Sociology, 14*, 126-146.

Mayhew, D. J. (1992). *Principles and guidelines in software user interface design*. New Jersey: Prentice Hall.

Mintzberg, H. (1979). *The structuring of organizations: A synthesis of the research*. Englewood Cliffs, NJ: Prentice Hall.

Morgan, G. (1997). *Images of organizations* (2nd ed.). Thousand Oaks, CA: Sage.

Nevis, E. C., DiBella, A. J., & Gould, J. M. (1995). Understanding organizations as learning systems. *MIT Sloan Management Review, 36*(2), 73-86.

Orlikowski, W. J., & Yates, J. (1994). Genre repertoire: The structuring of communicative practices in organizations. *Administrative Science Quarterly, 39,* 541-574.

Richardson, S. M., Courtney, J. F., & Paradice, D. B. (2001). An assessment of the Singerian approach to organizational learning: Cases from academia and the utility industry. *Information Systems Frontiers, 3*(1), 49-62.

Rittel, H. W. J., & Webber, M. M. (1973). Dilemmas in a general theory of planning. *Policy Sciences, 4*(2), 155-169.

Senge, P. M. (1990). The leader's new work: Building learning organizations. *Sloan Management Review, 38 (1),* 7-22.

Shanks, D. C., & Olson, D. A. (1995). The learning organization. *The Chief Executive, 101,* 57-64.

Slater, S. F., & Narver, J. C. (1995). Market orientation and the learning organization. *Journal of Marketing, 59*(3), 63-75.

Terveen, L., Selfridge, P., & Long, M. (1995). Living design memory: Framework, implementation, lessons learned. *Human-Computer Interaction, 10*(1), 1-37.

van der Krogt, F. J. (1998). Learning network theory: The tension between learning systems and work systems in organizations. *Human Resource Development Quarterly, 9*(2), 157-177.

von Krogh, G. (1998). Care in knowledge creation. *California Management Review, 40*(3), 133-153.

Walsh, J. P., & Ungson, G. R. (1991). Organizational memory. *Academy of Management Review, 16*(1), 57-91.

Waterman, R. H. (1993). *Adhocracy.* New York: W.W. Norton & Company.

Weick, K. E. (1979). *The social psychology of organizing* (2nd ed.). New York: Random House.

Wenger, E. C., & Snyder, W. M. (2000). Communities of practice: The organizational frontier. *Harvard Business Review, 78*(1), 139-145.

White, G. (1990). Natural language understanding and speech recognition. *Communications of the ACM, 33*(8), 72-82.

Chapter II

Information Technology and Hegelian Inquiring Organizations

Bongsug Chae
Kansas State University, USA

James F. Courtney
University of Central Florida, USA

John D. Haynes
University of Central Florida, USA

Abstract

This chapter demonstrates how Hegelian inquiring systems may be applied to wicked problem situations and knowledge work and how Hegelian inquiring organizations are well suited for the discontinuous environments of the new world of business (Malhotra, 1997, 2000). In addition, the chapter discusses how Hegelian organizations and how emerging information technologies can support Hegelian processes, especially the Hegelian dialectic. We claim that extant information systems (IS) are not suitable for wicked situations due to their rigidity, which stems from a philosophical basis of logical positivism, coupled with the prevailing functionalistic, technology-driven IS development models. The need for a new approach is suggested, based on a multiple perspective pluralistic approach.

Introduction

Churchman's (1971) inquiring systems have been proposed as the basis for learning or inquiring organizations (Courtney, Croasdell & Paradice, 1998). Previous work (Courtney, 2001) has suggested that the Singerian model is appropriate for decision making in complex ill-structured highly interconnected environments and applications of the Singer model in situations of at least moderate complexity have been explored (Richardson, Courtney & Paradice, 2001). Within the context of inquiring organizations, Malhotra (1997, 2000) defines today's organizational environments as increasingly more dynamic, discontinuous, and *wicked* and suggests the need for consideration of Hegelian models that can provide an organization or organizational unit(s) with multiple, diverse, and contradictory interpretations of data. This chapter continues the theme of adapting Churchman's models of inquiring systems by exploring the Hegelian model as it relates to inquiring organizations. It is argued that the Hegelian model is suitable for the environments Malhotra describes. This chapter first discusses the wicked nature of future business environments, then describes the Hegelian inquiring system and how it may be applied to ill-structured organizational situations. Next, information technology appropriate for use in Hegelian organizations is described, and some conclusions are drawn with respect to the need for a new approach to IS development in such organizations.

The Wicked Environments of the Future

As a result of many factors, among them globalization, deregulation, privatization, and advancements of information and communications technology, today's business environments are changing rapidly and discontinuously. The behavior of these new environments will be highly uncertain and unpredictable, what Rittel and Webber (1973) refer to as *wicked* situations. Mason and Mitroff (1981) identified characteristics of wicked problems found in strategic planning and policy making. These characteristics include interconnectedness, complicatedness, uncertainty, ambiguity, conflict, and social constraints. Wicked problems are accompanied by conflict of interest among individuals and teams and are intimately connected to each other. Therefore, there is no one single solution that can satisfy a wicked problem because it must also satisfy all other wicked problems. Most importantly wicked problems exist, not in a stable and predictable environment, but in a dynamic complex and unpredictable situation. Wicked problems require multiple interpretations since there is no knowable *correct* answer. To Ackoff (1999), real organizational problems are wicked and may be regarded as *messes*. Messes interact with each other and, thus, cannot be understood independently from other messes. They must be understood as highly complex ill-structured systems with strongly interacting components.

In such environments, the future of an organization depends on its ability to constantly question existing ways of doing things and to create new processes in order to respond quickly to dynamic changes. A number of researchers (e.g., Ackoff, 1999; Buckingham

Shum, 1996; Gordon & Karacapilidis, 1997; Malhotra, 1997, 2000; Mason & Mitroff, 1981; Rittel & Webber, 1973) suggest dialectics, argumentation and negotiation as a way of dealing with wicked situations. Ackoff (1999) notes that effective management of *messes* requires dissolving, not solving or resolving problems. Malhotra (1997, 2000) calls the new environment the world of *re-everything* and suggests that organizations must manage their knowledge effectively to survive re-everything and that the Hegelian approach may be the way to surface knowledge. The next section describes Hegelian Inquiring Systems and discusses their use in managing knowledge in wicked situations.

Hegelian Inquiring Systems (HIS) and Wicked Environments

Hegelian inquiring systems are based on dialectic, a participative process meant to dissolve conflicts rather than to find compromises. The result of the debate is to allow the decision maker to form a synthetic view of the issue. The inputs into the dialectic are complex and consist of a common data set plus two opposing worldviews, the thesis and antithesis, that characterize the deep positions of the two proponents. The data only takes on meaning through the worldviews; the data itself has no meaning. The purpose of the data is not to settle issues, but rather to surface the intense differences in background assumptions between two divergent positions. The operator in the system is the decision maker or observer of a debate by the two proponents. The observer must adopt one of the two pure positions (sets of assumptions) or form a new position through synthesis or some other process as a result of witnessing the debate (Mitroff & Linstone, 1993). The guarantor of this system is intense conflict. Ideally, the two adversarial views (assumptions) have no overlap. It is hoped that as a result of witnessing an intensely explicit debate between two polar positions that the observer will be in a much stronger position to know the assumptions of the two adversaries and thus clarify his or her own assumptions.

We propose that attacking wicked problems by forging a synthesis from a thesis and its antithesis is a form of knowledge work. Many researchers distinguish knowledge work from service work or procedural work, even though the concept itself remains somewhat vague and ill defined. Schultze (2000) suggests that knowledge work produces and reproduces information and knowledge. Buckingham Shum (1996) believes that knowledge work and wicked problems have similar properties, which are described as follows:

- Knowledge work is team work and is dominated by negotiation and argumentation.
- The space of knowledge work is unstable and thus goals, constraints, and solutions must be open to change.
- Knowledge work is interdisciplinary so that multiple assumptions and interpretations are inevitable.
- Knowledge work leads to cross-functional teams and flatter organizational structures.

We argue that knowledge work exists, not because of tame problems, but because of wicked problems. That is one of the reasons we can find knowledge workers in the areas where examples of Hegelian inquiry can be found, such as strategic planning, policy formulation, system analysis and design, competitive intelligence, legal issues and collective bargaining. Thus we propose that many knowledge problems can be addressed with the Hegelian conflictual approach and that ideal knowledge workers should possess the characteristics of the Hegelian *synthesist* (Kienholz, 1999). The synthesist asks *why not* (Kienholz, 1999) and *so what* (Churchman, 1971, p. 174), seeks conflict and synthesis, and sees likenesses in things looking unalike.

We conclude then that Hegelian inquiring systems may be well-suitable for wicked problems and knowledge work and that it may be fruitful to deploy Hegelian inquiring systems within organizations facing wicked environments.

Developing Hegelian Inquiring Organizations

The Hegelian approach is based on conflict, but within an organization, this conflict must be productive, not divisive. There is a need for open constructive dialogue and the expression of multiple viewpoints on an issue if an effective synthesis is to emerge. This section describes those features of Hegelian systems and how they may be obtained in practice (Table 1).

Toward Creative Conflict

Because it is intense conflict that guarantees the operation of the Hegelian inquiring system, conflict or disagreement is essential to Hegelian inquiring organizations. A number of management scholars (e.g., Eisenhardt, 1999; Eisenhardt, Kathwajy & Bourgeois, 1997; Leonard & Straus, 1997) recognize that conflict is essential to organizational innovation and decision effectiveness. Eisenhardt (1997, 1999) argues that the absence of conflict is not harmony but rather apathy and disengagement. Leonard and Straus (1997) point out that conflict is essential to innovation because innovation takes place when different ideas, perceptions, and ways of processing and judging information *collide*.

To guarantee creative conflict in an organization, first of all, the organization must adopt a structure that offers it. The adoption of certain structures encourages learning through multiple and antithetical interpretations and debates. Hegelian inquiring organizations cannot exist without such a structure, which can support learning connected to the purpose of the dialectic debate. A centralized mechanistic structure tends to reinforce past behaviors and discourage debate (Fiol & Lyles, 1985) and tends to form barriers to learning and establishment of relationships (Preskill & Torres, 1999). Under bureaucratic structures, people tend to avoid conflict and suppress diverse contradictory viewpoints. Thus, individuals fail to have a comprehensive picture of the whole and fail to see interrelationships in the world (problem) around them.

Structure that encourages debate requires a new role of leader as designer (Senge, 1990). Traditional views of leaders, characterized as heroes in the West and charismatic personas in the East, are the antithesis of the leader for Hegelian inquiring organizations. As designer, the leader is responsible for building appropriate structures and strategies for Hegelian inquiry and encouraging members to adopt systems thinking. Because of its flatter organizational structure, the Hegelian inquiring organization requires more active roles of middle managers, who have a better understanding of their teams and local environments than top management does.

In Hegelian inquiry, the energy for change comes from the broad perspective of the observer toward *progress* (Churchman, 1971, p. 178). Between the Hegelian synthesis and thesis and antithesis, there is the natural bent of humans toward progress and development. The synthesis is not the end of change. Rather it soon becomes one aspect of reality and a new thesis. Thus, Hegelian inquiry is restless and never ending, just like progress and development in the history of humankind.

Toward More Dialog

Even though an organization may have a suitable structure, employ systems thinking, and have a design that ensures more conflict, that conflict must be positive or else the Hegelian inquiring organization fails. Positive conflict is different from negative conflict in that win-win conditions among members and teams are sought. Negative conflict results in win-lose conditions among members and teams. The notion of "strongest possible disagreements" is often taken as "heated or authoritarian arguments" which is a view that derives from a literal interpretation of—and thereby misrepresents—the Hegelian dialectic. Churchman (1971, p. 163) points out that "the teleological approach to information—in keeping with the dialectical approach of an Hegelian inquiring system—emphasizes purpose (means and ends)."

Table 1. Guiding Principles and Design Guidelines for Hegelian Inquiring Organizations

Guiding Principles	Design Guidelines
Toward Creative Conflict	• Organic structure for learning & multiple interpretations and debates • Leader as designer using systems thinking • Significant role of middle-level managers
Toward More Dialogue	• Dialogue for positive conflict to emerge • Trust and respect among members & communities
Toward Open Systems	• Open-mindedness • Shifting the view of other communities and companies from competitors to collaborators • Not only intraorganizational but also interorganizational learning
Toward Wicked Learning	• Faster learning • Capability for radical organizational change • Updating organizational memory through unlearning and forgetting
Diverse, Contradictory Interpretations	• Promoting creativity and imagination • Leader as teacher encouraging members to surface their mental models

Haynes (1999) therefore considers that strong debates and disagreements must be tempered with trust and respect. In the Hegelian inquiring system, strong debates are agreed to as a teleological consideration by the organizational members. Thus to, for example, give a "full and frank" viewpoint is to already have understood that the receiver, or receiving group, appreciates that full and frank comments come from a depth of understanding that can potentially develop the subject under consideration.

Dialectic and positive conflict cannot exist without dialog. The concept of dialog comes from the Greek origin, *dia* (through) *logos* (meaning), and literally means when a group of people talk with one another such that the meaning (*logos*) moves through them (Ellinor & Gerard, 1998; Senge, 1992). Dialectic cannot deal with isolated propositions because isolated propositions introduce contradiction and destroy the dialectic process (Hodges, 1991). As the dialog develops, contradictions are resolved in the way in which a topic is modified (Arbnor & Bjerke, 1997). Thus, dialog is the basis of dialectic and may be viewed as collective reflection (Nonaka & Takeuchi, 1995; Senge, 1990). Dialog inquiry does not seek the correct answer but is meant to explore the question. Dialog is a core process of Hegelian inquiring organizations. The discipline of team learning, suggested by Senge as one of the five disciplines for building learning organizations, also starts with dialog, the capacity of members of a team to suspend assumptions and enter into genuine thinking together.

The more dialog occurs, the more *stories* are created, and hidden tacit knowledge is revealed. The stories help members understand not only others' cognition but also their emotions. Stories create a sense of shared understanding and belonging. Without dialog there is no positive conflict, no organizational knowledge creation, no story creation, and no progress.

Toward Open Systems

The Hegelian synthesis of integrating the opposites into a new and expanded worldview is the epitome of an open system (Courtney, Croasdell & Paradice, 1998). Hegelian inquiring organizations, as open systems, require open-mindedness. Levey and Levet (1994) note that "open-mindedness is a quality of mind that is open to the flow of experience without bias and editing, and respectfully tolerant of chaos and ambiguity. …Open-mindedness allows us to encompass a more global, systems view of a situation and to honor diversity" (p. 268).

This quality of open-mindedness is essential to learning in any complex system, especially for organizations in wicked environments. In wicked environments, the way corporations used to compete is gone for good (Moore, 1996), and the old "kill-the-competitor" mindset is no longer appropriate (Nadler, Shaw & Walton, 1995). Researchers (e.g., Fiol & Lyles, 1985; Moore, 1996) believe that organizations must align themselves with the environment to remain competitive and to survive over the long run. Hegelian inquiring organizations actively respond to external environments and collaborate with other organizations to take advantage of their core competencies (Prahalad & Hamel, 1990).

Dynamic environments and competitors are key sources for learning in Hegelian inquiring organizations. Some researchers view learning from the experience of others as the key capability of learning organizations (Levitt & March, 1988). Mason (1993) proposes that learning organizations must see competitors more as a means of learning than a hostile threat. Learning from the experiences and best practices of competitors is one of the five skills that learning organizations must possess (Garvin, 1993). One of the reasons for the success of Japanese businesses has been their skill at seeking inspiration in external ideas (Nevis, DiBella & Gould, 1995).

Toward Wicked Learning

In dynamic and uncertain environments, organizational learning becomes more and more complex. Thus, many researchers believe that learning organizations require double-loop learning (Argyris & Schon, 1996), generative learning (Senge, 1990), and higher-level learning (Fiol & Lyles, 1985). Double-loop learning occurs when underlying assumptions, norms, and objectives are open to debate and change (Argyris & Schon, 1996). Generative learning requires new ways of looking at the world (Senge, 1990). It emphasizes continuous experimentation and feedback in an ongoing examination of the way of organizations. Underlying assumptions and governing variables cannot be effectively questioned without another set against which to measure them. In other words, generative learning always requires an opposition of ideas (the dialectic) for comparison. The Hegelian synthesis, based on intrinsic motivation for change, exemplifies generative, double-loop learning (Courtney et al., 1998).

We argue that the more dynamic and uncertain organizational environments are, the more complex and radical organizational learning becomes. In this sense, organizational learning seems to be wicked. We view single-loop learning as tame learning and double-loop or generative learning as wicked learning. Tame learning seeks incremental change. In contrast, wicked learning seeks radical change. Consequently, wicked learning may result in a major change in strategic direction (Courtney et al., 1998).

Knowledge is that which Hegelian inquiring organizations create and deal with tends to be tacit, episodic, idiosyncratic, and abstract rather than explicit, semantic, communal, and concrete. Thus, it is short-term, dynamic, and unsanctioned. Hegelian knowledge must be dynamic because it exists in an environment of rapid change. It is unsanctioned because it may not be based on consensus. These aspects of Hegelian knowledge increase the importance of *unlearning* and selectively forgetting the past. Wicked learning involves unlearning and forgetting. Unlearning does not mean *not learning;* it actually means more effective learning through discarding obsolete and misleading knowledge (Hedberg, 1981). Huber (1991) believes that unlearning provides a chance for new organizational learning to take place. Also, dialog offers a path for successful unlearning (Fulmer, Gibbs & Keys, 1998). Forgetting is a process of deleting old knowledge and outdated assumptions from organizational memory. The process of forgetting keeps organizational memory updated. *Selective* forgetting can decrease irrelevant information and increase relevant information in organizational memory.

It is believed that the ability to learn faster than competitors is the primary competitive advantage (e.g., Brown, 1999; DeGeus, 1988). Without *appropriate* unlearning and selective forgetting, learning in Hegelian inquiring organizations becomes slower, and organizational memory suffers from lack of relevant information and overabundance of irrelevant information. Consequently, slow learning will result in organizations losing their competitive edge.

Diverse, Contradictory Interpretations

The existence of different views of the world is a natural phenomenon. People have different mental models and different experiences that influence their understanding of reality. By seeing explicitly two or more positions operating on the same data set, we have the opportunity to systematically witness the background assumptions that the proponents of different positions bring with them to convert data to information and knowledge. Huber (1991) notes that "because such development changes the range of the organization's potential behaviors" (p. 90), the more varied interpretations that are available, the more learning occurs. The greater the degree of uncertainty, the greater the need for more varied interpretations.

For more interpretations, the role of the leader is that of teacher who brings to the surface people's mental models of important issues and encourages members to develop their inquiry skills (Senge, 1990). Mental models are ingrained assumptions that tell us why two people may interpret and react differently to the same event (Kienholz, 1999). Hegelian inquiring organizations must not follow the adherence of the organization's view of "how things are done here" or current practices. Instead, such ways and practices must be re-examined and reassessed from multiple perspectives for their alignment with changing environments.

Senge (1990) states that one reason many of the best ideas in organizations never get into practice is that new insights may conflict with existing mental models. Therefore, Hegelian inquiring organizations need a knowledge-sharing open culture that encourages people to surface their underlying assumptions and to develop diverse contradictory perspectives. Courtney (2001) notes that as perspectives are developed, insight is gained and the mental models are updated. Further, as learning occurs and new knowledge is created, more intellectual solutions are available to the organization. "To conceive of knowledge as a collection of information seems to rob the concept of all its life   Knowledge resides in the user and not in the collection. It is how the user reacts to a collection of information that matters" (Churchman, 1971, p. 11). It is not computers or databases but human beings that provide multiple diverse interpretations. Thus, Hegelian inquiring organizations require much greater involvement of human imagination and creativity than other inquiring organizations in order to facilitate multiple contradictory interpretations of the data. Without them, there is no intense conflict, no synthesis, and no progress.

Information Systems in Hegelian Organizations

Several researchers have suggested IT applications that can enhance an organization's learning capabilities (e.g., Huber, 1991; Mason, 1993; Nonaka et al., 1998; Robey et al., 1995; Zuboff, 1988). The conflictual nature of Hegelian organizations requires a somewhat different type of information technology support to enable open constructive debate, the construction of individual and group interpretations of an issue, and democratic and participatory organizational structure. For example, Mason (1981) argues that many information systems are designed for decision making and decision taking, the purpose of which is to put an early closure to the debate about the appropriate course of action to be taken. Information systems based on decision making and decision taking may not be suitable for helping people solve wicked problems, as they may tend to discourage dialog and debate. Other researchers (e.g., Angehrn & Jelassi, 1994; Jones, 1994; Stohr & Konsynski, 1992; Weick & Meader, 1993; Whitaker, 1994) suggest that many DSS and GDSS have focused too much on the decisions and answers and have ignored interpretation and questions. These systems exhibit a relatively narrow conception of meetings (Bannon, 1997) and an inappropriate view of dialog.

Hegelian Information Systems

Information systems for supporting the Hegelian model have been the concern of some researchers, including Mitroff and Mason. Mason (1969) introduced the Hegelian approach to strategic planning. Mitroff (1971) developed a mathematical model of the Hegelian Dialectical Inquirer using Bayesian probability theory and Ackoff's Behavioral Theory of Communication. Nelson and Mitroff (1974) conducted an experiment concerned with the investigation of presentation formats for Dialectic Information Systems (DIS) that generate information for a decision maker by means of intense conflict between proponents of two radically opposed positions, theories, and points of view. Mason (1981) introduced systemic information systems, the purpose of which is to expose assumptions or views-of-the-world so that they may be examined and reconsidered. He stated that "an information system is said to be dialectical if it examines data completely and logically with at least two different and opposing sets of assumptions or from two different points of view" (p. 93).

Also, other researchers have suggested that advanced information technologies may contribute to removing barriers to Hegelian inquiry within an organization. Klein and Hirschheim (1985) propose different roles for information systems to support a Hegelian-like pluralist concept of inquiry by removing barriers such as limited access, cost of communication, and emotional inhibition. By applying Harbermas' theory to information systems, Lyytinen and Hirschheim (1988) argued that new forms of information systems need to be developed which facilitate discursive action and suggest the need for new and novel types of teleconferencing systems, GDSS, electronic brainstorming systems, and so forth. Based on Toulmin's (1958) work, Nissen (1989) recognized communicative and discursive elements of information systems use. Lyytinen (1992) also suggested the potential use of IS to harness discursive activity in organizations. Ngwenyama and Lyytinen (1997) provided groupware applications to support discursive and strategic as well as instrumental and communicative action.

Visual Tools

Visual tools are extremely useful in helping to see the processes and interactions within complex systems such as the wicked environments of Hegelian inquiring organizations. For example, cognitive mapping is a set of techniques for understanding people's perceptions about the structure of their environment. These perceptions are represented graphically in the form of box and arrow diagrams that show concepts (boxes) and relationships (arrows) between concepts (Sheetz et al., 1994). The cognitive map represents mental models that explain perceptions of the world. Cognitive maps are valuable tools for making thinking visible, and they are very effective in working with groups to discover all the members' perceptions. The role of cognitive maps goes beyond the representation of thinking and learning of an individual. Maps can be developed for groups and organizations by aggregating maps from individuals by direct group mapping and inference from documentary evidence that relates to an organization (Eden, 1992). Hodges's (1991) Dialectron is a prototype system that supports diametrically opposed cognitive maps of a problem domain and manages the dialog necessary to generate synthesis. Two cognitive mapping tools, COCOMAP (Lee, Courtney & O'Keefe, 1992) and Spider (Boland, Tenkasi & Te'eni, 1994) have been designed to allow organizational members to represent their interpretations and to facilitate dialog with others through exchanging and merging their cognitive maps. Other computer tools that have been developed for cognitive mapping and illustration of feedback loops include Belvedere, developed by the Learning Research and Development Center at the University of Pittsburgh, the COPE software package (Sheetz et al., 1994), and Decision Explorer by Scolari Software.

Also, other specific instruments like Schon and Rein's (1994) frame analysis and Kelly's repertoire grid technique (Shaw & Gaines, 1995) can be very useful for understanding the differences of individual phenomena. Schon and Rein (1994) suggested frame analysis to understand different actors' mental structures, appreciations, world making, or framing. Depending on one's frame, situations are imbued with different meanings. Advanced computer tools can be designed and used to support the analysis of various actors' frames. Based on personal construct psychology that emphasizes the idiographic nature of individual constructions of the world, Shaw and Gaines (1995) and their colleagues have introduced computer-based tools for eliciting and comparing different construction systems. Building on Kelly's concept of *learning experiments* Harri-Augstein and Thomas (1991) developed the idea of learning conversations. These tools and techniques would help people and groups understand their own frames—perspective making—as well as others'—perspective taking—and help develop mutual understanding of each other. Boland and Tenkasi (1995) proposed five classes of forum-based electronic communication systems to support knowledge work by helping construct strong frames within a community of knowing and exchange them between communities. For effective perspective taking, the terms *translation, marginal people,* and *boundary objects* developed by Star and Griesemer (1989) might offer social strategies for promoting the spread of knowledge between communities (Brown & Duguid, 1998).

Argumentation and Negotiation Systems

Some information systems have been designed to support argumentation and negotiation in groups using several different information technologies and techniques, such as hypertext, Internet technology, multimedia, and artificial intelligence. These systems help produce free debates and encourage dialog in groups. Ideally, they provide more multiple diverse perspectives on the focal information, and thus, group members find the differences among mental models of members. Finally, the group comes up with a new expanded solution to the problem. For example, Rittel (1970) developed the IBIS (Issue-Based Information Systems) notation to encourage debates among members by raising new issues. IBIS starts with a Question. The response to the Question is one or more Ideas. An Argument provides support for or against one or more of the Ideas. Based on Rittel's work, Conklin and Begeman (1988) designed the gIBIS system, a hypertext prototype of IBIS, to facilitate a team conducting debates by building a graphical argumentation structure. Corporate Memory System, Inc. (1993) developed a commercial collaborative system called QuestMap, a hypermedia groupware system. In this system, rationale and debates are stored as audio, video, reports, spreadsheets, and more. Hypermedia integrates all different forms of artifacts together. This kind of system not only provides free debates about wicked problems but also captures the debates so that they are available to support future decisions (Balasubramaniam & Sengupta, 1995; Hashim, 1991; Tweed, 1998).

In the field of Human-Computer Interaction there is ongoing research about argumentation-based design rationales and notations to support them. DRL (Decision Representation Language) and the QOC scheme (Questions, Options, and Criteria) are examples (Buckingham Shum, 1996). The DRL allows participants to explore Alternatives, back them up by Claims, and argue through Questions and Counter-Claims (Buckingham Shum, 1996). The QOC scheme is very similar to IBIS, starting with Questions. Options are alternative answers to the Questions. Criteria are used to assess the relative superiority of Options (Buckingham Shum, 1996).

There is also ongoing research on negotiation support systems (NSS) (e.g., Jain & Solomon, 2000; Jarke et al., 1996; Kersten & Noronha, 1999) to support, formalize, and help visualize heterogeneous viewpoints. Dialectical structured languages to support argumentation and negotiation have also been developed. For example, ARBAS (Action-Resource Based Argumentation Support) was developed to provide a computer-based platform for exchange of dialectical arguments between parties involved in a negotiated situation (Bodart et al., 1997).

Computational dialectics, the subject matter of which is mathematical models of norms of rational discourse, can serve to support Hegelian inquiry. Computational dialectics is concerned with modeling a large process of argumentation and designing computer systems for supporting argumentation and negotiation in groups. Examples are Zeno and D3E (Buckingham Shum, 1996). Zeno (Gordon & Karacapilidis, 1997) is a mediating system based on Rittel's IBIS model. The Zeno system offers assistance to mediators and other trusted third parties by providing an issue-based discussion forum or conferencing system. The Zeno system is designed to support the retrieval, use, and reuse of information practices and knowledge in cooperative distributed planning and decision-making procedures on the World Wide Web. The system consists of four layers: logic, argumentation framework, actions, and protocol. The logic layer formalizes the notions of consequence and contradiction. In the argumentation layer, concepts such as claim, supporting argument, counter-argument, and issue are defined. The action layer defines the possible kinds of actions. The protocol layer defines the rights and responsibilities of the participants to perform the actions in the action layer. Zeno provides another dimension of information technology support for *Virtual* Hegelian inquiring organizations through the World Wide Web and geographical information systems.

The Effects of Computer-Mediated Communication

It has been suggested that computer-mediated communication (CMC) may lead to democratizing effects on communications among members within and between organizations. Sproull and Kiesler (1991) claimed that computer-based communication could alleviate barriers and distortions in organizational communication and can create opportunities for new connections among people. CMC systems may equalize communication opportunities for all organizational members (Hiltz & Turoff, 1978; Kiesler, 1986). CMC and GDSS technology can lead to dispersion of power and influence and to reduced dominance by powerful members of the community (DeSanctis & Gallupe, 1987). Further emerging technologies such as those for collaborative work, multimedia communications, and information dissemination systems using intranet technology can be useful in Hegelian environments by helping to flatten the structure of organizations and promote dissemination of information to all members. Such technologies may help members of an organization to team build a shared vision and values. Ouksel, Mihavics and Chalos's (1997) simulation-based study indicates that learning in organizations with flatter structures is generally faster than in hierarchies. Therefore, such technologies are expected to enable organizational members and groups to increase the speed of their learning.

Many studies show that rich media are better suited to perform tasks that are high in ambiguity, such as those found in wicked domains. Daft and Lengel's (1986) study shows that equivocality resolution requires rich media, while uncertainty reduction occurs best in lean media. Rana and Turoff (1996) point out that a rich medium of communication is critical to the successful performance of group tasks involving conflictual approaches. High equivocality requires a rich medium of communication, such as face-to-face meetings. Today, face-to-face meetings can be simulated with advanced video conferencing systems supported by high-bandwidth computer networks. Such technologies enable members of an organizational unit or project team to collaborate across time and distance barriers while sitting in their offices (Balasubramanian, 1997).

Among available information technologies, hypermedia may be ideal for capturing knowledge that is hard to formalize and for linking ideas raised by team members (Buckingham Shum, 1996). Multimedia databases and advanced case-based reasoning techniques may be helpful for storing and retrieving dynamic and unsanctioned knowledge gained in Hegelian inquiring organizations (Kakola, 1995). Further combining multiple technologies, such as video-conferencing systems, multimedia communication, and multimedia databases, may offer the opportunity to produce more *stories,* capture them with their *drama* and *emotion,* and make them more accessible to organizational members, thereby promoting more effective dialogs and organizational progress.

Use and Implementation of Hegelian Information Systems

These technologies and tools discussed above should not be seen as an independent entity but instead as a socially constructed artifact (e.g., Barley, 1986; Bijker & Pinch, 1987) and inserted into sociotechnical *webs* (Kling, 1980). Therefore, they will both enable and constrain certain actions by organizational members (Orlikowski et al., 1995; Yates, 1997). There would be both intended and unintended consequences from implementing and using them, as already indicated by many recent empirical studies (Bijker, 1995; Orlikowski, 2000; von Hippel, 1988).

A strong relationship has been found between technology and organizational contexts or institutional conditions. Many collaborative technologies fail because of organizational contexts that are rigid, control oriented, bureaucratic, or too individualistic and competitive, rather than communal in nature (Orlikowski, 1992, 1993; Orlikowski, 2000; Orlikowski & Hofman, 1997). Applegate, DeSanctis, and Jackson (1995) reported that the successful implementation of groupware requires a cooperative culture. Also, organizational *defensive routines* which cannot deal with incongruent technological frames or mental models (Orlikowski & Gash, 1994) often result in IT failure (Argyris & Schon, 1996; Orlikowski & Gash, 1994) and *technological distanciation* where learning around technology does not occur (Henfridsson & Söderholm, 2000).

Orlikowski (2000) reported that where users' social practices correspond with the *Notes* designers' norms and visions of supporting collaboration through technology, a technology-in-practice may be enacted that more closely realizes those designers' intentions and their technology's properties. We believe that the *Spirit* (DeSanctis & Poole, 1994) of the technologies and tools discussed above is compatible with Hegelian open and cooperative structures. The perspective taking and "against defensive routine" culture can promote productive adaptations of information technology. In a Hegelian inquiring organization, key actors can share their different technological frames through early articulation, reflection, dialog, and negotiation. This greatly reduces the likelihood of unintended consequences and misunderstandings and delusions around the implementation and use of new information technology (Orlikowski & Gash, 1994). We further expect that this may reduce the likelihood of many IT failures caused by the power dynamics of key social networks (Bloomfield et al., 1997). With the proper technology-use mediation process (Orlikowski et al., 1995) through providing ongoing attention and resources, such as educational programs that promote productive adaptations (DeSanctis & Poole, 1994) and mediators, Hegelian inquiring organizations may achieve more desired consequences from deploying the technologies.

Next we turn to discuss the need of a new IS development model for such computerized systems discussed above after pointing out the problems with the traditional functionalistic IS development models that focus on information requirements and modeling for a computer-based artifact and often view information systems as a simple *plug-in* into any organizational settings.

The Need for a New Development Model

Researchers seem to agree that (1) wicked problems and wicked environments need the appreciation of multiple, diverse, and contradictory interpretations of the data, and (2) organizations need higher-level learning (double-loop learning, strategic learning, generative learning, and wicked learning) or *qualitative* change to be successful in wicked environments. However, many researchers also believe that (1) most information systems are rigid and mainly designed for single-loop learning (adaptive learning, lower-level learning, and tame learning), and (2) much of the rigidity of extant information systems stems from their philosophical basis in logical positivism and functionalistic technology-driven IS development models.

A growing number of researchers argue that extant information systems are rigid because they are machine-centered and designed on the logical positivistic assumption that the world is relatively predictable, and this can be portrayed by independent and dependent variables. This functionalistic approach, which has been dominant in the IS field, considers only the technical dimension of information systems, which are conceived as technical artifacts that may (or may not) have social and behavioral implications (Hirschheim, Klein & Lyytinen, 1996; Iivari, 1991; Lyytinen & Hirschheim, 1988).

This technology-oriented approach to IS development too often sees IS development as a narrow technological task (Wastell & Newman, 1996) and overemphasizes the design and construction of computer-based artifacts such that insufficient attention is given to the social and contextual aspects of IS development (Avison et al., 1998). This does not take into account the cultural, social, and political aspects of systems design (Lyytinen, 1987).

Along with these claims, a growing number of researchers suggest new views on information systems from different perspectives, such as critical social theory (Ngwenyama & Lee, 1997), hermeneutics (Boland, 1987; Lee, 1994; Myers, 1994), phenomenology (Boland, 1985), activity theory (Kuutti, 1996), constructionism, critical systems thinking (Ivanov, 1991; Jackson, 1992), and postmodernism. These different perspectives seem to provide different directions, yet one thing in common: they all take a social and humanistic view of IS development, rather than a mechanistic view. The social and humanistic view of information systems tends to pursue common principles, including user participation, pluralism, autonomy, privacy, social contexts, evolutionary change, emancipation, and democracy. For example, a substantial body of research views information systems as social constructs or social systems and information systems development as a social process (e.g., Davis et al., 1992; Hirschheim & Klein, 1994; Hirschheim et al., 1996; Lee, 1999; Myers, 1994; Newman & Robey, 1992).

Many researchers (e.g., Bjerknes & Bratteteig, 1995; Corbett et al., 1999; Ehn, 1989; Mumford, 1993) point out the problems arising from technically-led systems design and implementation methodologies and suggest more human actor participatory design practices. Hirschheim and Klein (1994) reformulated Mumford's ETHICS to achieve emancipatory principles, and Haynes (2000) proposes a model consistent with *perspectival* thinking.

In addition, it is argued that we need unconventional computer architectures for new dynamic knowledge bases with high contextuality created by today's organizations (Tuomi, 1995). Malhotra (2000) proposes a sense-making model whose philosophical bases are Churchman's (1971) Kantian and Hegelian inquiry systems. Following the tradition of multiple perspectives (e.g., Avison et al., 1998; Mitroff & Linstone 1993), Courtney (2001) points out that various perspectives offer much greater insights into the nature of the problem but that extant DSSs rely heavily on the technical perspective, failing to consider organizational and personal perspectives. Further, he calls for a greatly expanded view of DSS that supports not only technical perspectives but also humane aspects of decision making, organizational, individual, ethical, and aesthetic perspectives. It appears that we may need the process of *decision breaking* (a diverging process) prior to *decision making* (a converging or synthesizing process) to produce more intellectual solutions for wicked problems. Thus, it may lead us to consider designing *decision-breaking systems* and integrating them with existing *decision-making systems.*

Here it is argued that we need to examine our assumptions on extant IS development approaches and technologies and engage the Hegelian dialectic to devise a new paradigm. The synthesis would be the new paradigm of information systems for facilitating diverse contradictory interpretations and supporting various perspectives for the 21st century. We believe it is in line with Churchman's (1971) discussion of designs of Hegelian and, particularly, Singerian inquiry through a *sweeping-in* process which consists in bringing concepts and variables from variously different perspectives into an inquiry in order to both create and overcome inconsistencies.

We further predict that the new paradigm of information systems should not be knowledge-based but wisdom-based, what we call *wisdom-based information systems.* Wisdom is knowledge with moral and ethical concerns (Courtney, 2001). Ackoff (1999) sees that the distinction between doing things right and doing the right things is the same as that between information and knowledge and wisdom. He believes that information and knowledge contribute primarily to efficiency, and "for effectiveness wisdom is required" (p. 162). He defines wisdom as the ability to perceive and evaluate the long-run consequences of behavior. Wisdom sees a big picture and guides us where we are and what we need to do for the larger systems. Information and knowledge often change, but wisdom does not. It seeks a better sense of what is *good* for the larger systems and the nature of deep issues (Senge, 1995). Senge (1995) points out that in order for organizations to prosper over the long term they must contribute something to the larger systems (customers, communities, employees). Hegel himself is a paradigm source of instruction in relation to wisdom. The real strife for Hegel was the battle between the propositional world of the true and the false and what he called Speculative Judgement, or the unity of idea (or meaning). For Hegel, the unity of the idea, which is *ceteris paribus,* sought out for the purpose of wisdom as an agreement with other humans (rather than whether a particular piece of knowledge is either true or false) occurs in a special environment of trust and respect that fosters the genuine nature of humanity. "It is the nature of humanity to press onward to agreement with others: human nature only really exists in an achieved community of minds" (Hegel, 1977, p. 43).

This notion of wisdom in Hegel and its connection with a community of minds finds its fullest expression in what Hegel meant by *Spirit.*

"The Spirit of this world is a spiritual essence that is permeated by a self-consciousness which knows itself, and knows the essence as an actuality confronting it. But the existence of this world, as also the actuality of self-consciousness, rests on the process in which the latter divests itself of its personality, thereby creating its world." (Hegel, 1977, p. 297)

But this is not to be taken literally, rather it is to be taken in the very mode of wisdom that Hegel advocates, namely, as an essence (or essential thinking) which does not take its foundation from what happens to be true or what happens to be false. We happen to literally have a personality but Hegel is not advocating that we literally divest ourselves of it. What Hegel is saying is that in order to maintain the power inherent in self-consciousness, *per se,* we must be informed by that self-consciousness which both knows itself and knows the essence of what confronts it. Our personality only represents the outward literal signs of that self-consciousness. Self-consciousness finds its expression and most especially its power in a meeting of minds that forms for itself its own community. It is not so much the literal fact of the existence of the community but the experience of what being in a genuine community does to the individual (member's) expression of self-consciousness. When the members tune-in to each other, it is in that tuning-in that their own personality is divested; they are tuning-in to the rhythm of self-consciousness, a rhythm which cannot be discovered other than by experiencing ideas which are outside those of the individual personality. Part of the power of Hegelian self-consciousness is intuition, which is a natural and highly sought after outcome of wisdom.

From the above we can see why it is that to be ethical or possess wisdom is also to be spiritual. Mitroff and Denton (1999) believe that being spiritual means having a "basic feeling of being connected with one's complete self, others, and the entire universe" (p. 83)—interconnectedness. Their empirical study of spirituality in the workplace reports that senior executives and managers associated with organizations they perceive as more spiritual also see their organizations as more profitable, and they could deploy more of their full creativity, emotions, and intelligence in spiritual-based organizations. The authors claim that profits follow directly from being ethical, not the other way around.

In this sense, wisdom will be the core competency for organizations to remain competitive over the long run. Thus, it is suggested that it is not too early to consider the implications of wisdom and spirituality in the field of information systems. We believe that the wisdom-based information systems must be designed *ecologically* and deliver not only accounting data or financial information but also be concerned with corporate social responsibility, care, and trust to people within and between organizations. Spirituality resides in our everyday lives. Extant information systems are mainly designed to support problem-solving and goal-oriented tasks so they clearly lack support for many everyday activities. It means we need a radically different approach to the design of information systems. In addition, what we mean by *ecologically designed* is that the information system must be culturally and socially *sustainable* with human systems. Thus, the notion of wisdom-based information systems may add another critical principle—sustainable improvement—to the design and development of information systems, particularly global information systems, large-scale information systems, global IT infrastructure (the Internet), and so forth. As for this new principle, IS researchers and practitioners as system designers must stay away from any "contentment" and instead possess the "heroic mood" (Churchman, 1971, p. 202) to strive for a comprehensive rationality of their designs.

Summary

In summary, we have argued that organizations today face many wicked problems and wicked environments. Wicked problems and wicked environments require multiple diverse and contradictory interpretations of data and reality. These problems and environments require wicked learning (double-loop learning, strategic learning, generative learning, and higher-level learning). The Hegelian model is well-suited for wicked learning environments. Information technology to support cognitive mapping, negotiation, and argumentation may be helpful in creating and capturing diverse contradictory interpretations of data, leading to more effective forms of wicked learning. We thus believe that organizations should consider an Hegelian approach to problem solving and relevant information technology to support the dialect approach.

Furthermore, we have argued that the rigid structures of many extant information systems often result in difficulties when applied in wicked contexts, and much of the rigidity of extant information systems stems from their philosophical basis, logical positivism, and functionalistic technology-driven development models. Thus, there is the need to revisit our assumptions on extant information systems, and a new paradigm of information systems is needed for the 21st century that is social and humanistic rather then mechanistic and reductionistic. Wisdom is the core competency for the organization's long-term success, so the new information systems should be wisdom-based.

We further believe that a mechanistic paradigm of information systems today should turn over its position to a new paradigm arising from new emerging philosophical views on information systems development. As an alternative, we have suggested wisdom and spirituality as an additional principle for the design and development of information systems.

References

Ackoff, R. L. (1999). *Re-creating the corporation: A design of organizations for the 21st century.* New York: Oxford University Press.

Anghern, A., and Jelassi, T. (1994). DSS Research and Practice in Perspective. *Decision Support Systems*, 12, 267-275.

Applegate, L. M., DeSanctis, G., & Jackson, B. (1995). *Technology, teams, and organizations: Implementing groupware at Texaco.* Invited multimedia paper delivered at Harvard Business School Colloquium Multi-Media and the Boundaryless World.

Arbnor, I., & Bjerke, B. (1997). *Methodology for creating business knowledge.* Thousand Oaks, CA: Sage.

Argyris, C., & Schon, D. (1996). *Organizational learning II.* Reading, MA: Addison-Wesley.

Avison, D. E., Wood-Harper, A. T., Vidgen, R. T., & Wood, J. R. G. (1998). A further exploration into information systems development: The evolution of Multiview2. *Information Technology & People, 11*(2), 124-139.

Balasubramaniam, R., & Sengupta, K. (1995). Multimedia in a design rationale decision support system. *Decision Support Systems, 15,* 181-196.

Balasubramanian, V. (1997). Organizational learning and information systems. Retrieved September 2, 2004, from *http://eies.njit.edu/~333/orglrn.html*

Bannon, L. (1997). *Group decision support systems: An analysis and critique.* The 5th European Conference on Information Systems, Cork, (pp. 526-539).

Barley, S. (1986). Technology as an occasion for structuring: Evidence from observations of CT scanners and the social order of radiology departments. *Administration Science Quarterly, 31,* 78-108.

Bijker, W. E. (1995). Sociohistorical technology studies. In S. Jasanoff, G. E. Markle, J. C. Petersen, & T. Pinch (Eds.), *Handbook of science and technology studies* (pp. 230-256). Thousand Oaks: Sage.

Bijker, W. E., & Pinch, T. J. (1987). The social construction of facts and artefacts: Or how the sociology of science and the sociology of technology might benefit each other. In W. E. Bijker, T. P. Hughes, & T. J. Pinch (Eds.), *The social construction of technological systems: New directions in the sociology and history of technology* (pp. 17-50). Cambridge: MIT Press.

Bjerknes, G., & Bratteteig, T. (1995). User participation and democracy: A discussion of Scandinavian research on systems development. *Scandinavian Journal of Information Systems, 7*(1), 73-98.

Bloomfield, B. P., Coombs, R., Owen, J., & Taylor, P. (1997). Doctors as managers: Constructing systems and users in the national health service. In B. P. Bloomfield, R. Coombs, D. Knights, & D. Litter (Eds.), *Information technology and organizations* (pp. 112-134). Oxford: Oxford University Press.

Bodart, F., Bui, T., Melard, P., & Vanreusel, J. (1997). A system for argumentation support and organizational memory. Proceedings of the Thirty Annual Hawaii International Conference on Systems Sciences, IEEE Computer Society Press, Los Alamitos, CA, 524-532.

Boland, R. (1985). Phenomenology: A preferred approach to research in information systems. In E. Mumford, R. A. Hirschheim, G. Fitzgerald, & T. Woodharper (Eds.), *Research methods in information systems* (pp. 193-201). Amsterdam: North-Holland Publishers.

Boland, R. (1987). The in-formation of information systems. In R. Boland & R. Hirschheim (Eds.), *Wiley series in information systems* (pp. 132-142). Chichester, UK: John Wiley & Sons.

Boland, R., & Tenkasi, R. V. (1995). Perspective making and perspective taking in communities of knowing. *Organization Science, 6*(4), 350-372.

Boland, R., Tenkasi, R., & Te'eni, D. (1994). Designing information technology to support distributed cognition. *Organization Science, 5*(3), 456-475.

Brown, J. S. (1999). Sustaining the ecology of knowledge. *Leader to Leader, 12.*

Brown, J. S., & Duguid, P. (1998). Organizing knowledge. *California Management Review, 40*(3), 91-111.

Buckingham Shum, S. (1996). Design argumentation as design rationale. In A. Kent & J. Williams (Eds.), *The encyclopedia of computer science and technology* (pp. 95-128). New York: Marcel Dekker, Inc.

Churchman, C. W. (1971). *The design of inquiring systems.* New York: Basic Books.

Conklin, J., & Begeman, M. L. (1988). gIBIS: A hypertext tool for exploratory policy discussion. *ACM Transactions on Office Information Systems, 6*(4), 303-331.

Corbett, J. M., Faia-Correia, M., Patriotta, G., & Brigham, M. (1999). Back up the organization: How employees and information systems re-member organizational practice. *Proceedings of the Thirty-Second Annual Hawaii International Conference on Systems Science,* IEEE Computer Society Press, Los Alamitos, CA.

Courtney, J. F. (2001). Decision making and knowledge management in inquiring organizations: A new decision-making paradigm for DSS. *Decision Support Systems: Special Issue on Knowledge Management, 31,* 17-38.

Courtney, J. F., Croasdell, D., & Paradice, D. B. (1998). Inquiring organizations. *Australian Journal of Information Systems, 6*(1), 3-15.

Daft, R. L., & Lengel, R. H. (1986). Organizational information requirements, media richness and structural design. *Management Science, 32*(2), 554-571.

Davis, G. B., Lee, A. S., Nickles, K. R., Chatterjee, S., Hartung, R., & Wu, Y. (1992). Diagnosis of an information system failure: A framework and interpretive process. *Information & Management, 23,* 293-318.

DeGeus, A. (1988). Planning as learning. *Harvard Business Review 66*(2), 70-74.

DeSanctis, G., & Gallupe, R. B. (1987). A foundation for the study of group decision support systems. *Management Science, 33*(5), 589-609.

DeSanctis, G., & Poole, M. S. (1994). Capturing the complexity in advanced technology use: Adaptive structuration theory. *Organization Science, 5*(2), 121-147.

Eden, C. (1992). On the nature of cognitive maps. *Journal of Management Studies, 29*(3), 261-265.

Ehn, P. (1989). *Work-oriented design of computer artifacts.* Hillsdale, NJ: Lawrence Erlbaum.

Eisenhardt, K. (1999). Strategy as strategic decision making. *Sloan Management Review, 40*(3), 65-72.

Eisenhardt, K., Kathwajy, J., & Bourgeois, L. (1997). How management teams can have a good fight. *Harvard Business Review, 75*(4), 77-85.

Ellinor, L., & Gerard, G. (1998). Dialogue: Rediscover the transforming power of conversation. New York: John Wiley & Sons.

Fiol, C. M., & Lyles, M. A. (1985). Organizational learning. *Association of Management Review, 10*(4), 803-813.

Fulmer, R. M., Gibbs, P., & Keys, J. B. (1998). The second generation learning organizations: New tools for sustaining competitive advantage. *Organizational Dynamics, 27*(2), 6-15.

Garvin, D.A. (1993). Building Learning Organization. *Harvard Business Review, 71*(4), 78-91.

Gordon, T. F., & Karacapilidis, N. (1997). The Zeno argumentation framework. *Proceedings of the Sixth International Conference on Artificial Intelligence and Law*, 10-18.

Harri-Augstein, S., & Thomas, L. F. (1991). *Learning conversations: The self-organized learning way to personal and organisational growth.* London, New York: Routledge.

Hashim, S. (1991). WHAT: An argumentative groupware approach for organizing and documenting research activities. *Journal of Organizational Computing, 1*(3), 275-302.

Haynes, J. D. (1999). Phenomenological aspects of Churchman's Hegelian inquiring system. *Proceedings of the Fifth Americas Conference on Information Systems*, 633-635.

Haynes, J. D. (2000). *Perspectival thinking—For inquiring organizations.* New Zealand: Thisone.

Hedberg, B. (1981). How organizations learn and unlearn. In C. Nystrom & W. H. Starbuck (Eds.), *Handbook of organizational design*, Oxford University Press.

Hegel, G. W. F. (1977). *Phenomenology of spirit* (A.V. Miller, Trans.). Oxford University Press. (Original work published 1807.)

Henfridsson, O., & Söderholm, A. (2000). Barriers to learning: On organizational defenses and vicious circles in technological adaptation. *Accounting, Management and Information Technologies, 10*(1), 33-51.

Hiltz, S., & Turoff, M. (1978). *The networked nation.* Cambridge, MA: MIT Press.

Hirschheim, R., & Klein, H. K. (1994). Realizing emancipatory principles in information systems development: The case for ETHICS. *MIS Quarterly, 18*(1), 83-109.

Hirschheim, R., Klein, H., & Lyytinen, K. (1996). Exploring the intellectual structures of information systems development: A social action theoretic analysis. *Accounting, Management and Information Technology, 6*(1-2), 1-64.

Hodges, W. S. (1991). *Dialectron: A prototypical dialectic engine for the support of strategic planning and strategic decision making.* Unpublished doctoral dissertation, Texas A&M University.

Huber, G. (1991). Organizational learning: The contributing processes and literature. *Organization Science, 2*, 88-115.

Ivanov, K. (1991). Critical systems thinking and information technology. *Journal of Applied Systems Analysis, 18*, 39-55.

Jackson, M. C. (1992). An integrated programme for critical thinking in information systems research. *Journal of Information Systems, 2*, 83-95.

Jain, B. A., & Solomon, J. S. (2000). The effect of task complexity and conflict handling styles on computer-supported negotiations. *Information & Management, 37*, 161-168.

Jarke, M., Gebhardt, M., Jacobs, S., & Nissen, H. (1996). Conflict analysis across heterogeneous viewpoints: Formalization and visualization. *Proceedings of the*

Twenty-Ninth Annual Hawaii International Conference on Systems Sciences, IEEE Computer Society Press, Los Alamitos, CA, 199-208.

Jones, M. (1994). Information Technology for Group Decision Support: Beyond GDSS. *Journal of Organizational Computing,* 4(1), 23-39.

Kakola, T. (1995). Designing and deploying coordination technologies for fostering organizational working and learning. *Scandinavian Journal of Information Systems,* 7(2), 45-74.

Kersten, G. E., & Noronha, S. (1999). WWW-based negotiation support: Design, implementation, and use. *Decision Support Systems, 25,* 135-154.

Kienholz, A. (1999). Systems Rethinking: An inquiring systems approach to the art and practice of the learning organization. Foundations of information systems: Towards a philosophy of information technology. Retrieved September 2, 2004, from *http://www.cba.uh.edu/~parks/fis/inqre2a1.htm*

Kiesler, S. (1986). The hidden message in computer networks. *Harvard Business Review, 64*(1), 46-58.

Klein, H. K., & Hirschheim, R. (1985). Fundamental issues of decision support systems: A consequentialist perspective. *Decision Support Systems, 1,* 5-24.

Kling, R. (1980). Social analyses of computing: Theoretical perspectives in recent empirical research. *Computing Surveys, 12*(1), 61-110.

Kuutti, K. (1996). Activity theory as a potential framework for human-computer interaction research. In B. A. Nardi (Ed.), *Context and consciousness.* Cambridge: MIT Press.

Lee, A. (1994). Researching MIS. In W. Currie & B. Galliers (Eds.), *Rethinking management information systems* (pp. 7-27). Oxford: Oxford University Press.

Lee, A. (1999). Researching MIS. In W. Currie & B. Galliers (Eds.), *Rethinking management information systems* (pp. 7-27). Oxford: Oxford University Press.

Lee, A. S. (1994). Electronic mail as a medium for rich communication: An empirical investigation using hermeneutic interpretation. *MIS Quarterly, 18*(2), 143-157.

Lee, S., Courtney, J. F., & O'Keefe, R. M. (1992). A system for organizational learning using cognitive maps. *OMEGA: The International Journal of Management Science, 20*(1), 23-36.

Leonard, D., & Straus, S. (1997). Putting your company's whole brain to work. *Harvard Business Review, 75*(4), 111-121.

Levey, J., & Levet, M. (1994). Wisdom at work. In S. Chawla & J. Renesch (Eds.), *Learning organizations: Developing cultures for tomorrow's workplace.* Portland: Productivity Press.

Levitt, B., & March, J. G. (1988). Organizational learning. *Annual Review of Sociology, 14,* 126-146.

Lyytinen, K. (1987). Different perspectives on information systems: Problems and solutions. *ACM Computing Surveys,* 19(1), 5-43.

Lyytinen, K. (1992). Information systems and critical theory. In M. Alvesson & H. Willmott (Eds.), *Critical management studies* (pp. 159-180). London: Sage.

Lyytinen, K., & Hirschheim, R. (1988). Information systems as rational discourse: An application of Habermas's theory of communicative action. *Scandinavian Journal of Information Systems, 4*(1-2), 19-30.

Malhotra, Y. (1997). Knowledge management in inquiring organizations. Proceedings of the Third Americas Conference on Information Systems, 293-295.

Malhotra, Y. (2000). Knowledge management and new organization forms: A framework for business model innovation. *Information Resources Management Journal, 13*(1), 5-14.

Mason, R. M. (1993). Strategic information systems: Use of information technology in a learning organization. Proceedings of the Twenty-Sixth Annual Hawaii International Conference on Systems Sciences, IEEE Computer Society Press, Los Alamitos, CA, 840-849.

Mason, R. O. (1969). A dialectical approach to strategic planning. *Management Science, 15*(8), B403-B414.

Mason, R.O. (1981). Basic concepts for designing management information systems. In R.O. Mason & B. Swanson (Eds.), *Measurement for management decision* (pp. 81-95). MA: Addison-Wesley.

Mason, R. O., & Mitroff, I. I. (1981). Challenging strategic planning assumptions. New York: John Wiley & Sons.

Mitroff, I. I. (1971). A communication model of dialectical inquiring systems: A strategy for strategic planning. *Management Science, 17*(10), 634-648.

Mitroff, I. I., & Denton, E. (1999). A study of spirituality in the workplace. *Sloan Management Review, 40*(4), 83-92.

Mitroff, I. I., & Linstone, H. A. (1993). *The unbounded mind: Breaking the chains of traditional business thinking.* New York: Oxford University Press.

Moore, J. (1996). *The death of competition.* New York: HarperCollins.

Mumford, E. (1993). The participation of users in systems design: An account of the origin, evolution, and use of ETHICS method. In D. Schuler & A. Namioka (Eds.), *Participatory design: Principles and practices* (pp. 257-270). Hillside, NJ: Lawrence Erlbaum.

Myers, M. D. (1994). Dialectical hermeneutics: A theoretical framework for the implementation of information systems. *Information Systems Journal, 5,* 51-70.

Nadler, D. A., Shaw, R. B., & Walton, E. A. (1995). *Discontinuous change: Leading organizational transformation.* San Francisco: Jossey-Bass.

Nelson, J. A., & Mitroff, I. I. (1974). An experiment in dialectic information systems. *Journal of the American Society for Information Science, 25*(4), 252-262.

Nevis, E. C., DiBella, A. J., & Gould, J. M. (1995). Understanding organizations as learning systems. *Sloan Management Review, 36*(2), 73-85.

Newman, M., & Robey, D. (1992). A social process model of user-analyst relationships. *MIS Quarterly, 16*(2), 249-266.

Ngwenyama, O. K., & Lee, A. S. (1997). Communication richness in electronic mail: Critical social theory and the complexity of meaning. *MIS Quarterly, 21*(2), 145-167.

Ngwenyama, O., & Lyytinen, K. J. (1997). Groupware environments as action constitutive resources: A social action framework for analyzing groupware technologies. *Computer Supported Cooperative Work: The Journal of Collaborative Computing, 6,* 71-93.

Nissen, H. E. (1989). Information systems development for responsible action. In H. Klein & K. Kumar (Eds.), *Systems development for human progress* (pp. 91-113). Amsterdam: North-Holland.

Nonaka, I., & Takeuchi, H. (1995). The knowledge-creating company. Oxford: Oxford University Press.

Nonaka, I., Reinmoeller, P., and Senoo, D. (1998). The 'Art' of Knowledge: Systems to Capitalize on Market Knowledge. *European Management Journal,* 673-684.

Orlikowski, W. (2000). Using technology and constituting structures: A practice lens for studying technology in organizations. *Organization Science, 10*(2), 15-30.

Orlikowski, W. (1992). The duality of technology: Rethinking the concept of technology in organization. *Organization Science,* 3(2), 398-427.

Orlikowski, W. J., & Gash, D. C. (1994). Technological frame: Making sense of information technology in organizations. *ACM Transactions on Information Systems, 12*(2), 174-207.

Orlikowski, W., & Hoffman, J.D. (1997). An improvisational model for change management: The case of groupware technologies. *Sloan Management Review,* Winter, 11-21.

Orlikowski, W. J., Yates, J., Okamura, K., & Fujimoto, M. (1995). Shaping electronic communications: The metastructuring of technology in use. *Organization Science,* 6(4), 423-444.

Ouksel, A. M., Mihavics, K., & Chalos, P. (1997). Accounting information systems and organization learning. *Accounting, Management and Information Technology,* 7(1), 1-19.

Prahalad, C. K., & Hamel, G. (1990). The core competence of the corporation. *Harvard Business Review, 68*(3), 79-91.

Preskill, H., & Torres, R. (1999). The role of evaluation enquiry in creating learning organizations. In M. Easterby-Smith, J. Burgoyne, & L. Arqujo (Eds.), *Organizational learning and the learning organization* (pp. 93-114). Thousand Oaks, CA: Sage.

Rana, A. R., & Turoff, M. (1996). Inquiring systems' validation approaches as determinants of the media richness for technology supported group work. *Proceedings of the Second Americas Conference on Information Systems,* (pp. 440-442).

Richardson, S. M., Courtney, J. F., & Paradice, D. B. (2001). An assessment of the Singerian approach to organizational learning: Case from academia and the utility industry. *Information Systems Frontiers: Special Issue on Philosophical Reasoning in Information Systems Research, 3*(1), 49-62.

Rittel, H. (1970). Some principles for the design of an educational system for design. *DMG-DRS Journal: Design Research and Methods, 7*(2).

Rittel, H., & Webber, M. (1973). Dilemmas in a general theory of planning. *Policy Sciences, 4*, 155-169.

Schon, D. A., & Rein, M. (1994). *Frame reflection: Toward the resolution of intractable policy controversies.* New York: Basic Books.

Schultze, U. (2000). A confessional account of an ethnography about knowledge work. *MIS Quarterly, 24*(1), 3-42.

Senge, P. (1990). *The fifth discipline: The art and practice of the learning organization.* New York: Century Business.

Senge, P. (1992). Building Learning ORganizations. *Journal for Quality & Participation,* 15(2), 30-38.

Senge, P. (1995). Making a better world. *Executive Excellence, 12*(8), 18-19.

Shaw, M. L., & Gaines, B. (1995). Comparing constructions through the Web. *Proceedings of the Computer Supported Cooperative Learning.*

Sheetz, S. D., Tegarden, D. P., Kenneth, K., & Ilze, Z. (1994). A group support systems approach to cognitive mapping. *Journal of Management Information Systems, 11*(1), 31-57.

Sproull, L., & Kiesler, S. (1991). Computers, networks and work. *Scientific American, 265*(3), 84-91.

Star, S. L., & Griesemer, J. (1989). Institutional ecology, translations and boundary objects: Amateurs and professionals in Berkeley's museum of vertebrate zoology. *Social Studies of Science, 19*, 387-420.

Stohr, E.A., and Benn R. Konsynski. (1992). *Information Systems and Decision Processes,* Los Alimotos, CA: IEEE Computer Science Press.

Toulmin, S. (1958). *The uses of argument.* Cambridge: Cambridge University Press.

Tuomi, I. (1995). Abstraction and history from institutional amnesia to organizational memory. *Proceedings of the Twenty-Eighth Annual Hawaii International Conference on Systems Science,* IEEE Computer Society Press, Los Alamitos, CA, 303-312.

Tweed, C. (1998). Supporting argumentation practices in urban planning and design. *Computers, Environment and Urban Systems, 22*(4), 351-363.

von Hippel, E. (1988). *The sources of innovation.* New York: Oxford University Press.

Wastell, D., & Newman, M. (1996). Information systems design, stress and organizational change in the ambulance services: A tale of two cities. *Accounting, Management and Information Technology, 6*(4), 283-300.

Weick, K.E., & Meader, D.K. (1993). Sensemaking and group support systems. In L.M. Jessup & J.S. Valacich (Eds.), *Group support systems new perspectives* (pp. 230-254). New York: Macmillan Publishing Company.

Whitaker, R. (1994). GDSS' Formative Fundaments: An Interpretive Analysis. *CSCW: An International Journal,* 2(4), 241-262.

Yates, J. (1997). Using Giddens' structuration theory to information business history. *Business and Economic History, 26*(1), 159-183.

Zuboff, S. (1988). *In the age of the smart machine.* New York: Basic Books.

Chapter III

The Design and Evolution of Singerian Inquiring Organizations:
Inspiring Leadership for Wise Action

Alice Kienholz
Calgary, Canada

Abstract

In this chapter, Singerian inquiring organizations are further developed as the most appropriate type of inquiring organization for moving from knowledge management to wisdom by elaborating on the original knowledge management concepts and framework proposed by Croasdell, Courtney, and Paradice (1998). In moving from knowledge management to wisdom, the author has integrated some of the most classic and substantive thinking, research, and practices in the leadership and wisdom literature into the design of Singerian inquiring organizations.

Introduction

The purpose of this chapter is to offer some insights into the nature, origins, and development of wisdom and how such understanding can be applied to inspire leadership for wise thought and action through inquiring organizations--specifically, Singerian inquiring organizations. According to the designers of inquiring organizations, Courtney,

Croasdell, and Paradice (1996), inquiring organizations are comprised of special systems whose actions result in the creation of knowledge. Inquiring organizations are based on C. West Churchman's (1971) classic treatise, "The Design of Inquiring Systems," and provide a new perspective on the design of learning organizations and how this design can be justified. The five main historical and philosophically-based ways of thinking and coming to know that form these inquiring systems and, in turn, the inquiring organizations are ascribed to the philosophers Lock, Leibniz, Kant, Hegel, and E. A. Singer. As Courtney, Croasdell, and Paradice (1998) explain, Singerian inquiring organizations operate on the principle of metrology. Using a system of measures, the Singerian inquirer continuously monitors, refines, and revises data and information in order to achieve progress in the generation of valid knowledge. Rapid learning and unlearning, insightful thinking, and wise actions are vital as we move into the 21st century with its accelerating pace, technological changes, discontinuity, unpredictability, and complexity. Beginning in 1996, Courtney, Croasdell, and Paradice outlined five types of inquiring organizations based on each of Churchman's five inquiring systems. As Mason and Mitroff (1973) point out, dealing with ill-structured environments requires more substantive and dynamic systems of inquiry than the consensus building systems ascribed to Locke and Leibniz, which generally provide only one perspective of a problem and are thus not suited for dealing with wicked environments. Singerian inquiring organizations enable one to draw on not only the fact-oriented and functional Lockean and Leibnizian inquiring systems but also the more value-oriented and substantive Kantian and Hegelian inquiring systems. Singerian inquiring organizations are thus designed to be more efficacious in enabling the creation, acquisition, capture, sharing, adaptation, dissemination, and utilization of knowledge than any of the other four forms of inquiring organizations.

Recent literature in the management of information systems has focused on the progression of managing first data, then information, and, finally, knowledge. As this body of knowledge developed, a whole litany of knowledge management (KM) concepts and buzzwords ensued, including knowledge capture, creation, harvesting, utilization, sharing, dissemination, and so forth (Davenport & Prusak, 1998; Nonaka & Takeuchi, 1995). With such a substantial body of knowledge now available on knowledge management, some are looking to take this progression to the next level. This brings us to the pursuit of wisdom and how we might understand, develop, and apply it for leading and managing organizations or learning organizations. This chapter will, however, extend that pursuit to include a more integrative and dynamic goal that is more befitting such a high aspiration as wisdom, namely, Singerian inquiring organizations.

Evolution of Knowledge Management

From Knowledge Management to Knowledge Ecology

Malhotra (1998) poses two fundamental questions regarding knowledge management: (1) Can information systems be managed? (2) Can we therefore assume that knowledge can be managed? As he sees it, the concept of knowledge management is based on predictive models, yet people would be better served through the application of models capable of responding to organizational white-waters that demand the *anticipation of surprise*. What is needed, according to Malhotra (1998, 2002) then, is an organizational ecology capable of developing and sustaining what he refers to as *loose-tight* knowledge management systems. As he explains, these systems retain the idea of best practices through an ongoing process of construction and reconstruction of such practices. They are *loose* in that they allow for the continuous re-examination of the underlying assumptions of the best practices and the interpretation of this information. They are *tight* in that they also allow for efficiencies derived from the propagation and dissemination of the best practices.

As Malhotra (1998) points out, knowledge management systems as they are currently conceived are largely incapable of handling the kind of continuous learning and unlearning processes required by the increasing pace of discontinuous and radical change. Such discontinuous change requires the continuous examination and renewal of the basic assumptions underlying *best practices* stored in organizational knowledge bases. Otherwise, the hardwiring of such assumptions results in organizational insensitivity to the organization's changing environment, but identifying and being aware of our many assumptions is a daunting task. Understanding and awareness of the kinds of assumptions that an organization holds is made more lucid and apparent through an understanding of Churchman's five basic inquiring systems and the underlying assumptions on which each is based.

According to Krogh, Ichijo, and Nonaka (2000) knowledge cannot be managed, only enabled; thus, they propose enabling knowledge creation rather than managing it. They identify five knowledge enablers: (1) instill a knowledge vision, (2) manage conversation, (3) mobilize knowledge activists, (4) create the right context, and (5) globalize local knowledge. While they never mentioned leadership, *per se,* they did recommend that managers need to be caring and that a caring manager requires wisdom. This means that they must understand the needs of others as well as the needs of the group, the company, and society.

Churchman's (1971, 1979, 1982, 1994) critical systemic thinking provides a more holistic, substantive, and dynamic approach to addressing knowledge issues by going beyond the fact-oriented and functional assumptions of systems thinking to a more substantive value-oriented approach. Based on a Singerian system of inquiry, critical systemic thinking therefore includes both of these approaches and then takes it to the next level by also including its aesthetic, ethical, and spiritual dimensions. Courtney, Croasdell, and Paradice (1996), Malhotra, (1997), Flood (1999), and Kienholz (1999), therefore call for a rethinking of the assumptions underlying Senge's (1990) *The Fifth Discipline*. Learning organizations, as proposed by Senge (1990), are based on the assumption that systems thinking is fundamental to all the other disciplines. He describes these five disciplines as component technologies that are gradually converging to innovate learning organizations. They include, besides the fifth discipline of systems thinking, personal mastery, mental models, building shared vision, and team learning. It is here proposed that systems thinking is therefore a necessary but not sufficient component of the kind of efficacious evolving systems of inquiry that are required for today's learning organizations. Singerian inquiring organizations have the design potential to provide the kind of loose-tight knowledge management systems and efficacy needed to address the kind of complexity, discontinuous change, and the element of surprise that characterize the wicked environments of today's organizational reality.

Matthews (1997) also identifies similar concepts for moving from knowledge management to wisdom in the management of knowledge for a global water company, Anglian Waters, and its *University of Water* learning facility in the United Kingdom. Using the metaphor of a Double Helix for representing the development of wisdom, he delineates a progression of intellectual capital components, followed by their complementary behaviors (cb). Thus, beginning with *historical data and experience*, the cb would be *Analytical.* Moving to *information,* the cb would be *Interpretive.* For *knowledge*, the cb would be *Contemplative.* For *wisdom*, the cb is *Inspirational Understanding.* *Creativity* comes next, and its cb is *Insightful,* followed by *Innovation,* for which the cb is *Entrepreneurial.* This is followed by another *new data experience,* and once again, the cb is *Analytical. Historical data and experience, information, and knowledge* follow, and, finally, the cycle concludes with *progress and versatility.* As he sees it, organizations will need to create and use wisdom in making the change to being versatile organizations. He regards the process of change as a managed paradox. While there are demands for greater public involvement, greater employee involvement and support, and greater environmental investment, on the one hand, there are also demands for lower costs, less bureaucracy, less peripheral activity, greater focus, and fewer employees, on the other. Although Matthews never mentioned it, managing this paradox could be enabled through the application of Churchman's five inquiring systems such that each inquiring system is drawn on when it is the most appropriate for handling circumstances as they occur or for rigorously planning ahead. Thus, in Singerian inquiring systems terminology, they would be situationally responsive in any given circumstance. Matthews (1997) sees the end result of creating and sustaining knowledge for sustainable water management as wisdom creation and versatility with the stability of public service being matched with the change capability of entrepreneurial business. With this in mind, we turn now to finding ways of enabling wisdom through Singerian inquiring organizations.

The Evolution of Leadership Wisdom

From Knowledge Management/Ecology to Leadership for Enabling Wisdom in the Workplace

Robert Galvin (2000), who was at the helm of the Motorola Corporation for over 40 years, outlined 12 developmental endeavors for moving knowledge management toward wisdom. He based them on his belief that the greater value to be achieved under the rubric of managing knowledge and intellectual capital is to be found within us and our peers personally and not any, albeit, significant institutional policies and practices. These twelve endeavors are listed below with the present author's commentary in italics:

- Timely mastery, again and again, versus life-long learning, which, as he explains, implies a plodding pace where we have plenty of time to achieve learning.

- Teach to learn better, *since the best way to learn something is to teach it.*

- Be the best compared to your counterparts among your competitors.

- Appreciate that knowledge saves time and money.

- We now know that creative thinking can be taught and learned, thus *everyone can be creative.*

- Creativity is what differentiates the quality of our judgements.

- Counterintuitive thinking is more often right. *Thus, we need to examine our assumptions much of the time. Understanding Churchman's five main inquiring systems can be helpful here. See Harrison and Bramson (1982), The Art of Thinking, or Mitroff (1998),* Smart Thinking for Crazy Times.

- Search for the essence within relevant knowledge. *Again, the best system of inquiry for getting at essences is the Hegelian dialectic or the Synthesist mode of inquiry outlined by Harrison and Bramson (1982).*

- Practice our use of knowledge through recommendations. When we are not included among the decision makers on problems or issues of importance, we can state our recommendation to ourselves and then wait to see how our judgement held up. This is especially useful for junior employees for testing themselves.

- Strive for leadership through bold activation of what is known. Boldness is the acid test of whether we have used and processed knowledge wisely.

- Understand values and facts, including cultural variances. *This can be accomplished through application of Churchman's fact-oriented Lockean and Leibnizian inquiring systems and the value-oriented Kantian and Hegelian inquiring systems.*

- Strive for highest quality, particularly the quality of thinking (p. 59). *Quality of thinking is made more accessible and tangible through understanding the five inquiring systems. The fact-oriented and functional Lockean and Leibnizian systems are more simplistic and therefore appropriate for well-defined, well-structured matters. The Kantian and Hegelian systems, being more holistic, substantive, and value-oriented, are more suited to complex ill-structured discontinuous issues and situations. Singerian Pragmatism in its highest form, draws on all four systems and also considers the ethical, aesthetic, and spiritual dimensions of the matter.*

Historical/Philosophical/Theological Perspectives on Wisdom

In the East, wisdom and a holistic approach have been more of an integral part of the culture than in the West and are therefore more likely to form part of business practices. For example, wisdom is referred to in Buddhism as the thousand-petaled lotus since it is believed to consist of 972 facets or petals. While in the West, we recognize that wisdom is a many-faceted concept, there is less awareness of its parameters. Consequently, KM theorists and other academics, especially those outside of the humanities, arts, and fine arts have been reticent to consider it as an integral part of their discipline and to address it directly. Wisdom seems too vast and unwieldy, too abstract and complex, and somehow not relevant. Therefore, we in the business and scientific world have traditionally reverted to addressing and working with more concrete and tangible concepts like information and knowledge.

To date, KM theorists have reasoned that if information is more valuable than data, and knowledge is more valuable than information, "knowledge is power." Further reflection, however, lead them to the realization that it was the understanding and application of what was known that was of greater significance than the knowledge, *per se*. As Churchman (1971) put it, "To conceive of knowledge as a collection of information seems to rob the concept of all of its life. ...Knowledge resides in the user and not in the collection" (p. 10). In a similar vein, Nonaka and Takeuchi (1995) state that "knowledge, unlike information, is about beliefs and commitment" (p. 58). Galvin (2000) also observed that while the mastery of information processing hardware, software, and communications tools are vital for further managing knowledge and intellectual capital, they are more the *form* than the *substance* of the ultimate wisdom that we are pursuing when managing knowledge and intellectual capital.

Other recent publications, like *Working Wisdom: The Ultimate Value in the New Economy* by Dalla Costa (1995) and Matthews (1997) article, "What Lies Beyond Knowledge Management? Wisdom Creation and Versatility," are also beginning to show an appreciation of the fundamental significance of wisdom as the highest form of understanding and right action for inspiring leadership. Therefore, wisdom, or more precisely, wisdom in action, is increasingly being reflected in the business and KM literature as the highest goal to be striving toward for individual and organizational efficacy and evolution. This realization is nothing really new of course since it was known thousands of years ago in Western culture as is evident in the much quoted proverb: "Wisdom is the principle thing; therefore get wisdom: and with all thy getting, get understanding" (The Holy Bible, King James Version, Chapter IV, Verse VII). Similarly, the pre-eminence of wisdom as being among the highest virtues, and even the very purpose of life, has also been an integral part of Eastern culture for most of recorded history.

Thus, it behooves us to set our sights high and to seek after wisdom if we are to have any hope of realizing our potential as human beings and, in turn, leaders in the 21st century. Following in the style of a Singerian pragmatist, this pursuit then begins with Churchman (1982), who proposes to explicate and explain the meaning of thought in relation to wisdom through the metaphor of two conversationalists. As he so eloquently postulates, "Both thought and wisdom agree that the three cornerstones of philosophy, the Good, the True, and the Beautiful are closely intertwined; but Thought does emphasize the True, and Wisdom the Good and the Beautiful. In effect, Wisdom's ethics are based on the aesthetic" (p. i). Churchman further proposes putting a group of our ancestors together from whom we can draw, when we seek…good conversations with our ancestors. "They include: The I Ching, the Bhagavad Gita, the pre-Socratics, Plato, Aristotle, Epicurus, the Stoics, St. Paul, St. Augustine, St. Thomas, Spinoza, some Holy Books, and a selection of individuals from current history" (p. 6). Churchman further informs us that "the conversation is not only the attempt to understand what an ancestor says, but what his sayings mean in the design of our lives" (p. 5).

The Lineage Supporting Singerian Inquiring Organizations

Churchman's ideas come to us through the lineage of William James (see James, 1890). Churchman's mentor was Edgar A. Singer, who, in turn was, as William James put it, the "best all around student" in the philosophic business that he had had in his 30 years of teaching philosophy (Mitroff & Linstone, 1993). Following the completion of his Ph.D. at the University of Pennsylvania, Singer served as William James's assistant in the Department of Psychology at Harvard University for two years from 1895-1896. He then returned to his alma mater to teach in the Department of Philosophy and was appointed to a professorship in 1909. Singer's long and distinguished career in American philosophy produced many other outstanding scholars in addition to Churchman. Consequently, Singerian philosophy is evident in a wide range of disciplines, including philosophy, biology, psychology, ethics and religion, aesthetics, history, and systemic thinking (Clarke & Nahm, 1942).

Churchman, who completed BA, MA, and PhD degrees in the Department of Philosophy at the University of Pennsylvania, was also an assistant professor there, and from 1945 to 1948 served as Chairman of the Philosophy Department. Currently, Churchman is a professor emeritus, University of California, Berkeley, in the Haas School of Business and holds three Honorary Doctorates (Churchman, 2004). Churchman continues to publish and is currently working with the Institute for Management, Innovation and Organization (IMIO) at the Haas School of Business. Not surprisingly, Churchman is regarded as the leading philosopher of information systems.

Throughout his illustrious career, Churchman extended Singer's ideas significantly (i.e., see 1971, 1979, 1982, 1994), and it is through their innovative ideas that the philosophical basis for the modern systems approach was designed (Mitroff & Linstone, 1993). Churchman distinguishes himself in systems theory through his "critical systemic thinking" (Flood, 1999; Mitroff, 1998) by not only considering the matter of inquiring systems but by taking his deliberations to the next level and sweeping in the ethical and aesthetic and, most recently, the spiritual considerations. Courtney, Croasdell, and Paradice (1996) took the initiative to extend Churchman's inquiring systems for systems and organizations and applied them to learning organizations, building on the ideas of Mason and Mitroff (1973). In explaining their new perspective on learning organizations, they define inquiring organizations as "inquiring systems, or systems whose actions result in the creation of knowledge" (p. 1). Churchman's (1971) inquiring systems would thus supercede Senge's (1990) concept of systems thinking, which he based on systems theory and systems technology. Churchman's (1971) design of inquiring systems provides a more comprehensive and dynamic approach to thinking systemically by drawing on systems philosophy (see Kienholz, 1999). Croasdell, Courtney, and Paradice (1998) adapted Churchman's models of inquiring systems by explicating and explaining the philosophy of Singer as it applies to inquiring organizations. They refer to such organizations as Singerian inquiring organizations, which, in turn, constitute a central theme of this chapter.

As mentioned above, Churchman (1971) outlined five main traditions of inquiry that, as basic concepts for systems and organizations, are fundamental to Western philosophy. These he ascribed to the British philosopher John Locke, the German philosophers, Leibniz, Kant, and Hegel, and the American philosopher, Edgar A. Singer. Mitroff and Pondy (1974) and others later adapted these traditions of inquiry for use in public policy analysis and decision making. Allen Harrison and Robert Bramson, together with Nicholas Parlette and Susan Bramson (1997) then designed and developed an instrument that measured one's relative preference for these five inquiry modes. As they point out, the Inquiry Mode Questionnaire (InQ) is especially helpful in high knowledge fields that are characterized by complexity, discontinuous change and uncertainty (wicked environments). Being one of Churchman's main disciples, Ian Mitroff (1998) has continued to develop and apply Churchman's work in a variety of disciplines, including psychology, sociology, management, and information systems. Through the judicious application of Churchman's inquiring systems, we can better equip ourselves to approach any given situation or type of research in the most appropriate way. By knowing how we know and the guarantors that determine the truthfulness of each of the various ways of thinking and coming to know, we become more mindful of the kinds of assumptions that we bring to the processes used for individual, team, and organizational development and effectiveness. With this insight and understanding, we can more readily appreciate the appropriateness of alternative ways of thinking and coming to know that enable us to be situationally responsive and to provide *thought leadership* and, in turn, wise actions.

Through the five inquiring systems, we generate knowledge in terms of the assumptions we hold that underlie data collection, the kind of questions asked, and the problem solving and decision making approaches used. By understanding, appreciating, and applying the strategies, processes, and guarantors that constitute each of Churchman's inquiring systems and then integrating the ethical, aesthetic, and spiritual dimensions into the equation, researchers can better determine if they are asking the right questions for developing a comprehensive theory. Most importantly, however, it uncovers the deeper more fundamental and substantive value-oriented and human concerns of an ill-defined problem, issue, or situation (Kienholz, 2001).

A Psychological Perspective on Wisdom

The History of Psychology
"Psychology was originally the science of the soul.
First, it lost its soul-presumably in the 18th century.
Then it lost its mind, at the hand of the 19th century associationists.
Early in the 20th century it lost consciousness,
because of the Freudians and the behaviorists...
...We have now disposed of the brain and replaced it by a computing machine."
...Is the computer a tool? A liberator? A creator? A master? A monster?

Adapted from Robert B. Macleod (1963, p. 177). Note: Macleod attributed this quote to Woodworth whom he said had condensed the history of psychology into a few concise statements, which he then recounted as outlined above.

The use, misuse, abuse, and nonuse of data, information, and knowledge is fundamentally a psychological and social phenomenon. Therefore, we look to psychology and related disciplines for insight and answers to the increasing number of challenges engendered by these phenomena at the individual, organizational, and societal levels.

According to Robert Kegan, Harvard Professor of Education, "Ken Wilber is a national treasure. No one is working at the integration of Eastern and Western wisdom literature with such depth or breadth of mind and heart as he" (Testimonial taken from the back cover of Integral Psychology by Ken Wilber, 2000). So, whether you agree with Kegan's bold assertion or not, Ken Wilber is certainly a leading authority in the field. Wilber describes the evolution of wisdom as the highest level of human development from the perspective of consciousness, spirit, psychology, and therapy. This allows him to acknowledge the higher levels of spiritual development that are fundamental to understanding and developing such a lofty virtue as wisdom. As he points out, the great problem with psychology as it has historically unfolded is that different schools of psychology have regularly taken one aspect of the extraordinarily rich and multifaceted phenomenon of consciousness and declared it to be the only aspect worth studying. Wilber (2000) has provided a comprehensive definition of psychology as being the study of human consciousness and its manifestations in behavior. The *functions* of consciousness include perceiving, desiring, willing, and acting. The *structures* of consciousness, some facets of which can be unconscious, include body, mind, soul, and spirit. The *states* of consciousness include normal (e.g., waking, dreaming, sleeping) and altered (e.g., nonordinary and meditative). The *modes* of consciousness include aesthetic, moral, and scientific. The *development* of consciousness spans an entire spectrum from prepersonal to personal to transpersonal, subconscious to self-conscious to super-conscious, id to ego to spirit. The *relational* and *behavioral* aspects of consciousness refer to its mutual interaction with the objective, exterior world and the sociocultural world of shared values and perceptions (p. 1).

Thus, as Wilber (2000) explains, it is the goal of an integral psychology to endeavor to honor and embrace every legitimate aspect of human consciousness. With such an expansive and inclusive conceptualization of psychology, understanding and developing the highest stages of consciousness wherein wisdom resides is made much more likely. When comparing developmental stages of Eastern and Western forms of consciousness, Wilber found that orthodox Western psychological research begins to abandon us at the upper reaches of the spectrum of consciousness, and it becomes increasingly necessary to draw on the great sages and contemplatives of East, West, North and South (p. 10). Therefore, while we may learn from traditional psychological studies concerning the development of wisdom, we also need to consult other sources in our search for such metaphors of wisdom as the elusive *thousand-petaled lotus* aspired to in Buddhism.

In the West, the works of the French psychoanalyst Jacques Lacan have influenced nearly every field of the humanities and social sciences and provide some insight into Western intellectualism. In his major text, *Ecrits: A Selection,* Lacan (1969, 2002) provides a vehicle by which readers can exercise their perspicacity, one of the many facets of wisdom. As Palmier (1972) explains, it is through the spoken word that Lacan restores to us fragments of a teaching or of a truth, always in waiting or in retreat, always to come or withdrawn. According to John Muller and William Richardson in their reader's guide to *Ecrits*, the experience of reading Lacan is "infuriating" and "extraordinarily painful." In fact, Muller and Richardson (1982) even concede that "Summary and critique must wait for another day, when we have greater familiarity...with the seminars (many still unpublished) on which most of the *Ecrits* are based (p. 18). Thus, only after all the seminars are published and understood can *Ecrits* be fully and finally read.

What we learn from this is reflective of the lessons of life by which we come *to know*. Wisdom is a substantive and yet functional way of knowing and is *attained to* through a deep and abiding comprehension and appreciation of the whole and the parts that comprise it and how they all work together. Too often our need to know something is for the sake of imposing judgment or for appearing decisive, which reflects our simplistic and reductionistic predilection in the way we handle information and knowledge. All too often in our attempts to be efficient and to at least appear to make progress our judgments are based on incomplete information, misinterpretations, and unfounded assumptions. Lacan would therefore have us learn the importance of examining our assumptions. Examining our assumptions is one of the strategies of Churchman's Hegelian inquiring system and, in turn, the synthesist inquiry mode outlined by Harrison and Bramson (1982). With its preoccupation with the intellect (cognition), it is a necessary but not sufficient condition for wisdom.

With this philosophical, historical, theological, and psychological foundation in mind, this inquiry will move to the more conventional psychological literature to see what psychology's leading wisdom researchers can tell us about their understanding of the concept. Baltes and Staudinger (2000) characterize wisdom as a cognitive and metaheuristic (pragmatic) that organizes and orchestrates knowledge toward human excellence in mind and virtue, both individually and collectively. Paul Baltes and his team at the Max Planck Institute for Human Development in Berlin, Germany are major contributors to the psychological research on the study of wisdom, using a largely empirical approach. The Berlin Wisdom Paradigm, informed by a cultural-historical analysis, has defined wisdom as "an expert knowledge system concerning the fundamental pragmatics of life. These include knowledge and judgement about the meaning and conduct of life and the orchestration of human development toward excellence while attending conjointly to personal and collective well-being" (p. 136).

Birren and Fisher (1990) summarized the psychological literature on the nature, origins, and development of wisdom as follows:

"Wisdom is an emergent property of an individual's inward and external response to life experiences. A wise person has learned to balance the opposing valences of the three aspects of behavior: cognition, affect and volition. A wise person weighs the knowns and unknowns, resists overwhelming emotion while maintaining interest, and carefully chooses when and where to take action." (p. 331)

Thus, they propose that we attain wisdom through the development, balancing, and integration of the cognitive, affective, and conative elements of mind, and there is also a cognitive style component which is yet undefined.

By drawing on Churchman's five inquiring systems to provide the cognitive style component for our attainment of wisdom, we find a place to begin our quest for inspiring wise action in Singerian inquiring organizations. Furthermore, Harrison, Bramson, Parlette, and Bramson (1997) have designed an instrument, the Inquiry Mode Question-naire (InQ), that measures our relative preference for Churchman's five inquiring systems. This instrument can be used at the individual level to help people within organizations to, as Socrates admonished us, *know thyself.* It could also be paired with measures of personal development, based on those outlined in Wilber's (2000) cognitive, affective, social, and spiritual developmental charts. For example, Daniel Goleman's (1998) Emotional Competence Framework would serve well for emotional intelligence, as would some of Assagioli's (1973) (or his disciple's more recent works) for measuring and developing conative (willing/striving) propensity. Most recently, Malhotra and Galletta (2003) have elaborated the thinking on knowledge management systems that result in effective business performance to include such intervening variables as attention, motivation, commitment, creativity, and innovation. Conation (willing and striving) is closely linked to the more commonly used concepts of motivation and commitment. It is particularly pertinent and relevant here to point out that these two variables were measured through the development of a theoretical framework for measuring these constructs in knowledge management systems. Malhotra and Galletta (2003) also propose further research within diverse implementation contexts of KMS and organiza-tional knowledge management programs, which will advance the theoretical and empiri-cal development of the proposed framework.

Together, these instruments could provide a point of departure for beginning to measure progress in the evolution toward wise action in Singerian inquiring organizations. Furthermore, Dalla Costa (1995) has developed a Wisdom Index that could also be integrated into such an assessment battery. It includes an audit of ten dimensions of wisdom within four main categories, each having ten questions that can be answered as yes or no, which determine development within each aspect of wisdom for an organization or an individual within an organization. The questions provide a mirror for an organization to look frankly at the longer term issues that are vital to wise action and decision making.

They form part of Dalla Costa's leadership model and include (Perspective) timelessness, clarity and focus; (Values) compassionate detachment, truth and honesty, justice; (Action) unity and integration, intellectual and emotional harmony, equanimity; and (Support) substantial subjectivity and mentorship.

Another psychological approach to understanding wisdom, which is among those worthy of recommendation by Wilber (2000), comes from renowned psychoanalyst Erik Erikson (1963, 1982) who identified eight stages of psychosocial development with their attendant *crises* which, when successfully passed through, lead to the development of wisdom.

This framework could be adapted as a starting point for a framework for developing wise leaders. Building trust is essential for knowledge sharing, and as the *first of Erikson's developmental crises,* once resolved and established, can lay the foundation for hope in the quest for moving from knowledge management to wisdom. The *second stage* is characterized by the need for autonomy. With muscular maturation, the child experiments with knowing when to hold on and when to let go. If the crisis is not resolved satisfactorily, it can lead to feelings of shame and doubt, resulting in a compulsive personality. Successful resolution, however, enables self-control and willpower to function autonomously. (Willpower is conation—one of the elements of wisdom referred to above by Birren and Fisher, 1990.) Similarly, for the *third stage* of initiative versus guilt, one of the key prerequisites of the wise leader is a clear sense of purpose. A sense of purpose is developed where the inner struggle over the desire to take initiative and follow one's inner direction can be thwarted by being reprimanded or discouraged from following one's wishes. This leads to feelings of guilt, and if not satisfactorily resolved, can result in a person lacking any real purpose in life. The *fourth stage* involves the education of the person to sublimate the normal necessity to become mama and papa in a hurry and, instead, to win recognition by producing things and mastering skills and tasks. In so doing, the person develops a sense of industry wherein that person gradually replaces the wish to play with the desire to bring a productive project to completion. This is a most decisive stage, as it involves doing things beside and with others, and it provides a first sense of division of labor and differential opportunity so fundamental to the technological ethos of a culture. With adolescence comes the need to establish an identity. With the attendant physiological revolution that they must also contend with, adolescents are now primarily concerned with what they appear to be in the eyes of others, compared to what they, themselves, feel they are (peer pressure). They are also concerned with how to connect the roles and skills they have developed with the occupations available to them in the future. This integration takes place in the form of ego identity and involves more than the sum of the childhood identifications. This learning is provided by teachers, other adults in the community, and especially by older children. With successful resolution of the crises between achieving industry and thereby avoiding feelings of inferiority, the adolescent becomes competent and avoids inertia. The *fifth stage* is where the young adult must establish an identity or suffer role confusion. Strong doubt of one's sexual identity can lead to delinquent and outright psychotic episodes. In most cases, the inability to decide on an occupational identity is most disturbing to young people. Successful resolution of this stage results in fidelity and devotion, rather than repudiation. They have a clear, strong, and positive notion of

Table 1. Erikson Psychosocial Development

Stage	Characterized By	How Stage is Resolved Or Consequent Behavior
1. Infancy:	Basic Trust vs. Basic Mistrust	Hope or Withdrawal
2. Early childhood:	Autonomy vs. Shame and Doubt	Will or Compulsion
3. Play age:	Initiative vs. Guilt	Purpose or Inhibition
4. School age:	Industry vs. Inferiority	Competence or Inertia
5. Adolescence:	Identity vs. Identity Confusion	Fidelity or Repudiation
6. Young adulthood:	Intimacy vs. Isolation	Love or Exclusivity
7. Adulthood:	Generativity vs. Stagnation	Care or Rejectivity
8. Old age:	Integrity vs. Despair	Wisdom or Disdain

Adapted from Erickson (1963, pp. 247-274)

who they will be, if not who they are (know thyself). They are then ready to move on to the adult stages.

The *sixth stage* sees young adults eager to fuse their identity with that of others. It is time for intimacy and committing themselves to concrete affiliations and partnerships, which require the ethical strength to abide by such commitments with their inherent sacrifices and compromises. Failure to successfully resolve this stage can lead to isolation and the avoidance of relationships that lead to intimacy. Generativity is the *seventh stage* that must be successfully resolved to avoid stagnation or personal impoverishment in adulthood. This occurs through establishing and guiding the next generation, whether it be through one's own offspring or other forms of productivity and creativity. Successful resolution to this stage results in caring for the creatures of our world, rather than rejectivity. The *eighth and final stage* Erikson identifies is that of ego integrity versus despair. The fruits of the former seven stages are realized in those who have taken care of things and people and adapted themselves to the triumphs and disappointments of being the originator of others and/or the generator of products and ideas. Wisdom, as the highest virtue, is thereby attained after the successful resolution of the seven prerequisite virtues: hope, will, purpose, competence, fidelity, love, and care (Erikson, 1963, pp. 247-274).

These eight stages with their attendant crises were included in Wilber's (2000) developmental charts and have the potential for application at the organizational level. They could be used as a beginning point for an organizational development program that aims at bringing the whole organization to a level of integrity for operating wisely. Once this level is achieved, Wilber's (2000) seminal work on the higher stages of consciousness can provide direction for attaining higher levels of enlightenment.

In defining wisdom, Wilber (2000) states that "wisdom means the best that any era has to offer, and sensitive scholars have found that the perennial philosophers—from Plotinius to Shankara to Fa-tsang to Lady Tsogyal—are a storehouse of extraordinary wisdom" (p. 9). Wilber goes on to point out that:

"Reaching out to them is more than an embrace of some important truths. It is a way to affirm our continuity with the wisdom of the ages; a way to acknowledge our own ancestors; a way to transcend and include that which went before us, and thus flow with the current of the Kosmos; and most of all, a way to remind ourselves that even if we are standing on the shoulders of giants, we are standing on the shoulders of GIANTS, and we would do well to remember that." (p. 10)

Inspiring Leadership and Wise Action

Warren Bennis on Leadership

Warren Bennis (2003) defines management as "doing things right" and leadership as "doing the right thing" (p. 40). In Churchmanian terms, management processes, then, would operate more from a Lockean/Leibnizian form of thought, while leadership would require a higher order of reasoning, such as a Hegelian dialectic and a Kantian idealism. Therefore, it would follow that, as one moves from knowledge management toward wisdom, one would adopt more of a leadership perspective. If one can assume that the wise person would not only do the right things but that they would "do the right things right," then it would follow that wisdom would require expertise in both leadership and management. This sounds like Singerian pragmatism. The wise person would be both a leader and a manager but a leader first and foremost.

Warren Bennis (2003) is one of today's most distinguished authorities on leadership. As he points out, to become a leader, one must first become oneself. In order to become oneself, one must first, as Socrates admonished us, "know thyself." Thus, the big question of "who am I and why am I here" must be addressed at the onset. Bennis tends to differentiate between leaders and managers on many points, for example, as the difference between those who master the context (leaders) and those who surrender to it (managers). This is akin to thinking in terms of the more substantive value-oriented inquiring systems that Churchman (1971) ascribed to Kantian and Hegelian inquiring systems and the more fact-oriented functional inquiring systems of Locke and Leibniz. In addition to the need for mastering the context, Bennis lists several other factors that differentiate leaders from managers, including the need to know yourself, know the world, operate on instinct, and deploy yourself.

Bennis (2003) also lists a number of qualities that are more or less shared by all leaders:

1. A guiding purpose or vision. Leaders have a clear idea of what they want to do—professionally and personally—and they persist, regardless of setbacks or failures.

2. Passion. Includes the underlying passion for the promises of life, combined with a specific passion for a vocation, a profession, or a course of action. Leaders love what they do. When leaders communicate passion, they give hope and inspiration to others.

3. Integrity. Consists of three essential parts: self-knowledge, candor, and maturity.

    •   Self-knowledge, or knowing oneself, is among the most difficult challenges we face. As Bennis explains, once you know your strengths and weaknesses and what you want to do and why you want to do it, you can invent yourself and become who you really are.

    •   Candor is the key to self-knowledge. Candor is expressed through honesty of thought and action, a steadfast devotion to principle, and a sound and holistic personal quality. Leaders adhere to their standards and principles, regardless of current trends or fashions.

    •   Maturity is fundamental to a leader since leading involves more than just issuing orders or giving directions—command and control. Leaders need to have experienced life and grown through following first. They need to have learned to be dedicated, observant, capable of working with and learning from others; and while never servile, must always be truthful.

As a vital component of a leader's character, however, Bennis regards integrity as more of a product of leadership than an ingredient. Once leaders have located these three basic qualities in themselves, they are then able to nurture and foster them in others, and in so doing in the pursuit of their guiding purpose or vision, they become leaders. Curiosity and daring are two further qualities that Bennis identifies as fundamental to developing leadership capability (pp. 31-32). Warren Bennis was also one of the first to endorse Robert K. Greenleaf's seminal work on Servant Leadership, which is presented next.

Robert K. Greenleaf and Servant-Leadership

One of the most revolutionary and enlightened approaches to leadership today is attributed to Robert K. Greenleaf, who coined the term *servant-leadership* in his seminal essay "The Servant as Leader" (1970). Following a 40 year career at AT&T, he retired as director of management research and founded The Center for Applied Ethics, which later became The Greenleaf Center for Servant-Leadership.

In "The Servant as Leader," Greenleaf (1991) explained servant-leadership as follows:

"The Servant-leader is servant first ... It begins with the natural feeling that one wants to serve, to serve first. Then conscious choice brings one to aspire to lead...The difference manifests itself in the care taken by the servant-first to make sure that other people's highest priority needs are being served. The best test, and difficult to administer, is: do those served grow as persons: do they, while being served, become healthier, wiser, freer, more autonomous, more likely themselves to become servants? And, what is the effect on the least privileged in society: will they benefit or, at least, not be further deprived?" (pp. 19-25)

In addressing the relevance of servant-leadership for the 21st century, Bennis (2002) elucidates what he believes are the most crucial traits of the contemporary servant-leader in the workplace. These include trust, vision, meaning, and distributed leadership, all of which are fundamental concepts for servant-leadership. Bennis also delineates some other complementary concepts that enrich our understanding of what is needed for efficacious leaders in the 21st century. As he points out, as we become more authentic and attuned to the times, we are better able to lead in the transformation of our organizations. Authentic people are action-oriented. He believes that most leaders are either pragmatic dreamers or practical idealists. Thus, they see things not only as they are but as they should be and have the capacity to convert purpose and vision into action.

Bennis (2002) lists ten traits that tomorrow's leaders must learn to create an environment that embraces change so that it is understood as an opportunity rather than a threat.

1. *Successful leaders have self-awareness and self-esteem.* They have the diagnostic sensitivity and ability to be situationally responsive and to know when something new is required, when something must be unlearned, and the behavioral flexibility to change with the times.

2. *Leaders ensure that boundaries are porous and permeable.* This enables you to be in touch not only with the people in your organization but also with your customers, with society, and the outside world. These multiple perspectives allow you to see things before others do and to anticipate needed changes.

3. *Competitive advantage will be realized through the leadership of women.* By 2005, women are increasingly expected to hold top management positions, includ-

ing 50 percent in vice president of finance positions. Rather than become more macho, women's feminine traits will become more valued, since they contain the potential for improving the human condition. Thus, corporate cultures will have to change. It is not about being masculine or feminine but about having a particular set of attributes which all leaders share.

4.   *Leaders have a strongly defined sense of purpose and vision.* Leaders then increasingly find ways to clearly articulate their visions. Leaders do the right things, while managers do things right. Without knowing whether what you are doing is the most efficacious use of your time, one ends up keeping very busy doing many little things, all of which could have been accomplished in short order if one had bothered to ask a better question. When you are thinking about doing the right thing, you focus on the future, your dreams, missions, visions, strategic intents and purposes. When you are thinking about doing things right, your focus is on systems and processes. Managers ask *how to* questions about things and are interested in control and efficiency. Leaders ask *what and why* questions and are concerned with people and the long term. They nurture, develop, and empower the people in their organization. Leaders live their vision daily and create a culture that communicates and inspires others toward some worthy cause or powerful vision. The strength of an organization is determined by the extent to which their employees share that vision and know why they are there. As leaders live their vision and empower others to execute that vision in everything that they do, it then becomes anchored in realities and serves as a template for decision making.

5.   *Leaders generate trust.* Leaders need to communicate at a very personal level if they are to generate trust and show that they genuinely care. In order to generate and sustain trust, leaders must also demonstrate competence and constancy. Leaders have to take risks and be able to learn from their mistakes.

6.   *Leaders have a bias toward action.* Leaders need to be able to reflect and act and to know when it is appropriate to do either. Then they need to elicit feedback from their best and most trusted colleagues, who have the courage and honesty to tell them the truth and who they know are on side with them in pursuing the vision with passion.

7.   *Leaders create not just a vision but a vision with meaning.* A vision that has significance puts the players at the center of things, and when they truly share that vision, nothing will stop people from achieving their goal. Leaders must specify the steps required to achieve that vision and reward people for following those steps. It is also necessary to incorporate some feedback loops to ensure that the vision remains relevant and salient over time. It needs to be a dynamic vision, which can evolve and still retain its meaning.

8.   *Leaders must become very comfortable with advanced technology and the changes that it will bring.* Living in this high-tech high-touch world means that leaders will need to be competent in the use of advanced technology, while at the same time, possessing a high level of interpersonal competence.

9.   *Leaders must act big if they are small and small if they are big.* In the global economy, success is a matter of finding the right scale for a given organization and industry and then providing the appropriate structure and leadership. Small

companies are giving themselves a size advantage through networking, joint ventures, R&D consortia, and strategic partnerships, which allow them to cut across corporate and national boundaries and gain scale in marketing, purchasing, and manufacturing. Through new technologies, like computer-based manufacturing and distribution, elite marketing databases, and advanced telecommunications systems, they are able to build global markets quickly. While large corporations have advantages in economies of scale, resources, skilled workforce, know-how, and so forth, in order to remain competitive, they must find ways to re-create themselves as small independent units that are more manageable. This can take the form of a variety of initiatives, including reengineering, subcontracting, decentralization, and intrapreneuring.

10. *Ultimately, leaders make federations of corporations.* The best characteristics of big and small companies are found in most successful organizations. Thus, large corporations become federations, which provide both strength and flexibility. Corporate federations work on the same principles as nations. First, power is diffused to all the semiautonomous units, making them noncentralized, rather than just decentralized. Second, the decision making is shared between the units and the central authority rather than being dictated. Third, the company's operating principles are laid out in an overarching vision and purpose with some form of a compatible written constitution at the unit level. Fourth, the units need to know where their business, product, or geographical boundaries are. Fifth, power needs to be balanced between the units and the central authority and between the units themselves. Sixth, the units must be autonomous, while adhering to the federations universal operating principles. This results in a continuing tension, which is the most difficult characteristic of federalism. This is where leadership is critical to provide the delicate balance. Leaders of the new federal corporations must be a leader of leaders. You have to create an environment in which people at all levels are empowered to be leaders, and who, because they subscribe to your vision, can make effective decisions also. The leaders enunciate their company's performance standards clearly and then leave their associates to determine the best way to meet those standards. It is therefore up to the leader of federations to establish the why and the what —the overarching vision and purpose—but the other leaders must be responsible for the how (pp. 102-109).

Leaders and Heroes

McGee-Cooper and Trammell (2002) differentiate the traditional leadership model of leader as hero with servant-leadership. As they explain, the hero-as-leader is characterized by the champion who comes to the rescue to put out fires and save the company, whereas the servant-as-leader model is more concerned with fully tapping the brain power and potential for joy in the workplace that is overlooked by traditional leadership models. With the advent of the new millenium, more and more people are seeking deeper meaning in their work that goes beyond basic financial rewards and prestige. People want to make a difference, to support a worthy vision, and leave the planet in a better state than they found it. This organizational and spiritual awakening is also seen in the kind of shifts made evident in whom we choose to follow, how we lead, and the way in which we conjugate to address accelerating change. New ways of recruiting, rewarding, and leading will be needed to address the radical reductions happening in the workforce and the movement into the workforce of a new generation of employees with differing values and expectations.

Servant-leadership provides a new avenue for organizational learning by capitalizing on the knowledge and wisdom of all employees, not just the administration. Through servant leadership, big-picture information and business strategies are shared broadly throughout the company. When employees understand the basic assumptions and background information on problems, issues, and decisions, everyone has the opportunity to make meaningful contributions, thus empowering the hearts and minds of the entire organization toward realizing their vision. All employees thus enjoy true empowerment and greater job satisfaction, and the organization's individual and collective brain power is accessed, mobilized, and optimized. McGee-Cooper and Trammell (2002) also list five main ways of practicing servant-leadership: *listen without judgement, be authentic, build community, share power, and develop people.* "The magical synergy that results when egos are put aside, vision is shared, and a true learning organization takes root is something that brings incredible joy, satisfaction, and results to the participants and their organizations" (p. 150).

Singerian Heroic Mood

Heroic mood is integral to Singerian inquiring organizations (Croasdell, Courtney & Paradice, 1998). "As with all inquiring systems, Singerian inquiry includes a guarantor, which warrants that the system will generate greater knowledge of reality (progress) rather than its own form of illusion (process)" (p. 2). As Churchman (1971) explains, the guarantor for Singerian inquiring organizations is heroic mood. Heroic mood is a force toward progress and fulfillment that originates in the collective unconscious. It manifests as an attitude that risks security and comfort, with an impulse to challenge the status quo. It is predicated on the belief that understanding must precede progress through the promotion and sharing of knowledge, resulting in a concerted movement toward overall enlightenment.

Certainly, the understanding and application of wisdom will require a heroic effort. While the many facets of wisdom may not be readily quantifiable, there are a number of very efficacious qualitative research methods that could be applied to meet the ongoing measurement requirements of a Singerian Inquiring Organization. It should also be noted that Singerian inquiring organizations include both inquiry and advocacy, with asking the right questions to identify the real problem (inquiry), taking precedence over simply solving the apparent problem (advocacy).

Servant-leaders would therefore appear to adopt what Churchman (1971) has previously referred to as an *heroic mood* (p. 201) in achieving their vision. This would require that in addition to the five inquiring systems, the aesthetic, ethical, and spiritual dimensions would also be integrated into the mix. Thus, heroic mood is not about being a hero for the sake of inflating one's ego but rather for courageously rising to the challenge for serving one's fellow human beings and, being so, is in alignment with servant-leadership.

Dialogue and Singerian Inquiring Organizations

Singerian inquiring organizations that are oriented toward wise actions would assume that wisdom would also be created through dialogue. Isaacs and Senge (1999) define dialogue as "the art of thinking together" and as "listening and thinking beyond my position for something that goes beyond me and you." Dialogue provides the ability to explore beyond what is currently accepted as *given*. Dialogue also maintains a continuous mode of inquiry that regards the current state of knowledge—however proven it may be—as tentative. The result is not *a given problem* or *a specific solution* but rather a sharing of the various perspectives of the problem and the possible solutions. Mitroff (1998) refers to the surfacing of these multiple perspectives in terms of an ongoing process of divergence and convergence used in problem formulation. This process of knowledge sharing results in greater interpretative flexibility of the participants, thus yielding flexible schemas that give more knowledge creation, thereby enabling more wisdom creation per data set or body of information.

Wise communication also needs to ensure that everyone has the necessary communication skills to express themselves adequately and to know what to say and how to say it in order to be heard and not unnecessarily irritate others. This requires that we each examine our assumptions about our personal communication styles. The InQ Educational Materials, referred to earlier, address the importance of good communication skills for purposes of influence and persuasion through the judicious application of the various strategies that accompany each of the five inquiring systems. Workbook exercises guide participants through a series of activities which help them to recognize people's preferred thinking styles by the kinds of things each style, or inquiry mode, is likely to say and do. With this new awareness, individuals are able to *speak the language* of another and thus become more likely to be heard and to have their views appreciated. Further elaboration on listening to and observing another's language, speech, and behavior to enhance our communication skills is presented by renowned sociolinguist Deborah Tannen (1994). In *Talking from 9 to 5*, Tannen explicates and explains how women's and men's conversational styles affect who gets heard, who gets credit, and what gets done in the workplace. These powerful communication insights and skills enable men and women, coworkers, employees, bosses, and anyone who is trying to communicate with someone different from themselves, to become more sensitive and situationally responsive and thereby communicate more efficaciously.

Summary and Conclusions

This chapter develops a framework for moving from knowledge management in learning organizations to wisdom leadership/management in Singerian inquiring organizations. Courtney, Croasdell, and Paradice (1996) originated the concept of inquiring organizations and defined them as being special systems whose actions result in the creation of knowledge. There are five main kinds of inquiring organizations, which correspond to the five inquiring systems outlined by Churchman (1971) in his seminal work, *The Design of*

Inquiring Systems. These five inquiring systems and the subsequent inquiring organizations are ascribed to the philosophers Locke, Leibniz, Kant, Hegel and E. A. Singer. Hence, Singerian inquiring organizations are designed after the philosophy of the great American pragmatist, E. A. Singer. Recent literature in knowledge management has focused on the progression of managing first data, then information, and finally knowledge. With a substantial body of knowledge now available, some are looking to take this field to the next level, namely to the pursuit of wisdom for leading and managing organizations. Some, who have been alluded to above, have already anticipated this next step and provided ways and means by which this could be accomplished (i.e., Dalla Costa, 1995; Matthews, 1997; and Galvin, 2000).

In appreciating the importance of examining our assumptions, Malhotra (1998) and Krogh, Ichijo, and Nonaka (2000) have questioned whether knowledge can, in fact, be managed. Their study and reflection led them to the conclusion that, more correctly, it can be *enabled*. Matthews (1997) anticipated the importance of appreciating wisdom for organizational effectiveness. He draws on the psychological summary of the wisdom literature by Birren and Fisher (1990) to provide a framework for moving knowledge management to wisdom in order for organizations to become sufficiently versatile to manage the paradox they are facing. The paradox is evident in the demand for greater public and employee involvement along with environmental investment, which must be balanced with the demand for lower costs, less bureaucracy, and fewer employees. Motorola's former head, Robert Galvin (2000) also understands the importance of moving knowledge management toward wisdom and outlined 12 developmental endeavors to facilitate the process. Like Churchman (1971) and others, he recognizes that the greater value to be achieved in knowledge management is to be found within the people in the organization, rather than any institutional policies and practices.

While wisdom is more readily and directly integrated into the business sector in the East, in the West, business people are more likely to address the topic from a more concrete perspective, preferring to first deal with data, information, and knowledge before tackling such an esoteric topic as wisdom. Within the last ten years, however, wisdom has become more recognized in the west as a legitimate and valued goal for organizational efficacy and evolution.

The history and lineage of Singerian inquiring organizations dates back to the renowned Harvard philosopher and psychologist, William James (1890). Edgar A. Singer was his student and assistant, and later Singer was West Churchman's professor and mentor. Churchman (1971, 1979) extended Singer's ideas significantly, and it is through these innovative ideas that the modern systems approach developed. Later, Mason and Mitroff (1973) who had studied under Churchman, found further new and creative ways to apply Churchman's inquiring systems to the management of information systems. From their initiative, Courtney, Croasdell, and Paradice (1996) generated the idea of applying these inquiring systems to improving the efficacy of learning organizations, resulting in inquiring organizations. The present author has sought to extend and elaborate that work by introducing and integrating leading edge psychological and leadership perspectives into the equation for moving from knowledge management/ecology to wisdom.

Wilber's (2000) work on the integration of Eastern and Western wisdom literature shows the kind of depth and breadth of mind and heart that are needed to provide the leadership necessary for such a heroic undertaking. As he explains, the goal of an integral psychology is to honor and embrace every legitimate aspect of human consciousness. While we may learn from traditional psychological studies, concerning the development of wisdom, it is also necessary to consult other sources to inform us when it comes to the upper reaches of the spectrum of consciousness. The Berlin Wisdom Paradigm has defined wisdom as "an expert knowledge system concerning the fundamental pragmatics of life. These include knowledge and judgment about the meaning and conduct of life and the orchestration of human development toward excellence while attending conjointly to personal and collective well-being" (Baltes & Staudinger, 2000, p. 136). Birren and Fisher (1990) proposed that we attain wisdom through the development, balancing, and integration of the cognitive, affective, and conative elements of mind, and there is also a cognitive style component which is yet undefined. It is the present author's observation that a greater appreciation of the necessity of developing the heart (affection) and spirit (conation) is required in the equation, as compared to the amount of attention that is so often allotted to the, albeit necessary, intellect (cognition). Thus, while some of the greatest intellectuals may display remarkable knowledge, skill, and even insight, by denying the heart and spirit, they limit themselves from attaining true wisdom.

By drawing on Churchman's five inquiring systems to provide the cognitive style component for attaining wisdom, we find a place to begin to implement leadership wisdom and wise action in Singerian inquiring organizations. Measures of each of the elements comprising the development of wisdom are also available. Another psychological approach to understanding how wisdom develops has been provided by renowned psychoanalyst Erik Erikson (1963, 1982). Erikson identified eight stages of psychosocial development, their characteristics, and how each stage is resolved. Beginning with infancy, this stage is characterized by basic trust vs. basic mistrust, which is either resolved in the attainment of hope or consequently results in withdrawal. The eighth stage is generally achieved by the time one reaches old age and is characterized by integrity vs. despair. It is either resolved through the attainment of wisdom or results in feelings of disdain. These eight stages with their attendant crises could be used as a starting point for an organizational development program aimed at elevating the integrity of an organization for the attainment of wisdom at the organizational level.

Our understanding of the nature, origins, and development of wisdom has therefore evolved from a variety of sources. It draws on the philosophy, history, theology, psychology, management, and leadership literature. This chapter, then, proposes ways and means for inspiring, fostering, and enabling the development, use, measurement, and refinement of leadership wisdom through Singerian inquiring organizations.

Warren Bennis (2003) defines management as "doing things right" and leadership as "doing the right thing." Management would operate from a more Lockean and Leibnizian inquiring system and leadership from a more Kantian and Hegelian inquiring system. Presumably, wise leaders would not only do the right things, but also they would do them right. Therefore, it would follow that, as one moves from knowledge management toward leadership wisdom, one would adopt a balanced and integrated perspective so as to be situationally responsive and thereby in keeping with the role and purpose of Singerian inquiring organizations.

A framework for orchestrating this balanced and integrated approach of the best qualities of managers and leaders is explicated and explained by Hickman (1992). As he points out, while other kinds of organizations may accomplish their goals quite well from time to time, the optimal organization will create greater and more permanent value for everyone for the benefit and enlightenment of all. For Hickman, the optimal management/leadership environment, then, is the one that is balanced and integrated in terms of (1) its competitive strategy advantage, (2) its organizational culture/capability, (3) its external/internal change, (4) its individual effectiveness/style, and (5) its bottom-line performance/results. In playing out these five success factors, such an organization would enable (1) the implementation of changing game strategies, (2) cultural renewal, (3) the blending of stability and crisis, (4) the promotion of a dynamic approach, and (5) the balancing of tangible short-term with intangible long-term results. Therefore, what such optimal companies may actually need is a means by which to orchestrate the skills and abilities, talents and gifts of both the practical, analytic, and orderly mind of the manager and the experimental, visionary, and creative heart and soul of the leader. Orchestration is what Singerian inquiring organizations are all about.

References

Assagioli, R. (1973). *The act of will.* New York: Viking Press.

Baltes, P. B., & Staudinger, U. M. (2000). Wisdom: A metaheuristic (pragmatic) to orchestrate mind and virtue toward excellence. *American Psychologist, 55*(1), 122-136.

Bennis, W. (2002). Become a tomorrow leader. In L. C. Spears & M. Lawrence (Eds.), *Focus on leadership: Servant-leadership for the 21st century* (pp. 101-110). New York: John Wiley & Sons.

Bennis, W. (2003). *On becoming a leader.* Cambridge, MA: Perseus.

Birren, J., & Fisher, L. (1990). *The elements of wisdom: Overview and integration.* In R. Sternberg (Ed.), *Wisdom: Its nature, origins and development* (pp. 317-332). New York: Cambridge University Press.

Churchman, C. W. (1971). *The design of inquiring systems: Basic concepts of systems and organization.* New York: Basic Books.

Churchman, C. W. (1979). *The systems approach and its enemies.* New York: Basic Books.

Churchman, C. W. (1982). *Thought and wisdom.* Seaside, CA: Intersystems.

Churchman, C. W. (1994). Management science: Science of managing and managing of science. *Interfaces, 24*(4), 99-110.

Churchman, C. W. (2004). Global ethical management. Retrieved September 20, 2004, from *http://nature.berkeley.edu/~schultz/people/churchman_cv.html*

Clarke, F. P., & Nahm, M. C. (Eds.). (1942). *Philosophical essays in honor of Edgar Arthur Singer, Jr.* Philadelphia: University of Pennsylvania.

Courtney, J. F., Croasdell, D., & Paradice, D. (1996). Inquiring organizations. Foundations of information systems: Towards a philosophy of information technology. Retrieved September 20, 2004, from *http://www.cba.uh.edu/~parks/fis/fisart.htm*

Courtney, J. F., Croasdell, D., & Paradice, D. (1998). *Singerian inquiring organizations: Guiding principles and design guidelines for learning organizations.* Unpublished manuscript, Texas A&M University, Business Analysis and Research Department.

Dalla Costa, J. (1995). *Working wisdom: The ultimate value in the new economy.* Toronto: Stoddart.

Davenport, T. & Prusak, L. (1998). *Working knowledge: How organizations manage what they know.* Boston: Harvard Business School Press.

Erikson, E. (1963). *Childhood and society* (2nd ed.). New York: Norton.

Erikson, E. (1982). *The life cycle completed: A review.* New York: Norton.

Flood, R. L. (1999). *Rethinking the fifth discipline: Learning within the unknowable.* London: Routledge.

Galvin, R. (2000). Managing knowledge toward wisdom. In P. Krass (Ed.), *The book of management wisdom* (pp. 48-59). New York: John Wiley & Sons.

Goleman, D. (1998). *Working with emotional intelligence.* New York: Bantam Books.

Greenleaf, R. K. (1970, 1991). *The servant as leader.* Indianapolis: The Greenleaf Center.

Harrison, A. F., & Bramson, R. M. (1982). *The art of thinking.* New York: Berkley Books.

Harrison, A. F., Bramson, R. M., Parlette, N., & Bramson, S. (1997). Assessing your thinking profile: InQ. San Francisco: InQ Educational Materials.

Hickman, C. R. (1992). *Mind of a manager: Soul of a leader.* New York: John Wiley & Sons.

Isaacs, W., & Senge, P. (1999). *Dialogue and the art of thinking together: A pioneering approach to communicating in business and in life.* New York: Doubleday.

James, W. (1890). *Principles of psychology* (Vol. 1). New York: Henry Holt.

Kienholz, A. (1999). Systems rethinking: An inquiring systems approach to the art and practice of the learning organization. Foundations of information systems: Towards a philosophy of information technology. Retrieved September 20, 2004, from *http://www.cba.uh.edu/~parks/fis/fisart.htm*

Kienholz, A. (2001, June 8). *Churchman's inquiring systems and the creation of knowledge in psychology.* Proceedings of the Biennial Conference of the International Society for Theoretical Psychology, Calgary, Canada.

Krogh, G. V., Ichijo, K., & Nonaka, I. (2000). *Enabling knowledge creation: How to unlock the mystery of tacit knowledge and release the power of innovation.* New York: Oxford University Press.

Lacan, J. (1969). *Ecrits: A selection.* New York: Norton.

Lacan, J. (2004). *Ecrits: A selection* (Bruce Fink, Trans.). New York: Norton.

Macleod, R. B. (1963). Retrospect and prospect. In H. Gruber, G. Terrell & M. Wertheimer (Eds.), *Contemporary approaches in creative thinking: A symposium held at the University of Colorado* (p.177). New York: Atherton Press.

Malhotra, Y. (1997, August 15-17). *Knowledge management in inquiring organizations.* Proceedings of the 3rd American's Conference on Information Systems, Indianapolis, IN, USA (pp. 293-295).

Malhotra, Y. (1998, Feb. 2-25). *Toward a knowledge ecology for organizational white-waters.* Keynote Presentation for the Knowledge Ecology Fair 1998: Beyond Knowledge Management. Retrieved September 20, 2004, from *http://www.brint.com*

Malhotra, Y. (2000). Knowledge management and new organizational forms: A framework for business model innovation. *Information Resources Management Journal, 13*(1), 5-14.

Malhotra, Y. (2002). Information ecology and knowledge management: Toward a knowledge ecology for hyperturbulent organizational environments. *Encyclopaedia of Life Support Systems (EOLSS).* Oxford, UK: UNESCO/EOLSS Publishers.

Malhotra, Y., & Galletta, D. F. (2003, January 6-9). *Role of commitment and motivation in knowledge management systems implementation: Theory, conceptualization and measurement of antecedents of success.* Proceedings of the 36th Annual Hawaii International Conference on System Sciences, Hilton Waikoloa Village, Island of Hawaii, CD/ROM, 8 pages, Computer Society Press.

Mason, R. O., & Mitroff, I. I. (1973). A program for research on management information systems. *Management Science, 19*(5), 475-487.

Matthews, P. (1997). What lies beyond knowledge management? Wisdom creation and versatility. *Journal of Knowledge Management, 1*(3), 207-214.

McGee-Cooper, A., & Trammell, D. (2002). From hero-as-leader to servant-as-leader. In L. C. Spears & M. Lawrence (Eds.), *Focus on leadership: Servant-leadership for the 21st century* (pp. 141-151). New York: John Wiley & Sons.

Mitroff, I. I. (1998). *Smart thinking for crazy times: The art of solving the right problems.* San Francisco: Berrett-Koehler.

Mitroff, I. I., & Linstone, H. A. (1993). *The unbounded mind.* New York: Oxford University Press.

Mitroff, I. I., & Pondy, L. R. (1974). On the organization of inquiry. *Public Administration Review, 34,* 471-479.

Muller, J. P., & Richardson, W. J. (1982). *Lacan and language: A reader's guide to Ecrits.* New York: International Universities Press.

Nonaka, I., & Takeuchi, H. (1995). *The knowledge creating company.* New York: Oxford University Press.

Palmier, J. M. (1972). *Lacan.* Paris: Editions Universitaires.

Senge, P. (1990). *The fifth discipline: The art and practice of the learning organization.* New York: Doubleday.

Tannen, D. (1994). *Talking 9 to 5: How women's and men's conversational styles affect who gets heard, who gets credit, and what gets done at work.* New York: William Morrow.

Wilber, K. (2000). *Integral psychology: Consciousness, spirit, psychology, therapy.* Boston: Shambhala.

Chapter IV

Kantian Inquiring Systems: A Case Study

Ahmed Y. Mahfouz
Texas A&M University, USA

David B. Paradice
Florida State University, USA

Abstract

Kantian inquiring systems can be used as a model for learning organizations. Based on Churchman's (1971) inquiring systems and Courtney, Croasdell, and Paradice's (1998) inquiring organizations, this chapter discusses the Kantian inquiring system and applies it to an organization in the retail industry. Kantian systems take input, process the input using multiple models, and interpret the data in terms of the best fitting model. Accepted output from the system is integrated into the system's fact net. The guarantor of the system is the fit between the data and the model. The authors make recommendations in light of the Kantian inquiring system to the retail organization.

Introduction

Churchman (1971) described five inquiring systems, based on the work of five major Western philosophers: Leibniz, Locke, Kant, Hegel, and Singer. This chapter explores the

Kantian inquiring system and illustrates its principles in the context of an organization in the retail industry. The five parts of the model, *a priori* theory, input, process, output, and guarantor, draw from the works of Churchman (1971) and Courtney, Croasdell, and Paradice (1998). Each part will be illustrated in the context of the world's largest retail organization, Wal-Mart. Recommendations in light of the philosophical basis are also considered. A summary of the characteristics of the Kantian inquiring system is shown in Table 1.

Wal-Mart is suitable to explore as an example of an inquiring system and, specifically, a Kantian one for two reasons. First, Wal-Mart is a rich organization to study due to the fact that it is the largest retailer in the world and the largest employer in the United States after the federal government (Ortega, 1998; walmartstores.com, 2003). With 1,517 stores, 1,333 supercenters, 528 Sam's Clubs, 52 Neighborhood Markets, 1,297 international units, and sales of $244.5 billion in the fiscal year ending January 31, 2003, Wal-Mart hires more than 1,000,000 employees (called *associates*) in the United States and more than 1,300,000 worldwide, serving over 100 million customers weekly worldwide. Such a large organization provides complex interactions among employees, consumers, and suppliers that are very appropriate to examine in the context of an inquiring system and a learning organization. Second, several characteristics of the Kantian inquiring system are exemplified in the management and operations of Wal-Mart, as detailed in the chapter below. Since the purpose of this chapter is to examine Wal-Mart as a Kantian inquiring organization, only examples of a Kantian system are discussed, excluding examples that may pertain to other inquiring systems that could be employed by Wal-Mart in certain aspects of its managerial and operational levels.

Table 2 shows a comparison of the different types of the four Wal-Mart retail divisions. Wal-Mart Discount Stores offer a variety of retail merchandise, including clothing, automotive products, health and beauty aids, home furnishings, electronics, hardware, toys, sporting merchandise, lawn and garden items, pet supplies, jewelry, and housewares. Besides the retail offerings of its regular discount stores, the Wal-Mart Supercenter facilitates one-stop shopping and includes grocery items, a vision center, Tire & Lube Express, Radio Grill restaurant, photography shop and photo center, hair salon, bank, and placement agencies. Wal-Mart Markets provide groceries, pharmaceuticals, and general

Table 1. Kantian Inquiring Systems (Courtney, Croasdell & Paradice, 1998)

System	Characteristics
Given	Space-time framework
	Theories
Input	Internal and external
Process	Build models
	Create theories
	Interpret data
	Select the best model
Guarantor	Fit between data and model
Output	Fact nets

items. Sam's Clubs are a members-only warehouse offering large-volume merchandise at discount prices, such as bulk paper products, furniture, clothing, electronics, hardware and software, jewelry, and many other types of products for office and home use.

Wal-Mart's History

The story of Wal-Mart starts with the story of its founder Sam Walton (Ortega, 1998; Vance & Scott, 1994; walmartstores.com, 2003). Oklahoma-born and Missouri-raised, Walton graduated from the University of Missouri with a degree in economics in 1940. That same year, he started his career in the retail industry as a J.C. Penney's management trainee in Des Moines, Iowa. Management dismissed his suggestions and vision of selling high volume at low prices and in smaller communities. Five years later and using $25,000, Walton became a Newport, Arkansas-based franchisee for Ben Franklin, a chain of dime stores. Walton broke the franchise's rules by dealing directly with suppliers and passing the savings on to his customers.

Although Walton was soon successfully running a number of Ben Franklin stores, he opened the first Wal-Mart Discount City in Rogers, Arkansas in 1962, which coincidentally is the same year that Kmart and Target started. The first store had 18,000 square feet. Walton and his brothers continued to open stores in small towns with populations ranging from 5,000 to 25,000. This move would become a strategic Wal-Mart trademark in terms of demographics and geography (Thompson & Strickland, 1995). Early on, Wal-Mart recognized the profile of its consumer segment (Table 3).

Seven years later, the company was incorporated with 18 Wal-Marts and 15 Ben Franklins in Arkansas, Missouri, Kansas, and Oklahoma. Wal-Mart became a publicly held company in 1970 and opened its first distribution center and home office in Bentonville, Arkansas. In 1972, the company stock was listed on the New York Stock Exchange. In 1977, Wal-Mart made its first significant acquisition when it bought 16 Mohr-Value stores in Missouri and Illinois. That same year, based on data from the previous five years, Forbes ranked the nation's stores in the retail industry, and Wal-Mart emerged first in several categories: return on equity, return on capital, sales growth, and earnings growth. That same feat would repeat itself in present times in terms of revenue (#1), market value (#4), and number of employees (#1) across all of the top 500 Fortune companies and not just in the retail industry, as shown in Table 4.

Table 2. Comparison of Wal-Mart Retail Divisions (walmartstores.com, 2003)

	Discount Stores	Supercenters	Neighborhood Markets	Sam's Clubs
# of Stores	1,517	1,333	52	528
Sq. ft. (000)	40-125	109-230	42-55	110-130
# of Employees	150	350	90	125
# of Items	80,000	100,000	28,000	4,000

Table 3. Profile of Wal-Mart's Target Consumer (Mason & Mayer, 1987)

Characteristic	Profile
Price sensitivity	High
Desire to shop	Good
Adopters of fashion/technology	Late adopters
Mass merchandiser use	High
Need for in-store service	Little or none
Store loyalty	Low
Age and marital status	Young families
Income	Low to medium
Occupation	Blue-collar
Education	Down-scale

In 1978, Wal-Mart began operating its pharmacy, auto service center, and jewelry divisions, and acquired Hutchenson Shoe Company. There were 276 Wal-Mart stores by 1979 in 11 states, mostly in small towns. Sales had grown from $44 million in 1970 to $1.25 billion in 1979. Wal-Mart opened its first Sam's Club in Midwest City, Oklahoma in 1983. By 1988, the first Supercenter opened in Washington, Missouri. That same year, David Glass succeeded Walton as CEO. During the 1980s, Wal-Mart added 1,126 stores.

In 1990, Wal-Mart continued its growth and added new stores in California, Nevada, North Dakota, Pennsylvania, South Dakota, and Utah. It also acquired Western Merchandise, Inc. of Texas, a suppler of music, books, and video products to many of its stores. In 1991, Wal-Mart introduced its new store brand, Sam's American Choice, and the first products were beverages, colas, and fruit juices. That same year, it entered the international market, opening stores in Mexico. By 1992, Wal-Mart had 1,720 stores, some of which represented a change in policy by opening near big cities with large populations. On April 5, 1992, Walton passed away.

After dethroning Kmart and Sears, Wal-Mart became America's top company in the retail industry. Kathie Lee Gifford and Wal-Mart announced in 1996 the launch of the Kathie Lee women's apparel line, a Wal-Mart exclusive. Furthermore, Wal-Mart became the number one employer in the U.S. in 1997 after the federal government, with 680,000 associates, as well as 115,000 international associates. In 1998, it started the first Neighborhood Market store in Arkansas. The following year, Wal-Mart became the world's biggest private employer with 1,140,000 associates. In 2000, H. Lee Scott became president and CEO. In 2001, Wal-Mart achieved yet another feat: the biggest single-day sales record in history, totaling $1.25 billion on the day following Thanksgiving. In 2003, it posted record sales of $244.5 billion. Wal-Mart continues its phenomenal growth to the present day.

Table 4. Top Fortune 500 Companies Comparison ("Largest U.S. Corporations," 2003)

	Revenue ($ millions)	Market Value ($ millions)	Number of Employees
Wal-Mart Stores	247,000	218,000	1,300,000
General Motors	187,000	18,000	350,000
Exxon Mobil	182,000	231,000	93,000
Ford Motor	164,000	12,000	350,000
General Electric	132,000	256,000	315,000
The 500 Median	5,800	2,900	26,000

Inquiring Systems

"An Inquiring System...is a system of interrelated components for producing knowledge on a problem or issue of importance" (Mitroff & Linstone, 1993, p. 29). Furthermore, "Inquiry is an activity which produces knowledge" (Churchman, 1971, p. 8). Churchman (1971) defines a system as one that meets nine necessary conditions, as shown in Table 5. Wal-Mart is teleological since it has a set of goals: to maximize profit for shareholders and minimize costs. The measure of performance is the annual sales revenue (and reduced expenses). The client is composed of all consumers who potentially would buy products and services and those who actually do. The components are the products and services in all the stores, with senior management, local store managers, and associates as subcomponents. The environment consists of the business and legal environment, community reaction, competitors, and worldwide/global markets. The decision makers and designers are the board and top-level executives. The designer's intention is to maximize the value of Wal-Mart to shareholders and value of products and services to consumers. This intention is assumed to be stable and realizable.

Kantian Inquiring System

What is Given?

The Kantian inquiring system has both theoretical and empirical parts, which allow it to generate hypotheses. It requires a space-time framework (i.e., an *a priori* space and an *a priori* clock) in order to identify and examine the input and create those hypotheses. However, knowledge and hypotheses change over time. As a result, the system must continuously look into the environment for new knowledge and check it against existing knowledge. For example, Wal-Mart utilizes a process called *traiting*, which indexes

Table 5. Necessary Conditions for a System (Churchman, 1971)

Condition
Teleological
Measure of performance
Clients
Teleological components coproducing performance measure
Environment
Decision maker
Designer
Intention of designer to maximize system value to the client
Stability

product movement in the store to over a thousand stores and market traits. Traiting is an essential data warehousing and data mining tool (Westerman, 2001). Wal-Mart's appreciation and use of technology goes back a long time, as Wal-Mart designed an executive information system on an IBM platform in 1988. The traiting data are analyzed to see if any relationships or causality explains the reasons customers tend to buy specific products at certain locations and times. Location is significant since Wal-Mart has determined as part of its corporate strategy that the best location for setting up stores is small to medium size towns. Time is important since retail sales are seasonal, and having a full stock of merchandise during peak times, such as Christmas, is vital.

A Kantian inquiring system has a theoretical component, and one economic theory that Wal-Mart operates on is the principle of cost minimization. This principle involves reducing costs by using the least amount of inputs, such as labor and capital, to achieve a given level of output or result. Wal-Mart tries to cut its costs, such as overhead, in operations. For example, it hires 30% of its staff on a part-time basis. It runs 12-13 advertising circulars per year while competitors run 50-100 circulars per year. Also, executives share hotel rooms during their weekly visits to stores. Moreover, the demand of Wal-Mart customers is price elastic. Demand is price elastic when customers buy only on the basis of price. In other words, Wal-Mart customers are price sensitive. Wal-Mart lowers its prices to attract and keep those customers. These are all aspects of the environment assumed, or *given*.

Input

The Kantian inquiring system receives input. According to Churchman (1971), the system's input mechanism draws on characteristics from both the Leibnizian and Lockean systems. Even though it may seem contradictory, the system reflects both closed (Leibnizian) and open (Lockean) systems characteristics regarding its environment. In the case of an organization in the retail industry like Wal-Mart, the closed aspects are reflected in reliance on internal input from associates and local store managers. In many internal transaction processing situations, events or activities in the organization's environment are largely ignored. However, open systems aspects are also evident in a reliance on external input from the environment from customers and competitors.

Using internal and external inputs, an organization scans its environment, compares the inputs to existing knowledge, and creates new knowledge. For example, to receive internal input, Wal-Mart listens to associates and local store managers and incorporates their suggestions into its business strategy. This focus starts at the top, from senior management, and is interpreted at many levels within lower management. This way, management finds new and better ways to reduce costs and run the stores and operations more efficiently.

The internal input from associates and local store managers and the resulting implementation of those suggestions creates *single-loop learning*. Argyris and Schon (1996) defined single-loop learning as learning that addresses circumstances and problems based upon existing premises without changes in values and norms. For example, one of the programs used to involve associates is the *Yes We Can Sam* program. This program allows associates to suggest ways to simplify, improve, or eliminate work. In 1994, over 650 suggestions were implemented, resulting in estimated savings of over $85 million.

For external input from customers, Wal-Mart listens to their preferences and suggestions. This is an example of *double-loop learning*. Argyris and Schon (1996) defined double loop learning as learning that modifies or changes values, assumptions, theories, and strategies in an organization. Over the past few years, Wal-Mart realized that customers prefer one-stop shopping, whereby consumers can do all their shopping in one place. As a result, Wal-Mart has expanded and added new services and products. To meet these new customer needs, it created the Supercenter, which includes one-stop shopping opportunities, such as a pharmacy, a grocery department, Tire and Lube Express, a vision center, and so forth. Moreover, Wal-Mart listens to customers through traiting. Using inventory and sales data and regional customer preferences, local store managers can have some latitude in choosing which products to display. Managers are also given latitude to set prices to meet local market conditions. In remote areas where Wal-Mart has no direct competitors, prices tend to be slightly higher than Wal-Mart stores next to Kmart and other competitors.

External input could also be received from competitors. Wal-Mart observes its competitors closely and examines their business practices. This practice stems from the guiding principles that Sam Walton left as a legacy. He was known to visit competitors and even stay in their parking lots to observe their operations and their customers, according to Walton's biographer, Vance Trimble (1990). Walton would incorporate any new ideas and improvements he found into his own business strategy. For an example of a competitor as compared with Wal-Mart (Table 6).

The Kantian inquiring system self-examines to validate the axioms of the *a priori*. Then the system, through its sensuous intuition, individuates sensations (inputs). On recognizing an input, the system places it in context, allowing for multiple interpretations or views of the input. This ability is very important since the system draws upon several models and looks at causality. For example, a major competitor of Wal-Mart, Kmart saw a decline in its sales in the mid-nineties and on January 22, 2002, declared Chapter 11 bankruptcy due to slow holiday sales. This resulted in closing 284 stores in 48 states. Kmart could have determined at least two interpretations of its situation. First, Kmart's own inefficient way of running its operations contributed to the decline of sales. Second, competitors like Wal-Mart were being especially successful in adopting technology earlier and faster throughout their operations. Wal-Mart was one of the early adopters of electronic scanners at cash registers that were connected to a central inventory system and a satellite communications system (Brands, 1999). Bonczek, Holsapple, and Whinston (1981) stated that technological innovations enable organizations to grow and become better decision makers.

As input is interpreted and theories are created, the Kantian inquiring system builds its own models. It also searches for the best fitting model that works. For example, Wal-Mart uses a low cost leadership strategy. It sells at a lower price in comparison to competitors and controls cost in operations. If Wal-Mart wanted to launch an advertising campaign that builds on this strategy and on its mottos, "Everyday Low Prices" and "Price Rollbacks," it would need to select a campaign that best fits its image and low cost theme. If an ad campaign shows product selection and benefits (utility) and emphasizes low cost, then that campaign would be selected over an alternative advertising campaign that stresses hedonic characteristics of expensive products. The latter campaign would be more suitable for a company that targets consumers with high levels of discretionary income. In Kantian terms, an Executor oversees this process of determining model fit. If a part of a model, or the entire model, is not working, then it can be set aside until it works properly again or until a better fitting model is found. For example, if Wal-Mart implements an advertising campaign that does not seem to increase sales, the campaign must be replaced with a more suitable one.

Wal-Mart executives have looked at several ways (or models) to improve the distribution operations. In the terms of a Kantian inquiring system, it chooses the best fitting model

Table 6. Wal-Mart and Kmart (walmartstores.com, 2003; kmartcorp.com, 2003)

	Wal-Mart	Kmart
Headquarters	Bentonville, AR	Troy, MI
CEO	H. Lee Scott	Julian C. Day
Store Count	3,430	1,512
Employees	1,000,000+	170,000
Revenue ($ billions)	$244.5	$35
Product		
Breadth	Some	Some
Depth	Little	Little
Price	Inexpensive	Inexpensive
Customer Service	Low	Low
Store Size (sq. ft.)	96,883	110,000

for its needs: an internal distribution system that takes care of its inventory (Francis & White, 1995). It builds its own warehouses, so it can buy in large volumes. It builds stores close to these distribution centers within a few hundred miles radius. As a result, merchandise is delivered *just-in-time* to the stores. In 2003, over 80% of Wal-Mart's merchandise was shipped from 84 distribution centers: 33 general merchandise distribution centers, 25 grocery distribution centers, seven clothing distribution centers, and 15 specialty distribution centers. Specialty distribution centers handle items, such as jewelry, tires, optical, returned merchandise, and pharmaceuticals. In addition, some items come directly from suppliers.

Guarantor

The guarantor of the Kantian inquiring system is the degree of data/model fit (Mason & Mitroff, 1973). If the guarantor of the system fails to have a fit between the data and the model, failure could occur. In the case of Wal-Mart, part of the success is attributed to the fact that current management implements the original model based on success factors that Walton preached for years, such as low cost, good use of technology, and so forth. The organizational knowledge he left as a legacy became part of the organizational learning and memory of Wal-Mart.

Table 7 shows a summary of Walton's rules for building a business. The rules (# 2, 3, 4, 5, and 7) reveal the obvious fact that Walton stressed the great value of associates and their (internal) input. This type of organizational metaphor (Kendall & Kendall, 1993) is likened to a *family*, whereby workers support each other, share and exchange ideas, have specific roles, and strive to benefit the overall well-being of the organization. Walton stressed these rules to create a close corporate culture within the organization.

In addition, Walton had several personality characteristics and instituted many other policies and business practices that became part of Wal-Mart's organizational learning and memory (Collins & Porras, 1997). He was a rather flamboyant and charismatic leader, despite his humble personal life and standard of living in terms of a multibillionaire's wealth. For example, to celebrate the milestone of his associates' breaking the 8% profit level, he went down Wall Street in a grass skirt with a band of hula dancers. He usually led his associates to scream the Wal-Mart cheer. More importantly, he stressed change, experimentation, and improvement (Collins & Porras, 1997). For example, he was behind *A Store Within a Store* idea, whereby department managers have the latitude to operate their local department as if it were their own business. Walton gave out rewards to and publicly acknowledged associates who came up with ideas to improve operations and cut cost. His *VPI* (*Volume Producing Item*) program allows associates to experiment with new ideas in the stores. Great ideas are then published in Wal-Mart's company magazine and broadcast across Wal-Mart's satellite communications system. More importantly, as an organizational leader, Walton groomed his successor David Glass to follow successfully in his footsteps (Collins & Porras, 1997). This move manifests itself in successful corporate cultures, such as in the case of General Electric's CEO Jack Welch, who also prepared his successor Jeffrey R. Immelt well to replace him.

One of the ideas that Walton is sometimes credited with is having *people greeters* at store doors to welcome customers and create a friendlier shopping experience. Walton's son, Jim Walton, stated that some observers and scholars of corporate strategy used to say how ingenious his dad was in using such grand plans or strategies to better run operations (Collins & Porras, 1997). However, Jim Walton noted that his dad undertook such moves simply as a countermeasure to combat shoplifters, and the original idea was not even his! In Crowley, Louisiana, a Wal-Mart store manager had problems with shoplifters. He thought having an older gentleman or lady at the door would serve two purposes: greet honest shoppers with a friendly face and deter shoplifters from stealing. Walton simply copied the idea in all his stores as standard practice and competitive advantage (Collins & Porras, 1997). Jim Walton summed this up humorously: "Later, we all snickered at some writers who viewed Dad as a grand strategist who intuitively developed complex plans and implemented them with precision. Dad thrived on change, and no decision was ever sacred" (Walton & Huey, 1992, p. 90).

Hence, the business environment continuously changes, especially since the days when Walton founded the company. Fortunately, current top managers continue Walton's policy of *management by walking and flying around*, whereby they visit stores to get input from associates and regional managers. This way, top managers not only follow old traditions set by Walton, but they also avoid falling victim to old traditions that may no longer work.

As a result, the models of the system are updated as necessary and in order to make better sense of the data and arrive at improved decisions. Wal-Mart managers actually update these models with new information. For example, local store managers can submit their input via a computer communications technology called *Retail Link*. An important part of this platform is a decision support system (DSS) that helps managers in making decisions by allowing them to share data, store by store, item by item, and so forth. Also, part of the DSS is a question-based program that is tailored to provide all the details needed to make accurate decisions, regarding profits, sales, market share, and so on. Consequently, these techniques may facilitate better decision-making processes in such collaborative environments (Dennis et al., 1999).

Table 7. Walton's Rules for Building a Business (Walton & Huey, 1992)

1.	Commit to your business.
2.	Share profits with your associates; treat them as partners.
3.	Motivate your partners.
4.	Communicate everything you can to your partners.
5.	Appreciate everything your associates do for business.
6.	Celebrate your successes.
7.	Listen to everyone in your company.
8.	Exceed your customers' expectations.
9.	Control your expenses better than your competition.
10.	Swim upstream.

This ability to share and transfer knowledge among the store managers and headquarters of Wal-Mart helps to create new organizational knowledge. Ruggles (1997) classifies knowledge management tools as those which "enhance and enable knowledge generation, codification, and transfer" (p. 1). Retail Link, in this context, is both a generation and transfer tool. By sharing organizational knowledge this way, Wal-Mart as a retail organization is involved in *combination*, a mode of knowledge conversion that goes from tacit to explicit knowledge. Nonaka and Takeuchi (1995) define two types of knowledge: tacit and explicit. *Tacit knowledge* is subjective and comes out of experience. On the other hand, *explicit knowledge* is objective and comes out of rationality. Conversion is the result of the interaction between tacit and explicit knowledge. This conversion results in four modes of knowledge conversion, as shown in Figure 1.

Output

Output for the Kantian inquiring system for Wal-Mart in the form of fact nets results from data collected from multiple sources, such as Retail Link, traiting, and Walton's legacy. The fact net becomes a foundation that Wal-Mart draws on in its business strategy and decisions. Here, the Kantian system is similar to the Leibnizian system, since both generate fact nets as output. Adding new information to existing fact nets, creating new fact nets, and abandoning false fact nets are important tasks of the inquiring organization. This is analogous to a process of continuous improvement, development, and growth in the life cycle of an organization in the retail industry, like Wal-Mart.

Recommendations

Applying the Kantian inquiring system philosophy, Wal-Mart should continue to scan its environment for input and use this knowledge to create new organizational knowledge in running its operations so that it becomes more profitable.

An internal input, suggestions from associates and local store managers could be further captured in other media, richer than the one used in Retail Link. Dennis and Kinney (1998) suggest that performance is enhanced when richer types of media are used to accomplish a task. Their study involved computer-mediated and video communication. Wal-Mart could utilize video-conferencing technology so that richer information exchange takes place among its stores.

An external input, census data indicate an interesting demographic trend. The number of births in the U.S. in the nineties averaged 4.1 million a year, up from an average of 3.7 million annually in the preceding decade (Bureau of Statistics, 2000). This creates an opportunity to extend more lines into infants' and children's clothing, which are part of softgoods, one of three product categories constituting the majority of Wal-Mart's sales, as shown in Table 8 and Figure 2. This move would potentially generate increased sales revenue. In addition, Wal-Mart can take advantage of this change in demographics and create a more pleasant shopping experience by building temporary daycare centers

Figure 1. Modes of Knowledge Conversion (Nonaka & Takeuchi, 1995)

Knowledge From/To	**Tacit**	**Explicit**
Tacit	Socialization	Externalization
Explicit	Internalization	Combination

inside the stores. This is especially important since (representing more than half the workforce) females and especially mothers are time pressured and would like to reduce their distractions and, hence, time shopping, knowing their children are well-taken care of in the meantime.

In addition, external input shows great opportunities in private and licensed brand name labels and cobranding. Wal-Mart sells merchandise under its private store brands, such as Equate in health and beauty care, Ol' Roy in dog food, and Sam's American Choice and Great Value in many items including beverages and packaged food items. Other private brands include One Source, Puritan, No Boundaries, George, and Athletic Works. Sam's Choice is considered Wal-Mart's premium-quality line and offers an average of 26% price savings over comparable branded products. This strategy creates even greater avenues to venture further and offer more items with private labels in other product categories beyond what is currently offered, including toys, hardware, and so forth, especially when Wal-Mart is America's biggest toy seller.

Wal-Mart can also combine its marketing efforts in licensed products and with celebrities, in hardgoods (hardware) and softgoods (apparel), since they constitute a major portion of its sales, as shown in Table 8 and Figure 2. For example, the Kathie Lee Gifford clothing line was a successful venture in terms of sales and lead time. It took Wal-Mart one year to develop the line, while it took Kmart ten years to develop the Jaclyn Smith line. Wal-Mart could also look for a celebrity endorsement in gardening, hardware, and so forth, similar to Martha Stewart's presence in Kmart. Wal-Mart has already seen success in licensing products, such Faded Glory, General Electric, White Stag, Catalina, Starter, and Mary-Kate and Ashley. Another recommendation for Wal-Mart is to continue to capitalize on its cobranding ventures. It already has a cobranded credit card with Chase Manhattan. Other ventures could include cell phone plans or even apparel lines that are normally sold in department stores only. However, a strategic issue facing Wal-Mart here is how much it should invest in the brand label business, especially apparel lines, and what strategies it needs to implement. The basic items currently sold in the stores are relatively unchanging in both style and demand. Because basic lines are not subject to the whims of the latest *hot* fashion trends and are part of everyday use, their demand remains steady. However, for brand label apparel, individual fashions go in and out of style, and hence, demand is more cyclical and possibly less predictable. This cyclical demand may create greater market and financial risk. Also, designing a nonbasic line requires longer lead times and much more investment. Wal-Mart would have to weigh the costs and benefits and come up with the best fitting model of how to proceed with its new ventures and strategies in apparel lines.

Table 8. Wal-Mart Sales by Product Category (Wal-Mart Form 10-K, 2003)

Category	Percentage of Sales	Industry Average (%)
Grocery, candy, and tobacco	22	27
Hardgoods	21	20
Softgoods/domestics	18	22
Pharmaceuticals	9	2
Electronics and records	9	9
Sporting goods and toys	7	7
Health and beauty aids	7	7
Stationery	3	2
One hour photo	2	2
Shoes	1	1
Jewelry	1	1

Figure 2. Wal-Mart Sales by Major Product Categories (Wal-Mart Form 10-K, 2003)

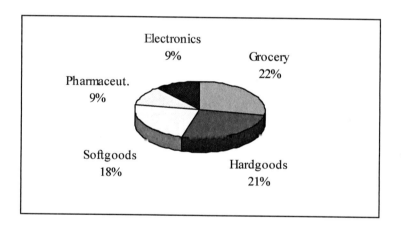

Furthermore, based on external input from census data, it is estimated that senior citizens will constitute the bulk of the U.S. population by the year 2030. Home delivery is expected to grow as the population of senior citizens continues to grow; which creates an opportunity for Wal-Mart. In order to cater to these demographic trends and expand into them further, new merchandise and a home delivery service, backed up by an appropriate advertising campaign, would need to be created. The inquiring system would select the best fitting model and create separate ad campaigns for infants and elderly. In addition, the retailing environment is increasingly becoming more online, which portends a change in the buying habits of customers. Even though Wal-Mart has a Web presence, another recommendation would be to expand further in electronic commerce and establish a bigger presence on the Internet to match its status as the world's largest retailer. Wal-Mart can also offer international shipping which is not currently offered. Greater varieties of existing products, along with offering new specialty products that are normally sold through competitor's mail order catalogs, can be advertised and offered on Wal-Mart's site.

Furthermore, external input indicates the global nature of business today. Senge and Sterman (1994) advise that the organization of the future act locally and think globally. Besides the stores Wal-Mart has in Argentina, China, Mexico, Brazil, Germany, Puerto Rico, Canada, Korea, and the United Kingdom, a recommendation would be to open more stores overseas in the European Union or in nations that are slowly adopting open and free markets, such as China and the former Soviet Union, or purchase existing retailers in those countries. In these emerging markets, Wal-Mart would need to deal with several challenging factors as shown in Table 9: entry strategy, cost/tax factors, demand factors, strategic factors, regulatory/economic factors, and sociopolitical factors (Luo, 2002). Hence, the Kantian inquiring system once again will have to select the best fitting model to combat such challenges and capitalize on the opportunities in those new emerging markets.

In addition, in terms of this global expansion, more expenditure on technology and especially intranets would be needed so that managers can share information (internal input) worldwide. In addition, an extranet could be established so that Wal-Mart can better communicate with suppliers globally, such as Proctor & Gamble. This way, the fact nets of the inquiring system's output would be updated with new information, and better models would be built and selected, such as those models used to set prices and determine product offerings in the stores.

External input from the environment shows that certain communities perceive Wal-Mart's expansion as a threat. When Wal-Mart opens stores nearby, several communities lose their downtown small businesses, such as drug, hardware, clothing, sporting goods, and fabric stores. This affects the small-town feel and atmosphere of many such communities. In recent news for example, union voters in California stopped Wal-Mart from opening a Supercenter in Inglewood in 2003. In 2004, the state of Vermont was named one of America's Most Endangered Historic Places to combat the arrival of Wal-Mart. On the other hand, Wal-Mart creates many jobs for the local community and results in increased business in major appliance and furniture, restaurants, and gasoline stations, due to increased traffic. To counterattack this negative sentiment, Wal-Mart needs to increase its social and environmental programs and engage in an advertising campaign to enhance its positive image. The Kantian inquiring system would select the best fitting strategy and campaign to promote Wal-Mart in a positive light. This strategy includes an increase in sponsorship of nonprofit organizations and financial donations to social causes, as well as the establishment of programs where employees can volunteer several hours a month to help the local community. In response to the environmental concerns, Wal-Mart can ask its manufacturers to improve their products by eliminating excessive packaging, converting to more recycled materials, and eliminating toxic inks and dyes. Wal-Mart can also establish more environmentally-friendly programs, similar to its *Green Coordinator,* which helps stores become more environmentally responsible and responsive.

Table 9. Challenges Facing Wal-Mart in Emerging Markets (Luo, 2002)

Factor Type	Subdimensions
Entry	Location and timing
Cost/Tax	Transportation, wages, land, construction, raw materials, financing, taxes, investment
Demand	Market size and growth, customer presence, local competition
Strategic	Investment infrastructure, manufacturing, workforce productivity, logistics
Regulatory/ Economic	Industrial policies, availability of certain special economic zones
Sociopolitical	Political instability, cultural barriers, local business practices, corruption, attitude to foreign business, community characteristics

Summary

In summary, given a space-time framework and theories, the Kantian inquiring system scans the environment for input, both internally and externally. It builds models, interprets the data, and then selects the best fitting model to achieve its goal. It must continue to scan for new information to be added and compared to existing knowledge. The system produces output in the form of fact nets. The system may fail if there is no fit between the data and the model. Wal-Mart is used an example of a retail organization to demonstrate several key aspects of the Kantian inquiring system. Wal-Mart is the world's largest retailer and continues to be very successful, implementing and illustrating several characteristics of the Kantian inquiring system.

References

Argyris, C., & Schon, D. (1996). *Organizational learning II: Theory, method, and practice.* Reading, MA: Addison-Wesley.

Bonczek, R. H., Holsapple, C. W, & Whinston, A. B. (1981). *Foundations of decision support systems.* New York: Academic Press.

Brands, H. W. (1999). *Masters of enterprise: Giants of American business from John Jacob Astor and J. P. Morgan to Bill Gates and Oprah Winfrey.* New York: The Free Press.

Bureau of Statistics. (2000). Retrieved September 23, 2004, from *http://stats.bls.gov/*

Churchman, C. W. (1971). *The Design of inquiring systems: Basic concepts of systems and organizations*. New York: Basic Books.

Collins, J. C., & Porras, J. I. (1994). *Built to last: Successful habits of visionary companies*. New York: HarperBusiness.

Courtney, J. F., Croasdell, D., & Paradice, D. B. (1998). Inquiring organizations. *Australian Journal of Information Systems, 6*, pp. 3-14. Retrieved September 23, 2004, from *Foundations of Information Systems: Towards a Philosophy of Information Technology, http://www.cba.uh.edu/~parks/fic/fic/htm*

Dennis, A. R., & Kinney, S. T. (1998). Testing media richness theory in the new media: The effects of cues, feedback, and task equivocality. *Information Systems Research, 9*(3), 256-274.

Dennis, A. R., Aronson, J. E., Heninger, W. G., & Walker, E. D. (1999). Structuring time and task in electronic brainstorming. *MIS Quarterly, 23*(1), 95-108.

Francis, M., & White, S. (1995). *The total quality corporation: How 10 major companies turned quality and environmental challenges to competitive advantage in the 1990s*. New York: Truman Talley Books/Dutton.

Kendall, J. E., & Kendall, K. E. (1993). Metaphors and methodologies: Living beyond the systems machine. *MIS Quarterly, 17*(2), 149-171.

Kmart. (2003). Retrieved September 23, 2004, from *http://www.kmartcorp.com/corp/story/index.stm*

Largest U.S. corporations. (2003). *Fortune, 147*(7), F1-F31.

Luo, Y. (2002). *Multinational enterprises in emerging markets*. Copenhagen, Denmark: Copenhagen Business School Press.

Mason, J. B., & Mayer, M. L. (1987). *Modern retailing: Theory and practice*. Plano, Texas: Business Publications.

Mason, R. O., & Mitroff, I. I. (1973). A program for research on management information systems. *Management Science, 19*(5), 475-487.

Mitroff, I. I., & Linstone, H. A. (1993). *The Unbounded mind: Breaking the chains of traditional business thinking*. New York: Oxford University Press.

Nonaka, I., & Takeuchi, H. (1995). *The knowledge-creating company: How Japanese companies create the dynamics of innovation*. New York: Oxford University Press.

Ortega, B. (1998). *In Sam we trust: The untold story of Sam Walton and how Wal-Mart is devouring America*. New York: Times Business.

Ruggles, R. (1997). Knowledge tools: Using technology to manage knowledge better. Retrieved September 23, 2004, from *http://www.businessinnovation.ey.com/mko/html/toolsrr.html*

Senge, P. M., & Sterman, J. D. (1994). Systems thinking and organizational learning: Acting locally and thinking globally in the organization of the future. In J. D. W. Morecroft & J. D. Sterman (Eds.), *Modeling for learning organizations* (pp. 194-215). Portland, OR: Productivity Press.

Thompson, A. A., Jr., & Strickland III, A. J. (1995). *Crafting and implementing strategy*. Chicago: Richard D. Irwin.

Trimble, H. T. (1990). *Sam Walton: The inside story of America's richest man*. New York: Dutton.

Vance, S. S., & Scott, R. V. (1994). *Wal-Mart: A history of Sam Walton's retail phenomenon*. New York: Twayne Publishers.

Wal-Mart Form 10-K. (2003). Retrieved September 23, 2004, from *http://www.walmartstores.com/*

Wal-Mart Stores, Inc. (2003). Retrieved September 23, 2004, from *http://www.walmartstores.com/*

Walton, S., & Huey, J. (1992). *Sam Walton: Made in America-my story*. New York: Doubleday.

Westerman, P. (2001). *Data warehousing: Using the Wal-Mart model*. San Francisco: Morgan Kaufmann Publishers.

Section II:

Systems, Applications, Developers, and Users

Chapter V

Email and Knowledge Creation:
Supporting Inquiring Systems and Enhancing Wisdom

Sharman Lichtenstein
Deakin University, Australia

Craig M. Parker
Deakin University, Australia

Margaret Cybulski
Deakin University, Australia

Abstract

The real promise of organizational communication technologies may lie in their potential to facilitate participative discourse between knowledge workers at all levels in distributed locations and time zones. Such discourse enables the exchange of sometimes conflicting viewpoints through which resolution and symbiosis, organizational knowledge can be built. This chapter presents a case study of a Singerian inquiring organization which illustrates how a fluid dynamic community of employees can use email to build knowledge, learn, make decisions, and enhance wisdom through a cycle of knowledge combination (divergence) and knowledge qualification (convergence). The chapter offers new theoretical perspectives on the enhancement of wisdom in inquiring organizations and provides practical insights into the use of email for supporting effective knowledge creation in inquiring organizations.

Introduction

In today's globalized business environment, many companies recognize the strategic role of the generation, capture, and dissemination of knowledge in developing inimitable competencies, innovations, and competitive advantages. In particular, the constant creation of new knowledge has been identified as a key business objective. While some experts see the value of ongoing knowledge creation in terms of accelerating innovation (Sharkie, 2003), others focus on its value for enhancing a firm's ability to act—the hallmark of a learning organization (Loermans, 2002; Senge, 1990). When such an approach uses a systematic method for justifying knowledge claims about complex social alternatives, the company evolves into an inquiring organization, employing inquiring systems.

Inquiring systems were originally conceptualized by the pragmatist philosopher Churchman (1971), who strongly believed that knowledge should be created for practical problem-solving purposes and that its creation should be ethically grounded. He specified five archetypal inquiring systems to assist with complex problem solving, each corresponding to a particular philosophy for discovering knowledge truth. A comprehensive view of inquiring systems proposes that they systematically generate knowledge, resolve complex problems, and enhance organizational learning capability, leading to continuous learning and improvement (Courtney, Chae & Hall, 2000).

In the past decade, a diverse body of knowledge has accumulated around identifying, understanding, and linking the key concepts of inquiring systems and organizations. Some of this work has focused on the development of design frameworks for inquiring systems. In a recent development, Hall, Paradice, and Courtney (2003) described a conceptual model for a Learning Organization Knowledge Management System (LOKMS) that portrays a design for an environmentally aware extended inquiring system. Their model shows how key information and knowledge can be continuously and systematically captured and employed to hypothesize and select new states or goals. To achieve these goals, alternative solutions are generated, each based on a recognized mode of inquiry. From among the alternatives, the best option is selected in a decision-making process. A key feature of LOKMS is its reliance on an organizational memory comprising a constantly verified and updated knowledge base and a store of extraneous accumulated knowledge which, while not immediately useful, may acquire validity at some future time. Monitoring of the external environment introduces new and updated knowledge into the organization.

While such designs appear promising, we still lack ways to *support* such organizations and systems and also need a greater understanding of the underlying concepts. One way to explore and understand the constructs and their support is to study environments where the systems are in evidence. We noticed in the discourse of the ubiquitous organizational tool electronic mail (email), the enactment of some of the key processes appearing in LOKMS—in particular, information and knowledge discovery, the creation of organizational knowledge from the resolution of multiple perspectives, decision support, and the building of organizational memory.

These knowledge processes were discovered in email conversations between people collaborating in distributed networks to solve practical problems. The linchpin knowledge process identified in the conversations was knowledge creation, suggesting to us that in the group appropriation of email for collaboratively solving problems, characteristics of inquiring systems might emerge through the patterns of discourse. We wondered whether discourse found in the simple tool, email, could support some of the components of inquiring systems and organizations. Reaching for wisdom, it was also worth considering whether email could support the enhancement of wisdom.

In this chapter, we explore the potential of email for supporting inquiring organizations and enhancing wisdom. We begin the chapter by looking at an information hierarchy that shows how data can be transformed into knowledge and wisdom. Knowledge creation and other key concepts of inquiring organizations and systems are then reviewed, guided by a simplified conceptual model of inquiring systems in inquiring organizations that incorporates wisdom development structures.

We then analyze how knowledge creation takes place in a collection of email conversations and how inquiring system characteristics emerge. A cycle of collaborative knowledge creation found in email conversations is described, highlighting a pattern of discourse interaction that may enhance wisdom. The chapter provides insights into how inquiring systems and wisdom can be enabled in organizations through specific discourse structures supported by email. This understanding highlights a previously overlooked value in email and also suggests potentially valuable design elements and interventions for inquiring organizations.

Knowledge Creation in Organizations

The Information Hierarchy

To understand how knowledge is created in organizations, we must first settle the meaning of knowledge in terms of its position within an information hierarchy. In Figure 1, we illustrate an information hierarchy developed by Barabba and Zaltman (1991) and Haeckel and Nolan (1993). According to Barabba and Zaltman, many codified observations or data are obtained from a marketplace of data which, when placed in a decision context, become information. By analyzing information, intelligence is developed. In developing high levels of certainty in intelligence (not necessarily 100%), we create knowledge. Through synthetic thinking about knowledge, a wise outcome is reached— that is, wisdom is achieved. Synthetic thinking involves synthesis, or the combining of ideas in such a way as to create a whole that is greater than the aggregation of its parts.

The value of data increases along the transformation path from data to wisdom, while the volume decreases. There are two distinct stages described: In the creation of collections of data, information is provided. When people use this information for a purpose, intelligence, knowledge, and wise decisions may be developed. What is emphasized in this model is Churchman's key observation that how users *react* to a collection of information alters outcomes and their meanings. Later in the chapter, we show how different modes of inquiry can systematically guide users in the way they create knowledge and even enhance wisdom.

We now proceed to explore how knowledge is created in organizations, how this is often linked with decision-making, and how, simultaneously, learning occurs.

How Knowledge is Created in Organizations

According to Nonaka (1994), knowledge is created from the interplay and transformations between the various knowledge types—individual or collective; tacit or explicit. The four basic transformations are socialization (the conversion of tacit knowledge to tacit knowledge); combination (the conversion of explicit knowledge to explicit knowledge); externalization (the conversion of tacit to explicit knowledge); and internalization

Figure 1. Information Hierarchy (based on Barabba & Zaltman, 1991; Haeckel & Nolan, 1993)

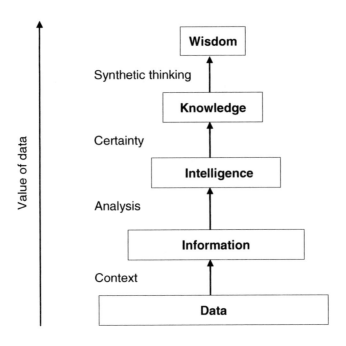

(the conversion of explicit to tacit knowledge). This remains the most well known model of knowledge creation, although many others exist.

Various scenarios stimulate knowledge creation. First, within and across the boundaries of organizations, knowledge can be created when insights and intuitions are shared, combined, or gleaned during social processes that typically involve discourse. Second, through regular sampling of external environmental data (for example, scanning the World Wide Web), new knowledge can be brought into the firm and existing organizational knowledge thus validated, updated, and extended. Third, new knowledge may be discovered through a knowledge discovery process from databases. As we have highlighted in the information hierarchy, knowledge originates with people who use information. Thus, most knowledge creation models show the expansion of a knowledge base through collective human activity and are fundamentally social models.

Clearly, participatory organizational groups and networks are particularly useful for this purpose. Such structures are increasingly prevalent in organizations, given the need to coordinate and/or integrate temporally and geographically distributed specialist knowledge for wider purposes, such as projects, and the trend toward participatory work practices. Increasingly, emerging network structures support self-organizing groups whose members cluster around programs, practices, projects, and tasks.

Social Knowledge Creation and Decision Making

The creation of organizational knowledge through collective human activity is closely related to decision making. Knowledge from different people must be assembled to solve problems and make decisions because the likelihood that one person will contain all the relevant knowledge is miniscule—given the current paradigm of specialized knowledge and the limitations (bounded rationality) of the human mind (Jensen & Meckling, 1992).

As today's organizations are plagued by complex changing circumstances and destabilized authority, there are often many considerations and alternatives when resolving associated *wicked* decision problems (Rittel & Webber, 1973; Weick, 2001). According to Courtney's (2001) new paradigm for decision making in such settings, the interplay of diverse perspectives may assist in resolving wicked decision problems by producing new insights and updating the mental models of stakeholders with one another's perspectives and unspoken assumptions. Dialogue is an important medium that enables diverse views to be heard and resolved.

Social Knowledge Creation and Learning

The link between social knowledge creation and learning is also important to note. Dialogue plays a critical role, in that valuable learning occurs as a result of the interactions occurring in group discourse and collaboration (Bakhtin, 1986; Roschelle, 1992; Stahl, 2002). According to Bakhtin, learning is closely linked to the process of multiple voices coming into contact with one another via verbalized utterances. He suggests that in an utterance, both speaker and listener learn. Stahl describes how social and individual learning are enhanced through discursive debate and a negotiated outcome. Highlighting the nature of interactions needed, Roschelle suggests that effective learning occurs through patterns of divergence and convergence in discourse during collaborative problem solving. Convergence is associated with processes of analysis—for example, testing concepts and solving problems; while divergence is associated with processes of synthesis—for example, generating alternatives and recognizing problems.

Various well known learning models incorporate the ideas of analysis/convergence and synthesis/divergence--for example, Carlsson, Keane, and Martin (1976) and Kolb (1985). Roschelle and other researchers report how the presence of authority in a problem-solving/decision-making conversation can force early convergence and stifle learning (Hubscher-Younger & Narayanan, 2003; Roschelle, 1992), suggesting more generally that conversations require cooperative conditions for optimal learning to take place. Learning is also enhanced *in situ* (e.g., Lave & Wenger, 1991). Amalgamating these findings:

"Collaborative conversations based around pragmatic problem solving and decision making can be highly valuable for learning purposes, if skills of synthesis and analysis are employed, and if authority does not intervene."

As organizations aim not only for new knowledge and learning but also wisdom in decisions and people, we now discuss the role that knowledge creation can play in leading to wise decisions and, more generally, wisdom.

From Knowledge Creation to Wisdom Enhancement

We review two perspectives of wisdom enhancement: making wise decisions and enhancing wisdom through an attitude of fallible knowing.

In order to make wise decisions, the information hierarchy suggests that analysis (convergence) and synthesis (divergence) are needed (Barabba & Zaltman, 1991; Haeckel & Nolan, 1993). Considering also the value to learning of collaborative problem-solving/decision-making conversations involving cycles of convergence and divergence as discussed previously, we propose a cycle of *wisdom enhancing* problem solving and decision making in discourse, as shown in Figure 2. The knowledge processes involved are knowledge sharing, creation, convergence and divergence. Wisdom is not *indefinitely* increased through this cycle, however, because, for example, too many cycles will lessen commitment to continue or follow through with a decision at the end.

Weick (2001) views wisdom as *a balanced attitude of fallible knowing*, a conceptualization originally espoused by Meacham (1990). Weick suggests that the influx of knowledge in dialogue adds to overly cautious participants' knowledge while removing some of the existing doubt, thereby increasing wisdom. Conversely, doubt raised by the input of new

Figure 2. Enhancing Wisdom in Decision Making in Discourse

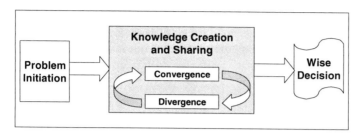

Figure 3. Wisdom as Fallible Knowing

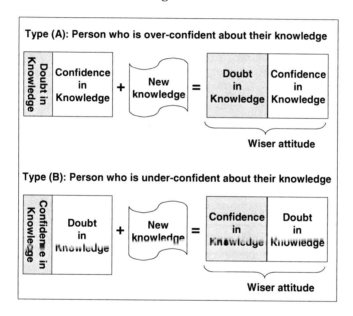

knowledge provided to overly confident participant attitudes increases wisdom. This effect is illustrated in Figure 3. Remaining mindful of ongoing fallibility in knowing during knowledge creation through a combination of acts of doubt and acts of confidence will ultimately lead, according to Weick, to wisdom.

We argue that in today's organizations, where specialization is the norm for distributing knowledge among workers, there tends to be greater doubt than confidence in domains that lie outside one's area of specialization. In such settings, gathering knowledge from others offsets excessive doubt by imbuing the recipient with new confidence once such knowledge is internalized. Confidence is also increased when knowledge creation is situated in practice, and the new knowledge created is highly relevant, accordingly. Furthermore, if this knowledge is collaboratively created, it can later be defended by those who constructed it, providing greater confidence in the validity of the knowledge within the organizational context.

Knowledge Creation in Inquiring Organizations

In this chapter, we are particularly concerned with social knowledge creation, decision making, and wisdom enhancement in inquiring systems. As we wish to review the concepts of inquiring systems and organizations, we begin by summarizing a complex design model of an inquiring system, LOKMS, introduced earlier and fully described in Hall, Paradice, and Courtney (2003). LOKMS comprises a staged view of how an inquiring system can reach a decision while simultaneously building and refreshing an organizational memory. The system aims to have verified knowledge in its memory, thus storing only concrete types of knowledge. Softer knowledge including semi-abstract types of knowledge, such as stories and artifacts, and abstract knowledge, such as organizational structure, roles, and culture, is not stored.

Simon's (2003) Intelligence-Design-Choice model underpins the three basic stages of LOKMS, comprising Intelligence—information discovery, hypothesis generation, and goal selection; Design--generation and analysis of alternatives developed from different modes of inquiry; and Choice—selection of the best option by a decision maker. In the Intelligence phase, key information and knowledge are continuously and systematically captured from knowledge sources and employed to hypothesize and select new states or goals. In the Design phase, alternative solutions and analyses are generated, each based on a different inquiry paradigm. In the Choice phase, one of the candidate solutions is selected. Feedback loops—and environmental and time-space checks for currency— are built in throughout. The model is fully explained in Hall, Paradice, and Courtney (2003).

LOKMS is a specific and complex design for an inquiring system. Our objective in this chapter is to show how discourse in email can support the basic elements of inquiring systems and enhance wisdom. For this purpose, in Figure 4 we provide a simplified conceptual model of how inquiring systems operate inside inquiring organizations, incorporating the wisdom enhancement principle of convergence-divergence in discourse, introduced in the previous section. This model encompasses the external environment and internal environment, which is comprised of the organizational memory, inquiring system knowledge flow domain, and philosophies guiding knowledge claim justification (knowledge creation) in the domain. We review each of these elements in more detail.

Organizational Memory

An organizational memory (OM) is a place to retain, integrate, and provide access to organizational knowledge. Most modern definitions for OM include people, processes, norms, standards, and technological repositories. Wickramasinghe (2003) found that although ideally OM should be composed of objective components (explicit knowledge), such as recorded knowledge in repositories, and subjective components (tacit knowledge), such as personal knowledge, the subjective component is typically missing in practice. In inquiring organizations, as shown in Figure 4, subjective knowledge is made available through interpersonal interaction in the group and participation in norms, processes, and standards. Knowledge that has been created in the inquiring system knowledge domain is returned to the OM, while knowledge in the OM is continually validated against scanned external knowledge.

The codified component of OM faces significant problems, such as its potential for sustaining indefinite growth. Another problem is that nowadays codified OM is often fractured into localized repositories (e.g., intranets) that grow in isolation and, to be

Figure 4. Supporting Inquiring Organizations and Wisdom Enhancement

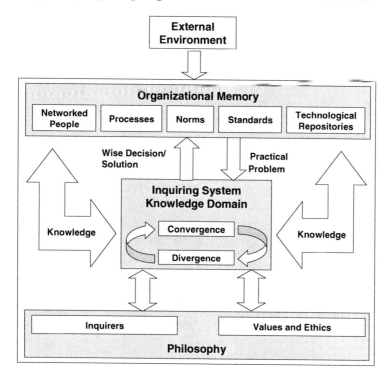

useful at a broader level at a future time, need reintegration or coordination. In inquiring systems, knowledge held in the OM is coordinated and/or integrated through pragmatic knowledge creation.

Inquiring System Knowledge Domain and Inquirers

A practical problem requiring a solution will lead problem solvers to tap into knowledge from OM and/or the external environment in order to develop a solution/decision. This knowledge creation activity occurs inside a knowledge work domain. Inquiring systems that support inquiring organizations in order to arrive at solutions or decisions are composed of inputs, operators, outputs, and *inquirers* that define particular modes of inquiry for ascertaining the truth of knowledge claims. Each inquirer represents a specific philosophy for determining knowledge—inductive and consensual (Locke); deductive and analytic (Leibniz); multiple realities (Kant); conflicting and dialectic (Hegel); and multiple perspectives (Singer).

Courtney, Chae, and Hall (2000) describe five types of inquiring organizations. Liebnizian and Lockean organizations are basically scientific with the first determining truth through theory and the second determining truth through empirics. A Liebnizian organization argues with formal logic, assumes cause and effect, and uses predetermined axioms. In contrast, a Lockean organization is empirically focused, valuing group observation, discourse, and validation in a social context in which group consensus is sought in order to meet group needs. Majority support provides validation of any given observation, input or other information, with an efficient solution sought to meet a group's current needs.

In the Kantian organization, the elements of Liebnizian (truth by theory) and Lockean (truth by empirics) are combined and enhanced through an analytical approach where various alternative models of meaning, explaining the data through a particular theory, are constructed and evaluated. A *best fit* is obtained through judgment in the particular context. The Hegelian organization takes a dialectic approach that assumes that through conflict of opposing views—thesis and antithesis—a solution better than either view can be synthesized.

Finally, the Singerian organization encompasses all the other types of inquiring organizations by enabling and resolving multiple competing viewpoints, aiming for the common good. Existing knowledge is challenged, and new information representing technical, organizational/social, personal, ethical, and aesthetic perspectives is *swept in* whenever current models fail to explain a particular situation. Discrepancies are analyzed using methods from the four previous inquirer styles with an emphasis on an ethical and practical approach.

The model depicted in Figure 4 also illustrates knowledge creation and learning as well as the wisdom enhancement cycle of convergence and divergence processes introduced earlier, which, we have argued, can enhance wisdom.

Level of Complexity of Knowledge Work Domain

The level of complexity of a knowledge work domain (Snowden, 2002) shapes and is shaped by the inquirer employed in that domain. In *complicated* domains, the relationships between cause of knowledge outcome and the outcome itself (that is, cause and effect) are already known, or knowable given sufficient resources. There is high predictive ability for knowledge outcomes in such domains, suggesting that the Liebnizian or Lockean inquiry approaches may be successful.

In *complex* domains, there are many interacting human agents, each with multiple identities. The interactions form patterns whose outcomes are unpredictable. However, the patterns can be recognized, disrupted, and reoriented, suggesting the potential for Kantian, Hegelian, or Singerian inquirers. In *chaotic* domains, while patterns of interaction are not emergent, they can be imposed as interventions. According to Snowden, people can mold complex or chaotic domains into known or knowable domains through applying regulation and order. The problem does not determine the inquiry style but rather, people do. Thus, there is always some opportunity to organize all these types of knowledge domains through appropriate management. Snowden further suggested that different managerial and leadership approaches are needed for each domain type.

Values and Ethics

Recent sociopolitical pressures have highlighted the role of ethical values in global healing (Simon, 2003), and ethical values are considered important to inquiring organizations. The values of an organization are embedded in knowledge work through the participants, whose individual values are recreated or reinforced as a result. Internally, a morally sound framework will contribute to increased intraorganizational trust with positive ramifications for open and cooperative team functioning, as required for collective inquiry. Network structures that enable equitable participation and addressing of diverse concerns are suggested.

Ethical organizations exhibit and reinforce values in all activities, including knowledge work. As there is often more than one set of personal values at play in collaborative problem solving, people with values lying outside the boundary of common or majority may be excluded and marginalized. However, with reflection upon this situation by a decision maker, group, or other agent, their views can be accommodated. This reflective process is termed system intervention by Midgley (2000), who suggests that the particular "boundary critique" policy adopted will affect the ethical nature of the organization.

We now proceed to explore these concepts empirically through a study of knowledge creation in discourse in email.

Support of Knowledge Creation and Inquiring Systems in Email Discourse

We conducted a case study involving the knowledge creation activities of a community of practice in a large Australian university, as found in email discourse. The results of this qualitative research are primarily based on a qualitative content analysis of the patterns of discourse involved in knowledge creation in 300 complete email conversations collected from a Eudora email archive in the community under study. Each conversation analyzed contained more than 10 messages and featured the creation of new organizational knowledge. Two of the authors were participants in the academic community while one was the archive owner. Thus, an ethnographic understanding of the context of the conversations was present during analysis, helping us to develop greater insights.

Knowledge Creation Cycle in Email Discourse

In LOKMS, the three basic stages are intelligence, design, and choice. In the email discourse studied, knowledge was created incrementally through discourse interactions that interwove the elements of intelligence, design, and choice. We identified a pattern of collaborative knowledge development and creation in the conversations studied, described in depth in Lichtenstein (2004) and shown in Figure 5. There are five underlying processes—*initiation, crystallization, sharing, qualification,* and *combination*--leading to the creation of new organizational knowledge. The life cycle is illustrated by the email conversation shown in Figure 6.

To summarize, transient virtual teams, operating more like microcommunities, are summoned through an initial message inspired by a need perceived to be of mutual interest to others in the group. This message becomes part of a knowledge trail consisting of successive related emails in one or more threads emanating from the first knowledge seed email. In the conversations, selected because knowledge development took place, knowledge is crystallized along the knowledge trail through processes of knowledge qualification and combination with reference to knowledge resources, including authorities, documents, contributions of insights, ideas, suggestions, and context by participants.

New participants are co-opted as needed for their decision-making power, interest, or additional knowledge. From time to time, participants are omitted from the circulation list. By the end of the knowledge trails, the tacit knowledge of participants has been shared and combined in useful ways, and new organizational knowledge has been created in the form of organized plans and innovation, decisions, and actions. As a result of the continuous learning occurring concurrently, new social and intellectual capital has also been created at individual and collective levels. Thus, there has been *knowledge integration* in which the specific knowledge held by individual participants has been

Figure 5. Collaborative Knowledge Creation Life Cycle in Email (Lichtenstein, 2004)

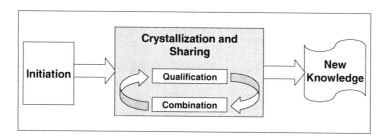

combined, imbued with collective meaning, and integrated into the group members' tacit knowledge in a potentially valuable way.

In the conversations studied, we observed that the impetus for the cycle of inquiry and knowledge creation arose from an individual (alone, or on behalf of a collective) raising issues for discussion, such as new directions, problems, challenges, or opportunities. These issues had diverse origins including the environment external to the organizational unit (for example, competitive threats and mandates from elsewhere in the organization, or outside the organization), the individual's own needs, or a perceived need of the organizational unit.

From Knowledge to Wisdom in Email Discourse

It is important to assess the value of the knowledge created in this way. A key advantage of email in this respect is its ability to access a wide variety of people's knowledge through its great reach. Thus, knowledgeable people were co-opted into discussions through the copy or forward facilities, when access was sought to newly needed knowledge. People were included in the initiating message or called upon during email discussions only when needed, including peers, decision makers, knowledge experts, administrators, and knowledge archivists. This may have enabled key people with little time and attention to contribute in a timely and economical fashion. The participation of decision makers also meant there was an extremely high likelihood that the created knowledge would have a practical immediate outcome—thereby motivating participants to develop a good solution, quickly.

The raising of a variety of viewpoints allowed assumptions and other issues to surface in the form of disagreement, for resolution. The time available for reflection between attendances on email enabled an important issue to be identified off-line, then raised in email discussion on the next attendance. Finally, issues could be relatively easily brought to the attention of key decision makers without the need for scheduled appointments, providing motivation for raising a concern in email that might otherwise remain unvoiced.

Figure 6. Sample of knowledge creation in email discourse

Ray (*initiation*): "I am planning to teach Subject A next year on week nights, instead of weekends. In order to do that, I need a free week night when there are no other classes for students. Bob, can you swap times with me for Subject B, and teach on weekends?"

Bob (*crystallization, sharing, combination*): "I wish I could help, Ray, but I can't do weekends, either. I've been thinking though of changing the teaching for Subject B. I've noticed students don't get much out of Tutorials in Subject B, so I might omit those and have a two hour seminar which I can put on at 4pm. You can then teach three hours of Subject A afterward at 6pm, Ray. What do you all think?"

Sue (*crystallization, sharing, qualification*): "As I recall, Marcia says all postgraduate subjects need three hours of class contact."

Marcia (*crystallization, sharing, qualification*): "Colleagues, yes, the students like three hours of class contact a week, to provide the understanding they need in the subject."

Ray (*crystallization, sharing*): "Maybe it is time to look at alternative ways that provide even better value?"

Marcia (*crystallization, sharing, qualification*): "Well, perhaps Bob can find an innovative way of doing that? Bob, I will leave it to you to come up with something."

Bob (*crystallization, sharing, combination*): "After some discussions with others about this, I suggest we have a two hour workshop each week at 4pm, and a two day workshop during the mid-semester break."

Marcia (*crystallization, sharing, qualification*): "Sounds good to me. What do you think, Sue and Ray?"

Sue (*crystallization, sharing, qualification*): "Good idea!"

Ray (*crystallization, sharing, qualification*): "Yup. Thanks, Bob."

Over and above the advantages discussed above, we suggest that the main value of the knowledge generated is to be found in the *method of resolution of multiple perspectives*. This resolution was driven by the emerging inquiry mode (as discussed later) as well as the cycles of qualification and combination.

Comparing the cycle in Figure 6 with the cycle of wise decision making in Figure 2 (and shown again in Figure 4), we observe a correspondence between the qualification and convergence processes in that current alternatives are being considered and judged, hastening decision closure. Similarly, there is a correspondence between the combination and the divergence processes in that new alternatives are offered for consideration, showing expansion. *We suggest that in general, the greater the number of cycles of qualification and combination, the wiser the resulting solution.* A caveat to this is that there will be a point of diminishing returns in repeating the cycle in that, eventually, cooperation in problem solving will diminish under perceived group dissonance.

According to the second perspective of wisdom as fallible knowing, expressed in Figure 3, it is through such combinations in email that an attitude of wisdom can be nurtured, in adding knowledge that balances doubt or confidence in knowing. An attitude of fallible knowing through email discourse is also encouraged at a collective level.

Mode of Inquiry and Decision Making

The mode of inquiry drove the resolution of diverse perspectives. We observed an eclectic array of inquirers: Hegelian (for example, new academic programs in development were considered both with and without particular content); Kantian (for example, reasoning about possible causes for enrolment trends); Singerian (for example, the synthesis of academic content for new units being developed from multiple contributions); Lockean (for example, analyzing enrollment information to make key enrollment decisions); and Leibnizian (for example, an analysis of the number of cars needed to transport employees to an event). We found the Singerian cycle to be the dominant inquirer for knowledge truth in the email conversations studied, with other inquirers utilized as needed. Importantly, the multiple discordant voices appearing in discourse acted as stimuli for the cycle of knowledge creation described.

However, we observed examples where more was needed to achieve closure in the email conversations. There were challenges to the knowledge base—or assumptions or problems—that were difficult to resolve. An impasse, in which no decision was possible as a consensual outcome was required, necessitated moving a discussion off-line. At times, a decision-making authority was brought into a conversation to guarantee resolution in an act of power (Lichtenstein, 2004), or this person simply observed the conversation until the "dust had settled" and then pronounced the outcome, providing a rationale based on assessment of the conversation.

Domain Complexity

We noticed significant disorder in the patterns of knowledge processes occurring, with chaotically (rather than linearly) ordered employee contributions to knowledge development. It is impossible in email, as it presently exists, to ensure linear development of a threaded discussion. After an initiator sent an initial message, a number of people responded at different times, possibly without reading the most current response. This resulted in quite fragmented discussions, which may have reduced the effectiveness of email-based decision making and knowledge creation. On the other hand, this may have encouraged the submission of diverse views, as the protocol of turn taking was simply not possible.

Yet, despite this obstacle, most conversations still resulted in successful outcomes. We recognized that the knowledge work in our email sample resembled the domain of complexity reviewed earlier. This pattern was observed in many of the conversations studied and ties into our finding that the dominant mode of inquiry was Singerian. As mentioned previously, Snowden (2002) suggests that complex domains are managed and led by the early identification of pattern formation, followed by disruption of any undesirable patterns, and stabilization of those desired. We observed signs of this type of management and leadership in the discourse interactions, although this did not appear to be planned. The leadership which emerged seemed to be based mainly on natural authority of a patriarchal or matriarchal nature and was obtained through the process of knowledge qualification, although at times an act of power was clearly linked to an actor with designated authority, as we discuss in the next section.

Organizational Memory and External Knowledge Resources

In our study, the important role that was played by an organization's memory and the external environment was observed because email participants often included knowledge resources of high quality to inform the decision-making process. For example, documents and hyperlinks from sources in organizational memory or outside the organization were included in emails and, in some cases, participants prepared documents over the course of the email conversation if needed. The knowledge of the participants themselves was available through email discourse—as far as participants were prepared to share and able to articulate such knowledge. The tacit knowledge of experts and decision makers who were not initially included in the conversation was accessed when needed. Similarly, affected knowledge stakeholders could be accessed when needed for their opinions or authorization by adding them to the list of email recipients.

The email discourse itself resulted in new codified knowledge being added to organizational memory because participants used the quote function to generate a knowledge trail. This trail provided a record of the way in which the issues and knowledge had developed over a conversation and acted as a reminder of the state of play, considering the lack of continuity inherent in communicating with an asynchronous medium. Possibly, it was an attempt to mimic threaded conversations on a message board in which entire discussions are always viewable. However, there was some confusion experienced whenever participants chose to respond without including the previously maintained knowledge trail.

A major concern with organizational memory repositories is the issue of ensuring that the knowledge retained is accurate. In the organizational unit studied, we found that key people "in the know"—as well as recent credible external information—were accessed for the most recent knowledge and information, while some current participants brought this knowledge with them as they were also participants in other groups (as mentioned earlier, such people can be termed *knowledge integrators*). Indeed, the degree of accuracy within the email conversations was largely dependent on participants' awareness of who was "in the know" in order to co-opt those experts or peers into the discussion (for example, via the copy feature of email).

A danger thus exists in that if current participants lack accurate knowledge as well as the knowledge of who has the accurate knowledge and is accessible to share it, inaccurate knowledge could be accepted and employed as fact. This is a likely advantage of the

LOKMS model, which attempts to link explicit knowledge to individuals who possess the requisite tacit knowledge. However, it was certainly true that in the email conversations in our empirical study there was usually an attempt to co-opt the needed people and thus correct possible errors in the knowledge being shared (and hence ensure that the resulting knowledge created had a greater chance of accuracy).

In some respects, we saw accuracy as enhanced through email via the rationales and results of the additional "information gathering" (the first phase of the LOKMS model) provided by participants. Even stored presumably static knowledge was not always taken as commonly agreed but rather consulted, queried, debated, and sometimes revised when arising in discussion—suggesting that such *static* knowledge is merely a starting point for developing a situated form of the knowledge. Because participants could view the rationale provided, for instance, they could assess more openly the accuracy of the facts or explicit knowledge on which a decision was being made. Further, we found that accuracy problems in email discourse were reduced to some extent because errors could be detected quite late in the cycle and be relatively easily corrected.

Values and Ethics in Knowledge Creation in Email

Importantly, in email, compared with face-to-face meetings and various synchronous collaborative tools, we discovered a strong sense of participatory and democratic involvement in decision making, with all participants given plenty of opportunity to reflect, formulate, and contribute individual opinions, as well as consider at leisure the other perspectives offered and formulate and contribute responses. Furthermore, the fact that key decision makers were accessible and accountable loaned credibility and weight to the decision-making processes involved—in particular, the qualification processes— as well as to the final knowledge outcome.

Participants clearly cooperated and collaborated in their efforts to build knowledge for a team-driven common purpose. There was generalized team spirit and determination to find a solution, however.

A further finding was that email encouraged only participants who felt they had "something genuine to say," or those who read their email in a timely manner, to contribute. Other participants effectively excluded themselves from the process by choosing to remain passive. This questions the true extent of participation provided by email.

Conclusion

This chapter aimed to explore the potential of email for supporting inquiring organizations and enhancing wisdom. We first reviewed how knowledge can be created when solving problems and making decisions in organizations during social processes involving discourse and circumstances in which this may lead to the enhancement of wisdom. In particular, the chapter highlights the value of a cycle of convergence and divergence in discourse for the promotion of learning and wisdom and the wisdom of maintaining an attitude of fallible knowing throughout knowledge creation and decision making. We also reviewed key concepts of inquiring organizations, highlighting the influences of different inquiry modes for guiding knowledge creation and decision making and introducing a conceptual model for supporting inquiring organizations (Figure 4) that incorporates the wisdom enhancement principle of cycles of convergence-divergence.

We reported an empirical study of knowledge creation in email from which emerged some of the key characteristics of inquiring systems. More specifically, we observed a cyclic knowledge creation life cycle (Figure 5) that highlights cycles of qualification (convergence) and combination (divergence), suggesting that wisdom may be enhanced through this email-enabled knowledge creation cycle.

The potential of email for supporting pragmatic collaborative knowledge creation, learning, and wisdom enhancement has been highlighted in this chapter. In looking for ways to promote the valuable patterns found, the structuring of collaborative spaces with negotiation discourse templates is one avenue to explore (Ing & Simmonds, 2000; Turoff et. al, 1999). A simpler idea is to train employees in the types of conversations that best promote learning, wise decisions, and wisdom in general. Leadership provides yet another path for influencing domains by modifying the complexity of knowledge work, thus encouraging different patterns of discourse.

We saw that the interplay of perspectives enabled the coordination and integration of tacit knowledge between organizational participants who, possessing only specialized knowledge, otherwise tended to remain isolated and unable to contribute to the larger goals of the organization. Participants also integrated their tacit knowledge with codified knowledge in knowledge trails and internal repositories. These findings are important because, as noted earlier, OM is piecemeal, and its fragments require integration or coordination, while it is generally difficult to access the subjective component of OM. An emerging key role for people possessing integrated knowledge was highlighted by the study. Such people can be termed *knowledge integrators*, and their increasing importance for collaborative learning and decision making suggests a shift away from valuing specialist knowledge toward valuing people with interdisciplinary and "big picture" understanding.

In closing, we remark an increasing need, in our times, for wisdom. The way forward may lie in giving people voices that are genuinely heard, as people strive to achieve their individual goals, together. This chapter has suggested that it is in the resulting symbiosis of individual ideas and judgments that wisdom, so greatly needed, may well be found.

References

Bakhtin, M. (1986). The problem of speech genres. In *Speech genres and other late essays* (V. McGee, Trans.). Austin, TX: University of Texas Press.

Barabba, V. P., & Zaltman, G. (1991). *Hearing the voice of the market: Competitive advantage through creative use of market information*. Boston: Harvard Business School Press.

Carlsson, B., Keane, P., & Martin, J. B. (1976). R&D organizations as learning systems. *Sloan Management Review, 17*(3), 1-15.

Churchman, C. W. (1971) *The design of inquiring systems: Basic concepts of systems and organization.* New York: Basic Books.

Courtney, J. F. (2001). Decision making and knowledge management in inquiring organizations: Toward a new decision-making paradigm for DSS. *Decision Support Systems, 31*(1), 17-38.

Courtney, J. F., Chae, B., & Hall, D. (2000). Developing inquiring organizations. *Knowledge and Innovation, 1*(1), 132-145.

Haeckel, S. H., & Nolan, R. L. (1993). Managing by wire. *Harvard Business Review, 71*(5), 122-132.

Hall, D., Paradice, D., & Courtney, J. F. (2003). Building a theoretical foundation for a learning-oriented knowledge management system. *Journal of Information Technology Theory and Application, 5*(2), 63-89.

Hubscher-Younger, T., & Narayanan, N. H. (2003). Authority and convergence in collaborative learning. *Computers & Education, 41*(4), 313-334.

Ing, D., & Simmonds, I. (2000, May). *Managing by wire, revisited* (White Paper). IBM Advanced Business Institute.

Jensen, M. C., & Meckling, W. H. (1992). Specific and general knowledge, and organizational structure. In L. Wering & H. Wijkander (Eds.), *Contract economics* (pp. 251-274). Oxford: Basil Blackwell.

Kolb, D. A. (1985). *LSI Learning Style Inventory.* Boston: McBer and Company.

Lave, J., & Wenger, E. (1991). *Situated learning: Legitimate peripheral participation.* Cambridge: Cambridge University Press.

Lichtenstein, S. (2004, January 5-8). Knowledge development and creation in email. In *Proceedings of the 37th Annual Hawaii International Conference on System Sciences (HICSS'04)*, Big Island, HI, USA. IEEE Computer Society.

Loermans, J. (2002). Synergizing the learning organization and knowledge management. *Journal of Knowledge Management, 6*(3), 285-294.

Meacham, J. A. (1990). The loss of wisdom. In R. J. Sternberg (Ed.), *Wisdom: Its nature, origins, and development* (181-212). Cambridge: Cambridge University Press.

Midgley, G. (2000). *Systemic intervention: Philosophy, methodology and practice.* New York: Kluwer Academic/Plenum.

Nonaka, I. (1994). A dynamic theory of organizational knowledge creation. *Organizational Science, 5*(1), 14-37.

Rittel, H. W. J., & Webber, M. M. (1973). Dilemmas in a general theory of planning. *Policy Sciences, 4*, 155-169.

Roschelle, J. (1992). Learning by collaborating: Convergent conceptual change. *Journal of the Learning Sciences, 2*(3), 235-276.

Senge, P. (1990). *The fifth discipline: The art and practice of the learning organization.* New York: Currency Doubleday.

Sharkie, R. (2003). Knowledge creation and its place in the development of sustainable competitive advantage. *Journal of Knowledge Management, 7*(1), 20-31.

Simon, P. (2003). *Healing America: Values and vison for the 21st century.* Orbis Books.

Snowden, D. (2002). Complex acts of knowing: Paradox and descriptive self-awareness. *Journal of Knowledge Management, 6*(2), 100-111.

Stahl, G. (2002). Rediscovering the collaboration. In T. Koschmann, R. Hall, & N. Miyaki (Eds.), *Carrying forward the conversation: Proceedings of CSCL2.* Mahwah, NJ: Lawrence Erlbaum.

Turoff, M., Hiltz, S. R., Bieber, M., Fjermestad, J., & Rana, A. (1999, January 5-8). Collaborative discourse structures in computer mediated group communications. In *Proceedings of the 32nd Annual Hawaii International Conference on System Sciences (HICSS'99)*, Maui, HI, USA. IEEE Society Press.

Weick, K. E. (2001). *Making sense of the organization.* Malden, MA: Blackwell Publishers.

Wickramasinghe, N. (2003). Do we practice what we preach: Are knowledge management systems in practice truly reflective of knowledge management systems in theory? *Business Process Management Journal, 9*(3), 295-316.

Chapter VI

Supporting the Complexity of Inquiring Organizations:
An Agent Approach

Dianne J. Hall
Auburn University, USA

Yi Guo
University of Michigan – Dearborn, USA

Abstract

This chapter examines the issue of technological support for inquiring organizations and suggests that the complexity of these organizations is best supported by a technology of equal complexity—that is, by agent technology. Agents and the complex systems in which they are active are ideal for supporting not only the activity of Churchman's inquirers but also those components necessary to ensure an effective environment. Accordingly, a multiagent system to support inquiring organizations is introduced. By explaining agent technology in simple terms and by defining inquirers and other components as agents working within a multiagent system, this chapter demystifies agent technology, enables researchers to grasp the complexity of inquiring organization support systems, and provides the foundation for inquiring organization support systems design.

Introduction

Organizations are operating in increasingly complex environments. Simply functioning effectively in these environments requires increasing amounts of information; creating, storing, and retrieving this information is of paramount importance. To effectively manage these tasks, organizations must adopt flexible technologies capable of withstanding dynamic environments and which enable the organization to maintain and evolve a reliable data store. A framework for such an organization is based on the philosophies underlying inquiring systems (Churchman, 1971); an organization that adopts the framework is known as an inquiring organization (Courtney, Croasdell & Paradice, 1998).

The inquiring organization is a complicated structure which has, as its primary task, creation and maintenance of knowledge. Learning is of paramount importance to such an organization and relies heavily on the organization's ability to manage its stores of data, information, and knowledge. Managing these stores requires not only the ability to store and retrieve but also to ensure integrity throughout organizational memory by reducing or eliminating redundancy, inconsistency, and temporal issues. This indicates a need for a complex knowledge creation system that also supports management of knowledge within the organization.

Further, any organization today must glean and analyze information from its complex environment. This requires that an organization be cognizant of its environment and has the ability to continuously scan for changing conditions. Once changing conditions are noted, the organization must be able to recognize whether the condition is immediately threatening (or opportunistic) and requires immediate action, is potentially actionable, bears watching, or can be ignored.

While Churchman's (1971) inquirers on which the concept of an inquiring organization is based are separate entities, they are discussed in terms of an overall knowledge creation and sharing system. To be successful in these endeavors, inquiring organization members require support from a system that also aids decision-making and information discovery, provides temporal guidance, and routinely provides feedback. An inquiring organization must, therefore, be able to scan the environment, interpret incoming information, assess its importance, decide whether action is necessary, and ultimately decide on a course of action in addition to looking for and creating opportunities to learn. This is a complex set of actions best accomplished by a knowledge creation system based in part on the knowledge creation capabilities of the inquirers and, in part, on an overall knowledge management system. This chapter suggests that agent technology is an appropriate method for conceptualizing, designing, and ultimately implementing this complex system.

Technological Support of an Inquiring Organization

The nature of inquiring organizations requires a supporting system that is active, proactive, and interactive. Furthermore, in accordance with the philosophies underlying the inquiring organization, more than one perspective should be included in the support process in order to achieve a more comprehensive understanding of the problem at hand. A system that can work with more than one perspective and, where applicable, knowledge and information are readily available, is capable of functioning in a scenario of complex and fuzzy problems as well as those problems of a more mundane nature. In order to support the dynamic nature of a wicked environment faced by today's organizations, a system must be able to go beyond a functional (action-oriented) process toward an achievement (goal-oriented) process.

Various techniques are feasible when working with complex issues. For instance, Huff and Lesser (1988) demonstrate how nonmonotonic reasoning can be used to assess the credibility of complex alternatives. Their system works with assumptions and is capable of revising those assumptions using its truth maintenance system, much like the inner workings of the Leibnizian or Lockean inquirers. The same need for reasoning in a complex and dynamic environment exists for inquiring organizations which have specific requirements for their support system.

Support Requirements for Inquiring Organizations

There are a number of characteristics that are crucial to the process underlying an inquiring organization. For instance, continuous information gathering is critical to the potential for knowledge creation in general. Without examining both that which is *known* to the organization and that which is new to the organization, challenges to existing assumptions and knowledge will not occur, and an opportunity for knowledge creation may be lost. Of course, this element is inconsequential if the knowledge within the system has not undergone diligent integrity checking both as environmental conditions change and as new information or knowledge is assimilated into the system. This requires the ability to recognize a changing environment and respond accordingly as well as warn the user against storage of information that potentially or directly conflicts with information in the knowledge base. Thus, truth maintenance (accuracy) is also a crucial characteristic that must be supported during design of an inquiring organization support system.

For inquiring organizations particularly, elements such as continuous information gathering and truth maintenance are critical requirements necessary to support the organization in its inquiry process. However, one must remain aware that the human element of the organization also requires support. It is recognized that humans are generally inefficient in gathering, storing, and most importantly, processing large amounts of information. Therefore, systems to support inquiring organizations must have a degree of autonomy, responsiveness, and proactiveness so that they are able to perform their functions in a continuous fashion as appropriate, reacting to changing conditions as well as to user requests and needs.

Because knowledge creation and management is a complex and highly social task often involving many individuals, organizational units, or supply chain partners, a support system must abide by interaction requirements, such as those interaction patterns (cooperation, negotiation, and coordination) evident in Churchman's (1971) inquirers. For instance, cooperation is the essence of the Lockean inquirer; the Singerian inquirer's measure refinement process is one of negotiation. Coordination exists within the guarantors of the Kantian, Hegelian, and Singerian systems.

The combination of dynamic requirements (continuous information gathering, feedback) and social requirements (interaction) require a technology that is capable of both. We believe that agent technology is an appropriate technological tool to conceptualize, design, and eventually implement such a system.

Applying agent technology to the development of inquiring organization support systems is quite natural given the level of sophistication of software agents today. For example, Chuang and Yadav (1997) developed an agent-based architecture to realize an adaptive decision support system proposed by them (Chuang & Yadav, 1996; Chuang & Yadav, 1998). Multiagent systems are used to support knowledge network and corporate memory (Aguirre, Brena & Cantu, 2001). The coordination issue in using multiagent systems to support knowledge management in supply chain systems is studied by Wu (2000) and Barbuceanu and Fox (1997). The use of agents in negotiation is also evident in the literature (Espinasse, Picolet & Chouraqui, 1997; Lee, Chang & Lee, 2000), as well as research into agent-based systems to support learning and knowledge sharing practices in community settings (Lee & Chong, 2003; Roda et al., 2003). However, in these efforts, there is no explicit support for inquiring organizations. Accordingly, this chapter begins the discussion of agents and multiagent systems specific to inquiring organization philosophy.

A Layman's Explanation of Agent Technology

Agent technology is based in artificial intelligence (Russell & Norvig, 1995, p. 3). A software agent (hereafter referred to simply as an agent) is a self-contained program capable of controlling its own decision-making and acting, based on its perception of its environment, in pursuit of one or more objectives (Jennings & Wooldridge, 1996). In particular, agents enjoy properties of autonomy, responsiveness, proactiveness, and social ability, which make an agent a "computer system, *situated* in some environment, that is capable of *flexible autonomous* action in order to meet its design objectives" (Jennings, Sycara & Wooldridge, 1998, p. 276). Two key distinguishing characteristics of agents are that they (1) are capable of handling relatively high-level tasks and (2) exist in an environment that may dynamically affect their problem-solving behavior and strategy. Agents are often referred to as intelligent entities with some degree of decision-making capability and a knowledge representation mechanism, characteristics which epitomize an inquiring organization's requirement to be autonomous, responsive, and proactive.

Further, discovery and information sharing is critical to facilitation of inquiring organizations and can be incorporated into a knowledge creation system by using an agent to proactively mine for new information or changing conditions (Chen, Qiuming & Chen, 2001). Mobile automated programs have been used on the Internet as discovery agents, and the capability of those agents continues to be enhanced by new developments (for example, Menczer, 2003). Thus, agents are appropriate for carrying out the tasks of continuous information gathering and checking for an inquiring organization.

Many researchers agree that autonomous agents and multiagent systems represent a new way of analyzing, designing, and implementing complex software systems (Jennings et al., 1998). The agent-based view offers a powerful repertoire of tools, techniques, and metaphors that have the potential to considerably improve the way people conceptualize and implement many types of software, including those designed for decision-making and information management. Multiagent systems, where the system is designed and implemented as several interacting agents, are "ideally suited to representing problems that have multiple problem solving methods, multiple perspectives and/or multiple problem solving entities" (Jennings et al., 1998, p. 277). This characteristic of agent-based systems meets the requirement for the social perspective in inquiring organizations. Further, the social perspective recognizes the need for and encourages use and growth of intellectual capital, which can be facilitated by the use of agents that provide services, such as discovery and data checking, to the user.

For example, a system has been developed to make sale policy recommendations (Symeonidis, Kehagias & Mitkas, 2003). In this system, a data agent continuously monitors and mines data in an Enterprise Resource Planning system based on customer and supplier profile attributes. It supplies new discoveries to other agents in this multiagent system (customer profile agent, supplier profile agent, and inventory pattern identification agent). Once a customer order arrives, the recommendation agent will make a recommendation based on the information received from the profile and pattern identification agents, who are trained regularly by newly added information. This system is multiperspective (supplier and customer), social in nature (cooperation between the agents to discover, disseminate, and process information), and illustrates the capability of agent systems to perform continuous information gathering and decision-making tasks.

The ability of agents (or any support system) to supply users with context-specific information may help lessen the effects of bounded rationality (Simon, 1957) by supplying a decision-making environment that includes access to relevant knowledge and information and routines for problem solving. Evaluating and interpreting the external environment is not rational, as both an individual's experience and mental models affect it. Individuals, in accordance with their own reality, interpret information about changes in the environment differently. Formal and informal communication can change an individual's perception of a given situation as ideas are exchanged and knowledge is transferred. Limiting the amount of information processed by the decision maker to that which is relevant and channeling problem solving to those individuals with related knowledge or expertise in the problem domain help to alleviate these limitations. This can be accomplished by using an agent (or agent system) whose task is to filter information relevant to the specific context at hand. This agent must be intelligent and endowed with the ability to recognize domain knowledge relevant to the decision context. Agent technology is capable of recognizing domain knowledge of any kind, despite its beginnings primarily in the domain of software requirements. This type of support is most relevant for domain-specific functional scenarios, such as scheduling problems.

Sometimes, however, it is more advantageous that the user is presented with a variety of information, both from within and outside the domain or context. This support for multiperspective decision-making is a requirement of an inquiring organization. For example, while new product discovery seems internal to the organization, understanding the potential impact outside the organization is crucial to maintaining the organization's social responsibility. In this case, the user should not only be made aware of context-specific items (e.g., cost of retooling, potential market share gain) but also outside concerns (e.g., environmental impact). Multiple domains may then come together for the user, providing that individual with perspectives that may not have been evident from within their own worldview.

Agent technology also has advantages of sophisticated patterns of interactions (cooperation, negotiation, and coordination). Although some agents can function independently, and in fact are designed to do so, it is when interacting with other agents and with organizational users that the system is truly taking advantage of the social potential of agent technology. For example, agents can be designed as teams with flexible relationships among them (Tambe, 1997). Agents can be used to support inquiring organization support systems that must interact with users and with other technologies (for instance, collaborative software). The varieties of agent characteristics listed above provide the foundation for the flexible dynamic support required by inquiring organizations.

An Agent Model for Inquiring Organizations

The Belief-Desire-Intention (BDI) model of agents, developed by Australian Artificial Intelligence Institute, has become one of the best known and most studied models for agents. The model is based on folk psychology in that BDI agents are characterized by a mental state with three components: beliefs, desires, and intentions (Rao & Georgeff, 1995). Generally, beliefs are what is contained in the agent's local knowledge base, and desires are what the agent is trying to achieve based on its beliefs. Intentions are currently adopted plans, which are predetermined sequences of actions (or subgoals) that can accomplish specified tasks. An agent's practical reasoning involves repeatedly updating its beliefs from information in the environment, deciding what options are available, filtering these options to determine new intentions, and acting on the basis of these intentions. In some cases, this reasoning may also include an effort to coordinate with other agents in the system in order to synthesize beliefs and desires into an achievable consensual plan of action.

Agent-oriented programming (Shoham, 1993) is a multiagent programming model in which agents are explicitly programmed in terms of mentalistic notions. In a multiagent system, agents can have different beliefs and goals, and there may be multiple instances of any given agent. Perspectives are implicitly embedded in a given agent's worldview; this worldview is similar to Churchman's (1971) use of Hegel's *Weltanschauung* and Singer's *natural image*. In this model, beliefs can be defined as the informative component of the agent's state. Agents acting under different perspectives each pay unique attention to various information items in the environment when collecting data according to that perspective; in other words, when perceiving the world.

These beliefs can be partitioned into two components. The first component contains the fundamentals of the particular perspective (worldview) on which the agent is to act; these are known as meta-beliefs. The other component contains the facts that the agent collects from the environment, which are interpreted through the lens of the meta-beliefs. Beliefs are parallel to the concept of a mental model. That is, they are continuously updated as the environment changes, yet the underlying foundations often remain undisturbed. Desires are the goals or motivations of the agent. By using certain decision criteria and other methods, the agent adopts the best intention/plan for the context.

The relationship between these components is shown in Figure 1; this figure depicts the internal structure of an agent which is comprised of beliefs and plans (Kinny, Georgeff & Rao, 1996). In order to make an agent more socially aware, a social component based on speech acts has been added (Dignum & van Linder, 1997). Contents of beliefs and/or plans can be similar among agents but will be interpreted differently (for instance, prioritizing) according to the belief component. Social plans may include a social network of cooperative agents. This network may, of course, be different for each agent and under different contexts. Implicit in the social plan is the need for the agent to act under direction

Figure 1. Internal Structure of an Agent

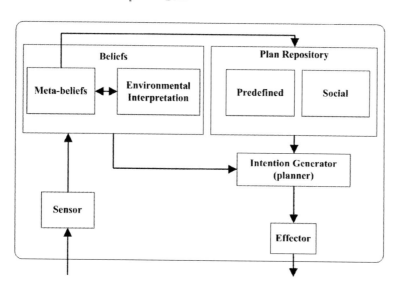

of any supervisory agent—explicit social plans are more detailed plans of communication and coordination required for the agent to carry out its task. The sensor is the component that reacts to changes in the environment to which the agent reacts; the effector implements the chosen plan.

Consider, for example, an agent based on the Lockean inquirer. The essence of the Lockean inquirer is to reach consensus about the interpretation of new information. Beginning only with a list of basic properties (categories), the inquirer views new information in relation to whether it does or does not fit existing categories defined earlier by the Lockean community. Learning about the new information requires that consensus is reached as to its classification or that a new classification is added. The agent's meta-belief is the store of classified observations against which new information is interpreted. Because of its social predisposition, a Lockean inquiring agent would have predefined plans of cooperation and explicit social plans that allow it to engage in compromise.

Contrast this with a Leibnizian inquiring agent, whose primary task is to analyze and react accordingly from within its own limited worldview and because of its closed nature does not have explicit social plans of negotiation, coordination, or cooperation. This type of agent is viable in structured problems, such as those requiring predefined plans based on known concrete variables. These two types of agents have different aptitudes and different worldviews. Table 1 shows the implementation of these agents in the traditional BDI beliefs and plans structure.

These two types of inquirers can be seen in the example of the agent-oriented air traffic management system (OASIS) (Kwok, Ma & Zhou, 2002) in which a given aircraft agent tries to fly along a certain flight path provided by the coordinates of a sequence of waypoints. This agent is best represented as Leibnizian because it pays attention only to facts related to its job — taking off, flying, and landing safely. These facts are information, such as wind and trajectories; it also follows rules regarding speed and altitude and defers to the sequencing agent when required.

On the other hand, a sequencer agent has a different goal of landing all aircraft safely in an optimal sequence; it is concerned with performance of aircraft, desired separation time,

Table 1. Differing BDI Beliefs and Plans Structure of Leibnizian and Lockean Agents

	Meta-beliefs	Predefined social plans	Explicit social plans
Leibnizian Agent	Axioms, fact net	If candidate = axiom Accept Else if candidate = fact net Accept Else Store as potential	None
Lockean Agent	Classified observations	If observation = classification Accept Else Enter mediation	Cooperation, consensus-seeking

wind field, runway situation, safety of crew, passengers, ground personnel, and so on. This has a social perspective that is representative of a Lockean inquirer. The sequencer agent must find that point at which all variables are in consensus that an individual aircraft may land in safety without disrupting the patterns of landings of other aircraft or the patterns of ground crews. This may require negotiation and cooperation with other agents as well as the overall task of coordinating flights.

The sequencer agent and the aircraft agent have different intentions and desires, thus different perceptions of the world (beliefs). Regardless, they must work together to accomplish the goal of a safe landing and hence must be able to develop an understanding of each other's perspectives, a process in an inquiring organization referred to as perspective synthesis.

A Lockean Cooperative Agent System Example

The above flight example illustrates why a cooperative system is necessary. Agents can work in isolation but, like people, are most productive in cooperative groups. This requires not only developing inquiring agents, which are procedural agents representing and implementing the logic of Churchman's (1971) inquirers but also developing agents whose primary function is to facilitate the successful operation of inquiring agents. For example, an interface agent to interact with the user is a possibility; a coordination agent is generally present in an agent system to control activity.

Sometimes treated as a natural extension of objects, agents are capable of concurrent actions and semantic knowledge and of exhibiting social behaviors (Wooldridge, 1997); these behaviors make agents suitable for higher-level tasks. Further, agents can work with each other to perform a multitude of functions. Multiagent systems are collections of agents with emergent behaviors. Inquiring systems can be conceptualized and implemented into multiagent systems and provide effective decision and knowledge management support because (1) the knowledge needed for knowledge creation and decision making is stored, continuously checked for integrity, and constantly generated; and (2) each of the inquirers imposes a decision process which is thought to be helpful in specific contexts (from structured to ill-structured problems). This approach has been proven constructive (Vahidov & Elrod, 1999). Perhaps the most natural inquirer to use in demonstrating the idea of cooperation is the Lockean inquirer.

The Lockean inquirer is an open system that uses as its basis a set of elementary labels or properties used to place observations into categories. By definition, a Lockean community shares common goals, beliefs, and values. Therefore, any problem considered by the Lockean community should be one of a strong consensual context. Conflict of any consequence does not exist because the goals of each member are the same, although the perception of the path necessary to attain the goal may differ between members. An example of a problem appropriate for a Lockean system would be the definition of a five-year plan. Each committee member is sent the outline for the plan and is expected to determine whether that outline fits with the existing goals and missions of the organization (classified observations). If all members agree that the outline of the five-year plan fits the organization's goals, the plan becomes part of the organization and is stored as a classified observation. If the plan does not meet with consensus among members, the committee chair attempts to alleviate differences in order to reach consensus. If the chair does not believe that consensus is possible, the plan is disregarded at that point in time and is stored as an unclassified observation for later discussion. The Lockean inquirer clearly encourages and supports socially oriented knowledge development.

A Multiagent Lockean Inquiring System

To move from a procedural schema such as that presented above toward an agent system, one must first conceptualize the Lockean community members as agents. Despite being members of the same community and thereby sharing many of the same beliefs and goals, these agents are not simply duplications of each other. Although there may be multiples of a given agent (e.g., multiple committee members), there will also be agents with differing tasks (e.g., the interface agent, the library agent).

A multiagent Lockean inquiring system must incorporate both cooperation among the community of agents and coordination of the system in general. Coordination requires agents whose tasks are to coordinate the system and to provide an interface between the system user and the system itself. To continue the five-year example described above, one may conceive of a chairman agent to coordinate the plan analysis process, a librarian agent in charge of organizational memory, an interface agent to provide the user with system interactivity, and a host of Lockean agents representing the committee members. The chairman agent is the one to determine whether consensus has been reached initially, to call for mediation if needed, and to determine whether consensus can be reached following mediation. The librarian agent is responsible for placing observations into the knowledge stores or retrieving observations when necessary. The interface agent, in itself a multiagent system, is responsible for producing and controlling the interface for the user, which may include input, query, and display capabilities. The Lockean agents conduct the plan analysis.

When the system user wishes to examine the 5-year plan, he or she interacts with the interface agent to query the system regarding whether the plan has potential to reach the organization's objectives. The interface agent then passes the query through the query agent into the Lockean community, where the chairman agent begins the analysis process. The chairman agent passes the plan through to the contingent of Lockean inquiring agents for analysis; each agent examines and interprets the plan and reaches a decision as to the plan's merit. During this time, the inquiring agents may request additional information directly from the librarian agent as appropriate, or may request additional information from the user, in which case the chairman would pass the request through to the user by way of the interface agent system. Once an inquiring agent reaches a decision, it communicates its findings to the chairman agent who then decides whether mediation is required. Following the cycle of mediation and analysis as necessary, the

Figure 2. A Lockean Multiagent System

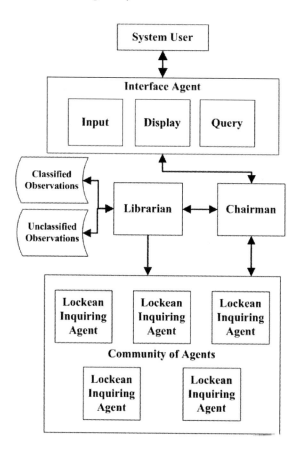

observation is passed to the librarian agent for storage. This iterative process involves not only the agent system but also the user who will ultimately approve the outcome. Figure 2 depicts a possible implementation of a multiagent Lockean inquiring system.

In addition to the complex multiagent system in which the inquiring agents reside, any one of the inquirers may be designed as a multiagent system itself. This multiple-agent concept is evident in Churchman's (1971) work. For instance, the Hegelian inquirer has the Over-observer that synthesizes the assumptions of two Leibnizian systems (a minimum of three agents) and the Kantian inquirer has the Executor to scrutinize model output from the Kantian model agent and adjust model use as necessary (a minimum of two agents). This further demonstrates the benefits of using an agent-based approach to support inquiring organizations.

Because agents, like objects, are used as abstraction tools in conceptualization and design, we can conceptualize a system at different levels. In our discussion thus far, we have conceptualized the structure of a Lockean multiagent inquiring system that includes inquiring agents (Figure 2); we have also examined a specific internal structure for single agents (Figure 1, Table 1). This descent through levels is required to reach granularity for implementation purposes (i.e., one simple agent that can be constructed as the basis for a multiagent system). Although simple agents must first be constructed, both simple and multiagent sets are building blocks for more complex structures. For example, Leibnizian inquirers, once constructed, can be used to facilitate Hegelian inquirers. At the highest level, we envision abstract entities representing the inquirers and other necessary agents; from there, we can combine agent types to form context-specific structures. We will use this approach to conceptualize a multiagent system for inquiring organizations.

A Multiagent Cooperative System for Inquiring Organizations

In the context of an inquiring organization, it is not enough to choose one type of inquirer on which to base the system. Because each of Churchman's inquirers functions best in particular situations (as discussed in previous sections) and, in many cases, incorporates elements of other inquirers, an inquiring organization's knowledge creation system must be comprised of all the inquirers, working together to achieve the ultimate result for the organization. It is necessary, therefore, to create a multiagent system that combines the five inquirers with other agents to facilitate an inquiring organization's needs. Thus, an inquiring organization can be conceptualized as a multiagent system—a collection of inquiring and supporting agents. We start with a depiction of an inquiring organization as a collaborative high-level structure with abstract entities representing an interface agent, a resource coordination agent, and five inquiring agents, each representing one of Churchman's (1971) inquirers (Figure 3).

The interface agent is necessary for the user to interact with the system; the resource coordination agent is required to break down tasks, make assignments, allocate resources, and attend to conflict management as necessary. The role of a resource agent can be strong or weak, depending on the level and type of coupling among agents. A strong resource agent (depicted in Figure 3 as being above the inquiring agents) may not be necessary if the agents will solve resource coordination issues among themselves through friendly negotiation as is frequently the case in a collaborative system. In such a system, agents do not generally possess conflicting goals or compete over resources, except where the resource is critical and unavailable.

The collective goal of the inquiring organization agent system is to provide relevant accurate information by maintaining a consistent knowledge base and by providing organizational strategies for processes, such as decision-making or goal setting; each organization, or unit within an organization, may choose to structure the system

Figure 3. Inquiring Organization Structure with Abstract Entities

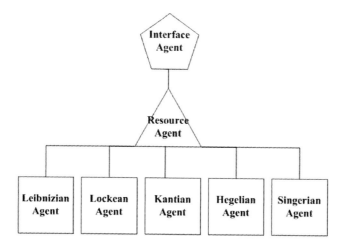

differently to fit its specific needs. The multiagent system is itself an organization; the relationship among the entities defines that organization. Thus, from the abstract organization in Figure 3, a more concrete representation may be drawn.

For a particular organization or organizational unit, there may be multiples of various inquiring agents or support components. For example, a team-oriented unit may engage more Lockean agents and forego Hegelian agents; an engineering unit may prefer the analysis capabilities of the Kantian agent. The Lockean-oriented organization may not have a need for a strong resource coordinator, whereas a strongly conflictual unit (for instance, organizational members frequently engaged in negotiation) would likely require an agent to handle inevitable conflict.

In a more complex setting, one organization may engage more than one arrangement of agents. Figure 4 depicts an organization that uses two different inquiring structures: a Hegelian-oriented structure and a Lockean-oriented structure. Each has different uses and is invoked at different times. For instance, when considering a five-year plan, such as that described above, the Lockean structure would be invoked. On the other hand, employee/management negotiations are likely to require that the Hegelian system is invoked. Note that each of these structures also contains Leibnizian inquirers, perhaps to facilitate structured problem analysis. These are only two of many possible structures an organization might employ. It is probable that an organization would utilize many configurations to meet its various needs; the ability to employ different configurations exemplifies the recursive property of the multiagent system concept. We can see that it is the characteristics of an organization or organizational unit and the nature of its processes that will dictate its configuration (i.e., the specific number and type of inquiring agents and supporting agents). Use of various agent configurations thus reflects the uniqueness of a given organization.

One of the many assets of agent technology is the ability to move, multiply, and restructure its agent configurations as required by any given context. Unlike other technologies, which, once established, remain fairly static (for instance, a database), agent-based technologies are free flowing and dynamic. Although we focus in this work on a minimal system, it is possible for an agent-based system to contain hundreds of agents with the ability to work with, or on behalf of, the others.

Each task that an organization finds itself engaging in can be facilitated by rearranging an agent structure to one suitable for that task. We know from Churchman's work, for instance, that the Leibnizian inquirer works best in structured situations. Therefore, an agent system with a Leibnizian orientation is likely to be formed when a procedural structured problem is being analyzed. However, if in the course of the analysis the problem changes from structured to unstructured, the system may dynamically restructure itself (for instance, by adding several Singerian inquiring agents) to respond to the new stimulus. This flexibility allows the inquirers to work in sync for the benefit of the organization and to reflect the uniqueness of both the situation and the organization.

Designing a Multiagent System to Support Inquiring Organizations

While abstraction is a useful tool for conceptualization, designing a multiagent system requires greater detail and a model on which to build. In their work on learning-oriented knowledge management systems, Hall, Paradice, and Courtney (2003) conceptualize a model based on Churchman's (1971) inquiring systems. They propose that, in addition to the inquirers themselves, there are several components that are necessary to support the operation of the inquirers. While they proposed a comprehensive model of which inquiring systems is a part, we are concerned only with those components that directly support all of the inquirers in their knowledge creation tasks. These components comprise what we will call the integrity checking process that allows an inquiring organization to expand its organizational memory with accurate timely knowledge. These components are concerned with integrity of knowledge stored and knowledge generated within the system. A *basis verifier* is critical to all the inquirers, as they depend on their knowledge bases to create new knowledge and analyze information. If any of the information in a knowledge base is incorrect, the system will reach the wrong conclusion about an item when it is compared to an incorrect base item. Additionally, it will reach the wrong conclusion with all items subsequently compared to any aspect of the base built on the initial erroneous conclusion. An *environmental verifier* is also critical for

Figure 4. Inquiring Organization With Context Specific Agent Structures

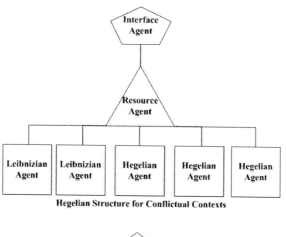

Hegelian Structure for Conflictual Contexts

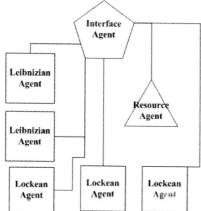

Lockean Structure for Consensual Contexts

much the same reason. It varies from a basis verifier in that, rather than continuously comparing knowledge in the store against itself, it reviews incoming information or newly created knowledge to determine whether changes have occurred in the environment that would, in turn, affect the validity of other stored knowledge components. Commonly, knowledge becomes outdated as an organization's processes or resources (particularly technology) mature. A *self-adaptation verifier* allows the system to support management by preparing reports of recommended action in the face of new knowledge, especially in response to changing environmental variables, which make this component a critical facet of functioning in a turbulent environment. This component monitors knowledge base changes to identify new relationships or new knowledge that arises from newly stored knowledge or changing information. Prevention of storage or use of knowledge based on error is inherently obvious; however, many systems have been designed that do not verify the accuracy of their internal models and therefore propagate incorrect information. A component such as an *analysis integrity verifier* can warn a user of potential problems with information or knowledge that the user wants to store. The *time/space component* plays an important role in the efficiency of the organization as well as integrity of the organization's knowledge base. Its primary function is to follow time-critical missions of the organization and to ensure that all temporal considerations of the organization are met. Additionally, it works to maintain time-sensitive knowledge and information such that outdated information is removed and information nearing its expiration is flagged and possibly sent to the self-adaptation verifier for action. Together, these five components comprise the integrity process that surrounds the inquirers, forming the basis of an inquiring organization's knowledge creation process.

In addition to the inquirers and their support components, an inquiring organization agent system must include not only an interface agent to provide the user access to the system but also an element of decision support. This may be in the form of query capabilities, such as those in the interface agent, but may also be more complicated, perhaps guiding the user through a strategic process. Further, any organization must be aware of its environment and the new information opportunities it may afford, but an inquiring organization with a learning foundation is particularly well served to engage in environmental scanning. This gives rise to a need for a discovery agent.

It becomes obvious that one could continue to conceive of *necessary* or *ideal* capabilities from which any organization would benefit. However, the capabilities outlined above serve well to demonstrate the concept of a multiagent inquiring organization agent system, as well as serve as a shell of an implementation of the learning-oriented knowledge management system proposed by Hall et al. (2003). Accordingly, these components are the basis for the multiagent system for inquiring organizations depicted in Figure 5.

Each of the entities in the figure have distinct tasks but work together to achieve the goal of knowledge creation and decision support within the inquiring organization. Organizational memory is shown here as centralized; this is for illustration simplicity only. The knowledge base can be centralized or distributed over the organization; in addition, each inquiring agent can also have local memory to facilitate faster processing.

The interface agent is included here to present the need for human-computer interaction, as it is important to recognize the importance of the user's input into an inquiring system. Even though the system may be multiagent, one interface agent may well be able to carry out the task of facilitating the interface between the users and agents. For instance, the user may query organizational memory, after which the interface agent will engage the appropriate agent or agent system to obtain all available information from the knowledge base. On receiving this information, the interface agent will display the result to the user.

The interface agent will also pass any new observation, data, or models that the user wants to add to the knowledge base to the strategy or librarian agents for processing. To prepare input from the user for storage in organizational memory, for instance, the tasks of the interface agent may include displaying an input form once the user chooses to add information or an observation to organizational memory, constructing the assertion in a proper form for storage in organizational memory, and issuing a request for assertion to the librarian agent. This process is iterative; many queries may pass between the user and the interface agent (and thereby between the interface agent and other agents) until the user is satisfied with the outcome, and integrity checks have not been violated.

The strategy agent's function is to differentiate between five inquirers and their representative agents based on the type of problem being considered. It will make a determination as to the problem type and structure and call on the most appropriate inquirer for analysis. The strategy agent may also examine the results of the analysis and call on a different inquirer if appropriate and interact with the librarian, interface, and discovery agents as necessary to facilitate information flow. In addition, this agent functions as a decision support or expert system support component for the user when required by providing problem-solving strategies to the user.

The inquiring agents are charged primarily with knowledge creation. Each inquirer functions here as described by Churchman (1971). Although depicted in the figure as one agent per inquirer, an organization may have many agents representing one of the inquirers (e.g., see Figure 4) depending on their needs. However, a true inquiring organization cannot be without all five inquirers. Specific characteristics of each inquirer must be considered when designing appropriate agents and agent systems. For example, agents representing both the thesis and antithesis components would be included in a design representing the Hegelian system, and agents representing both data integrity

Figure 5. A Multiagent System for Inquiring Organizations

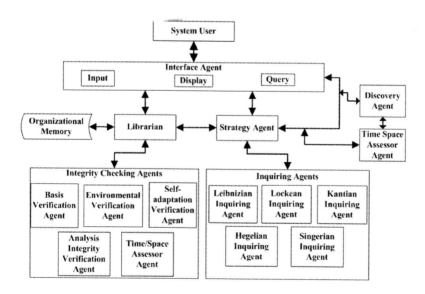

verifiers and alternative perspective generators would be present in a design representing the Singerian system (refer to Hall et al., 2003 for details).

The task of the discovery agent is to routinely scan the external environment of the organization for changes that warrant consideration or action. Like the Intelligence Gathering Unit in Hall et al.'s (2003) model, this agent is yet another multiagent system that may contain, in addition to discovery capabilities, the ability to hypothesize regarding the relevance and/or urgency of incoming information or the ability to advise the user when changes are observed. It interacts with all other agents depending on its current operating mode. For instance, it may be invoked by the interface agent to respond directly to a user query for new information or by the strategy agent to provide additional information to the inquirers. If it is operating in scanning mode and discovers potentially relevant information, it may initiate interaction with another agent as appropriate.

The task of the time/space assessor agent in the overall system is to provide the strategy agent and the discovery agent with a temporal foundation to facilitate the efficiency of the organization. In this capacity, the agent functions from a process orientation (Can the organization implement the suggestion in time?); its primary function as a member of the integrity checking community is to determine whether information in organizational memory is still applicable.

Integrity checking in this complex environment is a challenge. The integrity-checking agents will carry out the tasks of the components discussed above to ensure the validity of organizational memory. The goal of this multiagent subsystem is to maintain accuracy and consistency of the knowledge base and to guide the process as applicable. Operations of this agent include validating, asserting, warning, deducing, and monitoring.

For example, suppose that a user recently learned that a competitor is planning a price drop. The user believes that this is a crucial piece of information and wants it inserted into the knowledge base. Through the interface agent's input facility, the user will submit the information which is then appropriately formatted for both analysis and storage and passed to the chairman agent for processing. The chairman agent passes it on to the Lockean inquiring agents, who reach an agreement as to the proper classification of the item (in this case, perhaps, "potential market share loss"). The chairman will then pass the observation, along with its classification, to the librarian agent. It will then be examined against existing knowledge. If the observation is neither contradictory to nor a duplication of existing knowledge, it will be inserted into organizational memory; if its basis is questionable, the user may be asked if an override is desired—this occurs in the form of a warning issued via the interface agent. Depending on the depth of the agent, screening may occur to ensure the incoming information's applicability to the current context if, for instance, a result set is being built for the user. The agent will also investigate newly acquired information against existing information to deduce new relationships.

Existing Agent Technology to Support Integrity Checking Components

Although each of the agents above has specific and vital roles within an inquiring organization multiagent system, it is the integrity-checking component that is perhaps the most vital, particularly in the spirit of Churchman's (1971) inquiring systems. It is because of this importance that we look into the feasibility of supporting this agent subsystem with extant agent technology. This task is facilitated by the flexibility and portability of the concepts behind agent technology. Agents currently exist that parallel most, if not all, of the functions listed in the above components.

Knowledge engineering, an AI subfield, focuses on systematically capturing and representing domain knowledge, or knowledge facilitation (Fowler, 2000). Effort in this field has resulted in, for instance, production systems called expert systems. Because it is impractical to list all the AI/agent techniques that may potentially be applied to building or selecting agents for inquiring organizations, some common techniques are assumed herein and not directly addressed. For example, search algorithms, planning, inferring logical languages, and resource model representations are widely used in various agents, such as Retriever (Fragoudis & Likothanassis, 1999) and Softbot (Etzioni & Weld, 1994). Three techniques with special applications are discussed below. Table 2 summarizes the discussion.

The integrity checking agents are charged with maintaining the validity of knowledge created and stored. Techniques to maintain truth in a knowledge base are the basis for any evolving system and any inquirer with a locally operated knowledge base. Truth Maintenance System (TMS) techniques have been studied and developed since the late 1970s (Russell & Norvig, 1995) and can be used to improve knowledge base integrity. We can conceptualize a knowledge base in its simplest form as a collection of logical sentences. Some sentences become outdated or not applicable because of the passing of time or changes that have occurred. Therefore, in addition to retrieving information, we also want to have the ability to remove outdated information or information that is no longer valid. The challenge is to not introduce any inconsistencies or degrade the system when deleting sentences.

In AI, the process of keeping track of which additional propositions need to be retracted is the principle behind truth maintenance (Russell & Norvig, 1995). A TMS is capable of keeping track of dependencies between sentences so that retraction will be more efficient. Naturally, the major task of such a program is to use dependency-directed backtracking and avoid inefficient chronological backtracking. A second task is to provide explanations of propositions, which is critical to the analysis integrity verifier. A proof is one kind of explanation; if the proof is not accomplished successfully, assumptions are provided to explain why the proof is not possible. A third task of a TMS is default reasoning, which is useful for the self-adaptation verifier, and the last task for a TMS is to ameliorate possible inconsistencies by adding sentences.

The self-adaptation verifier not only passively produces reports at the arrival of new information but also actively makes recommendations. In order to do so, it needs to be able to learn over time. Maes's (1994) agent is a personal assistant agent designed to control incoming e-mails; learning via a neural network makes this agent a perfect example of what a self-adaptation verifier should do to achieve the goal of learning. There are many techniques developed in machine learning, such as data mining (Cho, Kyeong & Hie, 2003) and neural networks, observation, human feedback, or learning from other entities (Hu & Wellman, 1998) that can be used to implement the self-adaptation verifier. It is quite possible that an environmental verifier will also have learning capability. Because the environment is essentially dynamic, it is impossible for an agent to consider and respond to every stimulus. A more desirable behavior is to focus on relevant information and be proactive in the search for information. Learning is necessary for an agent to determine what is relevant to the current context and what is not.

Because its task involves monitoring changes occurring in environment, there is a need for the environmental verifier be able to move through different environments and through different perspectives. Agent mobility is a popular area of agent research and predicted to be the future of the Internet (Kotz & Gray, 1999). The environmental verifier can send small programs (robots or crawlers) to retrieve new information from relevant locations in a distributed inquiring organization or from locations external to the organization (such as Internet search engine robots) (Menczer, 2003). Mobility is also valuable for the basis verifier that is in charge of maintaining global consistency across a decentralized knowledge base. There are arguments for the trade-off between the increased complexity of mobility and the benefits that mobility provides. These trade-offs must be considered before mobile agents are implemented.

Table 2. Summary of AI/Agent Techniques that Support theIntegrity Checking Feature of the Inquiring Organization

Agents of the Integrity Checking Component	Critical Requirements	Techniques
Basis Verifier	Accuracy of system basis	Truth maintenance
Environmental Verifier	Knowledge store continually reviewed for accuracy in changing environments	Perception, learning, and mobility
Self-adaptation Verifier	New action requirements	Default reasoning and learning
Analysis Integrity Verifier	Prevents assimilation in error; prevents other knowledge store components from being assimilated because of an error	Proof and explanation
Time/Space Assessor	Time/space assessment	Temporal logic

Conclusion

In this chapter, we propose that agent technology can be used to support knowledge creation and management in an inquiring organization. Inquiring Systems Theory (Churchman, 1971) provides a basis for our conceptualization of an inquiring organization and its components; agent technology is used as the technological design framework. The concept of agent technology has been used to conceptualize and model agents and multiagent systems that serve to support the foundations of an inquiring organization and its characteristics.

Although we focus on the technological design aspect of inquiring organizations, we not only embrace Churchman's admonitions to maintain multiple perspectives, flexibility, learning, and social orientation by designing agents to represent different tasks and perspectives but also strongly advocate and design for the human element in an inquiring organization.

Humans play an indispensable role in these systems. The most obvious is that the modeling and design processes require input from human experts. Individuals provide the domain knowledge to be captured and verify the correctness of its representation during system design, construction, and implementation. The elements and models inherent in the design and use of a system must be understandable by all stakeholders (Kilov, 2002) and therefore depend not only on the expertise of the designers but the expertise and direction of the users as well. For instance, the rules for filtering relevant data need to be defined by system users in their specific domain context. While agents may play a large role in producing relevant information, there will always be a need for the system user to decide whether a piece of information is relevant to a specific context and on the assessment of the degree of importance. Ultimately, of course, the function of choice (that is, the decision) resides with the organizational member. The system described here is a *support* system; the object of that support is the system user. Thus, system users are not diminished by the system but rather empowered by it. The system described here will not simply automate but will *informate* (Zuboff, 1985).

The system conceptualized here has the ability to facilitate all components of a knowledge management system: knowledge creation, knowledge storage and retrieval, knowledge transfer, and knowledge application (Alavi & Leidner, 2001). These concepts are important to any organization desiring to exploit its knowledge resources but are particularly suited to inquiry. We believe that this support system framework will lead to a sustainable materialization of and support for the emerging form of an inquiring organization.

References

Aguirre, J. L., Brena, R., & Cantu, F. J. (2001). Multiagent-based knowledge networks. *Expert Systems with Applications, 20*(1), 65-75.

Alavi, M., & Leidner, D. E. (2001). Knowledge management and knowledge management systems: Conceptual foundations and research issues. *MIS Quarterly, 25*(1), 107-136.

Barbuceanu, M., & Fox, M. S. (1997, February 5-8). *Integrating communicative action, conversations and decision theory to coordinate agents*. Proceedings of the Autonomous Agents Conference, Marina Del Rey, CA.

Chen, M., Qiuming, Z., & Chen, Z. (2001). An integrated interactive environment for knowledge discovery from heterogeneous data resources. *Information and Software Technology, 43*(1), 487-496.

Cho, Y. H., Kyeong, K. J., & Hie, K. S. (2003). A personalized recommender system based on Web usage mining and decision tree deduction. *Expert Systems with Applications, 23*(3), 329-342.

Chuang, T. T., & Yadav, S. B. (1996, August 16-18). *A conceptual model of an adaptive decision support system (ADSS)*. Proceeding of the Second Americas Conference on Information Systems.

Chuang, T. T., & Yadav, S. B. (1997, August 15-17). *An agent-based architecture of an adaptive decision support system*. Proceedings of the Third Americas Conference on Information Systems.

Chuang, T.-T., & Yadav, S. B. (1998). The development of an adaptive decision support system. *Decision Support Systems, 24*(2), 73-87.

Churchman, C. W. (1971). *The design of inquiring systems: Basic concepts of systems and organizations*. New York: Basic Books.

Courtney, J. F., Croasdell, D. T., & Paradice, D. B. (1998). Inquiring organizations. *Australian Journal of Information Systems, 6*(1), 3-15.

Dignum, F., & van Linder, B. (1997). Modelling social agents: Communication as action. In M. Wooldridge, J. Muller, & N. Jennings (Eds.), *Intelligent agent III* (Vol. LNAI, pp. 205-218). New York: Springer-Verlag.

Espinasse, B., Picolet, G., & Chouraqui, E. (1997). Negotiation support systems: A multi-criteria and multi-agent approach. *European Journal of Operational Research, 103*(2), 389-409.

Etzioni, O., & Weld, D. (1994). A Softbot-based interface to the Internet. *Communications of the ACM, 37*(7), 72-77.

Fowler, A. (2000). The role of AI-based technology in support of the knowledge management value activity cycle. *Journal of Strategic Information Systems, 9*, 107-128.

Fragoudis, D., & Likothanassis, S. D. (1999, December 13-15). *Retriever: An agent for intelligent information recovery*. Proceedings of the 20th International Conference on Information Systems.

Hall, D. J., Paradice, D. B., & Courtney, J. F. (2003). Building a theoretical foundation for a learning-oriented knowledge management system. *Journal of Information Technology Theory and Application (JITTA), 5*(2), 63-89.

Hu, J., & Wellman, M. P. (1998). *Online learning about other agents in a dynamic multiagent system*. Proceedings of the Second International Conference on Autonomous Agents, Minneapolis, MN.

Huff, K. E., & Lesser, V. R. (1988, November 28-30). *A plan-based intelligent assistant that supports software development.* Proceedings of the ACM SIGSOFT/SIGPLAN Software Engineering Symposium on Practical Software Development Environments, Boston, MA.

Jennings, N. R., & Wooldridge, M. J. (1996). Software agent. *IEEE Review, 42*(1), 17-20.

Jennings, N. R., Sycara, K., & Wooldridge, M. (1998). A roadmap of agent research and development. *Autonomous Agents and Multi-Agent Systems, 1,* 275-306.

Kilov, H. (2002). *Business models: A guide for business and IT.* Upper Saddle River, NJ: Prentice Hall.

Kinny, D., Georgeff, M., & Rao, A. (1996, January 22-25). *A methodology and modelling technique for systems of BDI agents.* Proceedings of the Seventh European Workshop on Modelling Autonomous Agents in a Multi-Agent World, MAAMAW'96.

Kotz, D., & Gray, R. S. (1999). Mobile agents and the future of the Internet. *ACM Operations System Review, 33*(3), 7-13.

Kwok, R. C., Ma, J., & Zhou, D. (2002). Improving group decision-making: A fuzzy GSS approach. *IEEE Transactions on Systems, Man, and Cybernetics - Part C, 32*(1), 54-63.

Lee, K. J., Chang, Y. S., & Lee, J. K. (2000). Time-bound negotiation framework for electronic commerce agents. *Decision Support Systems, 28*(4), 319-331.

Lee, Y., & Chong, Q. (2003). Multi-agent systems support for community-based learning. *Interacting with Computers, 15*(1), 33-55.

Maes, P. (1994). Agents that reduce work and information overload. *Communications of the ACM, 37*(7), 31-40.

Menczer, F. (2003). Complementing search engines with online Web mining agents. *Decision Support Systems, 35*(2), 195-212.

Rao, A. S., & Georgeff, M. P. (1995, June 12-14). *BDI agents: From theory to practice.* Proceedings of the First International Conference on Multi-Agent Systems, San Francisco, CA.

Roda, C., Angehrn, A., Nabeth, T., & Razmerita, L. (2003). Using conversational agents to support the adoption of knowledge sharing practices. *Interacting with Computers, 15*(1), 57-89.

Russell, S. J., & Norvig, P. (1995). *Artificial intelligence: A modern approach.* Upper Saddle River, NJ: Prentice Hall.

Shoham, Y. (1993). Agent-oriented programming. *Artificial Intelligence, 60,* 51-92.

Simon, H. A. (1957). *Models of man: social and rational.* New York: Wiley.

Symeonidis, A. L., Kehagias, D. D., & Mitkas, P. (2003). Intelligent policy recommendations on enterprise resource planning by the use of agent technology and data mining techniques. *Expert Systems with Applications, 25*(4), 589-602.

Tambe, M. (1997). Toward flexible teamwork. *Journal of Artificial Intelligence Research, 7,* 83-124.

Vahidov, R., & Elrod, R. (1999). Incorporating critique and argumentation in DSS. *Decision Support Systems, 26*(3), 249-258.

Wooldridge, M. J. (1997). Agent-based software engineering. *IEEE Proceedings on Software Engineering, 144*(1), 26-37.

Wu, I.-L. (2000). Model management system for IRT-based test construction decision support system. *Decision Support Systems, 27*(4), 443-458.

Zuboff, S. (1985). Automate/informate: The two faces of intelligent technology. *Organizational Dynamics, 14*(2), 5-18.

Chapter VII

Knowledge Creation in Inquiring Organizations Using KDD:
Re-Focusing Research on the Analyst

John D. Murray
Georgia Southern University, USA

Thomas L. Case
Georgia Southern University, USA

Adrian B. Gardiner
Georgia Southern University, USA

Abstract

Churchman (1971) emphasized the continual learning nature of organizations as part of their ontological fabric. Accordingly, he proffered the view of organizations as inquiring systems whose actions result in the creation of knowledge. To this end, many modern organizations have attempted to create knowledge by using technologies, such as Data Mining and Knowledge Discovery in Databases (KDD). Although quite powerful, these technologies depend heavily upon the skill and insights of the analyst. We propose that the role of the analyst in the application of these technologies is poorly understood. To advance our understanding in this regard, we dedicate the first part of this chapter to describing the KDD process and relate it to the five philosophical perspectives of organizational knowledge acquisition, as originally discussed by Churchman (1971). In the second part of the chapter, we draw parallels between the process of knowledge acquisition via KDD with the concept of information foraging (Pirolli & Card, 1999). Information foraging theory is offered as a research lens through which we can investigate the role of human judgment in KDD. These insights lead us to propose a number of areas for possible future research. Based on our insights into information foraging and knowledge creation, the chapter concludes by introducing a new organizational metaphor into corporate epistemology: inquiring organizations as knowledge foragers.

Introduction

In his classic work, Churchman (1971) characterizes any organization that produces knowledge as an inquiring system. Inquiring organizations, therefore, are learning organizations modeled on the theories of inquiring systems (Courtney, Croasdell & Paradice, 1998). Accordingly, central to an inquiring organization's viability within the marketplace is its ability to learn: to better serve its constituency, inquiring organizations must continuously update and revise their knowledge (Courtney et al., 1998).

Churchman (1971) further asserts that the knowledge of an organization is more than merely a collection of information held in its archives: rather, it consists of the shared explicit and tacit information that is meaningful, or useful, in helping the organization meet its goals. As a result, meaningful information is normally distributed throughout an organization's infrastructure, as it is generally held by an organization's employees, or more precisely, the users of that information (see also, Courtney, 2001). Because of the dynamic nature of any human-centered enterprise, the process of updating and maintaining organizational knowledge is a task that is ongoing and evolutionary. Clearly, this process lies at the very foundation of an organization's ontological fabric.

Churchman (1971) also generalized to organizations five distinct philosophical perspectives that were originally put forward to describe the general nature of knowledge acquisition. Specifically, he took the philosophical perspectives of Leibniz, Locke, Kant, Hegel, and Singer and instantiated them within the context of organizational decision making. By doing so, he showed how each perspective translates into a distinct approach toward knowledge aggregation and management (see also, Courtney, 2001).

The primary focus of this chapter is to illustrate how a relatively new knowledge-generating technology, Data Mining (DM), can be integrated into Churchman's (1971) taxonomy of inquiring systems. Data Mining (more broadly known as Knowledge Discovery in Databases, or KDD) refers to a set of automated techniques that can be applied to discover relationships among variables in large databases. Many companies have implemented KDD technologies in the hope of discovering knowledge that will lead to actionable approaches for enhancing corporate revenue. Indeed, Heinrichs and Lim (2003) recently argued that the use of data mining tools has the potential to enhance decision support capability and thereby improve an organization's "strategic perfor-mance capability" (i.e., become a source for competitive advantage).

According to Frawley, Piatetsky-Shapiro, and Matheus (1992), when a KDD algorithm is applied successfully, it results in "the nontrivial extraction of implicit, previously unknown, and potentially useful information from the data" (p. 37). KDD applications may be used within companies, for example, to gain a better understanding of consumer purchasing behavior (Brachman & Anand, 1996), or to identify possible fraud (Cox et al., 1997). The types of databases that are frequently mined contain information about consumers or clients, their purchases or other expenditures, as well as a wide range of other variables about the target population (e.g., demographic information).

In this chapter, we first discuss the process by which DM and KDD techniques generate new knowledge. Second, we position KDD techniques within Churchman's (1971) taxonomy of inquiring systems. Third, we make the case that these processes, like any knowledge generation enterprise, must be viewed primarily as a human-centered activity: one that is only as effective as the human user (or analyst, in this case). Accordingly, our primary thesis is that the role of the human analyst in using KDD technologies presents a fruitful area for research. Fourth, we assert that the process an analyst follows in KDD is, in a number of ways, analogous to Pirolli and Card's (1999) concept of information foraging. We therefore explore the potential of using information foraging theory as a research lens through which we can investigate the role of human judgment in KDD. The chapter concludes highlighting a number of potential research avenues blending KDD, information foraging, and cognitive psychology.

The KDD Process

Feldens et al. (1998) characterize the KDD process as strongly application-oriented, iterative, interactive and nonlinear. It is often described as consisting of five major phases:

1.   Task and Data Discovery
2.   Data Cleaning
3.   Model Development
4.   Data Analysis
5.   Output Generation

Each phase is multifaceted and can involve numerous subphases. However, below is a brief explanation of each phase.

KDD goals are outcomes of the Task and Data Discovery phase. During this phase, goal-relevant task requirements (and applications that might result from KDD task completion) are identified. KDD analysts also develop an understanding of the structure, coverage, and quality of available data sets.

Data quality and coverage deficiencies relative to KDD tasks and goals are addressed during the Data Cleaning phase. The KDD analyst's background knowledge and judgment can play a crucial role in this phase. For example, analysts that perceive available data as being of poor quality may allow crucial indicators of interesting phenomena to be overlooked or dismissed as anomalies or outliers.

Once the analyst has identified KDD tasks and has assembled and cleaned task-relevant data, they are positioned to interact with the data. This interaction often involves the formation of hypotheses and development of models. However, analysts rarely start the Model Development phase with a formally specified hypothesis they wish to confirm or disconfirm. Instead, their behavior during this phase may be better characterized as that of a *data archeologist* who surveys the data landscape and by leveraging experience and background knowledge, decides where to dig. As the analyst sifts through the data, fragments that seem to fit together are identified, and hypotheses evolve to explain their meaning. Ultimately, an empirical-based explanatory model of the data patterns may emerge.

Data Analysis and Model Development activities are typically intertwined in KDD. KDD analysts typically leverage various analytical approaches to identify artifacts (explanatory models), including regression, decision trees, neural nets, and case-based reasoning. Moreover, both algorithm-based and visualization-based analysis tools may be used to assist analysts with model development tasks.

Output Generation involves the translation of insights resulting from model development and data analysis into reports and actionable recommendations. Output generation is typically supported by a variety of presentation and data transformation tools that assist analysts in making the case that previously unknown and potentially useful information has been discovered in the data.

One tool frequently used by analysts across the latter stages of the KDD process is OLAP (On-Line Analytical Processing). OLAP is software that allows analysts without technical database knowledge to browse data stored within a database in a user-friendly way. OLAP facilitates data retrieval by allowing the analyst to choose from a list of established data views, depending on what information the analyst wants to know about at the time. Thus, OLAP can be considered a type of decision support system (DSS) tool that allows the analyst to search efficiently and intuitively through a large data set.

The power of OLAP comes from the ability it gives the analyst to change quickly and easily the data view in front of them: by either providing more detail (e.g., drilling down into the data set) or changing to view related information (e.g., changing the displayed dimensions). For example, after an initial inspection of a dataset, an analyst may notice a trend that is either unexplained or of potential interest (in a way, a *scent* captures the analyst's attention). However, the analyst may initially have only limited insights into whether this trend is significant or what factors have contributed to it. Rather than having to wait until further relevant information is retrieved from the database by a database expert, the analyst using OLAP can quickly change the data view to view data about factors they may feel have contributed to the trend. Alternatively, they may wish to drill down in order to see whether the trend is isolated or whether it is more pervasive.

The data analyst is a human user of data mining tools that is intimately involved in all steps of the KDD process. As Brachman and Anand (1996) note: "Knowledge discovery is a *knowledge-intensive* task consisting of *complex interactions, protracted over time,* between a *human* and a (large) database supported by a *heterogeneous suite of tools*" (pp. 39-40).

From the broadest perspective, a KDD analyst queries a database to extract relevant data in response to a prespecified task or goal. The analyst then analyzes the extracted subset of the database using data analysis and/or visualization tools in order to gain insights about the data. The analyst subsequently uses presentation tools to disseminate insights about the data to a broader audience; this broader audience typically includes the individuals that specified the KDD task or goal(s).

Because the analyst is intimately involved with the KDD process, the analyst's background knowledge, characteristics, and psychological make-up are likely to have a significant impact on the KDD process and ultimately its success. Background and psychological differences, for example, may impact how KDD tasks, goals, and available data are perceived. Individual differences are also likely to influence the extent to which particular subsets of data extracted from the database are perceived to be relevant to the KDD tasks (potential sources of new patterns of useful information). Cognitive biases are also likely to influence model selection and refinement processes, as well as the nature of insights that result from the application of data analysis and visualization tools. An analyst's background knowledge or domain expertise is also likely to influence how insights about the data are communicated to broader audiences and used as inputs for future KDD activities.

KDD and Churchman's Taxonomy

Clearly, KDD is a process used to generate new knowledge. Through interacting with available datasets, the analyst becomes more knowledgeable and has the opportunity to validate new assumptions or perceptions of causal networks. Much of this knowledge will remain tacit (i.e., contained in the analyst's mind) but may also become explicit (recorded or written down). The methods and procedures used in KDD approaches can be integrated with Churchman's (1971) discussion of five theoretical views of knowledge generation. Recall that Churchman's articulated models were based on the classic philosophies of Leibniz, Locke, Kant, Hegel, and Singer. We refer the reader to Churchman's (1971) original work for a complete description of each view.

At first glance, KDD appears to bear the strongest resemblance to the Lockean and Kantian approaches, as articulated by Churchman (see also, Courtney, 2001). The Lockean approach is a relatively open style of generating new knowledge. Data in the form of new observations are collected, and then new knowledge is generated via inductive logic. Consensus from the Lockean community serves as a check that the new knowledge is both valid and accurate. As noted by Courtney (2001),

"The primary knowledge management tools in Lockean organizations are repositories, such as data warehouses, for storing observations, data mining for analyzing

observations, and groupware tools, such as electronic meeting software and e-mail, for facilitating the communication process and the development of shared meaning." (p. 27)

This observation highlights the significant overlap existing between KDD and Lockean inquiry.

The Kantian approach to inquiry relies upon the comparison of multiple models or perspectives that surround a particular problem or issue. These models arise from consideration of different types of observations or data—from both within and outside the system. Like KDD analysts, Kantian inquirers are capable of constructing multiple explanatory models of the decision situation. New knowledge results from what essentially reduces to a goodness-of-fit process—a highly analytical method of comparing each model or perspective with other perspectives to see which best explains the variance in problem-relevant data. The decision style exhibited in Kantian inquiry is both theoretical and empirical and is likely to be an approach used by many KDD analysts who serve as data archeologists.

With its strong association with the classic scientific method, KDD fits well with the Lockean approach. New observations (i.e., data from outside an organization's knowledge base) are sought and related to other data in the search for meaningful causal connections that manifest in the form of reliable patterns and associations. The Kantian approach is also appropriate in that KDD procedures frequently rely on procedures that generate and compare multiple models in order to determine which one best characterizes the emergent associations. The observations on which these models are based can originate from both within the organization's archived knowledge or be adopted from external sources. Sophisticated statistical procedures, like structural equation modeling, bear strong resemblance to the spirit of the Kantian approach.

Courtney (2001), however, alludes to potential limitations of applying the Kantian approach to KDD. As noted by Courtney (2001), because the Kantian approach "is based on the belief that problems can be modeled analytically. There is little or no emphasis on human interpretation of the problem, nor on human involvement" (p. 28). This view suggests that the Kantian approach only requires knowledge management tools whose functionality includes capabilities of maintaining problem-relevant data and the development of alternative explanatory models. Arguably, because fully automated data mining tools could fulfill this function, the Kantian approach may not be fully consistent with KDD processes in which human analysts play a pivotal role.

The open-endedness of the data discovery process inherent in KDD limits the applicability of the Leibnizian approach to the KDD process. Although KDD analysts, like Leibnizian inquirers, may use formal logic and mathematical analysis to make inferences about cause-and-effect relationships, they are not limited by access to internally generated data and knowledge. Taking this view, new knowledge results from the generation of logical conclusions from knowledge already inherent in the organization's archives—that is, *new* observations are not brought into the database. All new knowledge must be consistent with a set of axioms that define the core structure of the organization. Another distinction between KDD and Leibnizian inquiry lies in the importance of tacit knowledge: knowledge within a person's head that is difficult to express or codify (Nonaka & Takeuchi, 1995). As noted by Courtney (2001), tacit knowledge is afforded little importance within Leibnizian organizations (p. 26). In contrast, the effectiveness of KDD is typically driven by tacit knowledge. Analyst-centered KDD is consistent with Churchman's (1971) allusions to libraries and library users, noting that "the state of knowledge resides in the combined system consisting of the library and an astute and adept human user" (p. 9).

The Hegelian view is not directly applicable to the KDD process described in the previous section. Hegelian inquiry creates knowledge via a process of debate between antithetical ideas about a topic. After one thesis is advanced, compelling arguments for a diametrically opposite viewpoint are developed. An objective third-party analyzes the debate between the antithetical views and resolves them via a synthesis that reflects the most plausible aspects of both. This process bears little resemblance to the KDD process. As noted previously, many techniques applied within DM and KDD involve statistical exploration and operate on actual data that exists within and outside the organization's database. Although their colleagues may question the inferences made by KDD analysts, the KDD process does not require the development and resolution of conflicting viewpoints of the data.

The Singerian view transcends the other four approaches by arguing that new knowledge arises out of a consideration of a holistic mixture of specific observations (individual datum), implicit knowledge held by organizational employees, and ethical and personal characteristics of the user/analyst. The Singerian view, therefore, also clearly supports the notion of placing the analyst at the center of research into knowledge production (e.g., KDD research). This approach has been recognized as being highly suited for wicked problems (Rittel & Webber, 1973; see also, Courtney, 2001) and it applies to those DM and KDD processes that must consider both human and environmental factors during data interpretation. The Singerian approach is a combination of functional, interpretive, and critical views. As noted by Courtney (2001), "knowledge of all types must be supported in this environment, both tacit and explicit, both deep and shallow, both declarative and procedural, both exoteric and esoteric...every genre of software is required in the Singerian organization" (p. 28). As Churchman (1971) and Mitroff and Linstone (1993) note, the Singerian approach *sweeps in* all other inquiry and knowledge creation approaches; it will employ any or all of them to a particular decision-making process as well as information from both internal and external sources.

The overlap between the Singerian approach and KDD is evident in Mitroff and Linstone's (1993) discussion of the management of real-life problems. These researchers maintain that a combination of technical (T), organizational and social (O), and personal and individual (P) factors are crucial to managing and solving real-world problems. They also contend that successful implementation of problem solutions "depends first and foremost on the use of human resources" (p. 102). Courtney (2001) adds, "the personal perspective is based on individual experiences, intuition, personal factors, and attitudes about risk, among other things...in a complex scenario, given the same external information, no two people might reach the same conclusion, as their background, training, experience, values, ethics, and mores, may differ" (p. 30). Singerian inquiry's emphasis on organizational and social (O) factors, as well as personal and individual (P) perspectives in problem-solving situations is consistent with our contention that research focused on the analyst's interaction with data within the KDD process has considerable potential to help us better understand knowledge creation processes in inquiring organizations.

Limitations of DM and KDD Research

Research on the use of KDD is on the rise (e.g., Fayyad et al., 1996). To date, however, most KDD research has centered on the tools and algorithms used to mine data. Although numerous researchers recognize that the characteristics and expertise of the users of KDD tools are important to the success of KDD, relatively little attention has been devoted to elucidating the psychological demands of the KDD task, identifying user-oriented issues that are important to the task, or to articulating the points in the KDD process where human decision making and judgment are important. The popularity of OLAP reminds us of the central role the analyst plays within the KDD process.

The importance of human involvement in KDD has not, however, been overlooked by all KDD researchers. For example, Brachman and Anand (1996), Elder and Pregibon (1996), and Klosgen (1996) collectively characterize KDD as a human endeavor, which is guided and interpreted via human judgment. Specifically, Brachman and Anand (1996) contend that to "discover data," researchers must "understand the exact nature of the interaction between a human and data that leads to the discovery of knowledge" (p. 40). Klosgen (1996) also notes that the KDD process is analyst driven, rather than being tool driven. He maintains that any algorithm or automated system used in KDD must take on an "assistant" role (p. 269) because KDD is a discovery process that depends, first and foremost, on the goals of the analyst.

There is clearly considerable weight of opinion that KDD research should not lose sight of the central role of the analyst. The overlap between KDD and Lockean, Kantian, and Singerian inquiry processes, we previously described, also tend to underscore the importance of the analyst in knowledge creation. Courtney (2001) describes a new decision-making paradigm for DSS that is centered on decision makers' mental models. Courtney concurs with Churchman (1971) and Mitroff and Linstone (1993) that

"This model and the data selected by it (and hence the problems selected for solution) are strongly inseparable. Our mental model, either personally or collectively, determines what data and what perspectives we examine in a world of overabundant data sources and a plethora of ways of viewing that data." (pp. 30-31)

It therefore stands to reason that recentering KDD research on the analyst and the analyst's interaction with data (e.g., when using OLAP) is necessary to appropriately recognize KDD's role in inquiring organizations. The focus upon the analyst opens the door to new and potentially very rich avenues of research capable of deepening our understanding of the determinants of KDD success. We also argue that significant research is likely to be facilitated when the similarities between the KDD process and other forms of human information processing present in inquiring organizations (e.g., scttings/tasks requirlng problem solving, decision making, etc.) are recognized.

KDD as Information Foraging

In this section, we have chosen to apply Pirolli and Card's (1999) information foraging theory (IFT) to assist in the development of a descriptive conceptual model of the KDD process. IFT seeks to understand how strategies and technologies for information seeking, gathering, and consumption are adapted to the flux of information within the environment. An example of information foraging is the use of a search engine to locate relevant information on the Internet. IFT provides rather compelling evidence that inquiring organizations should not overlook the central role of the analyst in KDD. We contend that the process an analyst follows in KDD is, in a number of ways, analogous to the concept of information foraging.

Pirolli and Card argue that people will modify their information search strategies, or the structure of the task environment, to maximize their rate of gaining valuable information. Improved information foraging returns translate into a greater yield of relevant information per unit of effort needed to obtain it. IFT maintains that cognitive strategies that result in greater yields without additional effort will, over time, replace cognitive strategies limited by lesser yields. Arguably, from an evolutionary perspective, this choice of behavior is optimal as it maximizes the chances of survival within an environment where survival is contingent upon an organism's ability to balance the cost of information search with expected returns.

The roots of IFT lie in *Optimal Foraging Theory* (Stephens & Krebs, 1986). This theory accounts for how organisms adapt their behavior and biological structure to environmental changes in the context of searching for food. Important to this theory is the notion that food environments are often patchy: food is distributed throughout an environment in clusters or patches, with some patches being richer food sources than others. In this kind of environment, the organism must strategize about how much of its resources should be devoted to harvesting food *within* a patch, in contrast to seeking out new patches (*between-patch* activities). Within-patch foraging will continue to occur as long as the organism perceives that the effort needed to harvest the food supply in the patch to be greater than the energy needed to seek out a new patch. When the energy required to continue to extract food from a current patch is perceived to be more than that required to move to (and begin harvesting) a new patch, the organism's best strategy is to move to a different patch and begin foraging.

Optimal Foraging Theory maintains that species that develop superior foraging strategies will have an evolutionary advantage over those with inferior strategies. Such species will be able to acquire an adequate food supply more efficiently (with less energy expenditure) than competitors for the same food sources, thereby better positioning themselves for survival in tough times or harsh environments. Survivors are likely to have better cognitive strategies regarding within-patch and between-patch activities than nonsurvivors.

Optimal Foraging Theory is most relevant to situations where many types of foods are available, but these foods vary with respect to profitability (i.e., the food's nutritional value minus the resources needed by the organism to obtain and handle it). In general, an organism will make decisions about what kinds of foods to pursue and do so by considering which foods are most profitable in the current environment.

It is important to note that some organisms leverage technologies in their foraging activities, which may contribute to an improved ability to harvest food more efficiently within a particular patch. The use of such tools in foraging may contribute to the survival potential of a species relative to other species competing for the same food sources (Pianka, 1997). Sea otters living off the coast of northern California and in other habitats, for example, commonly manipulate rocks in order to facilitate access to shellfish. In addition, tool use by Brown Capuchins (chimpanzees) in food foraging is hypothesized to provide this primate species with an evolutionary advantage in its habitats (Bionski, Quatrone & Swartz, 2000). Tool use also suggests that some species may possess more cognitively complex foraging strategies than others.

Pirolli and Card (1999) noted multiple parallels between food foraging behavior and information foraging on the Internet. For example, like many food environments, information on the Web appears in a patchy environment: valuable information is unevenly distributed throughout Web-based locations, and the information seeker must decide whether to put forth resources to harvest the known information in one location or risk obtaining an unknown amount of information by following the perceived scent of potential information in other locations. Furthermore, like many food environments, information on the Internet varies enormously in its profitability. Some information is highly relevant to the seeker's goal, whereas other information is largely irrelevant.

Pirolli and Card created an artificial information forager that was designed to seek out particular documents on the Internet. This forager, which was inspired by Anderson's (1993) ACT-R model of human cognition, was endowed with mental characteristics that have been argued to describe the way humans solve problems and retrieve and use information from memory. The researchers had previously tracked the minimum number of steps (links in the Internet) to obtain the target documents and their artificial forager was found to take a similar (and highly efficient) route. In terms of contrast, the researchers had human volunteers search for the same documents and found human performance to be highly similar to that of the artificial forager, lending support to the notion that human information foraging behavior typically strives to optimize information yield. Such behavior is less likely to be consistent with the notion of satisficing.

The parallels between food foraging and information foraging can also be extended to KDD. Given that a data analyst using OLAP is faced constantly with the decision as to what data will be viewed (e.g., the choice of navigation path through the data set), and how long the current data set will be viewed for (i.e., the choice whether to move to a different data view immediately, or at a later time), there are arguably a number of parallels between OLAP use and information foraging. Moreover, KDD usually takes place in a patchy environment, where an analyst must make decisions pertaining to where to engage deeper drilling efforts (within-patch searching), as opposed to looking elsewhere in the database for other potential useful subsets of information (between-patch searching). Furthermore, like many food environments, the information of interest in KDD varies enormously in its profitability. That is, information contained within database subsets varies in relevance to the analyst's overall question/task and in the amount of effort required by the analyst to obtain and understand that information. In addition, KDD tools (analysis, visualization, etc.) are used by analysts to determine whether a particular database subset (data patch) is a fruitful source of new information about the target population or if it should be abandoned in favor of another subset with greater information yield potential. Effective tool use (and well-designed tools) can better position an analyst and employer for KDD success, thereby enhancing the organization's survival potential in today's brutally competitive markets.

Using IFT as a descriptive conceptual model from which to understand KDD is limited, in part, by the scant research directed at investigating the rationality and behaviors of information foraging. These matters are still very much an open research question. Notwithstanding the immaturity of research into information foraging, we contend that IFT is still useful as a basis for making predictions about expected KDD behavior, identifying factors analysts may be sensitive to during the KDD process, and for expressing hypothesized tests of rationality. For example, taking into consideration IFT, we would expect the following behavior to be exhibited by analysts during the KDD process:

- Analysts will strive to obtain the most useful (i.e., profitable) information possible to the current task;

- Analysts will perceive the most profitable information as information that overlaps highly with what is desired but involves minimal costs in obtaining and under-standing it;

- Analysts will often modify their strategies (i.e., change what they are doing) in order to efficiently obtain profitable information; they will also react to changing perceptions in profitability; and

- Analysts' search strategies that result in more profitable information will, over time, be implemented more often than strategies that result in less profitable information yields.

Other predictions of analyst behavior could address: data set navigation strategies, hypothesis development, hypothesis testing, the effect of learning and expertise, and the rationality of causal reasoning.

As noted in our description of the KDD process, the analyst often searches for information that meets *a priori* defined criteria. Pirolli and Card (1999) would label this search pattern a *diet* model, where information is sought that meets predefined criteria. However, there are other types of search strategies that may also accurately depict KDD analysts' behavior. For example, *scent* models search for information on the basis of obvious proximal cues (e.g., keywords) or statistical correlations. Alternatively, *patch* models are driven by the search for pre-existing clusters of information; visualization tools might assist analysts that employ patch models. It is possible that different search strategies are closely tied to specific forms of KDD (data mining). Further exploration of the extent to which alternative information foraging models best depict the KDD process may provide valuable insights into knowledge creation processes in inquiring organizations.

As animals do in their search for food, the analyst will hold critical assumptions that undoubtedly influence the way the task is perceived and executed. *Decision assumptions* comprise the analyst's definition of the task at hand; *currency assumptions* pertain to ideas about the value of specific types of information; and *constraint assumptions* involve known limitations of the task itself, the technology used to execute the task, or of the user. Like decision makers' mental models that play a central role in the new decision-making paradigm for DSS described by Courtney (2001), these assumptions play a critical role in IFT. Investigating how they pertain to KDD activities should enhance our understanding of how analysts obtain, interact with, and interpret data during the KDD process.

The information foraging approach is also quite useful because it embraces aspects of the KDD task that are problematic to the basic KDD model. In particular, most KDD analysts start with some rudimentary or skeletal hypothesis, but that hypothesis is quickly modified as extracted data sets are examined and analyzed. As the analyst interacts or becomes familiar with the data, specific ideas about potential outcomes become more refined (Brachman & Anand, 1996). In addition, the process is dialectic, with the analyst asking different questions while becoming familiarized with the client's needs, products, company structure, and interacts with task-relevant data. IFT provides insight into fundamental evolutionary forces that may be driving such inquiry and knowledge creation processes.

There are limitations of this approach to understanding KDD as well. Most notably, the information foraging approach may be viewed as being overly focused on the individual. It generally fails to take into account the role of communication and cooperation with others that could assist the data analyst in completing the KDD task (Montovoni, 2001). Such communication/cooperation could be especially valuable to the analyst during data analysis and interpretation (e.g., Simoudis, Livezey & Kerber, 1996). Today's organizational ecology enables individual information foragers to tap into online communities to obtain insights and to identify strategies beyond their own immediate capabilities. As such, it represents an important departure from foraging strategies developed by nonhuman animals. Also, whereas much of the previous information foraging research has focused on the productive search for information, KDD must be viewed as a process that encompasses much more than the mere search for information. The heart of KDD rests in the examination, consideration, and interpretation of the information that is obtained. As mentioned earlier, the analyst is not just a data miner but is more similar to a data archeologist who classifies and interprets this information (Brachman & Anand, 1996) or to a member of an inquiring organization that is actively engaged in knowledge creation processes.

Potential Research Avenues Blending KDD, Information Foraging, and Cognitive Psychology

This chapter has proposed a new agenda for analyst-centered research into KDD (vis-à-vis a more traditional technology-focused research approach). In this section, we go further and articulate a number of promising themes that can form a focus for future empirical/theoretical inquiry. These themes blend psychological theory and methodology with KDD and also reflect issues highlighted by IFT research. By articulating these themes, our hope is to encourage research that explores the psychological mechanisms that describe the interaction of the analyst with KDD tools, such as OLAP. Such research has the potential to shed new light on the KDD process itself (a descriptive approach) and potentially highlight opportunities to improve the state of the art in KDD tool design (a prescriptive approach).

Although our five themes and ensuing questions far from represent an exhaustive set of researchable issues, they squarely focus the attention of KDD research on analysts and their interaction with the data. The five themes are as follows:

Theme 1: Attention Processes

The first theme pertains to questions that address how an analyst perceives information relevant to the KDD task. One specific question very central to this issue concerns the perception of information diagnosticity. For example, are there general criteria for defining a fruitful data patch? Conversely, at what point is an analyst's line of inquiry likely to be abandoned because the analyst judges that the data patch is *not* worthy of further pursuit? Similarly, a second question addresses what general principles govern an analyst's perception of a data set's profitability: that is, how do analysts know, or judge, that information revealed through their interaction with a data set is more useful than other information? Are analyst's perceptions of profitability similar to a more objective reality-based determination of profitability, or are they driven by higher-order cognitive processes (e.g., Lockean, Kantian, or Singerian inquiry processes) that are best suited to philosophical explanations? A third question asks whether analysts are biased to attend to more profitable information in a data set, even though greater information yield might result from harvesting readily available but *less* profitable information (low hanging fruit)?

Theme 2: Decision Processes

Once useful information is attended to and encoded, the analyst must ultimately process (i.e., think about) and interpret the information yielded from the data set. There are a host of questions that relate to this theme, not the least of which is what kinds of decisions and strategies do analysts employ in determining when useful information has been encountered? A related question is how the process of decision making proceeds? Is it an incremental process, whereby evidence from data queries accumulates slowly; or is it more like an insight-based process where an answer or solution emerges suddenly? (Metcalf, 1986). Are monotonic reasoning processes at work when analysts discover new insights or do truth-maintenance systems slow down the emergence of new insights? (Reichgelt, 1991).

Another question pertains to the type of information that is most influential in a decision. For example, there is a body of research that addresses the situation when a global look at a data set provides a different perspective than a more detailed view of the data. This is known as Simpson's Paradox. Given that analysts make decisions regarding when to drill deeper, in what situations or in what kinds of task settings does this bias exist? (Curley & Browne, 2001; Lin, 2002; Spellman, Price & Logan, 2001). A related question asks whether there are aspects of an analyst's decision process that are amenable to automation. Another question related to decision processes goes beyond the individual decision maker to settings where multiple analysts are working together on a single problem. A number of previous research streams suggest that group communication processes can either enhance or inhibit the KDD process (e.g., Choi & Kim, 1999; Lam & Schaubroeck, 2000; see also related work by Weldon & Bellinger, 1997).

Theme 3: KDD Tool Use/Selection

Questions related to this theme revolve around the selection of analysis and visualization tools used to conduct the data query. What tools (analysis and visualization) do the best job of assisting the analyst (and other information foragers) in defining the usefulness of a data patch? Furthermore, are analysts predisposed toward KDD tools that yield useful information with minimal effort and energy expenditure? Do analysts naturally gravitate toward tools that facilitate optimal information foraging? Once within a data patch, how does the analyst make decisions about selecting appropriate visualization and presentation tools to convey the information contained within the patch? Also of interest is whether analysts modify their information foraging strategies and behaviors in response to KDD tools.

Theme 4: Individual Differences

Research questions within this theme focus on how analysts may differ in ways relevant to the other three themes. Of course, an obvious issue here is that of the wisdom/expertise of the data analyst. Do expert and novice analysts differ in their attention and decision processes as well as tool selection? Can appropriately structured tools reduce gaps between novice and expert in the quality of decisions they make in the KDD process? Larger questions to be explored are the characteristics of *wise* KDD analysts and whether analyst wisdom is due solely to greater experience and familiarity with KDD processes and environments. If experience is a primary predictor of expert/novice differences, how does greater experience affect analyst interactions with data sets and other KDD processes?

A key question for inquiring organizations focuses on the predisposition of KDD analysts to use the different inquiring styles described by Churchman (1971). Kienholz (1999) describes the Inquiry Mode Questionnaire (InQ) that can be used to classify analysts as Synthesists (Hegelian inquirers), Idealists (Kantian inquirers), Analysts (Leibnizian inquirers), Realists (Lockean inquirers), or Pragmatists (Singerian inquirers). The use of this questionnaire to assess expert/novice differences, information foraging strategies, and preferences for KDD tools could yield data with significant implications for inquiring organizations.

Undoubtedly, the above list of themes and questions ultimately falls short by not including other important topics. For example, many questions involve the interaction of the themes stated above. Analyst expertise, for instance, will most likely interact with attentional, decisional, and tool selection questions. In addition, there are issues that fail to fit cleanly into any of the above themes—like how variables that are external to the analysis focus (e.g., time pressure, stress, task ambiguity) affect analyst behavior (Driskell & Salas, 1991; Inzana et al., 1996). However, the themes presented above constitute a new and arguably better path for inquiring organizations that do not overlook the notion that data mining and other KDD processes are human-oriented endeavors.

Theme 5: Ethical and Privacy Issues

As personal information about individuals becomes increasingly available to industry, issues of privacy loom to the forefront in the minds of consumers, marketers, and researchers. Although there is some disagreement among these groups about the degree of threat associated with companies building data repositories that are replete with personal information, there is little dispute that the need for privacy protection is urgent (Estivill-Castro, Brankovic & Dowe, 1999). Even if one believes that the gathering institution owns information in a consumer database, there is frequently a substantial level of mistrust on the part of customers pertaining to what companies will do with the data.

By recentering the focus of KDD research to the analyst and the analyst's interactions with data sets, researchers can begin to explore how analysts manage ethical concerns pertaining to the data with which they work. An analyst may not be in a position to decide what kinds of information about customers should be captured, stored, or internally disseminated within the analyst's employing organization. The analyst may not have any say in the KDD tasks that are assigned. Indeed, the analyst is likely to be given an assignment and implicitly (or explicitly) charged with the task of "digging as deep" as possible to find a desired answer or to unearth new insights. Despite these constraints, expecting analysts to be governed by ethical considerations as they engage in KDD activities is consistent with Singerian inquiry that Churchman (1971) favors above all others.

A host of ethical and empirical questions are highlighted when attention is turned to privacy issues in KDD (e.g., Brankovic & Estivill-Castro, 1999; O'Leary, 1995; Wahlstrom & Roddick, 2000). Much of this work supports the notion that analysts should be aware of the potentially sensitive nature of the data they are analyzing, while also realizing that a primary constraint on their work is not to violate privacy. Understanding how analysts manage the delicate balance between looking for answers and protecting privacy is another important area of research for analyst-focused KDD researchers.

Inquiring Organizations as Knowledge Foragers

In the first generation of Knowledge Management (KM), the focus was on knowledge integration (McElroy, 2003). An underlying assumption was that valuable knowledge already existed. The primary purpose of KM was therefore to codify this knowledge (McElroy, 2003). In contrast, the focus of the second generation of KM (from the mid-1990s) also included knowledge production and therefore required making explicit a commitment to a specific corporate epistemology, which, in turn, forces an organization to define what constitutes truthful knowledge (theories of truth) and to also consider how truth claims will be evaluated (McElroy, 2003). Accordingly, Van Krogh, Roos, and Slocum (1994) describe corporate epistemology as the theory of how and why organizations know. A central tenet of this theory is that organizations are viewed as adaptive (living) things (McElroy, 2003).

Given that IFT addresses how individuals seek out knowledge, this theory appears especially relevant to the second generation of KM with its emphasis on how knowledge is obtained. Therefore, we believe it is reasonable and valuable to abstract the concept of information foraging to the organizational level. Accordingly, we propose to introduce a new concept to organizational and KM theory: *knowledge foraging*. We believe that knowledge foraging constitutes an important and fundamental epistemic behavior that characterizes an organization in terms of its fundamental role as a knowledge producer (inquiring organization).

Like IFT, the concept of knowledge foraging is rooted in optimal foraging theory (OFT) and includes an evolutionary perspective: inquiring organizations will, over time, gravitate toward knowledge foraging strategies and processes that maximize learning and knowledge yields. Accordingly, organizations that develop effective knowledge strategies and processes will increase their chances of survival over competitors with suboptimal strategies/processes. In addition, these organizations will be more able to adapt and respond to changes within their competitive environments and be better able to deal with wicked environments. It also follows that the development of effective knowledge foraging strategies is likely to be a source of sustainable competitive advantage, as continually updating, revising, and questioning existing knowledge will facilitate accomplishment of an organization's overall purpose for existence.

Organizations that are effective knowledge foragers possess characteristics ascribed to learning organizations: well-developed core competencies, continuous improvement, and the ability to renew and revitalize (Senge, 1992). Like inquiring organizations, effective knowledge foragers are systems with inputs, processes, outputs, and guarantors (Churchman, 1971). A key guarantor for effective knowledge foragers is the ability to monitor and continually assess the fit between knowledge foraging strategies and processes and the larger environmental context in which they compete.

Effective knowledge foragers share characteristics of effective inquiring organizations. As noted by Courtney et al. (1998), "effective inquiring organizations create knowledge and learn from behaviors to adjust to changing circumstances" (p. 1). Such learning propels the organization toward progress through what Churchman (1971, p. 201) refers to as a heroic mood, which is created by the collective unconscious. The knowledge foraging concept supports the possibility that this heroic mood may result from fundamental evolutionary processes designed to increase the organization's survivability within a competitive environment that can be characterized as wicked and unpredictable. As noted by Malhotra (1998), "knowledge management caters to the critical issues of organizational adaptation, survival, and competence in the face of increasingly discontinuous environmental change." Essentially, it embodies organizational processes that seek a synergistic combination of data, information processing capacity from information technologies, and the creative and innovative capacity of human beings. The concept of knowledge foraging suggests that evolutionary forces that help to ensure survivability via the maximization of knowledge yields may guide these organizational processes.

Knowledge foraging organizations include individual information foragers, some of which may be engaged in KDD processes. As inquiring organizations, knowledge foragers may also count the full range of inquirer types (Hegelian, Liebnizian, Lockean, Kantian, and Singerian) among its members. The knowledge foraging concept would include the possibility that the most effective mix of inquiry approaches may vary in response to changes in an organization's competitive environment. The optimal mix for one organization (or environment) may be suboptimal for another organization (or environment). Environmental changes are likely to trigger changes in optimal mix of inquiry approaches. Organizations that readily adapt to environmental changes may do so because they are able to quickly develop and embrace new knowledge foraging strategies.

Arguably, the introduction of the knowledge foraging concept to corporate epistemology represents only a small departure from Churchman's (1971) depiction of Singerian organizations as organizations with the broadest and most comprehensive form of inquiry and knowledge creation systems. As noted by Kienholz (1999), Singerian inquirers (Pragmatists) are able to draw upon whatever inquiry mode (Hegelian, Leibnizian, Lockean, or Kantian) or combination of inquiry modes that best suit the needs of the moment. In the long run, research evidence may support Churchman's implication that Singerian organizations are a superior organizational form because they respect, value, and behave ethically toward all constituencies. Such a finding would not be inconsistent with the knowledge foraging concept: if Singerian inquiry were, in fact, observed to provide organizations with sustainable competitive advantage across time, there would be support for the notion that this organizational form provides the foundation for an optimal knowledge foraging strategy. Note, however, that the evolutionary emphasis of the knowledge foraging concept would also entertain the possibility that major changes in the competitive environment could result in Singerian inquiry being superseded by other knowledge foraging strategies that are better suited to new environmental conditions.

Conclusion

This chapter has proposed a new agenda for analyst-centered research into KDD within inquiring organizations. It maintains that further research focused on the analyst's interaction with data within the KDD process can provide substantial insights into the knowledge creation processes utilized by many modern organizations. Moreover, we argued that such research would very likely shed further light on how organizations potentially operationalize Lockean, Kantian, and Singerian knowledge creation processes. We have also highlighted that IFT supports the view that fundamental evolutionary forces geared toward maximizing information yields may guide KDD processes. We also extended the notion of IFT beyond individual information foraging theory by introducing the new concept of *knowledge foraging*. We predict that knowledge foraging will shortly become an important construct within organization theory and Knowledge Management, as we believe it holds the potential to greatly aid our understanding of how knowledge management processes within inquiring organizations mature and evolve.

References

Anderson, J. R. (1993). Problem solving and learning. *American Psychologist, 48,* 35-44.

Bionski, S., Quatrone, R. P., & Swartz, H. (2000). Substrate and tool use by Brown Capuchins in Suriname: Ecological contexts and cognitive bases. *American Anthropologist, 102*(4), 741-761.

Brachman, R. J., & Anand, T. (1996). The process of knowledge discovery in databases. In U. M. Fayyad, G. Piatetsky-Shapiro, P. Smyth, & R. Uthurusamy (Eds.), *Advances in knowledge discovery and data mining* (pp. 37–57), Menlo Park, CA: AAAI Press/MIT Press.

Brankovic, L., & Estivill-Castro, V. (1999, July 14-16). *Privacy issues in knowledge discovery and data mining.* In C.R. Simpson (Ed.), Proceedings of the First Australian Institute of Computer Ethics International Conference on Computer Ethics (pp. 89-99), Melbourne, Australia.

Choi, J. N., & Kim, M. U. (1999). The organizational application of groupthink and its limitations in organizations. *Journal of Applied Psychology, 84,* 297-306.

Churchman, C. W. (1971). *The design of inquiring systems: Basic concepts of systems and organizations.* New York: Basic Books.

Courtney, J. F. (2001). Decision making and knowledge management in inquiring organizations: Toward a new decision-making paradigm for DSS. *Decision Support Systems, 31,* 17-38.

Courtney, J. F., Croasdell, D. T., Paradice, D. B. (1998). Inquiring organizations. *Australian Journal of Information Systems, 6,* 3-15. Reprinted in *Foundations of infor-*

mation systems: Towards a philosophy of information technology. Retrieved September 25, 2004, from *http://www.cba.uh.edu/~parks/fix/fis.htm*

Cox, K. C., Eick, S. G., Wills, G. J., & Brachman, R. J. (1997). Visual data mining: Recognizing telephone calling fraud. *Data Mining and Knowledge Discovery, 1*, 225-231.

Curley, S. P., & Browne, G. J., (2001). Normative and descriptive analyses of Simpson's paradox in decision making. *Organizational Behavior and Human Decision Processes, 84*, 308-333.

Datta, A., & Thomas, H. (1999). The cube data model: A conceptual model and algebra for on-line analytical processing in data warehouses. *Decision Support Systems, 27*, 289-301.

Driskell, J. E., & Salas, E. (1991). Group decision making under stress. *Journal of Applied Psychology, 76*, 473-478.

Elder, J. F., IV, & Pregibon, D. (1996). A statistical perspective on knowledge discovery in databases. In U. M. Fayyad, G. Piatetsky-Shapiro, P. Smyth, & R. Uthurusamy (Eds.), *Advances in knowledge discovery and data mining* (pp. 83-113), Menlo Park, CA: AAAI Press/MIT Press.

Estivill-Castro, V., Brankovic, L., & Dowe, D. L. (1999). Privacy in data mining. Privacy - Law and Policy Reporter, 9(3): 33-35, Septermber 1999.

Fayyad, U. M., Piatetsky-Shapiro, G., Smyth, P., & Uthurusamy, R. (Eds.). (1996). *Advances in knowledge discovery and data mining*. Menlo Park, CA: AAAI Press/ MIT Press.

Feldens, M. A., de Moraes, R. L., Pavan, A., Castilho, J. M. V. (1998). *Towards a methodology for the discovery of useful knowledge combining data mining, data warehousing and visualization*. Proceedings of the Conferência Latino Americana de Informática, Quito, Equador.

Frawley, W., Piatetsky-Shapiro, G., & Matheus, C. (1992). Knowledge discovery in databases: An overview. *AI Magazine, 14*(3), 57-70.

Gunderloy, M., & Sneath, T. (2001). *SQL server developer's guide to OLAP with analysis services*. Almeda, CA. Sybex.

Heinrichs, J. H., & Lim, J. (2003). Integrating Web-based data mining tools with business models for knowledge management. *Decision Support Systems, 35*, 103-112.

Holyoak, K. J. (1995). Problem solving. In E. E. Smith & D. N. Osherson (Eds.), *An invitation to cognitive science* (Vol. 3: *Thinking,* 2nd ed.) (pp. 267–296). Cambridge, MA: MIT Press.

Inzana, C. M., Driskell, J. E., Salas, E., & Johnston, J. H. (1996). Effects of preparatory information on enhancing performance under stress. *Journal of Applied Psychology, 81*, 429-435.

Kienholz, A. (1999). Systems rethinking: An inquiring systems approach to the art and practice of the learning organization. Retrieved September 25, 2004, from *http://www.bauer.uh.edu/parks/fis/inqre2a1.htm*

Klosgen, W. (1996). Explora: A multipattern and multistrategy discovery assistant. In U. M. Fayyad, G. Piatetsky-Shapiro, P. Smyth, & R. Uthurusamy (Eds.), *Advances in knowledge discovery and data mining* (pp. 249–271), Menlo Park, CA: AAAI Press/MIT Press.

Lam, S. S. K., & Schaubroeck, J. (2000). Improving group decisions by better pooling information: A comparative advantage of group decision support systems. *Journal of Applied Psychology, 85,* 565-573.

Lin, A. (2002). *Sensitivity to conditional contingencies in the use of on-line analytical processing.* Unpublished honour's thesis, The University of New South Wales, School of Information Systems, Technology and Management, Australia.

Louie, T. A., Curren, M. T., & Harich, K. R. (2000). "I knew we would win": Hindsight bias for favorable and unfavorable team decision outcomes. *Journal of Applied Psychology, 85,* 262-272.

Mackinnon, M. J., & Glick, N. (1999). Data mining and knowledge discovery in databases: An overview. *Australia and New Zealand Journal of Statistics, 41,* 255-275.

Malhotra, Y. (1997, August 15-17). *Knowledge management in inquiring organizations.* Proceedings of the 3rd Americas Conference on Information Systems (Philosophy of Information Systems Minitrack)(pp. 293-295), Indianapolis, IN.

Malhotra, Y. (1998). Knowledge management for the new world of business. Retrieved September 25, 2004, from *http://www.brint.com/km/whatis.htm*

McElroy, M., W. (2003). *The new knowledge management: Complexity, learning, and sustainable innovation.* Boston: KMCI Press, Butterworth-Heinemann.

Metcalf, J. (1986). Premonitions of insight predict impending error. *Journal of Experimental Psychology: Learning, Memory, & Cognition, 12,* 623-634.

Mitroff, I., & Linstone, H. A. (1993). *The unbounded mind: Breaking the chains of traditional business thinking.* New York: Oxford University Press.

Montovoni, G. (2001). The psychological construction of the internet: From information foraging to social gathering to cultural meditation. *CyberPsychology and Behavior, 4,* 47-56.

Nonaka, I., & Takeuchi, H. (1995). *The knowledge creating company.* New York: Oxford University Press.

O'Leary, D. E. (1995). Some privacy issues in knowledge discovery. *IEEE Expert, 10,* 48-52.

Pianka, P. (1997). Animal foraging: Past, present, and future. *Trends in Ecology and Evolution, 12*(9), 360-364.

Pirolli, P., & Card, S. (1999). Information foraging. *Psychological Review, 106,* 643-675.

Reichgelt, H. (1991). Knowledge representation: An AI perspective. New York: Ablex.

Rittel, H. W. J., & Webber, M. M. (1973). Dilemmas in a general theory of planning. *Policy Sciences, 4,* 155-169.

Senge, P. M. (1992). *The fifth discipline: The art and practice of the learning organization.* New York: Doubleday.

Simoudis, E., Livezey, B., & Kerber, R. (1996). Integrating inductive and deductive reasoning for data mining. In U. M. Fayyad, G. Piatetsky-Shapiro, P. Smyth, & R. Uthurusamy (Eds.), *Advances in knowledge discovery and data mining* (pp. 353–373), Menlo Park, CA: AAAI Press/MIT Press.

Spellman, B. A., Price, C. M., & Logan, J. M., (2001). How two causes are different from one: The use of (un)conditional information in Simpson's paradox. *Memory & Cognition, 29,* 193-208.

Van Krogh, G., Roos, J., & Slocum, K. (1994). An essay on corporate epistemology. *Strategic Management Journal, 15,* 53-71.

Wahlstrom, K., & Roddick, J. F., (2000). *On the impact of knowledge discovery and data mining.* In J. Barlow & M. Warren (Eds.), Australian Institute of Computer Ethics Conference. AICE, 2000, Canberra, November 11.

Weldon, M. S., & Bellinger, K. D. (1997). Collective memory: Collaborative and individual processes in remembering. *Journal of Experimental Psychology: Learning, Memory, and Cognition, 23,* 1160-1175.

Chapter VIII

Using Inquiring Practice and Uncovering Exformation for Information Systems Development

Martina Sophia Lundin
Copenhagen Business School, Denmark

Morten Thanning Vendelø
Copenhagen Business School, Denmark

Abstract

One of the oldest themes in information systems (IS) research concerns the relationship between developers and users of information systems. Over the years, IS scholars and IS practitioners have addressed the problem in a variety of ways, often focusing on how the use of social techniques can improve understanding between the two parties. Users, however, still find themselves working with systems, which do not match their requirements, needs, and expectations. We suggest that the problematic developer-user dynamic can be addressed by introducing an inquiring practice approach to information systems development. Consequently, this chapter conceptualizes a new way of understanding information systems development through the lenses of inquiring practice, Socratic dialogue, and the uncovering of exformation. We show that by applying this approach, we can enhance the inquiring capabilities of organizations, and thereby facilitate design and development of better information systems.

Introduction

One of the oldest themes in information systems (IS) research concerns the relationship between developers and users of information systems. Over the years, the theme has been addressed in a variety of ways by IS scholars and IS practitioners, for example, as a systems development problem (Fitzgerald, Russo & Stolterman, 2002; Hirschheim, Klein & Lyytinen, 1995; Mumford, 1996; Wood-Harper, Antill & Avison, 1985), as a problem that can be solved through end-user computing (Jarke, 1986), or by engaging in participatory design (Ehn, 1988; Greenbaum & Kyng, 1991). No matter how the problem is addressed, the underlying theme always seems to be how understanding between the two parties can be improved, typically through the use of various social techniques. The results, however, are not convincing. Users still find themselves working with systems which match neither their requirements nor their expectations.

We believe that attempts to address the problematic developer-user dynamic can be aided by a return to fundamental systems theory and the key questions raised by this body of knowledge. Churchman (1968) provides an example of such a key question in his book *Challenge to Reason.* He says, "How can we design improvement in large systems without understanding the whole system, and if the answer is that we cannot, how is it possible to understand the whole system?" (p. 3).

We argue that in aiming to develop improved information systems, we need to strive for an understanding of the whole system, and thus we pose the question: How can we facilitate a progression towards this understanding? For our part, we have chosen to focus on an inquiring practice approach to information systems development. In this chapter, we conceptualize a new way of looking at the theme through the lenses of inquiring practice, Socratic dialogue, and the uncovering of exformation. We suggest that by applying this approach, we can enhance the inquiring capabilities of organizations, and thereby facilitate the design and development of better information systems. In order to fulfill this purpose, the chapter proceeds in the following manner. First, we elaborate on the problems related to communication and understanding between developers and users of information systems, describe how conventional approaches to information systems development have dealt with the developer-user communication problem, and explain why it is appropriate to regard developers and users of information systems as belonging to different communities of practice. Second, we present the Socratic dialogue method and demonstrate how this approach to communication between different communities of practice is likely to enhance their inquiring capabilities. Third, we develop a model for how to apply Socratic dialogue method in information systems development practice, and thereafter we apply the model to a case of information systems development in order to demonstrate how developers and users can benefit from the use of Socratic dialogue method. For this purpose, we use the FX-system case, which describes the developer-user communication difficulties encountered by the Danish software firm, Unique, while developing a Foreign Exchange System for West Bank. Finally, we conclude and identify the point of arrival for our inquiring endeavor.

Inquiring Practice and Information Systems Research

The idea of inquiring organizations originates from the works on inquiring systems by Churchman (1971). The concept of inquiring organizations has predominantly attracted attention from scholars working in the fields of organization theory (Mirvis, 1996; Richardson, Courtney & Paradice, 2001), information systems research (Courtney, 2001; Klein & Hirschheim, 2001), and, more recently, knowledge management (Malhotra, 1997). While scholars of organization theory have focused on organizational learning, scholars of information systems research have addressed decision support systems and information systems development. The decision support systems approach focuses on building inquiring information systems for inquiring organizations, whereas the information systems development approach focuses on how organizations can take on an inquiring perspective when designing and developing information systems. Although differing in their focus, both approaches share the intention of creating viable alternatives to the rational choice approach to development and use of information systems in organizations. In their seminal article on management of information systems (MIS), Mason and Mitroff (1973) suggest "that the current philosophy underlying the design of MIS has presupposed a greatly restricted view of 'knowledge', 'effectiveness', 'action' and 'purpose'" and "that to date much of the research and development work on MIS has assumed only one underlying psychological type, one class of problems, one or two methods of generating evidence, and finally, one mode or method of presentation" (p. 475). Mason and Mitroff (1973) maintain that a one thinking-sensation approach tends to dominate the design of MIS in such a way that they only produce systems for one kind of people. Accordingly they suggest other methods to explore the variables in a systematic fashion. One variable offered by Mason and Mitroff (1973) is Singerian-Churchmanian IS, also defined as learning systems.

We find that the same type of philosophy prevails in the field of design and development of information systems and suggest that a new approach to this must take its point of departure in focusing on what we have labeled the developer-user communication problem. Belardo, Ballou, and Pazer (2004) recently articulated a similar point of view, noting that one of the most significant factors in the difficulty of producing information systems that satisfactorily meet user needs "is ineffective communication between the user group and the development group" (p. 43).

Developer-User Communication Problem

Developers and users of information systems have different backgrounds. Typically developers are employed in IS departments where they work and socialize with other IS professionals with whom they share language, concepts, and so on. Users, on the other hand, work in a context where vocation-specific languages and practices dominate. Although they may use information systems to carry out large sections of their duties, they seldom find themselves occupying the same world as IS professionals. Hence, when developers and users meet with the purpose of designing information systems, they both find themselves introduced to worlds which they have little knowledge of. Just like sellers and buyers of high-tech products who, by Darr and Talmud (2003), are found not to have a common image of product use and thus, to reach that common image, they must communicate contextual knowledge rooted in engineering practice, implying that an intense dialogue must take place between seller and buyer.

Developer-User Communication Problem in Conventional Information Systems Development Methodologies

Information systems are designed and developed for different purposes, and a variety of methodologies have been conceptualized to assist developers in designing and developing them. The methodologies are "coherent and integrated sets of methods, techniques, and tools to assist the developer" (Hirschheim, 1985, p. 80), and typically they comprise the two major tasks of systems analysis and systems development. According to Hirschheim (1985) "systems analysis is the process of collecting, organizing, analyzing facts about a particular system and the environment in which it operates" (p. 80), whereas systems development includes "requirements analysis, requirements specification, system design and systems implementation" (p. 80). Typically, a methodology includes a predetermined set of tasks, grouped into stages according to a prespecified method by use of tools and techniques. We find that the methodologies are characterized by a preoccupation with technicalities rather than with deep involvement of humans in the process. It is possible to observe this characteristic in the methodologies even when we take into account a sample including sociotechnical methodologies (Wood-Harper et al., 1985), participatory design methodologies (Greenbaum & Kyng, 1991), and structured methodologies (Yourdon, 1989). Even within the participatory design approach, humans and the interaction between them are described at a very abstract level, for example, when describing how user participation can take place in systems design and development processes. Mumford and Weir (1979) end up with a diagrammatical representation of the process, thereby not addressing the content of the process.

From our perspective, developers and users of information systems belong to different communities of practice (Brown & Duguid, 1991, 1998; Wenger, 1998) who are unlikely to have the same view on several factors. For example, the other party, its organization, and the information system to be developed, but they share an interest in getting the information system developed. Knowledge creation and knowledge sharing within and between communities of practice have been widely discussed for some years. Brown & Duguid (1991), for example, argue that working, learning, and innovating are interrelated, and to understand this, we must study formations and changes within the communities that actually do the work. Brown and Duguid (1998) stress the difficulties with the absence of interaction between different communities of practice, and they argue that innovations, including new information systems, emerge when different communities share and discuss experiences and best practices.

The Socratic Dialogue

Our point of departure is the speculation about how communication and understanding between developers and users coming from two different communities of practice can be improved. Maruyama (1974) states that the difficulty in cross-disciplinary communication lies not so much in the fact that communicating parties use different vocabularies or language to talk about the same thing but rather in the fact that they use different structuring of reasoning. If they use different structures of reasoning and different terminologies, which communication method could be applied? Furthermore, Maruyama argues that when communicating parties remain unaware that they use different structures of reasoning but are aware of their communication difficulties, each party will tend to perceive communication difficulties as resulting from the other parties being illogical, lacking intelligence, or even insincerity. Consequently, we wanted to advance a method that can facilitate the development of a better understanding of this communication problem, and we found the Socratic dialogue method (Apatow, 1999; Hansen, 2000).

Background

The Socratic dialogue is a group discussion method that aims to identify hidden and taken for granted assumptions, as participants learn to think together with others and to strive to reach understanding of the others at a fundamental level, including understanding of their values and beliefs.

The idea of Socratic dialogue originates from the German philosopher Leonard Nelson who developed and used it as a pedagogical tool for adult education in the early 1920s (Hansen, 2002), and as far as we know, it has never before been applied in an information systems context. As a group discussion method, Socratic dialogue aims at creating an elaborate and deep common understanding of information and ideas from a specific context. In the dialogue, the participants advance their own thoughts, expecting others reflection to improve them rather than threaten them. Ergo, the participants in the dialogue must have an interest in expressing their own basic values, as well as in understanding the basic values of others concerning specific issues. From an existential point of view, this means that everyone involved must go back to the very basics of the problem being addressed. If the values and beliefs do not concern the participants from an existential perspective, we cannot say that they are involved in a Socratic dialogue.

The Method of Socratic Dialogue

The Socratic dialogue begins with the formulation of a question, which all parties agree is relevant in the specific situation (Hansen, 2000). Thereafter, each participant provides a concrete example of what comes to mind when they consider the chosen question. Second, the group collectively selects the example, which it thinks provides the best outset for the dialogue. In the dialogue, the group now begins to form a main statement about the chosen question. In this process, it uses the chosen example as its point of departure. With the main statement as a background, the group then elaborates with values and assumptions underlying the statement. This inquiry into each participant's arguments and basic assumptions leads to further deepening of the premises and values that until now have been argued for. Hence, at this point in the process, the original statement has been revised several times, and more fundamental philosophical problems have been attached to the chosen question. Still, the focus of the group is on reaching the objective, namely, to find a common statement on the question. Finally, the group engages in testing the validity of the statement. This testing happens not only against the originally chosen example but also against the other examples mentioned by the participants. Thus, the testing enables the participants to reach a more general statement.

Modified Model of Socratic Dialogue Method

For several reasons, the original Socratic dialogue method needs to be modified in order to fit the information systems design and development context. First, the original method points out that the process must be given unlimited time for the parties to reach a statement that suits all. In a user-developer situation, one must face the fact that there is limited time for dialogue. Deadlines are reality, and both parties must be aware of this. Second, the original model argues that there is no need for reaching a common agreement. The objective here is the process. In our case, the objective must be more than this because users and developers need to reach a common understanding to afford product arrival. Third, in an information systems context, the starting question is unlikely to be philosophical in character. Hence, we arrived with the following picture of the Socratic dialogue method for information systems development.

Exformation: The Product of Socratic Dialogue

In relation to the Socratic dialogue, one must ask what output it produces, what is the role of this output in the information systems design and development process, and what makes the output of Socratic dialogue crucial? Using Nørretranders (1991),[1] we suggest that the output take the form of exformation. "Exformation is the history of a statement, information is the product of history. Both are meaningless without each other—

Figure 1. Socratic Dialogue Method for Information Systems Development

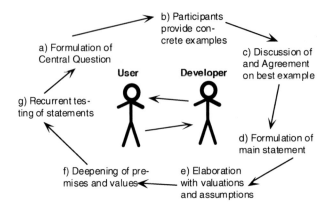

information without exformation is empty talk; exformation without information is not exformation, but only thrown away information" (p. 131).

The basic hypothesis is that information or knowledge exchanged between communities of practice is only a small and limited part of the knowledge creation process. The awareness of exformation as the context, the history, and the process behind the creation of information and knowledge needs as much attention as the information or knowledge itself. Exformation is an abbreviated form of explicitly discarded information. More specifically, Nørretranders (1991) states that "Exformation is everything we do not actually say but have in our heads when or before we say anything at all. Information is the measurable, demonstrable utterance we actually come out with" (p. 127).

Hence, from the information content of a message alone, there is no way of measuring how much information it contains. Nørretranders (1991) argues that exformation is produced in a process of chucking away information, and it is this process which is evident in automatic behavior of expertise (riding a bicycle, playing the piano) and which is therefore the most precious. Some might argue that exformation is similar to tacit knowledge (Nonaka, 1994). Yet, unlike tacit knowledge, exformation does not exist as something we know but cannot tell (Nonaka, 1994). Instead, exformation describes a person's nondisclosed thoughts, values, and assumptions concerning a given situation or task, and thus we maintain that talking about exformation rather than about tacit knowledge has relevance. We believe that the disclosure of exformation in the Socratic dialogue is highly beneficial for the conceptualization and design of information systems, as it enables developers and users of future information systems to produce intelligent understandings of the other party.

Case: Design and Development of the FX-System

Unique is a rapidly growing Danish software firm occupied with design, development, and implementation of advanced turn-key software applications for industrial, scientific, and administrative purposes.[2]

In the spring in year X, salesmen in Unique discovered that West Bank wanted to purchase a Foreign Exchange System (FX-system). Yet, Unique did not have an FX-system, and West Bank wanted a *ready to go* FX-system. In order to address this demand, Unique decided to perceive West Bank as a potential sponsor for the development of an FX-system, which the firm subsequently could refine and sell as an off-the-shelf FX-system. Therefore, Unique initiated activities aimed at selling an FX-system to West Bank. These activities focused on explaining to West Bank that Unique knew what an FX-system was and that the firm had almost finished development of such a system. For this purpose, the manager of the Financial Services Division in Unique initiated development of a prototype of an FX-system. One of the systems developers in the division later explained how the prototype was developed:

First, we spend three days on development of a prototype generator for Presentation Manager. This generator could pick text-files and display them on a screen with fancy colors. Then, we ordered sales-material from other suppliers of FX-systems, and reproduced their user-interface. In total, we designed 20 screens with different colors and of different size. Also, they showed numbers in the different screen fields, but it was impossible to make changes in the numbers. Thereafter, we implemented the prototype as an extension to our system for online trade with stocks and bonds, because we had to have some screens with moving numbers to demonstrate a working system.

When presenting the prototype to West Bank, employees from Unique informed them that the FX-system was almost finished but that the user-interface had yet to be completed, and therefore it was impossible to demonstrate a working version of the FX-system. Also, Unique arranged that currency dealers from those customers who already used other financial systems sold by the firm answered questions from West Bank about the functionality of the FX-system. Using this approach, Unique succeeded in persuading West Bank to buy "their" FX-system, and in June, Unique and West Bank signed a contract stating that an FX-system was to be delivered to West Bank in December that very same year.

The contract signed with West Bank included some general provisions of the contract and three pages with one-liners describing the functions to be included in the FX-system. Mainly, these three pages had their outset in the sales material collected from other suppliers of FX-systems and then mixed to compose a presentation of Unique's FX-system. Hence, the contract only provided a few conceptual guidelines for design of the system.

Development and Delivery of the FX-System

Nobody in Unique knew much about foreign currency trading; also, they had no time to develop a requirement specification for the system, as the project team (six to seven systems developers) had to observe a tight deadline for delivery of the system to West Bank. Hence, the project team assumed that trade with foreign currencies was almost similar to trade with stocks and bonds, which they had some experience with. Therefore, the project team copied the source-code from Unique's systems for this activity, changed the headlines in the user-interface, and started editing the code to facilitate what they believed was FX-operations. By the end of July, the project team delivered the first modules of the FX-system to West Bank, but the delivery was not successful, as Unique did not deliver what West Bank expected. However, users in West Bank had difficulties in explaining exactly what they expected. Given the problems, the management of Unique assigned a new project manager. He discovered that no plans existed for the FX-project, that project management was almost absent, and that to some systems developers, OS/2 constituted new technology. Furthermore, representatives of West Bank explained to the new project manager that West Bank expected delivery of an FX-system similar to the one specified in the contract, which in their opinion, was not what Unique delivered. Yet, the contract did not specify the FX-system apart from stating the different sub-systems to be included in the FX-system. This problem was compounded by the fact that West Bank had difficulties in specifying exactly what kind of system they wanted. Also, the new project manager realized that the schedule for the FX-project was not realistic when considering the large number of tasks to be accomplished.

A New Start on the FX-Project

With the above mentioned problems in mind, the new project manager developed a revised project plan, which divided the FX-system into subsystems and initiated development of the system from scratch. Furthermore, he explained to the top management that Unique had to perceive the project as a collaboration with West Bank. Thus, he initiated regular meetings between systems developers from Unique and users from West Bank, as he realized that Unique needed the currency dealers to tell the project team about their demands to the FX-system, since none of the system developers assigned to the project knew anything about foreign exchange. Six months later, the systems developers were in a position to produce parts of the FX-system, which were accepted by West Bank. However, at that point in time, the project was half a year behind schedule. Also, the new project manager conducted regular meetings with representatives of West Bank, as he wanted them to realize that the contract was unrealistic and to accept a revision of it. The strategy succeeded slowly as the representatives of West Bank learned that Unique did not know how to develop an FX-system. Yet, West Bank was not likely to accept a revision of the contract, as they felt that they would then have to accept a less advanced FX-system.

In the fall one year after initiation of the project, Unique faced new problems in the FX-project. The system often broke down due to problems with the software produced by Unique. The project team experienced that somehow these problems were related to the fact that West Bank did not know what they wanted and constantly changed their demands for the FX-system. In order to identify solutions to the problems, the project team intensified its meetings with users from West Bank, and thereby Unique managed to restore West Bank's confidence in the firm, as well as in persuading West Bank to stay in the project. In the end, Unique managed to develop and deliver the FX-system to West Bank, although it took more than one and a half years of extra work to finish the project, which in total meant a project which lasted for two years.

Interpretation of the Case

In the present paragraph, we interpret the FX-case through the Socratic dialogue model presented above. First, we identify communicative acts, which we find are representative for the case. Second, we interpret the acts with the use of the model, thereby we identify how the communicating parties acted and reacted in the process, and we seek to explain how their acting and reacting influenced the process over time. Third, we speculate how the process might have evolved if the Socratic dialogue had been applied.

Identifying Communicative Acts

For the purpose of interpretation of the case, we needed communicative acts representative for the case. Hence, we began our analysis by looking for such acts in the case. As communicative acts, we defined points in time where either of the involved parties "send messages" to the other party leading to some kind of response. As our first example, we identify the point in time where developers in Unique make contact with West Bank and suggest themselves as potential suppliers of an FX-system to West Bank. West Bank, which we now term the user, responds by agreeing to visit Unique on-site and see a presentation of the system. In total, we identified eight communicative acts. These, however, vary with regard to both content and form. Foremost, it is important to note that the form changes significantly after the first unsuccessful delivery of modules of the FX-system. We therefore talk about phase 1 initial communicative acts and phase 2 adapted communicative acts.

Initial Communicative Acts

As the first five communicative acts, we have identified the following:

Example A1:

- Developers make contact to users and suggest their firm as supplier of an FX-system
- Users accept invitation to visit developers' site and take a look at the system

Example A2:

- Developers present the proposed system to the users
- Users accept the proposed system as a suitable response to their needs

Example A3:

- Users pose questions regarding technical and functional aspects of the proposed system
- Developers answer the technical questions, and the currency dealers borrowed from existing customers answer questions about functional aspects of the system

Example A4:

- Developers write up contract about sale and delivery of the FX-system
- Users sign contract and buy the proposed FX-system

Example A5:

- Developers initiate development of the proposed FX-system
- Users passively await delivery of the FX-system

Looking at these communicative acts, it appears that they all have a similar form and content. Starting with the form, it can be observed that the communication is initiated by the developer-side as it approaches the user-side and suggests itself as an appropriate supplier of the FX-system that the user-side is looking for. From the developer-side, this gives the communicative acts a focus on convincing the user-side about the appropriateness in choosing it as the FX-system supplier. Also, it gives the communicative acts a flavor of being orchestrated by the developer-side constantly looking for the user's approval of its points of view.

As the dialogue evolves, the developer-side increasingly focuses on getting the user-side to confirm that it is on the right track regarding the proposed FX-system. This happens even though the developer-side must have some doubts about their actual capacity to deliver the proposed FX-system. In other words, no uncertainty is revealed and communicated by the developer-side. Viewing this from a Singerian perspective, it would be perceived as a highly unethical act. We do not claim that the developer-side knew that it would be difficult to deliver the system, but we assume that they must have had some doubt and that this doubt could have been articulated in an early stage of the dialogue. However, little dialogue about the users' requirements to the system took place in the initial stages of the process.

When interpreting the communicative acts in the light of the Socratic dialogue, we are afforded the following picture. The central question is formulated by the developer-side and is never tested in the dialogue with the user-side. The central question may be formulated as "We have an excellent FX-system here, don't you think?" If we then move on to Step 2 in the Socratic dialogue, the provision of concrete examples, it happens as the developer-side demonstrates the constructed FX-system to the user-side, and experiences that the user-side accepts the shown system as a suitable response to its needs, not even questioning the existence of the system. In neither of these two examples does the user-side inquire about the developer-side's understanding of its demands to such a system. Instead, "feedback" from users continuously confirmed the developers' formulation of the central question.

Adapted Communicative Acts

As the final three communicative acts, we have identified the following:

Step B1:

- Users respond to delivery by stating that this is not an FX-system

- Developers respond by assigning a new project manager who reorganizes the project team

Step B2:

- Developers begin to inquire into the users' demands to the system
- Users accept the developers' invitation to inquiring dialogue

Step B3:

- Developers suggest a step-by-step procedure for identification of the demands of the users, based on the one-liner contractual descriptions of the functionality of the FX-system
- Users engage in this activity by joining the dialogue with the developers

When looking at these three communicative acts, it appears that the initial failure by the developer-side to deliver what the user-side expected had an impact on how the dialogue evolved. In the adapted phase, far more open-ended communicative acts dominate. The weaknesses of the developer-side, which used to be hidden, are now obvious and need to be dealt with if the project is to continue. However, these inquiries from the user-side only emerged as the developer-side failed to fulfill the user-side's expectations to the delivery of the first modules of the system. The reorganization of the managerial setup following the failed delivery provided for initiation of an inquiring dialogue between the two parties.

Viewing the adapted communicative acts in the light of the Socratic dialogue, we can say that the new project manager initiates reformulation of the central question. Basically, the developer-side says: "What does an FX-system look like?" And essentially, the user-side replies: "That is actually a very good question." Here we witnesses a break point in the way the developer-side approaches the problem of developing the FX-system, and the user-side responds by accepting that this break with the prior pattern of communicative acts is highly needed. Hence, a new central question is being formulated through the involvement of both parties.

As the Socratic dialogue proceeds, the step-by-step procedure for identification of the user-side's needs implies inquiring into the meaning of the one-liner descriptions of the various functions in the proposed FX-system. If we perceive these one-liners as high-level abstractions containing a huge amount of exformation, it obviously becomes important that each party's interpretation of the one-liner is revealed, as most likely each interpretation is unknown to the other party. Hence, in this instance, the Socratic dialogue is about transforming abstractions to raw data. This happened as the involved parties provided concrete examples of how they interpret the one-liners. Examples may have been elaborated by provision of counter-examples or more detailed examples. Then, as the parties discuss and agree on best concrete examples, they obtain verification of their reciprocal understanding. Of course, the parties can never be sure of their full common understanding, and that is exactly why continuous dialogue is important.

Based on these discussions and agreements, formulation of main statements about the functionalities could take place. The main statements then serve as the basis for elaboration about the content of the functionalities to be included in the system. We cannot say much about E and F in the model, although we would expect that uncovering of crucial and case related exformation takes place here. We are however quite sure that in the FX-case testing of statements happened as modules were delivered and accepted or rejected by the users.

An important insight, which emerged in the adapted phase is that the user-side had a very vague picture of their demands to the FX-system. We see this in the fact that the user-side constantly changes its requirements to the system, and this uncertainty may have influenced them to not inquire about the presented FX-system in the initial phase.

Closure on Case Interpretation

Our interpretation of the FX-case has demonstrated that inquiring practice based on Socratic dialogue can make a difference in the quality of the output produced in IS development processes. The question that, of course, emerges is whether the developer-side had succeeded if the initial communicative acts with the user-side had started with an inquiring approach. Although we emphasize the importance of an inquiring approach in the user-developer communication, we cannot neglect that this kind of dialogue may foster uncertainty and anxiety in and among participants. However, all face-off actions demand boldness and courage, and we must take into account that our behavior may influence our counterparts to perceive us as less trustworthy. Another question is whether it was the developer-side that held the key to the initiative of inquiring practice.

Addressing the first question, we acknowledge that West Bank openly expressed that it was looking for a complete FX-system and that it would not buy a turn-key delivery. Yet, we maintain that the possibility for succeeding with an inquiring approach depends on the perspective taken by the counterpart, whether that be a developer or a user. Therefore, if West Bank had responded positively to an inquiring approach taken by Unique, we submit that the firm would have succeeded with this approach.

So, why did an inquiring approach not develop earlier on? Of course, the developers were quite street-wise in the initial phases, but on the other hand, the users did not act intelligently. They did not pose critical questions, and thereby they did not insist on engaging in an inquiring practice. In a Socratic dialogue perspective, neither the developers nor the users took responsibility for their own organization. We thus maintain that inquiring practice is always a two-way responsibility, which however might be provoked by one of the involved parties. Every stage must include inquiry, reflection, and active listening, with active listening including both listening to the counterpart and, perhaps even more important, listening to oneself.

Until now, we have argued for the Socratic dialogue method, but little has been said about how to initiate this method. From an information systems development point of view, we believe that the initiative must come from the developer-side, and in a sales context, it is probably the seller who has the greatest interest in implementing this kind of dialogue. We are aware of the problems arising when one party explicitly tries to introduce a philosophical tool in this situation, mainly, because tradition and norms tells us that this is not the way of conducting business. Therefore, we suggest that the developer-side initiates this in a manner that tells the user-side that it is important to open up ones basic thoughts and values without experiencing that these issues are too simple to highlight. Hence, the developer-side must state early on an example that is *in line* with the Socratic dialogue method.

Closure: Socratic Dialogue and Wisdom

In this chapter, we have argued for a more intelligent way of organizing the cross-disciplinary dialogue between developers and users of information systems. For this purpose, we identified Socratic dialogue method and argued that it can be used in an information systems development context. The Socratic dialogue method enhances the inquiring capabilities of organizations, and thereby it allows for uncovering of exformation, which is crucial if developers and users of information systems are to obtain a more advanced understanding of one another's positions. We argue that instead of asking, "Did we get the information and knowledge we searched for?" one should ask, "Did we uncover exformation in this dialogue that can facilitate the development of this system?" Consequently, Socratic dialogue is a new way of approaching the process rather than a tool.

When organizations apply Socratic dialogue in the developer-user communication, there is a high possibility that both parties will display exformation of a far more substantial kind than the information usually being developed and exchanged. Also, viewing developers and users from the point of view of inquiring communities of practice could, in fact, produce more open flows of information in organizations and thereby provide for more innovation in organizations. Therefore, we suggest that Socratic dialogue is useful beyond the area of application dealt with in the present chapter. It could be applied both among sellers and buyers of high-tech products and in the process of creating new management practice in organizations. Because this philosophical approach opens for a new way of viewing cross-disciplinary communication, regardless of business field or vocation function, Socratic dialogue can bring about exformation being held inside people—exformation that is crucial in order to understand and share knowledge between communities. Hopefully, this dialogue can help us not only to facilitate understanding but also to develop a new type of language in management and organizations (Lundin & Rasmussen, 2002). As with information flows, flows of often used words and phrases in a community make us unaware of their meaning for other groups of people. We simply forget to reflect on it and then take it for granted. By learning and developing our choice of semantics together with others in a Socratic dialogue, we can become more aware of what we actually communicate in and between these inquiring communities.

We realize that our attempt to apply the Socratic dialogue in an information systems context is only the first move in a new endeavor aimed at formulating a new methodology for use in this context. Hopefully, further research will help refine and modify the methodology and also through experiments in real-life environments, as it is important to remember that the Socratic dialogue method was originally developed for a different context with the aim of creating a methodology that facilitates critical reflection about issues that, at the first glance, may seem obvious to us. Yet, it is by reflecting over precisely those kind of questions that we can discover exformation and thereby arrive at a better understanding of our counterparts.

References

Apatow, R. (1999). Socratic dialogue. *Executive Excellence, 16*(5), 10-11.

Belardo, S., Ballou, D. P., & Pazer, H. L. (2004). Analysis and design of information systems: A knowledge quality perspective. In K. V. Andersen & M. T. Vendelø (Eds.), *The past and future of information systems* (pp. 43-59). Oxford: Elsevier Butterworth-Heinemann.

Brown, J. S., & Duguid, P. (1991). Organizational learning and communities of practice: Towards a unified view of working, learning, and innovation. *Organization Science, 2*(1), 40-57.

Brown, J. S., & Duguid, P. (1998). Organizing knowledge. *California Management Review, 40*(3), 90-111.

Churchman, C. W. (1968). *Challenge to reason.* New York: McGraw-Hill.

Churchman, C. W. (1971). *The design of inquiring systems: Basic concepts of systems and organization.* New York: Basic Books.

Courtney, J. F. (2001). Decision making and knowledge management in inquiring organizations: Toward a new decision-making paradigm in DSS. *Decision Support Systems, 31*(1), 17-38.

Darr, A., & Talmud, I. (2003). The structure of knowledge and seller-buyer networks in markets for emergent technologies. *Organization Studies, 24*(3), 443-461.

Ehn, P. (1988). *Work-oriented design of computer artifacts.* Stockholm: Arbetslivscentrum.

Enderud, H. (1987). Dataindsamling i organisationssociologien: En note om informationsorienteret respondent-udvælgelse. In T. Broch, K. Krarup, P. K. Larsen, & Olaf Rieper (Eds.), *Kvalitative metoder i dansk samfundsforskning – Lejerbosymposiet 1978. 2. udgave* (pp. 145-159). København: Nyt fra Samfundsvidenskaberne.

Fitzgerald, B., Russo, N. L., & Stolterman, E. (2002). *Information systems development: Methods in action.* New York: McGraw-Hill.

Greenbaum, J., & Kyng, M. (1991). *Design at work: Cooperative design of computer systems.* Hillsdale: Lawrence Erlbaum.

Hansen, F. T. (2000). *Den sokratiske dialoggruppe – et værktøj til værdiafklaring.* København: Gyldendal.

Hansen, F. T. (2002). *Det filosofiske liv – et dannelsesideal for existenspædagogikken.* København: Gyldendal.

Hirschheim, R. A. (1985). *Office automation: A social and organizational perspective.* Chichester: Wiley.

Hirschheim, R., Klein, H. K., & Lyytinen, K. (1995). *Information systems development and data modeling: Conceptual and philosophical foundations.* Cambridge, MA: Cambridge University Press.

Jarke, M. (Ed.). (1986). *Managers, micros and mainframes: Integrating systems for end-users.* Chichester: Wiley.

Klein, H. K., & Hirschheim, R. A. (2001). Choosing between competing design ideas in information systems development. *Information Systems Frontiers, 3*(1), 75-90.

Lundin, M. S., & Rasmussen, L. B. (2002). A radical Scandinavian ("Øresundsk") approach to inquiring organizations: A critique of ICT in knowledge management. In K. Brunnstein & J. Berleur (Eds.). *Human choice and computers: Issues of choice and quality of life in the information society* (pp. 293-304). Dordrecht: Kluwer Academic.

Malhotra, Y. (1997, August 15-17). *Knowledge management in inquiring organizations.* Proceedings of 3rd Americas Conference on Information Systems (pp. 253-274), Indianapolis, IN.

Maruyama, M. (1974). Paradigms and communication. *Technological Forecasting and Social Change, 6,* 3-32.

Mason, R. O., & Mitroff, I. I. (1973). A program for research on management information systems. *Management Science, 19*(5), 475-487.

Mirvis, P. H. (1996). Historical foundations of organizational learning. *Journal of Organizational Change, 9*(1), 13-31.

Mumford, E. (1996). *Systems design: Ethical tools for ethical change.* Basingstoke: Macmillan.

Mumford, E., & Weir, M. (1979). *Computer systems in work design: The ETHICS method.* London: Associated Business Press.

Nonaka, I. (1994). A dynamic theory of organizational knowledge creation. *Organization Science, 5*(1), 14-37.

Nørretranders, T. (1991). *Mærk Verden – en beretning om bevidsthed.* København: Gyldendal³.

Richardson, S. M., Courtney, J. F., & Paradice, D. B. (2001). An assessment of the Singerian inquiring organizational model: Cases from academia and the utility industry. *Information Systems Frontiers, 1*(1), 49-62.

Van Maanen, J. (1988). *Tales of the field: On writing ethnography.* Chicago: University of Chicago Press.

Wenger, E. (1998). *Communities of practice: Learning, meaning and identity.* Cambridge, MA: Cambridge University Press.

Wood-Harper, A. T., Antill, L., & Avison, D. E. (1985). *Information systems definition: The multiview approach.* Oxford: Blackwell.

Yourdon, E. (1989). *Modern structured analysis.* Englewood Cliffs: Prentice Hall.

Endnotes

1   Quotations from Nørretranders (1991) were translated from Danish to English by the authors.

2   Appendix A gives more information about the case study.

3   This book is published in English as: Nørretranders, T. (1998). The user illusion: Cutting consciousness down to size. London: Allen Lane.

Appendix A: Case Methodology

The case—Design and Development of an FX-system—is borrowed from a longitudinal study of new business creation in the Danish software firm Unique. The case study took place over a period of two years and used an explorative approach to study three different cases of new business creation in the firm. One case was Financial Products, of which the present case constituted one central activity. The main source of empirical evidences in the study was qualitative data gathered on-site in the organization. Several data generation techniques of ethnographic nature (Van Maanen, 1988) were employed, such as semi-structured interviews, informal talks, direct observations, collection and review of documents, and social contact. Hence, multiple sources of evidence were used in order to collect evidences conveying the same facts. Yet, interviews with members of the organization lasting from one to two hours were the main source of empirical evidence. For the Financial Products case, a total of 12 interviews were conducted. Selection of interviewees for the case happened based on information obtained from either prior interviews or written material collected in the firm. Also, a knowledge-based sampling method was used by asking interviewees to suggest others who had knowledge of, or were involved in, certain aspects of the case. Especially, the selection focused on people believed to hold central positions in each case; that is, interviewees were selected based on their information value (Enderud, 1987). Occasionally, people, who for different reasons had left the organization, were interviewed in order to obtain information about issues which people inside the organization were reluctant to talk about. Most interviews were taped and transcribed, but occasionally tape recording did not take place. Instead, interviews were recorded in shorthand notes. After transcription interview texts were handed over to interviewees in order to ensure that they could review and correct or add information in the interviews.

Another important source of empirical evidences were written material collected in various ways. Some documents were easily accessible in the organization. Such documents included annual reports, organization charts, messages from management to the employees, memos, strategic plans, firm journals, and news clipping. Some interviewees allowed the researcher to go through their personal files and handed over to him documents related to the cases studied. Finally, a kind kitchen midden technique was used, as occasionally the researcher was moved to offices previously occupied by people who had left the organization without removing their files and collection of documents. A couple of times the researcher took the liberty to go through these files and record information of interest to the case study.

Based on the empirical evidences gathered using the different data generation techniques described above, write up of chronological case stories took place in order to reveal the progression in the processes. Before writing up the cases, the researcher went through the empirical evidences in order to get an initial impression of the data and write notes about the activities and people involved in each case. Thereafter, a write up of the first draft took place, followed by two to three revisions of each case, and a final write up occurred on completion of the collection of empirical evidences.

Section III:

Wisdom, Mindfulness, Awareness, and Wise Action

Chapter IX

Avoiding Epistemological Myopia

Robert M. Mason
Florida State University, USA

Abstract

Organizational approaches to knowledge management are unlikely to lead to organizational wisdom unless the organization increases its awareness of factors that contribute to epistemological myopia—a nearsightedness that limits what and how the organization knows and how it learns. Contributors to this myopia include organizational learning pathologies, an unquestioning acceptance of fundamental concepts, such as time, and measuring success as the absence of failure. In many instances, the vocabulary, language, and business methods used by an organization, society, or culture reify these pathological factors and thereby further hamper the potential for learning. By raising our awareness of these contributors and the factors that support their reification and continued acceptance, we seek either to avoid these limitations or to develop corrective lenses that can extend the organization's vision and enable it to resolve issues with greater clarity. The conceptual frameworks used in this chapter are drawn from four distinct areas of study: systems theory, organizational knowledge and learning, the organization as a learning community and community of practice, and linguistic relativity. The underlying theme is the organization as an inquiring system—a system that seeks to learn and become more knowledgeable. Because learning processes are culturally biased, and the bias is reinforced by a culture's values, language, and vocabulary, the premise is that these biases and values constrain the organization's epistemological methods and processes.   The potential solutions to epistemological myopia include deliberate nurturing of cultural diversity, the institutionalization of Singerian approaches to inquiry, and the fostering of managed risk in experiments that do not guarantee success. While few organizations exhibit all of these desirable characteristics, there are some examples from the literature and practice that provide confidence that organizations can avoid epistemological myopia.

Introduction

In examining organizations as learning systems, we acknowledge that considerable prior work (mostly from an economic perspective) has contributed to the increased attention given to organizational knowledge and learning. Much of this can be traced to the resource-based view (RBV) of the firm (Penrose, 1959) and from the more recent knowledge-based view (KBV) of the organization. The knowledge-based view of the firm, anticipated by Drucker (1988), may be viewed as a special case of the RBV with a focus on knowledge as an organizational resource (Grant, 1996a, 1996b). In this view, knowledge is seen as an increasingly important asset for firms, especially in technology-driven growth economies. Technology often is applied to add value to existing products and services and is the basis for creating new products and services. Survival in a technically and economically dynamic environment requires not only knowledge but also knowledge renewal. Learning—the continuing renewal of the knowledge asset—is necessary for competitiveness, and some have even argued that it is the *only* basis for sustained competitive advantage (Stata, 1989).

Because knowledge management and organizational learning are viewed as critical functions in many firms, information technology and information systems should be supportive of these functions. Consequently, the concept of knowledge management activities became popular both as a way for a firm to appropriate its own internal knowledge and for consulting firms to improve the efficiency of delivering services to their clients. Both approaches have been examined in cases and practice-oriented summaries (e.g., Davenport & Prusak, 1998). The information systems community has benefited from the research summaries of the foundations of organizational learning (Huber, 1991) and knowledge management (Alavi & Leidner, 2001).

This chapter acknowledges these economic and information technology motivated reviews of knowledge management and learning by organizations, but it is aimed toward the gap between the philosophical foundations of learning systems and the unstated assumptions that tend to guide knowledge management practice. Churchman (1971) provides the philosophical inspiration for our discussion about organizational epistemology with his view of organizations as inquiring systems. Beginning with the metaphor of sight as a medium for knowledge and knowing, we seek to illuminate issues that constrain and limit organizations in their inquiring activities. The intent is to identify and explore methods that enable organizations to fully realize their potential as learning systems.

In addition to Churchman, the theoretical foundation for our discussion is motivated by and constructed from fundamental systems concepts such as von Bertalanffy (1968), whose idea of a higher organism includes deliberately disrupting the status quo in order to learn. The learning model perspective is that of the Kolb (1984b) experiential learning cycle, which is robust and flexible enough to accommodate principles of other learning models. Finally, we consider the organization as a community of practice (Wenger, 1998) in which social activities shape the organization's learning processes and identity.

Each of these readings invokes the metaphor of the organization as a living inquiring organism and as exhibiting behavior that reflects a particular epistemological viewpoint. The central thesis is that this learning behavior, just as a human's learning behavior, can reflect a myopic epistemology, and this myopia can limit the organization's ability to see clearly and to understand and interpret its environment. Being mindful of the possibility of myopia can help the organization avoid the accompanying limitations to learning and understanding.

Our motivation is to enable organizations to fully realize their potential as learning systems. We posit that these myopic limitations may be overcome by changes in organizational processes and practices. We further posit that *corrective lenses* or *vision exercises*, developed from an understanding of the interactions among culture, learning, and organizational practice, can reduce epistemological myopia.

To present this argument, we begin with a brief discussion of the nature of epistemological myopia. For our purposes, we use the term loosely to refer to a range of conditions that limit learning and knowledge acquisition. As metaphor, it suggests ways of examining the nature of organizations as systems that learn and manage knowledge.

Next, we argue that effective organizations, indeed, are learning systems, organisms that interact with their environment and use feedback to adjust their behavior to succeed in this environment. Particularly recently, organizational success is associated with creating and managing knowledge, so learning organizations have a competitive advantage over organizations that do not learn. Indeed, learning organizations may be the only survivors in a competitive environment that rewards innovation and continuous improvement. We further argue that *effective* learning organisms not only adjust their behavior to match their environmental needs, they additionally engage in behavior that might be called disruptive—they deliberately create disequilibria in order to explore, experiment, and play with alternative arrangements with their environment.

Next, we discuss ways that organizations can become foiled in their learning efforts. By omission or commission, organizations engage in behavior that is consistent with a myopic epistemology. To understand how these behaviors arise, we consider organizations from a systems perspective and examine learning from three conceptual frameworks—the experiential learning model of Kolb, the relationship of learning with culture and language, and learning as a social phenomenon that occurs in communities. Each perspective or framework enables us to identify ways in which myopia may arise or be reinforced.

Finally, we suggest that organizations can develop deliberate policies and actions that change their behavior, correcting their epistemological myopia. With this clearer vision, the organization becomes more like the inquiring system envisioned by Churchman. The chapter concludes with suggestions for further research and implications for management practice.

Nature of Epistemological Myopia

Myopia is a particular visual pathology, a deviation from *normal* sight, in which images are formed in front of the retina instead of on the retina. Someone with myopia is referred to as *nearsighted*; they are able to see nearby objects with greater acuity than ones at a distance.

Rather than using *myopia* in its more precise meaning, this chapter uses the term more loosely to encompass a range of visual deficiencies that might more precisely be labeled as *blind spots, having blinders on,* or *tunnel vision. Epistemological myopia* therefore is shorthand for a range of deviations from *normal* epistemology, indicating that an organization's nature of knowledge and knowing is limited by correctable factors. This limitation may be associated with what the organism knows and how it knows it, with how it acquires new knowledge (learns), or with what it accepts to be adequate evidence of knowledge.

With this use of the term myopia , the following paragraphs examine an inquiring organization using three complementary conceptual models. First, we view an organization as a learning *system* and compare its behavior to systems fundamentals. Second, we use a general model of learning to view the organization as an entity that engages in the activities that comprise this learning model. Finally, we view the inquiring organization as a community (social system) of learning and practice and examine the factors that may affect learning from this viewpoint. For each of these perspectives, we identify the deviations or pathologies that can be associated with *epistemological myopia*. Each conceptual model draws from existing literature and focuses on one or a few sources from each field rather than attempting to be comprehensive.

The theoretical foundation for our discussion of the system model of an organization is based on Churchman (1971). This systems perspective is further motivated by the fundamental systems concepts of von Bertalanffy (1968), in which the higher (living) organisms deliberately disrupt the status quo in order to learn. The learning model perspective is that of the Kolb (1984) experiential learning cycle, which has been applied frequently to organizational learning. Finally, for consideration of the organization as a community of practice, we draw from Wenger (1998), who emphasizes that social activities shape the organization's processes of learning and identity formation.

Each of these readings invokes the metaphor of the organization as a living organism. As our focus is on the inquiring organization, we will use *organization* often instead of the more general *organism*, remembering that some of the discussion is at the metaphor level and may not be suited to a precise mapping.

The chapter concludes by identifying research issues raised by considering these epistemological pathologies. The final discussion reviews practical implications and suggests activities that may help organizations avoid epistemological myopia.

Organizations as Learning Systems

Organizations have long been considered systems. To analyze them as systems, we specify their boundaries, their inputs (raw materials they use), their processes of transformation (their value-creating activities), and their outputs (products and services). From this systems viewpoint, we model organizations as systems with feedback mechanisms that provide information on the impact of their actions on the environment. This fundamental conceptual model of the firm as a closed loop system is part of the foundation for management information systems (e.g., McLeod & Schell, 2004). Managers use feedback to make judgments about modifying their actions in order for the organization to adapt to its environment. This ability to adapt and learn is seen as essential for a goal-seeking system; it is essential for the system's survival.

This feedback control model is a useful model for a large part of organizational activities. It provides a view of the organization that succeeds in adapting to its environment and in meeting the expectations of its customers. As in Maslow's (1962) hierarchy of needs, feedback control may be viewed as a necessary condition for survival, but it is an insufficient condition for an inquiring organization—it is not the highest need for an inquiring organization.

A review of system theory (von Bertalanffy, 1968) provides a reminder of one of the fundamental issues with which early systems researchers and thinkers struggled—how organisms approach learning and how feedback is used in learning. A somewhat robotic view of an organism's approach to learning is that learning occurs by way of repeated stimulus response behavior, in a kind of Skinnerian or Pavlovian repetition that leads to portfolios of behavior consistent with survival and with the achievement of the organization's objectives. In this view, reactive learning is an essential component of an organism's efforts to maintain homeostasis, or a dynamic equilibrium with its environment. Behavior is aimed toward achieving this dynamic equilibrium, and the goal of the organism is to learn what behavior enables and supports this homeostatic state.

However, such views have been criticized as leaving no room for explanations of play, exploration, and creativity—the very essence of learning or striving for a higher level of existence. The criticism is that homeostasis is a state more appropriate as a goal for a closed system. In a closed system, the second law of thermodynamics posits that entropy (or disorder) continues to increase toward an ultimate state of zero differential energy. At this point, with no energy differential, the system is incapable of work and may be considered "dead."

Instead of viewing an organism as a closed system, tending toward disorder and decay and eventual death, the contrasting view is that of the organism as an open system. In this view, the organization is a system that not only interacts with and adapts to its environment, but more importantly, it also engages in activities that are intended to change the environment. In other words, it learns through a series of exploratory, experimental, and even playful behaviors that are intended to disturb equilibrium. Much as Stata (1989) later argues for learning as the only basis for competitive sustainable advantage, von Bertalanffy (1968) argued that this active behavior of seeking to disrupt the equilibrium is normal for a living organism. "Life is not maintenance or restoration of equilibrium but is essentially maintenance of disequilibria" (p. 191). To behave otherwise is to lead to decay and death. From a systems standpoint, the organization disturbs its environment and thereby assures that simple feedback control is inadequate. In this approach, the organization is creating an unstable equilibrium, requiring that it exercises an active control mechanism (rather than simple cybernetic feedback control) for its continuity and survival. This desire to disrupt the status quo is observed in all higher forms of life; von Bertalanffy (citing Hebb) notes that even rats have been observed to behave in ways that disrupt equilibrium (*op. cit.*, p. 209).

In summary, the normal state of an organism (including human organizations) is to create a circle of disrupting equilibrium, exercising *active* control, and thus engaging in a virtuous cycle of active control and learning. If an organism is not disrupting equilibrium, it is missing an opportunity to learn, and we identify this as our first organizational pathology associated with epistemological myopia—pathology about how organizational members view the goal of the organization:

Pathology 1: Limiting the organization's goal to that of seeking a dynamically stable equilibrium and using feedback control as the mechanism to achieve and maintain this equilibrium.

If an organization's leaders, who have the responsibility for articulating its goal, define this goal only in dynamically stable terms, the organization may experience short-run success by adapting to the immediate demands of the environment. It will not realize the longer-term success of an inquiring organization.

Consider the history of Digital Equipment Corporation (DEC), which pioneered minicomputers and networks. DEC's founder and leader, Ken Olsen, in one famous quote, said "There is no reason for any individual to have a computer in his home" (Olsen, 1977). Among many analyses of the failure of DEC, one might view it as one of the founder's myopic visions of the market for microcomputers and a dependence on establishing and maintaining a stable set of loyal and reliable customers (Schein, 2003).

An inquiring organization will intersperse periods of stable equilibrium (opportunities for incremental learning and progress) with activities that disrupt equilibrium (opportunities for discontinuous learning). The organization in these latter periods develops skills that enable it not only to adapt to environmental demands but also to shape the environment to its own goals.

How can an organization introduce these periods of disequilibria? It must continually question the mental models it uses to collect and interpret data. Models of learning provide clues about how this can be accomplished.

How Organizations Learn

For this discussion, we may view organizational learning from three perspectives. A simple high-level model posits that individual learning and organizational learning are similar and can be linked (Dixon, 1999; Kim, 1993). We begin with one such model, the Kolb experiential learning cycle. We can assume that organizations learn as the individuals in the organization learn (Huber, 1991). However, individual learning depends on culture and language, so we must examine the influence of these factors on learning. Additionally, because global organizations comprise individuals from multiple cultures, we expect that organizational knowledge can emerge from encompassing the collective knowledge of these cultures. Finally, we note that organizations are social structures, and the learning processes involve not only individual learning but also the organizational practices that enable the sharing of individual knowledge.

Learning Model: The Kolb Experiential Learning Cycle

Of the many models of the learning process, the Kolb (1984b) experiential learning model, formalized in the 1980s, is one of the most widely studied and cited. Although developed for individuals, it was used as a basis to understand organizational learning even before being published in its current form (Carlsson, Keane et al., 1976). With the model's emphasis on experience as the basis of learning, it is particularly applicable to organizational learning (e.g., Dixon, 1999; Kim, 1993), and its simplicity makes it helpful in illustrating our discussion of inquiring organizations. Kolb developed the model as a synthesis of the work of several researchers, including Piaget, Lewin, and Guilford. As shown in Figure 1, Kolb posits that experiential learning occurs along two dimensions: abstract-concrete and active-reflective. Learning requires completion of each of four activities: abstract conceptualization, active experimentation, concrete experience, and reflective observation, and the cycle is recursive.

Individuals have learning preferences, and the *learning style inventory* (LSI) (Kolb, 1984a; see http://trgmcber.haygroup.com/ for the latest version) is a widely accepted means of measuring preferences for learning—that is, preferences for taking in and processing information in the learning process. Considerable research suggests that different learning style preferences are associated with different career choices. As one might imagine, individuals who are more thoughtful and prefer to reflect and work with abstractions gravitate toward careers that reward such behavior (e.g., academics). Individuals who prefer more active learning and seeing concrete results tend toward work that rewards these activities (e.g., entrepreneurial endeavors or management).

We generally visualize the process proceeding clockwise around the model so that *active experimentation* is informed by an *abstract conceptualization*, then the results of this experimentation become data, or *concrete experience*, and this experience is the basis for *reflective observation* on the significance of these data and experiences. The cycle is completed (and begins again) when the individual compares reflections and observations with the abstract concept with which the process began. It is recursive with continuing learning taking place as the cycle is repeated.

Organizations and individuals have learning preferences and may begin the process with any one of the activities. An observer hearing a lecture or viewing a work of art may form a mental model related to the subject of the lecture or art. After exploring further (experimenting), getting additional information about the subject (concrete experience), the observer may reflect on this additional experience (reflective observation). The result may be that the original mental model is modified or reinforced.

The model reflects the scientific method and should be familiar to anyone who does positivist research. A researcher normally begins with a theory (abstract concept), then tests the theory through an experiment (active experimentation), obtains data from the test (concrete experience), and finally analyzes the data and compares the results with the theory (reflective observation). The outcome of the cycle may be a modification of the theory to fit the data or a statement that further supports the theory. In either case, the researcher has *learned* by completing the cycle.

The significance of this model for epistemological myopia is that learning requires all four activities. Myopia occurs when (a) the organization avoids or skips one of the activities, (b) fails to link two adjacent activities, or (c) becomes stuck by cycling between adjacent activities. Any of these three behaviors results in stunted or limited learning.

Avoiding concrete experience, for example, results in an untested theory, an abstraction that may have intellectual appeal but whose validity has not been demonstrated and that may not withstand an application in the physical world. An organization that has a theoretically ideal project plan but never implements it does not learn.

The complementary failure is the failure to reflect on concrete experience. An organization or person may have considerable concrete experience, but if the entity does not reflect on this experience (reflective observation), there is no learning. (An old witticism captures this when it says of a job applicant: "this person does not have ten years' experience—only one year's experience ten times.") Without the reflection step in the cycle, the practitioner does not learn but simply is accumulating concrete experience.

The most familiar aspect of this incomplete learning is that an individual or organization experiences single-loop learning but not double-loop learning (Argyris & Schon, 1978,1996). Single-loop learning occurs when the organism learns incrementally (e.g., increases efficiency through a learning curve). Double-loop learning requires that the organism learn discontinuously by challenging and possibly changing its model of reality (McKee, 1992). From the Kolb model, this can be understood by observing what happens if an organization gets stuck by cycling between adjacent activities. For example, an organization that tries something different (experiments), gets unsatisfactory results, simply tries again with a modified set of values, then continues this cycle of trial and error, can be seen to be stuck in the upper left corner of the learning cycle in Figure 1. This behavior might lead to incremental learning (single-loop learning and progress along the learning curve), which in itself can be valuable. Without examining the fundamental assumptions, however, there is no basis for complete (double-loop) learning.

Pathology 2: Incomplete learning cycle—not completing the entire learning process, either by omitting one or more of the steps in the Kolb learning cycle or by being stuck in one quadrant of the cycle.

Figure 1. Kolb Experiential Learning Model

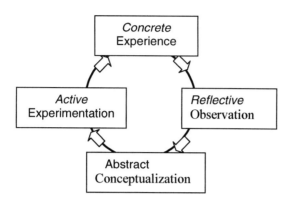

Research at Proctor and Gamble (Carlsson, Keane et al., 1976) indicated that R&D teams that followed the complete learning model performed well. The model also provided a way to understand problems that required additional attention. Without attention to each activity in the model, teams could end up idea poor, *unable to learn from mistakes*, or *unable to recognize problems/opportunities*.

To assure a complete organizational learning cycle, leaders should examine processes at the operational control, management control, and strategic levels to assure that each of the steps is a part of the business practice. The inquiring organization not only designs its work activities according to a plan (abstract concept), it continually reassesses this plan based on the results of prior efforts and changes in the environment.

Finally, an organization must *learn to learn*. An organization may develop the capability for triple-loop, or *deutero* learning (Argyris & Schon, 1978, 1996), but this capability may be associated with organizational culture. The complex relationships among learning, language, and culture are not fully understood but deserve some background discussion.

Learning, Language, and Culture

Language, thought, and culture are closely related (Gumperz & Levinson, 1996). This simple statement reflects the general acceptance of a range of scientific and philosophic communities over the past several generations as these communities have debated exactly what can be said about the relationships among these areas. If we are to manage knowledge and if organizations are to be learning organizations, we must recognize that the relationship exists. We will explore briefly two aspects of this connection: the relationship between learning and culture and the relationship between language and thought. Much of the work has been done on distinct national and ethnic cultures and their languages; we believe much of the results are relevant to the cultural aspects of organizations, and this is explored in the next section as we examine the nature of organizations as communities of practice.

Culture and Learning

Hall (1966) summarizes the relationship between learning and culture by saying,

"Once people have learned to learn in a given way it is extremely difficult to learn in any other way...Culture reflects the way one learns." (p. 47)

Learning is a complex process, and despite decades of research, there still is much to understand about how individual learning is facilitated. In 1930, Vygotsky and Luria proposed a culture-centered approach to learning (Vygotsky, Rieber et al., 1987), and later work has demonstrated the empirical significance of this approach (Forman, Minick et al., 1993; Kozulin, 1998). This viewpoint posits that culture mediates how individuals learn, and evidence indicates that lasting effects occur from an early age. In the formative years of a child, sociocultural activities shape cognitive processes and different cultures result in different processes. A child's early cultural environment provides for different systems of mediated learning experiences, and these different experiences are revealed later as differences in how the individuals as adults perceive and make sense of the world. In effect, distinct cultures are associated with different worldviews, and these different worldviews mediate how individuals from these cultures learn. That different worldviews exist may be revealed in simple tasks, such as the classification of objects according to their similarity.

Churchman views classification and the more basic task of making comparisons as fundamental to a Singerian inquiring system. Such a system begins with the fundamental capability to judge equalities, or alternatively, to discern differences (Churchman, 1971, p. 186). With this capability, one has the basic capability to place objects and events into categories, thereby distinguishing what is known and familiar from what is new and maybe not yet categorized.

An example of cognitive differences is demonstrated in asking British and Mayan speakers to classify objects (a task such as "is object A more like object B or object C?"). British speakers tend to use shape as a primary classification heuristic, and Mayan speakers tend to use similarities in material as a basis for classification. Interestingly, the authors determined that small children used shapes in both cultures; the shift to the use of distinct differentiators occurred before age eight (Lucy, 1996, p. 51).

Other studies have demonstrated that early formal education also makes a difference in how adults perceive the world (Kozulin, 1998). Studies of young adults, who have completed schooling in one culture and move to another culture, indicate that the nature of the initial formal schooling makes a difference. This difference goes beyond a difference in knowledge base and seems to be associated with the basic skills by which one learns new concepts. In the studies reviewed, the young adults exhibited specific difficulties associated with coding schema, concepts, graphic, and symbolic devices used in communication of ideas (e.g., tables, ordering, plans, and maps). The difficulties extend to cognitive activities, such as the ability to identify or define problems (that is, the ability to apply their knowledge to a set of data and infer the implicit question or issue), the ability to work with multiple sources of information, and so forth. In short, the young adults were missing the cognitive antecedents that would enable them to excel in their new environments (Kozulin, 1998).

Language: Both Cultural Expression and a Vehicle for Learning

What are we to make of this relationship between culture and learning? The fundamental proposition that links language, thought, and culture—and a concept that is widely debated in the field of linguistic relativity—is that the *semantic structures of languages are fundamentally distinct*. This strong position has several broad consequences. If accepted, it means that *true* translations from one language are impossible. It also suggests that speakers of distinct languages think and act differently. In essence, it says that the interlocking of culture, language, and thought makes it likely that each language has associated with it a distinct worldview that influences how speakers perceive and make sense of the world.

Historically, the fundamental concept may be traced to 19th century authors (e.g., Humboldt & Heath, 1988), but the most frequently referenced (and often misunderstood) statement is the more recent Sapir-Whorf hypothesis. According to this concept, "users of markedly different grammars are pointed by their grammars toward different types of observations and different evaluations of externally similar acts of observation, and hence are not equivalent as observers, but must arrive at somewhat different views of the world" (Whorf & Carroll, 1956, p. 221).

In its extreme interpretations, the concept was taken to mean that language was fundamental to thought and presupposes thought by making possible abstract (symbolic) thought. In this interpretation, if a language does not have a word for a concept, then the speaker of that language (assuming no other language) would have no way to think about this concept. This challenges some intuitive thought and seems inconsistent with some of the evidence of hardwired linguistic patterns in language across the globe. (A recent survey of this work by Chomsky and others is presented in a recent book by Baker, 2001.) However, the concept caught the attention of a broad range of scientists, including linguists, psychologists, and anthropologists. At some point, the idea became somewhat corrupt and was seen as an attack on the methods of anthropologists, who— it was argued—were simply struggling with translation difficulties (Gumperz & Levinson, 1996, p. 3). The more recent cognitive science position is that there are some basic roots (universals) across languages but that sense making, meaning, and discourse are influenced by differences between languages. In other words, universals such as *objects* may be perceived similarly across languages, but *relationships* among objects and communication about these and other abstractions may be expressed from a distinctive worldview that is associated with a particular culture or language. Moreover, using Whorf's terminology, different languages point us toward different types of observations and toward different evaluations of what we observe. Language draws our attention to particular features of the physical world and enables us to make sense of what we observe within the context of our experiences in the culture as expressed by our language. In short, different languages point us to different salient features and lead us toward different interpretations of our observations.

It is this latter statement that deserves our attention: knowledge management not only is about storing and accessing knowledge, it is also about knowledge creation. Reality and knowledge are socially constructed (Berger & Luckman, 1966), thus knowledge creation in an organization emerges from a social process of exchange among individuals. If the organization comprises individuals who have similar cultural backgrounds, these individuals will learn differently, and they will perceive the world differently because of their distinct languages. In such an organization, the knowledge and shared meaning that emerge may encompass the cultural knowledge and experience of those within the organization. Generally, group diversity has been positively associated with group creativity, but the organizational culture and the mechanisms by which members of the group exchange information can influence the degree to which a group or organization will be able to capture or appropriate the range of knowledge among its members (Woodman, Sawyer et al., 1993).

Consequently, we may infer that an organization may experience epistemological myopia if it restricts itself to members with the same or similar cultural backgrounds.

Pathology 3: Organizations comprising members from a single cultural background or having the same native language.

Pathology 4: Assuming that the metaphysics of one's own organization is the only way to understand and make sense of the physical universe.

Digital Equipment Corporation (DEC), noted earlier for exhibiting Pathology 1, may also be cited as an example of an organization that exhibits these pathologies. DEC's staff and management were predominantly from engineering backgrounds. In the series of analyses in a recent book on DEC, the significance of a relatively closed corporate culture frequently was mentioned as a contributing factor to the company's demise but ironically as part of its legacy as its executives became part of other organizations. As another irony, the firm's initial successes in technology leadership and market growth supported this closed culture by reinforcing the leaders' beliefs that their worldview and their practices were the bases for these successes (Schein, 2003).

Is Diversity Enough?

From this discussion, one can argue that a heterogeneous group may help avoid epistemological myopia, but is something else also required? In other words, having a heterogeneous group might be a *necessary* condition to avoid epistemological myopia, but it may not be a *sufficient* condition.

As one might expect, diversity itself is insufficient, as has been shown by a longitudinal study of homogenous and heterogeneous teams (Watson, Kumar et al., 1993). In this study, less diverse teams were able to be more effective sooner, but after about two-thirds of the way through the 17-week study, the diverse teams had developed processes that enabled them to be more productive. At the conclusion of the study, overall performances for the homogeneous and heterogeneous teams were similar. However, the diverse teams improved their process and performance more quickly than did the homogeneous teams and had higher scores on two task elements: identifying problem perspectives and generating alternative solutions (Watson, Kumar et al., 1993, p. 499). It is evident that a homogeneous group, one in which all members share similar backgrounds, can begin applying its knowledge to a task faster than a heterogeneous group. However, once the group develops processes for information exchange, the diverse group is more likely to develop creative solutions to problems and to use a wider range of approaches in trying to solve problems. Consequently, along with members from diverse cultures, an inquiring organization must establish an internal culture that encourages the exchange of knowledge and complementary information.

A recent study of knowledge management systems concluded that knowledge management systems (KMSs) rarely, if ever, take culture into account in their design and use (Mason, 2003). Instead, a common critical success factor for such systems appears to be a strong corporate culture in which use of the KMS is expected, and ethnic and national cultures are subsumed in the organizational culture. This finding is not necessarily in conflict with the pathology identified above—a corporate culture that encourages the sharing of information is a necessary condition to avoid such a pathology—but an organization that neglects the knowledge and learning differences embedded in its members' native cultures is unlikely to benefit from the complete range of knowledge available to it.

Language presents a current snapshot of culture. Words and grammar capture prior experiences and their significance. To truly understand a language is to understand the culture associated with that language. Importantly for our discussion, language may be viewed as a means toward constructing reality among the speakers, not simply as a means of communicating an external objectively verifiable reality. Even if such an objective reality exists, the relationships among the physical entities in this reality, and how one makes sense of these relationships (i.e., the abstractions that constructed about the physical objects), depend on language and grammar. Different languages and grammars reveal different underlying values in how they deal with abstract concepts and the relationships among physical objects.

Time: Example of How Different Cultures Place Value on Abstract Concepts

A vivid example of how these differences are expressed is the socially constructed concept of *time*. Whorf uses Hopi and English to demonstrate an extreme difference. In the Hopi language, not only is there no word corresponding to the abstract concept *time*, there is no clue (e.g., tense) about when something happened. (It is almost as though the Hopi are the ultimate existential communicators--everything is in the present.) For English, and to a great extent the Western world, the concept of time performs a critical role in organizing our lives and creating systems. Yet, according to Whorf, the Hopi language nonetheless "is capable of accounting for and describing correctly, in a pragmatic or operational sense, all observable phenomena of the universe" (Whorf & Carroll, 1956, p. 58).

Time and space are culturally associated but not always in exactly the way that Einstein posited for the physical world. The relationship of objects in space often implies a temporal or procedural relationship as well, and this can lead to differences in classification, in conceptual models of the physical world, and in how ideas are communicated (Bowerman, 1996; Levinson, 1996).

The Western world generally views time as a precious (scarce) commodity, as a raw material for accomplishing a goal or meeting a target. Common epigrams reflect this view: "Time is money" (Benjamin Franklin); "don't waste time"; and so forth.

Time is one of the foundations for measuring the value of other socially constructed abstractions, so that Western business students easily understand the "time value of money" and the notion that by reducing the duration for a task, we have improved the "benefit-cost" ratio of the output. Franklin's dictum is reflected in modern economic theory and is invoked whenever one seeks an improved way of accomplishing a task.

Because time is one of the fundamental socially constructed concepts that govern economics, the Western world has been preoccupied with structuring it to increasingly higher precision (classifying it into smaller and smaller increments). This capability has enabled increasingly complex systems in which components work together with an efficiency that would amaze a visitor from an earlier era (e.g., Gleick, 1999). However, such systems are closely coupled, and any variation can lead to the failure of an entire network. Sometimes we see the impact of this preoccupation with efficiency, as when weather closes a single hub airport for a few hours, causing days of disruption in air travel, or when a failure in a power line leads to widespread power outages in the power grid.

Given the dominance of western thought in the world's economy, one would think that time would be viewed similarly among developed countries in the western hemisphere, but there are variations and distinctions. Most of these distinctions are curiosities, but the style by which different cultures organize time can lead to misunderstandings and lack of effective communications within an organization (Bluedorn, 2002; Hall, 1966). An example is how individuals structure tasks over time. Individuals who are polychronic tend to engage in multiple activities simultaneously (e.g., an executive who reads or signs papers during a staff meeting); individuals who are monochronic engage in a single task at a time and do not move to the next task until the first one has been completed.

Pathology 5: Organizations comprising members from multiple cultures try to structure time in only monochronic or polychronic ways.

While polychronic and monochronic are individual characteristics and exist on a scale rather than being a binary variable, different national cultures tend toward one end or the other of the scale. Germanic and English cultures tend to be monochronic; Latin and Mediterranean cultures tend toward the polychronic end of the scale. Without having an awareness of these characteristics, a person from one end of the scale can be frustrated in trying to work with a person from the other end of the scale. In the extreme, either can lead to dysfunctional actions and not simply to myopia.

An example of this frustration is the story about an American attaché in a Latin country who wanted to call on the minister who was his counterpart. After some difficulty, he made an appointment. He arrived a few minutes ahead of time, as is the custom in the United States. The appointed time came, but the attaché continued to wait. His anxiety increased until after forty-five mintues, he protested in strong language ("damned sick and tired" of this type of treatment) (Hall, 1959, pp. 4-5). As Hall notes, the attaché's stay in the country was not a happy one.

The author has personal experience that confirms the significant difference between U.S. and Latin views of time. On a visit to Brazil as an invited lecturer several years ago, two of us avoided having an experience similar to attaché's only because one of his hosts had warned us ahead of time. "If you make an appointment to meet someone for dinner at 10:30 or 11 (they eat late in Brazil), don't be surprised if they don't show up until 11:30 or 12. If by 1 A.M. they still have not shown up, then perhaps something has happened, and they are not coming. This is the Brazilian way." We also experienced it at one particular stop on our lecture tour when we arrived late and expected to rush into the lecture hall to the hundred or so people waiting. Instead of rushing in to accommodate the crowd, as we would have been inclined to do based on U.S. protocol, the director of the research organization ushered us into his office for a cup of coffee and 20 minutes of conversation while the audience continued to wait patiently.

An inquiring organization both creates knowledge and seeks knowledge externally. Different time perspectives can create myopia by inhibiting communication among the members and inhibiting the acquisition of knowledge from outside. Most organizations recognize the necessity for different values of time by creating project teams that have project timelines and milestones for outcomes that are urgent and forming research groups for which timelines and outcomes are not directly linked to time as a measure of success.

This discussion has emphasized *time* as a source of misunderstanding and potential difficulty in communication and exchange of knowledge. There are other examples of national cultural differences (Hall, 1959, 1966; Hofstede, 1980), each of which can lead to difficulties in understanding and inhibit the creation of knowledge. By acknowledging these cultural differences and affirming their value, the inquiring organization may benefit from all the knowledge available.

Organizations as Communities of Knowing and Practice

Each of the above pathologies is a socially created idea, so why can the organization not simply change ideas and avoid the pathologies? The answer is that it can, but not simply.

The prior beliefs of an organization are part of the organization's identity and enable the organization to maintain a culture which can be extremely productive but which can resist change. The work practices of the organization, the processes by which the organization creates value, are also the means by which members of the organization come to make sense of their experiences and to give meaning to their actions (Wenger, 1998). Ideas and values are abstractions, but the community reifies these abstractions, and they become critical actors in how members of the organization establish identity and how they generate and use knowledge. To change, the organization may need to change work practices so that the abstraction of accepting and valuing multiple cultures is put into practice.

As one example, many organizations have a community value of always succeeding, and it would be viewed as almost nonsensical to propose a risky project, one that is not likely to succeed. Nonetheless, undertaking risky projects is one way to learn, and some have argued that failure should be part of a learning strategy (Sitkin, 1996).

Pathology 6: Undertaking only projects that have a high probability of success.

A few years ago two major lighting firms, one in the U.S. and one in Japan, decided to undertake a joint venture. The origin of the project was an idea hatched from a dinner conversation between the CEOs of the two firms. An initial investigation by a small group of engineers from each firm came back with the recommendation that there would be little hope of success. When the executive of the U.S. engineering group reported this to his CEO, the CEO's response to the executive was, "This is not the right answer. Make this happen." As might be expected, the venture came together. After operating for several years, it eventually was dissolved.

After the venture had been in operation for about three years, the author asked the executive of the U.S. firm (the one responsible for "making it happen") about his judgment at this point in time about its success. "Has it been a success?" I asked.

The executive was equivocal, so I persisted. "Has it been a financial success?" "No," was his answer. "Well, has it achieved the technical exchanges you expected?" He hesitated but again answered, "No." "Then why are you not willing to say that it has been a failure," I asked. "Because," he said, "we have learned so much."

Inquiring organizations have learned to manage risk. They undertake endeavors that may not succeed but may provide major opportunities for learning.

Summary and Discussion

Avoiding and Correcting Myopia

The premise of this discussion has been that organizations can become more like the Singerian inquiring organization envisioned by Churchman by acknowledging sources of epistemological myopia. By recognizing the sources, actions (changes in practice) can lead to changes in how the organization perceives its role and in how its members identify themselves.

Table 1 presents some of the organizational characteristics identified with a myopic epistemology and how an inquiring organization might view these characteristics. While it is clear that changes in outlook are critical, changes in practice will be how an organization is able to avoid myopia. An organization cannot make changes overnight, nor can it go to the extremes of always seeking to disrupt the status quo. One can expect continual tensions between the need for change and the need for a dynamic equilibrium and between the desire for classification (precision and detail for depth of understanding within a worldview) and the necessity for a softer focus (enabling other perspectives and worldviews to come into focus) to avoid myopia.

For an organization to change, it needs to be aware of how its present culture and current practices may be limiting its epistemology and contributing to myopia. Self-awareness can be difficult, but executives might begin the process by conducting an *epistemological audit*. Such an audit—basically addressing a series of questions about how the organization collects, interprets, and uses information and knowledge—can aid in revealing hidden assumptions in the organizational routines and practices that may contribute to myopia. External benchmarks, evaluators, and reviewers can be helpful in providing a basis for comparison to the organization's own internal audit. Table 2 presents an outline of such an audit.

Resources are necessary to make the changes in practice, to experiment with alternative worldviews, and to accommodate and embrace multiple cultures. Thus, a corollary to what has been presented here is that an organization that recognizes its own myopia must have or develop slack resources in order to make the transition to an open Singerian learning organization.

Implications for Research

The power of metaphor lies in provoking thought and discussion, and the purpose of this discussion is to stimulate organizational executives and organizational observers to reflect on the epistemology embedded in the organization's culture and routine activities. Nonetheless, the discussion suggests some paths of research that might prove valuable in developing a more structured understanding of epistemological myopia in organizations.

Table 1. Impact of Epistemological Myopia on Views of Organizational Success

Organizational Characteristics	Myopic Epistemology Interpretation	Singerian Epistemology Interpretation
System behavior	Possibly closed	Open
System goal	Stable equilibrium	Unstable equilibrium; disequilibrium necessary for learning
Control approach	Feedback, cybernetic	Active
Culture	Create single culture for learning	Embrace multiple cultures for learning
Unbroken series of project successes	Operational triumph of control approaches	Missed opportunities for learning
Unsuccessful project	Failure of controls	Normal and expected; some are necessary for continued learning
Out of bounds behavior; needs that were not anticipated	Contributes to inefficiencies; avoids surprises by trying to anticipate all needs	Opportunities for learning
Strong corporate culture	Shared corporate culture is necessary for effective knowledge management	Acknowledging distinct cultures (a corporate multicultural environment) may be a necessary step in learning
Value of time	"Time is money" and short term measures provide feedback that can assure long term success. Monochronic organization of time	Time is socially constructed and is only one dimension; "timeless" worldview may enrich understanding and redefine success. Embraces range of monochronic and polychronic time organizations

Case studies would be a useful way to study the culture and practices of organizations that have survived changes in competition, technology, and economic conditions. *The Wall Street Journal* recently highlighted one such company, GKN, a 245-year old British company that seems to have avoided many of the traps of epistemological myopia (Michaels, 2004).

Organizational epistemology can be more precisely developed as a concept. Such a step is necessary if this metaphor is to become more than a provocative basis to initiate discussions about how organizations learn.

One approach would be to better articulate the elements of epistemology for an organizational context. This chapter has provided some ideas for how these elements can be identified. A complementary approach would be to examine organizations as a value chain of knowledge developing, storage, interpreting, and distribution systems (Alavi, 2001). By testing and validating questions, such as those in Table 2, then using these to perform an audit on the processes in this value chain, the hidden assumptions in the organization's epistemology might be more visible. One might speculate on what such an approach might reveal, as in the following postulates.

Table 2. Outline for an Epistemological Audit

Area	Possible Questions	Sources of Information (Internal)*
System behavior	Do the leaders of the organization see their role as maintaining equilibrium or as creating disequilibrium?	CEO and top management team Board
	Are strategic controls in place that focus on correcting errors, or do the controls focus on managing risk of uncertain projects?	CEO and top management team
Attitude toward failed projects	Did the project fail because our controls were inadequate? Are these failures opportunities to learn? Are we learning from these experiences?	CEO and top management team Middle management Project leaders
Time	Does the organization have mechanisms that enable it to tolerate (or even embrace) both monochronic and polychronic behavior without individual frustration and stress?	HR Department Middle management Project leaders
Cultural diversity	Does the organization have a policy of hiring based on finding qualified persons from different cultural backgrounds?	HR Department
	Are culturally different worldviews seen as opportunities for learning, or are they "corrected" by others in the organization?	New members of the organization
Learning Activities	Can each of the four activities in the Kolb learning model be identified?	Middle management Project leaders
	Are there sufficient resources (time) for reflection, or is the prevailing value on efficiency without time for contemplation?	Middle management Project leaders Staff
	Is there an effective way for staff suggestions to be evaluated?	HR Middle management Staff
	Is there a formal post audit for projects?	Middle management Project leaders

* External sources, such as benchmarks, may also be used.

Postulate 1:   An epistemological audit can be developed that will reveal qualitative differences between organizations according to their Singerian inquiring properties (or, conversely, according to their epistemological myopia).

Postulate 2:   When organizations are ranked or classified according to the degree of myopia, the executives in the more myopic organizations will view their organization as having a corporate culture that diminishes the significance of national cultures and ethnic backgrounds in the organization's performance. Conversely, executives in the Singerian inquiring organizations will view their organizational culture as embracing differences in ethnic backgrounds and national cultures and using these differences to create value.

Postulate 3:   Compared with more myopic organizations, Singerian inquiring organizations will have slack resources, or will have resources devoted to reflective activities, such as project post audit reviews.

Postulate 4:   Compared with more myopic organizations, Singerian inquiring organizations will exhibit behaviors that explicitly disrupt their own status quo in organizational structure, worldview, processes, and product-market mix.

Postulate 5:   Compared with more myopic organizations, members of Singerian inquiring organizations will be more comfortable with tensions arising from different cultures, worldviews, and the disruptive activities that are part of the organization's culture.

Conclusion

The concept of epistemological myopia focuses attention on the sometimes hidden assumptions that affect organizational learning. As a metaphor for how organizations acquire, interpret, and value knowledge about their environments, epistemological myopia raises awareness and can initiate discussions of organizational culture and practice that can inhibit learning. The concept has the potential for identifying areas of research on organizational learning that can improve both our understanding of organizational effectiveness in a highly competitive and dynamic environment and how organizational leaders can develop organizations that can thrive in such environments.

References

Alavi, M., & Leidner, D. E. (2001). Review: Knowledge management and knowledge management systems: Conceptual foundations and research issues. *MIS Quarterly, 25*(1), 107-136.

Argyris, C., & Schon, D. A. (1978). *Organizational learning: A theory of action perspective.* Reading, MA: Addison-Wesley.

Argyris, C., & Schon, D. A. (1996). *Organizational learning II: Theory, method, and practice.* Reading, MA: Addison-Wesley.

Baker, M. C. (2001). *The atoms of language.* New York: Basic Books.

Berger, P. L., & Luckman, T. (1966). *The social construction of reality.* Garden City, NJ: Doubleday.

Bluedorn, A. C. (2002). *The human organization of time: Temporal realities and experience.* Stanford, CA: Stanford Business Books.

Bowerman, M. (1996). The origins of children's spatial semantic categories: Cognitive versus linguistic determinants. In J. J. Gumperz & S. C. Levinson (Eds.), *Rethinking linguistic relativity* (pp. 145-176). Cambridge, UK: Cambridge University Press.

Carlsson, B., Keane, P., et al. (1976). R&D organizations as learning systems. *Sloan Management Review, 17*(3), 1-14.

Churchman, C. W. (1971). *The design of inquiring systems: Basic concepts of systems and organization.* New York: Basic Books.

Davenport, T. H., & Prusak, L. (1998). *Working knowledge: How organizations manage what they know.* Boston: Harvard Business School Press.

Dixon, N. (1999). *The organizational learning cycle. How we can learn collectively.* London: McGraw-Hill.

Drucker, P. F. (1988). The coming of the new organization. *Harvard Business Review, 66*(1), 45.

Forman, E. A., Minick, N., et al. (1993). *Contexts for learning: Sociocultural dynamics in children's development.* New York: Oxford University Press.

Gleick, J. (1999). *Faster: The acceleration of just about everything.* New York: Pantheon Books.

Grant, R. M. (1996a). Prospering in dynamically-competitive environments: Organizational capability as knowledge integration. *Organization Science, 7*(4), 375.

Grant, R. M. (1996b). Toward a knowledge-based theory of the firm. *Strategic Management Journal, 17,* 109-122.

Gumperz, J. J., & Levinson, S. C. (1996). *Rethinking linguistic relativity.* Cambridge, UK: Cambridge University Press.

Hall, E. T. (1959). *The silent language.* New York: Doubleday.

Hall, E. T. (1966). *The hidden dimension.* Garden City, NY: Doubleday.

Hofstede, G. H. (1980). *Culture's consequences, international differences in work-related values.* Thousand Oaks, CA: Sage.

Huber, G. (1991). Organizational learning: The contributing processes and literatures. *Organization Science, 2*(1), 88-115.

Humboldt, W., & Heath, P. L. (1988). *On language: The diversity of human language-structure and its influence on the mental development of mankind.* Cambridge, UK: Cambridge University Press.

Kim, D. H. (1993). The link between individual and organizational learning. *Sloan Management Review, 35*(1), 37-50.

Kolb, D. A. (1984a). Learning Style Inventory, Hay McBer Group. Retrieved September 25, 2004, from *http://trgmcber.haygroup.com/*

Kolb, D. A. (1984b). *Experiential learning: Experience as the source of learning and development.* Englewood Cliffs, NJ: Prentice Hall.

Kozulin, A. (1998). *Psychological tools: A sociocultural approach to education.* Cambridge, MA: Harvard University Press.

Levinson, S. C. (1996). Relativity in spatial conception and description. In J. J. Gumperz & S. C. Levinson (Eds.), *Rethinking linguistic relativity* (pp. 177-202).Cambridge, UK: Cambridge University Press.

Lucy, J. A. (1996). The scope of linguistic relativity. In J. J. Gumperz & S. C. Levinson (Eds.), *Rethinking linguistic relativity* (pp. 37-69).Cambridge, UK: Cambridge University Press.

Maslow, A. H. (1962). *Toward a psychology of being.* Princeton, NJ: Van Nostrand.

Mason, R. M. (2003). Culture-free or culture-bound? A boundary spanning perspective on learning in knowledge management systems. *Journal of Global Information Management, 11*(4), 20-36.

McKee, D. (1992). An organizational learning approach to product innovation. *Journal of Product Innovation Management, 9*(3), 232-245.

McLeod, R. J., & Schell, G. (2004). *Management information systems* (9th ed.). Upper Saddle River, NJ: Pearson Prentice Hall.

Michaels, D. (2004, March 16). A British survivor goes from nuts to aerospace push. *The Wall Street Journal,* 1.

Olsen, K. (1977). The quotations page. Retrieved September 25, 2004, from *http:// www.quotationspage.com/quotes/Ken_Olsen/*

Penrose, E. T. (1959). *The theory of the growth of the firm.* Oxford: Blackwell.

Schein, E. H. (2003). *DEC is dead, long live DEC: The lasting legacy of Digital Equipment Corporation.* San Francisco: Berrett-Koehler.

Sitkin, S. B. (1996). Learning through failure: The strategy of small losses. In M. D. Cohen & Lee S. Sproull (Eds.), *Organizational learning* (pp. 541-577). Thousand Oaks, CA: Sage.

Stata, R. (1989). Organizational learning: The key to management innovation. *Sloan Management Review, 30*(3), 63-74.

von Bertalanffy, L. (1968). *General systems theory.* New York: George Braziller.

Vygotsky, L. S., Rieber, R.W., et al. (1987). *The collected works of L. S. Vygotsky.* New York: Plenum Press.

Watson, W. E., Kumar, K., et al. (1993). Cultural diversity's impact on interaction process and performance: Comparing homogeneous and diverse task groups. *Academy of Management Journal, 36*(3): 590-602.

Wenger, E. (1998). *Communities of practice: Learning, meaning and identity.* Cambridge, UK: Cambridge University Press.

Whorf, B. L., & Carroll, J. B. (1956). *Language, thought, and reality: Selected writings.* Cambridge: Technology Press of Massachusetts Institute of Technology.

Woodman, R. W., Sawyer, J. E., et al. (1993). Toward a theory of organizational creativity. *Academy of Management Review, 18*(2), 293-321.

Chapter X

Inquiring Organizations and the Wisdom of Tacit Knowledge for a Heideggerian Inquiring System:
The Sixth Sense

John D. Haynes
University of Central Florida, USA

Abstract

C. West Churchman's five inquiring systems are considered in the light of Polanyi's distinction between tacit knowing and practical thinking. It is suggested that the five inquiring systems, as distinct and crucial elements of the learning organization, can be divided into two perspectives: the modes of tacit knowing and the levels of practical thinking. While practical thinking is of great importance to the day-to-day management and the analysis of past events of an organization, tacit knowing critically contributes to the sustainable growth and future direction of an organization through its connection with (1) intuition, (2) holism, and (3) ethics. As an example of tacit knowing, particularly in terms of ethics and intuition, a sixth inquiring system is proposed, namely, a Heideggerian inquiring system (HIS). What characterizes a HIS is, together with traditional methods of analysis of what is known, *an organizational culture directed to the aim of discovering what is* unknown *in terms of products, markets, and competitive strategies and, most particularly, the capacities of organizational members. An existing real-world organizational example of an HIS is provided, examined, and discussed.*

Introduction

Practical thinking that results in practical applications is largely governed by logic and is directed to what is *known*, whereas tacit thought, that at least has theoretical consequences, is enhanced by certain capacities that support it and certain beliefs that underpin it and is mostly directed to what is *unknown*. In terms of capacities, Churchman (1981) makes the point that "wisdom is thought combined with a concern for ethics" (p. 9). We extend this idea to wisdom is thought underpinned by ethics and supported by the capacity for intuition. Indeed, it is argued in this chapter that ethics itself is underpinned by intuition. We define an ethical approach as action that results in good consequences for all concerned, as distinct from a moral approach that is prescriptive by adhering to sets of rules in advance of action. The question of what constitutes *good consequences for all* in advance of action is, it is suggested, largely intuitive.

This chapter indicates that Churchman's five inquiring systems each articulate themselves through two perspectives: (1) as modes of tacit knowing and (2) as varying levels of practical thinking. The claim of this chapter accordingly places pragmatism into one of those two perspectives, that of practical thinking, rather than as Kienholz's (1999) asserts, the viewpoint which "sees four levels at once" (p. 9). Seeing all four levels at once clearly entails intuition of which no mention—or any mention of any capacity of a similar vein—is entailed in the classically defined Singerian inquiring system. Nor does Kienholz provide any persuasive arguments as to why Singerian inquiring systems should or could see all four levels at once.

In other words, this chapter disagrees that pragmatism (as one of the five inquiring system types) is able to see each of the other four inquiring system types at once. Instead, it is the mode of tacit knowing that is capable of seeing—in that elevated sense— inquiring system types, including its own type (that is, seeing all *five* levels at once).

In order to make this point abundantly clear, a new inquiring system is proposed, a Heideggerian inquiring system (Haynes, 2000b), which, along with its own necessary practical thinking (systems that analyze what is *known*), is essentially defined in terms of tacit knowing—in relation to ethics and intuition—and is largely applied to what is *unknown*.

Polanyi's Practical Thinking and Tacit Knowing

From Haynes (1999, pp. 56-60), we can begin to appreciate Polanyi's distinction between practical thinking and tacit knowing (also referred to as, respectively, practical and theoretical knowledge in Polanyi, 1967, pp. 5, 6) with a paradox that Polanyi himself discovered in Plato's work, the *Meno*. Prosch (1986) mentions that:

"To search for the solution to a problem, Plato told us there [the Meno], would seem to be absurd, since, if you know what you are looking for, then there is no problem. If you do not know what you are looking for, then you cannot expect to find anything. Polanyi maintained that this was a genuine paradox. Because, 'to see a problem is to see something that is hidden. It is to have the intimation of the coherence of hitherto not comprehended particulars.' Yet in spite of the apparent contradiction, involved in claiming to be able to see a problem, pointed out by Plato long ago, Polanyi noted that people have continued for two thousand years to see and solve many problems. What the Meno really shows, therefore, said Polanyi, is not that knowing is impossible (as indeed Plato also thought it did not show) but 'that if all knowledge is explicit, i.e., capable of being clearly stated, then we cannot know a problem or look for a solution.'[1] Since we apparently do know good problems that can be solved, knowing a problem must be, he held, a kind of tacit knowledge, like the knowledge we have of a face or a class, a knowledge of which we cannot give a fully explicit account, but which nonetheless does exist." (p. 96)

In above the passage, Polanyi is giving an example of tacit knowing. For more abundant proof, Polanyi (1967) says precisely this in his *Tacit Dimension*, "the kind of tacit knowledge that solves the paradox of the *Meno* consists in the intimation of something hidden, which we may yet discover" (pp. 22-23). Another way of appreciating how tacit knowing solves the paradox of the *Meno* is to consider a situation where rational thinking is argued not to apply. Flemons (1991) in *Completing Distinctions* notes a situation based on Taoist principles where rational knowledge is argued to be of no use. Consider the following passage:

"If we are up against a mystery, then we dare act only on the most modest assumptions. The modern scientific program has held that we must act on the basis of knowledge ... but if we are up against a mystery, then knowledge is relatively small, and the ancient program is the right one: act on the basis of ignorance."[2] (p. 70)

In other words from the above passage, the meaning is that in acting from ignorance we are not contaminating our intuition (inner teaching) with our rational knowledge (outer teaching). In this strict sense then, ignorance can be of assistance in coming to know what is unknown. When we translate this point to our capacity for intuition, we can appreciate that genuine intuition is not contaminated by what is *known*. It is a genuine apprehension of what is *unknown*; were it otherwise, then it would not be intuitive.

On the other hand, practical knowledge for Polanyi does not have any hidden aspects to it. Practical knowledge gives rise to rational thinking or practical thinking. In the *Tacit Dimension* (Polanyi, 1967, pp. 32-33), Polanyi states that things for which practical knowledge is appropriate are "less real" than things for which tacit knowing applies. He gives the example of cobblestones as being more real [than tacitly known things] in the sense of being more tangible but less real in the sense that they have no hiddenness to them. Polanyi's views of the objects of practical knowledge align fairly closely with Heidegger's concept of a thing. Joseph Kockelmans (1984), in his book *On the Truth of Being: Reflections on Heidegger's Later Philosophy*, had this to say about a third conception of a Heideggerian thing that I conclude is close to Polanyi's object of practical knowledge:

"The thing is nothing but formed matter; and this conception also holds good for both natural and man made things. This conception accounts for the thingly element we find in every work of art." (pp. 175-176)

If an object then is *thingly,* it exhibits an absence of hiddenness if, and only if, it is the pure *thingliness* of the object that we are considering. Under such circumstances, it is a candidate for being an object of practical knowledge. Drawing on definitions from Kienholz (1999, p. 9, Table 1), we can determine that objects of practical knowledge are subject to the laws of cause and effect, are capable of event analysis, and are thereby the practical thinking domain of the *realist*. Similarly, objects of practical knowledge are observed objectively, are highly conducive to pattern analysis, and are, accordingly, a practical thinking domain of the *analyst*. Finally, objects of practical knowledge are above all objects of expediency and are perfect for tactical rearrangement—but so too are the outcomes of the *idealist* and the *synthesist*. Accordingly, the practical thinking of the *pragmatist* sees practical knowledge and interprets (as a category mistake) the mode of tacit knowing in the same way. The heart of this misconception is clearly located in the view that pragmatism wants to isolate "kinds of truth." This is a damning claim that, in the end, gives away pragmatism's own inability to *tacitly know* itself! Accordingly, pragmatism has no sense of truth as essence! So, what is the essence of pragmatism? By its own tenets, the answer arises that it depends on what kind of truth you take! Consider the following quotation from Rorty (1982):

"Pragmatism cuts across this transcendental/empirical distinction by questioning the common presupposition that there is an invidious distinction to be drawn between kinds of truths. For the pragmatist, true sentences are not true because they correspond to reality, and so there is no need to worry what sort of reality, if any, a given sentence corresponds to; no need to worry about what 'makes' it true. ... So the pragmatist sees no need to worry about whether Plato or Kant was right in thinking that something non-

spatio-temporal made moral judgments true, nor about whether the absence of such a thing means that such judgments are merely expressions of 'emotion' or 'merely conventional' or 'merely subjective.'" (p. 2)

Tacit Knowing as Intuition

The paradox of the *Meno* is a key metaphor for enacting innovative solutions to maintain the sustainable growth of an organization in the face of uncertainty. Accordingly, if we apply each of the five inquiring system types to the problem of the paradox of the *Meno*, then we discover that only the synthesist and the idealist can solve it. The key ingredient for both synthesist and idealist is intuition. In the case of the synthesist, making a distinction between appearance and reality (a key feature of a synthesist) already presupposes that intuition is operational. Since by definition appearance cannot at the same time be real, then it must be intuited to be other than real insofar as it appears to be real. Similarly, the idealist presupposes intuition to enable its key feature of the development of a personal vision through inquiry and reflection. A vision holds the potential for a real creation; it is fluid and capable of either vanishing or being brought into being. Accordingly, it is not capable of pragmatic manipulation (pragmatist), or part-like pattern analysis (analyst) or object-like analysis (realist). Alternatively, the idealist reflects on the vision and thus provides the necessary intuition for the vision's further enhancement. On this basis, the idealist and synthesist are two modes of tacit knowing and the pragmatist, analyst, and realist are three levels of practical thinking.

Tacit Knowing as Holism

Both the synthesist and the idealist develop a viewpoint out of which they create, respectively, their mental models and personal visions (Kienholz, 1999, p. 9, Table 1). The viewpoint, so-called, is essentially an ethic, namely, our own systems of accepted convictions, from within which we speak with conviction, or what I take to be an instance of a belief in our own beliefs. But a belief in our own beliefs arises out of the *whole* system of acceptances, not from one piece of knowledge, not one reasoned bit, not one logical element or group of logical elements but the *whole system*.

Tacit Knowing as Ethics

The power of an individual ethic arises because it is respectful of the whole system of acceptances. The *emergence* of an ethic for an individual—ethic being a belief in the good of things: action that both benefits the individual self and others in that one action—is not sidetracked by any individual desire. Nor is it sidetracked by any set of instances of self-gratification but subsumes all of these desires and groups into the whole system of beliefs and takes its grounding from that synthesis. In this way, an ethic develops independently of any logical or reasoned process. We do not condition our ethic by analyzing it; rather, our ethic arises out of the integration of all of our beliefs and desires. So, our ethic is distilled and distinctly nonlogical, nonreasoned, and independent of intellectual processes. Our ethic retains its capacity for intuition because it is independent of reasoning and therefore emerges out of a deep sense of care. We are all born with this deep sense of care. The quicker the emergence, I would suggest, the purer is the process of its being grounded and continuation for being grounded. One can imagine a paradigm case of an individual not being able to produce an ethic from which to base intuitions. Such a case would arise where certain obsessions and biases of self-gratification precluded a synthesis of the whole of the individual beliefs.

Consider now why the question "why does ethics ground intuition and logic and reasoning do not?" already contains the seeds of its own answer, or already provides a viewing of the tacit hiddenness of the answer (Haynes, 1999), nor does it depend on the arrangement of words. I argue in Polanyian terms that a recognition of the hiddenness is still possible given further rearrangements, such as: Does intuition come from ethics or logic and reasoning?

I have indicated that for Polanyi ethics arises or emerges from a distillation of beliefs and that such a distillation must have at some stage brought together both opposing and consistent beliefs. It is the critical nature of *emergence* that provides the clues to the recognition of hiddenness. Polanyi, as Webb (1988) notes, does "discuss a further major concept... that of 'emergence'" (p. 48). But Webb further comments that Lonergan "makes better use of it than Polanyi succeeded in doing" (p. 48). In *Philosophers of Consciousness*, Webb (1988) indicates Lonergan's extension to Polanyi's concept of emergence was the recognition that things that are viewed as recognized as having hidden qualities have "proportionate beings...[and have]...'parallel structures' to our knowing" (p. 78). Webb further comments of Lonergan's contribution that by "proportionate being, he says, is intrinsically intelligible because it is precisely that which we are able to inquire into" (p. 79). In other words, there is something in the question itself that triggers a *response* in the system of beliefs. What does this mean? It means that in asking a question for which we can recognize a hidden answer, we are putting forward a question that has already been asked at an *unconscious level*. At this unconscious level, the asking has been "sorted out"[3] and we, as an individual, are now putting that question forward for the *conscious level* of our being to apprehend. This is the way tacit knowing is both recognized as hidden and how it makes itself manifest as a process of uncovering what is hidden.

For C. West Churchman (1981) "the moral spirit puts us in touch with life" (p. 80). Churchman's use here of *moral spirit* is essentially referring to ethics (that is, that which seeks the good in humankind, as opposed to morals which is taken to be living one's life on the basis of rules). The point is made abundantly clear that Churchman meant *moral spirit* to refer to a (Heideggerian) higher self or being, in that Churchman embraced this terminology to refer to a deeper connection with all levels of nature. Accordingly, Churchman (1981) quotes the Upanishads and the *Bhagavad Gita*: "the Self is the fish born in the water, the plant growing in the Earth" (*op. cit.*, p. 80) in this connection.

An Inquiring System Example of Tacit Knowing as Intuition

C. West Churchman had five philosophical organizational inquirers, which he viewed through the lens of systems theory: Leibniz, Locke, Kant, Hegel, and Singer. In two seminal papers, Courtney, Croasdell, and Paradice (1998) and Courtney (2001), we find summaries of each philosopher's approach grounded in systems theory and perspective highlighted philosophically now crystallized as an inquiring organization. As an example of tacit knowing born out as ethics and intuition, this chapter draws upon Courtney's paper entailing extending the Table of Inquiring Organizational Characteristics (Courtney, 2001, p. 25, Table 1) to its sixth element: a Heideggerian inquiring system.

We suggest, for practical purposes in the context of Courtney's (following Churchman) inquiring organization, that we consider the Being that Heidegger speaks of as the "Realm of Intuition." So, we have the everyday-world (Heidegger's being) where humans in an information system apply everyday practical thinking and the realm-of-intuition (Heidegger's Being) on which humans in an information system draw inspiration.

The everyday-world constitutes explicitness, while the realm-of-intuition contextually is located in implicitness. In the everyday-world, we use our analytical abilities, our calculation capacity, and our ability to understand and think through things (objects). In the everyday-world, we deal with knowledge: what is *already known* and *known to us*. In the realm-of-intuition, we deal with what is *yet to be known* or *what is known* but not yet connected to *what is unknown*. From the realm-of-intuition, we develop holistic thinking abilities in relation to Heideggerian things-in-themselves (concepts). A very special feature of a concept is that it is able to reconcile opposites. This is a crucial characteristic in relation to decision making in apparently no-win contexts. For a more thorough treatment of these issues in the form of *Perspectival Thinking*, see Haynes (2000a).

In the everyday-world, logic is the operative methodology and through logic, logical opposites cannot be reconciled. An interesting feature of the experience of being human, the experience of Heidegger's dasein, is that the lessons we learn from our experiences come after the test. Clearly, this is apparently contradictory! How can you learn a lesson after the lesson has been tested? But in the realm-of-intuition (that is from the perspective of intuitional thinking) that is precisely what happens. Something happens in our lives which perhaps is traumatic and that is the test. Do we survive it? How do we survive it? What follows is the lesson. In the everyday-world we study our lessons, and then we are tested (examined) on what we know. The everyday-world is concerned with knowledge; the realm-of-intuition is concerned with what arises out of *what is unknown*, or what is unknown but not yet connected to *what is known*. In this context, the exam coming before the lesson, while not logical, is nevertheless not illogical, it is rather nonlogical (that is, it is not constrained by logical, or rational, considerations). Here is a case of an apparently logical opposite: an exam and its lesson that is reconciled in opposition to what is considered logical by virtue of a nonlogical solution or reconciliation in terms of its (modal) reversal with the exam preceding the lesson. This point has profound implications for human decision making in an information system!

Tacit Knowing and Phenomenology

When Polanyi (1967) says "tacit knowledge... consists in the intimation of something hidden, which we may yet discover" (pp. 22-23), he is, it is suggested, maintaining a phenomenological stance for tacit knowing. This is so because, for him, knowledge is implicit or hidden together with the recognition that it is the subject's intuition that at some level recognizes the tacitness of the knowledge. But hidden knowledge is, in a very important sense, yet to be discovered knowledge, which falls into the category of the realm-of-intuition.

The same hiddenness arises for Heidegger. Consider Heidegger's famous comment that a good question is more important than its consequent answer. In other words, the human recognizes that knowledge or *the path* or *the way* to take to solve a problem is, in a very important sense, hidden already in the question that articulates the problem in the first place. Heidegger considered this point from the perspective of phenomenology, that to ask a penetrating question is to already have come to an opinion on its answer.

Polanyi saw the nature and importance of a good (insightful) question for thinkers in general, or more precisely for their values, assumptions, and belief systems. As Haynes (1999) notes:

"Polanyi's individual is—in a paradigm way—always grounded in an ethic of goodness or what benefits all individuals, as if the concern for all individuals allows each separate individual intuition to 'flow' better. For example Webb notes (Webb, 1988, p. 28): '[in relation to] human existence for Michael Polanyi... the individual is grounded in values and ethics, rather than in logic and reason.' Why is it that ethics provides a different ground which is more fertile for intuition than to that of logic and reason for Polanyi? To uncover the hiddenness within this question we need to turn to Polanyi himself. In Personal Knowledge, (Polanyi, 1962, p. 267) the answer, already implicit in the previous question, is revealed:

Our mind lives in action, and any attempt to specify its presuppositions produces a set of axioms which cannot tell us why we should accept them.... Our basic beliefs are indubitable only in the sense that we believe them to be so. Otherwise they are not beliefs, but merely somebody's [some one else's] states of mind. This then is our liberation from objectivism: to realize that we can voice our ultimate convictions only from within our convictions—from within the whole system of acceptances that are logically prior to any particular assertion of our own, prior to the holding of any particular piece of knowledge." (p. 3)

From Haynes above, we can see that the question, "Why does ethics ground intuition and logic and reasoning do not?" already contains the seeds of its own answer, or already provides a viewing of the hiddenness of the answer. In terms of this chapter, those seeds grow in the realm-of-intuition. For more support for this conclusion, consider the following passage from Heidegger (1977a):

"Language is never primarily the expression of thinking, feeling, and willing. Language is the primal dimension within which man's essence is first able to correspond at all to Being. This primal corresponding, expressly carried out, is thinking. Through thinking, we first learn to dwell in the realm in which there comes to pass the restorative surmounting of the destining of Being." (p. 41)

Heidegger above is referring to thinking as a process. Language is the explicit outcome of thinking as a process. But the process itself is implicit, thought as a process is the *realm* we *first learn to dwell in*. Intuitive thinking is that realm, or, as we have developed in this chapter, the realm-of-intuition.

As we draw on the realm-of-intuition to answer a certain question, we discover that there is something in the question itself that triggers a *response* in our system of beliefs. In this realm-of-intuition, the asking is being worked through in terms of *what is unknown*. Later, the *working through* is made explicit (is revealed as a solution) for our *conscious level* (our Heideggerian being).

Basis for a Heideggerian Inquiring System

An inquiring organization is a paradigm case of a social system bound to technology. In such an information system, Polanyian practical thinking, or as Courtney (2001) notes if we may paraphrase him, a "Science of Knowledge" approach is of "limited value in solving unstructured complex management problems" (p. 23). Courtney (2001) goes on to say:

"Exoteric knowledge is applicable to broad domains, and in some cases, might be considered 'common sense'. It is applicable to complex, unstructured problems." (p. 23)

As experience has shown, and what is also clearly recognized implicitly in Courtney's work, common sense is not so common at all, nor does a technological or computer solution assist us: computer technology hopelessly fails to emulate common sense. It is little wonder that a positivistic solution is of no use whatsoever in emulating common sense. But intuition and ethical enlightenment is of assistance in serving a common purpose for giving us, as humans in an inquiring organization, a basis for acting in a common sense way to complex decision making. Why? Because firstly, the realm-of-intuition provides inspiration in the form of alternative courses of action to what we do not know. Secondly, the realm-of-intuition concerns itself with what we know but do not yet connect to what we do not know. Such a connection clearly entails what would be, in any event, describing what we have come to know as common sense.

The Polanyian concepts of hiddenness, emergence, and "tacitness grounded in ethics rather than logic" allows us to see a wider perspective for an inquiring organization and, as such, provides us with a ground for acting on the basis of common sense.

Goethe's and Steiner's Intuitive Thinking

As we noted from Polanyi, originality comes from tacit knowing, or in common sense terms, from an ability to be able to discriminate without the use of knowledge. Consider the following passage by Bortoft (1996) describing Goethe's position:

"Discovery in Science is always a perception of meaning, and it could not be otherwise. The essence of a discovery is therefore in the nonempirical factor in cognition. The recognition that meaning is a primary datum of cognitive experience brings a considerable simplification to the philosophy of science. Of course, the meaning in question may be several stages removed from the meaning in everyday cognition, and at a much more comprehensive level." (p. 57)

In Steiner (1995) too, we see the following passage echoes the nature of meaning and theme in relation to cognitive experiences of the *higher states* and the *everyday states*:

"Moral efficacy depends on knowledge of the phenomenal world with which one is dealing. This knowledge must therefore be sought in a branch of general scientific knowledge. Hence, along with the faculty for moral ideas and imagination, moral action presupposes the capacity to transform the world of percepts without interrupting its coherence in natural law." (pp. 182-183)

For Goethe, discovery in science is always a perception, rather than a conception, since conceiving is intuitive. For Steiner, "transformation of the phenomenal world" (i.e., this chapter's sense of the everyday-world) requires a capacity to transform percepts (i.e., what is perceived in the phenomenal world) as distinct from what could be conceived from intuition.

A Heideggerian Inquiring System

The basis for a Heideggerian inquiring system is the theme of implicitness and explicitness as manifest in Heidegger's distinction between Being (the realm-of-intuition) and being (or being-in-the-world). In Being, Heidegger's essential thinking finds its dwelling, and in being, Heidegger's calculative thinking is characteristic. Consider the following passages from Heidegger. Of calculative thinking, Heidegger says (Kaufmann, 1975):

"All calculation makes the calculable 'come out' in the sum so as to use the sum for the next count. Nothing counts for calculation save for what can be calculated. Any particular thing is only what it 'adds up to,' and any count ensures the further progress of counting. This process is continually using up numbers and is itself a continual self-consumption. The 'coming out' of the calculation with the help of what-is counts as the explanation of the latter's Being. Calculation uses everything that 'is' as units of computation, in advance, and, in the computation, uses up its stock of units. This consumption of what-is reveals the consuming nature of calculation. Only because number can be multiplied indefinitely ... is it possible for the consuming nature of calculation to hide behind its 'products' and give calculative thought the appearance of 'productivity' ... Calculative thought places itself under compulsion to master everything in the logical terms of its procedure." (pp. 261-262)

Of essential thinking, Heidegger says (Kaufmann, 1975):

"The thought of Being seeks no hold in what-is. Essential Thinking looks for the slow signs of the incalculable and sees in this the unforeseeable coming of the ineluctable. Such thinking is mindful of the truth of Being and thus helps the Being of truth to make a place for itself in man's history. This help effects no results because it has no need of effect. Essential thinking helps as the simple inwardness of existence, insofar as this inwardness, although unable to exercise such thinking or only having theoretical knowledge of it, kindles its own kind." (pp. 263-264)

The theme of implicitness is the realm-of-intuition or tacit knowing or essential thinking or the fruit of being grounded by ethics, and the theme of explicitness is practical thinking or calculative thinking or the everyday-world of being. An organization cannot ignore calculative thinking; it is the necessary means by which an analysis of what is known about the organization and what the organization gathers to support its financial growth takes place. In an organization, essential thinking supports calculative thinking. The primary point that a Heideggerian inquiring system makes is that calculative thinking is not sufficient for the complexities of organizational growth in an uncertain world. In order to make sense of uncertainty, intuition is required. We have seen how Heidegger draws out the essential thinking elements of intuition and how Polanyi views intuition in terms of tacit knowing.

We are now in a position to see how a real-world example also draws on what is, essentially, intuitional capacities.

Example of a Heideggerian Inquiring System: Jack Welch and GE

When Jack Welch was CIO of General Electric (GE), he enacted at least two key strategies (Pearlson & Saunders, 2004, p. 26) that essentially conform to an intuitional approach as outlined above in the Heideggerian inquiring system:

1. The Bottom 10 percent method, and
2. The DYB, Destroy Your Business approach

In the Bottom 10 Percent, employees, appropriately in the following category, were made aware that they were ranked as being within the bottom 10% of all employees. This then allowed those certain employees the freedom to be responsible for themselves concerning what they should do. Should they leave the organization or stay? The decision to stay really entailed that they considered themselves better than their ranking. If their decision to stay was correct, it drew upon self-reflection after a period of self-criticism, but it also entailed an element of intuition or, at the very least, a hunch that they could succeed. If they did succeed in their decision to stay, the organization would reinforce the intuitional capacity of their decision in the second approach that Welch introduced.

In relation to the second case, DYB, or Destroy Your Business, Welch introduced an approach whereby organizational members could think up every realistic possible way in which a competitor could destroy their own organization (that is, GE). Again, the organization had to participate in self-organizational criticism, self-organizational reflection, and most importantly, draw upon what had not happened, what was at that time *unknown*: the possibility of some event taking place from a competitor. Clearly, the DYB approach, if it was to succeed, was highly intuitional.

DYB is a highly participative activity, which brings the partaking organizational member into the "life of the organization" (Churchman, 1981, p. 113). Being within the *life* of the organization is a higher sense of *connectedness* insofar as it enables the being of each organizational member to resonate in that mode of connectedness. This is a powerful ground for the growth of intuitional capacities. It is also, as Churchman notes, possible that each contribution in this kind of situation of life "partaking," bears itself out as "freedom with responsibility" (Churchman, 1981, p. 113). When this kind of participative responsible intuition (that is understood to have freedom) is supported by a sense of ethics—as we find in a Heideggerian inquiring system—then a deeper connection is made to the outside world of clients and customers, and from that, the building of the reputation of the organization. But it should be noted that an organization that wishes to instantiate organizationally within themselves this culture of ethics and intuition must do so by senior management example.

Both of Welch's approaches relied on intuition, self-discipline, self-criticism, self-reflection, and self-inquiry, both at the individual organizational member level and collectively throughout the organization. The point that a Heideggerian inquiring system makes is that the wisdom of essential thinking and the continued application of ethics will greatly enhance such an approach as taken initially by Welch. Why? Because to be ethical entails being self-critical and self-reflective in such a way, of course, that you are being true to yourself. For an organization to be collectively and individually intuitive entails that the organization itself must encourage organizational self-reflection and organizational self-inquiry. In asking the serious questions of reflection and inquiry come surprising answers, answers that turn out to draw on the unknown. As we have previously mentioned, Heidegger maintained that a good question already contains the seeds of its own answer. In the case of the Heideggerian inquiring system, those seeds are to be found in intuition and nurtured by a sense and performance of ethics.

For an organization, this inquiry and reflection needs to be directed to the organizational business goals. For an organization to encourage this process, especially as a culture, requires wisdom, a wisdom that sees beyond immediate needs and determines that coming to terms with what is *unknown* does not always spring from what is *known*.

There is a further connection between intuition and tacit knowing that is instructive to mention by way of passing--the connection between rational thought and the emotions in reconciliation as the underlying foundation of intuition. Consider Jack Welch in terms of his emotions. If you have ever met Welch, or at least have seen him on a video or on TV, you will immediately notice that one of his primary characteristics is his charisma. This charisma is the force of his emotional state! Somehow he is able to reconcile that emotional state with his intellect—it is perfect (or at least near perfect) harnessing of his energies. He achieves it very successfully. Haynes (2000a) would argue that Welch has reached a state—and certainly achieved that state during his reign as CIO of GE--of perspectival thinking. Consider, as the upshot of the above position, the following quotation from Haynes (2000a) in relation to the connection between tacit knowing, intuition and thought (rational thought), and emotion:

"The nature of tacit knowing and its underlying intuitional capacity to implicitly 'connect' with other humans is crucial to an Inquiring Organisation. Most humans are aware, as an underlying sense, or perhaps in an unconscious way, that they are connected in the synthesized mode of thought and emotion with, at least, other human beings [ask any mother who loves her child if this is not so!]. Perspectival Thinking intensifies that awareness through the emotions by strengthening and expanding the connections." (pp. v-vi)

We are now in a position to add the sixth element (the sixth sense) to Churchman's philosophical inquiring organizers: a Heideggerian inquiring system. Using the categories from Courtney (2001, Table 1, p. 25), we have what is illustrated in Table 1.

Table 1. Summary of Inquiring Organization Characteristics

Heideggerian Inquiring System	
Decision-Making Style:	Intuitional (in combination with traditional methods)
Knowledge/Perspective/Mode:	Ethical and intuitional tempered by critical self and organizational reflection and inquiry
Knowledge Creation Process:	Implicit as unknown knowledge; explicit as a demonstration of known knowledge or original action, or explicit as a new connection for existing knowledge
Information Technology:	Complex (possibly neural) networks and traditional analytical systems

Conclusion

This chapter has consistently put forward the view with sufficient support from the generic phenomenologists, Polanyi (and brief support from) Goethe and Steiner, that the basis for a Heideggerian inquiring system is the theme of implicitness and explicitness as manifest in Heidegger's distinction between Being (the realm-of-intuition) and being (or being-in-the-world). In Being, Heidegger's essential thinking finds its dwelling, and, in being, Heidegger's calculative thinking is characteristic. Essential thinking is the ground for intuition, and intuition is the ground for ethics. Both an ethical and an intuitive approach to organizational learning require an environment that nurtures these capacities while at the same time provides for the self-discipline of critical self and organizational reflection and inquiry.

Intuitive thinking (Goethe and Steiner), tacit knowing (Polanyi), and essential thinking (Heidegger) all point to a way in which what is *unknown (implicit)* can be made manifest as *knowable (explicit)*. Is an intuitional Heideggerian inquiring system approach of benefit to an inquiring organization, that is, an organization that is interested in solutions to complex unstructured problems? It is suggested that an inquiring organization would profoundly benefit from such an approach that is unattainable from a logical (or positivistic) approach that only relies on what is *already known*.

All managers are vitally aware of how important intuition is as a guiding principle for, and a foundation for the vision of, their organizations. If they are not, then clearly they are missing out on a key human capacity! Yet, ever so ironically, the literature is relatively silent on how intuition can be integrated into effective academic research made more effective within a learning organization! It is hoped that the examples and discussion provided above in this chapter, namely, of approaches used by Jack Welch as an exemplar of a Heideggerian inquiring system (particularly during his time as CIO of GE), illuminate how pervasive and effective (given the full support of the Heideggerian inquiring system vis-à-vis its context as an organization) such an HIS approach can be.

References

Bortoft, H. (1996). *The wholeness of nature: Goethe's way toward a science of conscious participation in nature.* Hudson, NY: Lindisfarne Press.

Churchman, C. W. (1971). *The design of inquiring systems: Basic concepts of systems and organizations.* New York: Basic Books.

Churchman, C. W. (1981). *Thought and wisdom.* West Germany: Intersystems Publications.

Courtney, J. F. (2001). Decision making and knowledge management in inquiring organizations: Toward a new decision-making paradigm for DSS. *Decision Support Systems.*

Courtney, J. F., Croasdell, D., & Paradice, D. (1986). Inquiring organizations. Foundations of information systems: Towards a philosophy of information technology. Retrieved September 25, 2004, from *http://www.cba.uh.edu/~parks/fis/fisart.htm*

Courtney, J. F., Croasdell, D., & Paradice, D. (1998). Inquiring organizations. *Australian Journal of Information Systems, 6*(1), 75-91.

Croasdell, D., Courtney, J. F., & Paradice, D. (1998). Singererian organizations: Guiding principles and design guidelines for learning organizations. AMCIS.

Flemons, D. G. (1991). *Completing distinctions.* Boston: Shambhala Books.

Haynes, J. D. (1999). Practical and tacit knowing as a foundation of information systems. *Australian Journal of Information Systems, 6*(2). Available at *http://www.uow.edu.au/ajis/vol62p5.html*

Haynes, J. D. (2000a). *Perspectival thinking: For inquiring organisations.* New Zealand: ThisOne and Company.

Haynes, J. D. (2000b). Inquiring organizations and tacit knowing. *Philosophical Foundations of Information Systems, AMCIS 2001,* 1544-1547.

Heidegger, M. (1977). *Being and time* (J. Macquarie & E. Robinson, Trans.). UK: Basil Blackwell.

Heidegger, M. (1977). *The question concerning technology and other essays* (W. Lovitt, Trans.). New York: Harper Torchbooks.

Kaufmann, W. (1975). Heidegger, M, The Way Back to the Ground of Metaphysics, in "Quest For Being", in Kaufman's *Existentialism From Dosteousky to Sartre,* A Meridian Book, New American Library, USA.

Kienholz, A. (1999). Systems rethinking: An inquiring systems approach to the art and practice of the learning organization. Foundations of information systems. Retrieved September 26, 2004, from *http://www.cba.uh.edu/~parks/fis/fisart.htm*

Kockelmans, J. J. (1984). *On the truth of being: Reflections on Heidegger's later philosophy.* Bloomington, IN: Indiana University Press.

Pearlson, K. E., & Saunders, C. S. (2004). *Managing information and using information systems: A strategic approach* (2nd ed.). John Wiley & Sons.

Polanyi, M. (1962). *Personal knowledge: Towards a post critical philosophy.* Chicago: University of Chicago Press.

Polanyi, M. (1967). *The tacit dimension.* Garden City, NY: Anchor Books, Doubleday.

Polanyi, M., & Prosh, H. (1975). *Meaning.* Chicago: University of Chicago Press.

Prosch, H. (1986). *Michael Polanyi: A critical exposition.* New York: University of New York Press.

Rorty, R. (1982). Consequences of pragmatism. Retrieved September 26, 2004, from *http://www.marxists.org/reference/subject/philosophy/works/rorty.htm*

Steiner, R. (1995). *Intuitive thinking as a spiritual path: A philosophy of freedom.* Hudson, NY: Anthroposophic Press.

Webb, E. (1988). *Philosophers of consciousness: Polanyi, et al.* University of Washington Press.

Endnotes

[1] *Tacit Dimension* (Polanyi, 1967, p. 22)

[2] Quoted from Wendel Berry, in *Home Economics*, North Point Press, San Francisco, 1987, pp. 4-5.

[3] Or more precisely, placed within the context of the synthesis of the whole system of beliefs.

Chapter XI

Mindfulness:
An Essential Quality of Integrated Wisdom

Kay Fielden
UNITEC, New Zealand

Abstract

In this chapter, mindfulness as an essential quality of integrated wisdom within inquiring organizations is discussed. A holistic, rather than a scientific view, of knowledge is adopted. The discussion is also underpinned by a pragmatic approach that incorporates rational, emotional, psychological, and spiritual perspectives. While multiple worldviews are considered, the discussion is situated in an integrated participatory paradigm. A plan for developing mindfulness within organizations is described that includes consideration of multilayered development and ordered, unordered, and disordered organizational arenas. Complexities abound when both individual and group maturity levels on developmental layers diverge widely. Integrated wisdom is only achieved when consensual alignment is achieved. Integrated wisdom allows for this complex mix, is aware of the appropriate level and type of communication and or interaction required, and acts accordingly without prejudice or judgment. Implications for the future of mindfulness as a necessary skill for integrated wisdom are also explored.

Introduction

Snowden (2002) suggests that we have moved into the third generation of knowledge management (KM)--one that sees knowledge as both *thing* and *flow* (p. 12). This third generation of knowledge management requires diverse approaches to knowledge management.

The main contention in this chapter is that third generation approaches to knowledge management require many management skills drawn from multiple scenarios, management *spaces*, and worldviews. No longer can we rely on knowledge as fact (whether tacit or explicit) that can be managed, stored, retrieved, manipulated, reported, and acted on.

As we move into the fifth central domain of disorder (Kurtz & Snowden, 2003) (Figure 2) mindful knowledge workers are essential. No longer can knowledge workers rely on the basic assumptions of order, rational choice, and intentional capability.

In this chapter, the multiple characteristics of mindfulness are incorporated into an integrated whole. Characteristics of wisdom are then described and the notion of integrated wisdom explored. The link between a holistic view of mindfulness and integrated wisdom is then established.

The Cynefin framework (Kurtz & Snowden, 2003) (Figure 2) is described briefly as a sense-making device in managing complexity in organizations. Distinctions are made in this sense-making device of the difference between unordered spaces (complexity and chaos), order (knowable and known domains), and a fifth central domain of disorder where the only thing that is known is that there *is* no knowledge of thing or process. It is in this fifth central space that this discussion on mindfulness is situated, and it is knowledge gained about how particular domains of disorder operate effectively that characterizes the third generation of knowledge management.

The distinct elements of mindfulness required in domain of disorder are mapped on a timeline from initial entry into the domain, during the process of learning how this particular domain of disorder operates, and then to final outcomes for the domain.

Finally, implications for the future in developing third generation knowledge management skills to work effectively in these domains of disorder are discussed.

Mindfulness Defined

Mindfulness is a counterfoil to mental rigidity. While concentration focuses attention, mindfulness determines on what the attention will be focused (Figure 1). Mindfulness also detects when attention strays. Mindfulness is an act of neutral observation, where we are aware of distractions and refocus as distractions occur. Mindfulness usually requires immersion in the process at hand for a state of meta-awareness to emerge. Meta-awareness is being aware of what is happening as participation occurs.

Mindfulness and Cognitive Maturity

Meta-awareness and presencing can be classified as mindful dimensions only achieved with some degree of cognitive maturity. Both require awareness of what is happening while it is happening. Both require a *detached self* to notice and learn from the process being experienced. It appears that meta-awareness and presencing belong at a high cognitive level (but not necessarily high spiritual, emotional, or psychological levels), one achieved through mindful practice, training, and integrated wisdom.

Meta-Awareness

Meta-awareness is achieved most frequently in both Eastern and Western spiritual traditions through meditation and/or prayer. Meta-awareness is achieved by designers, artists, and innovators by immersion in a particular creative act so that *flow* (Csikszentmihalyi, 1979) is experienced. Meta-awareness is a skill seldom taught, learned, or practiced in Western spirituality.

Meta-awareness is an essential cognitively mature characteristic of mindfulness.

Figure 1. Qualities of Mindfulness

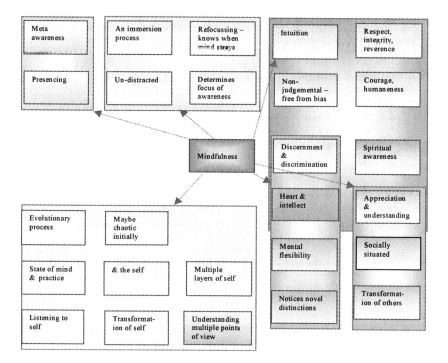

Presencing

Scharmer (2000) describes *presencing* as "learning from the future as it emerges" rather than from reflecting on past experiences (p. 18). Presencing, therefore, is the embodiment of foresight when applied to knowledge management practices in organizations. Presencing is also a necessary quality of mindfulness, related to but different from meta-awareness. Meta-awareness is being aware of what is happening as it happens, while presencing is the ability to learn from the future as it emerges. Both meta-awareness and presencing are situated on the same timeline continuum and, as well, on similar levels of conceptual abstraction as we form sense-making models of the world (Figure 3).

Mindfulness and Spirituality

Zukav (1989) believes that intuition is "the voice of the soul" (p. 83). Without intuition, we do not have access to whole solutions as they emerge, nor do we have a mechanism that enables deep and powerful contact with the divine. The mindful practitioner is more likely to embrace the spiritual dimensions of mindfulness for richness, humaneness, transformative powers, reverence, integrity, and respect. The mindful practitioner includes reflective spiritual activities as a key element of learning to practice in a mindful manner.

Mindfulness and the Self

The mindful knowledge management practitioner develops a greater self-awareness, understands the rational, emotional, spiritual, and psychological self in the process of knowing and in relationship to known facts. As awareness of multiple layers of self emerge, so maturity within and across self-layers emerges. The mindful self is aware of mindfulness as an evolutionary process. The mindful self also knows and is aware of the likelihood of chaos, especially on entry to domains of disorder (Figure 2).

Mindfulness and the Socially Situated Intellect

Fine-tuning discernment and discrimination occurs as the mindful intellect matures. Heart and intellect can and do operate together in an integrated manner for greater appreciation and understanding of socially situated knowing. The mindful intellect notices and acts upon novel distinctions with greater flexibility, more assurance and in less time. The socially situated self is transformed by mindful interactions with others. Mindful interactions have an empowering effect on all those within the social situation.

Partial Views of Mindfulness

Many authors have presented partial views of mindfulness.

Socially Situated Knowing

Reason and Bradbury (2001) identify socially situated knowledge as a characteristic of knowledge. Butler (2001) identifies contexts of practice that include both social settings and the minds of the knowers. Langer (2000) limits her studies in cognitive psychology to the simple act of drawing novel distinctions in the domain of rational thought. She suggests that drawing novel distinctions can lead to a heightened state of involvement and wakefulness or of being present.

The Spiritual View

Goodenough and Woodruff (2001), on the other hand, are concerned with the link between science and cardinal virtues of courage, fair-mindedness, humaneness, and reverence and that this link is rendered coherent by mindful reflection. They also suggest that this represents intellectual and spiritual collaboration and that mindfulness is both a state of mind and a practice that goes beyond the intellect touching all facets of humanness. These authors do not, however, dwell on the intellectual or meta-awareness qualities of mindfulness.

Waddock (2001) is concerned only with the spiritual qualities of integrity, respect, and reverence, rather than with any spiritual practices to achieve mindfulness.

The Humane Quality View of Mindfulness

Braud and Anderson (1998) suggest that mindfulness core qualities are heart and intellect, discernment and discrimination, appreciation and understanding, and transformation of self and transformation of others. This appears to be a partial picture of mindfulness at a lower cognitive level than meta-awareness and presencing. These core qualities contain a mix of spiritual, socially situated, and intellectually mindful characteristics.

Initial States of Mindfulness

Initial states of confusion are identified by Wheatley (2001b) as characteristic of mindful engagement. She also suggests that listening, rather than engaging in our own inner dialog in our heads, is a necessary precursor to mindful engagement and immersion

(Wheatley, 2001a). Wheatley states that if we do not listen to self, others, and our surroundings, we cannot be *present* in our social interactions.

Mindfulness and Multiple World Views

In regarding mindfulness as both a state of mind and a practice, one can start to envision mindfulness as an integrated whole. Essential qualities of mindfulness understood by multiple religious traditions, including Buddhism, Confucianism, Hinduism, and the ancient Greeks, are mindfulness as the path; mindfulness as observation free from bias, need, and prejudice; and mindfulness as immersion—a deep understanding of self and the beings of others.

Reason and Bradbury (2001) suggest that there is a continuum of competing worldviews (Table 1a-c) ranging from mechanistic to mind-matter views. This discussion on mindfulness is situated in the shaded areas on this continuum in Table 1c.

Ontologically, the chapter is situated in a participatory context. Active participation is essential for presence, which in turn is a necessary quality of mindfulness. Active participation, in the sense of *being present* means involvement of the whole self, not necessarily physical activity. To a lesser extent, and still important, mindfulness is situated in the pan-psychic realm where consciousness and matter arise together, and reality is self-organized, emergent, complex, evolutionary, and systemic. It is really important to note that the context for this chapter is not situated in reality as social construction, in an ideal world, or in a mechanistic world.

Epistemologically, knowledge as an essential element of mindfulness resides not only in human minds but also in a wider ecology of mind. Knowledge also occurs through active participation. We know our world as we act within it with critical subjectivity. While mindfulness is an important element of a mechanistic, idealistic, and socially constructed world, these are not the focus for this discussion.

Methodologically, the worldview influences on mindfulness arise from intuition (classified as idealist by Reason and Bradbury's competing worldviews), compassionate inquiry, and cooperative forms of action inquiry.

Axiologically, the discussion places mindfulness within a worldview that encompasses intrinsic value, self-realization, and practical and experiential knowing.

The major philosophical problem in situating mindfulness across these competing worldviews is that such views are fundamentally opposed to the dominant mechanistic perspective and must struggle for acceptance.

Major contributions to the affairs of the world in positioning mindfulness, thus, are that it draws attention to the contribution of consciousness and social relations in our world; provides a re-enchantment of the world; and honors the rights of more than human beings.

Such an integrated stance on mindfulness challenges us to discover a new form of knowing and methodologies that honor integration of mind and matter, politics, and epistemology. Mindfulness—being ever present, ever aware, places enormous demands on IS educators, practitioners, researchers, and consultants. Mindfulness is not taught in either the undergraduate or the postgraduate IS curriculum—apart from requesting that reflection take place.

Mindfulness is a quality and a process, a way of being and experiencing, a way of listening, and a way of reflecting. Mindfulness almost seems too much for mortal human beings. Spiritual practitioners from many traditions—both from East and West—have recognized this for centuries. Mindfulness for them emerges through dedication to spiritual practices—prayer, meditation, contemplation, devotion, and integrity.

Mindfulness and the Domain of Disorder

Kurtz and Snowdon (2003) suggest that it is only within the *domain of disorder* that effective consensual decision making based on an understanding of the complex nature of knowledge can be made. The development of mindfulness is essential to leverage advantages to be gained by understanding the complex nature of knowledge within the domain of disorder. Entering this domain, whether it is as a training activity or imposed by external pressures from the environment, may be a chaotic process (Figure 2). Individuals within organizations find themselves in spaces where nothing is known. (Perhaps critical incident and trauma training could inform this part of the process.)

The mindful practitioner, knowing the experience of initial chaos and the fight or flight syndrome, accepts this state of being as normal and becomes immersed in the process. The mindful practitioner knows there is something to learn in uncharted territory, and solutions may come from ordered or unordered (Snowden, 2002) worlds. The mindful practitioner knows that boundaries or phase shifting may occur from any domain, either

Table 1a. Mechanisitic Worldview (based on Reason and Bradbury, 2001)

	Dualism	**Materialism**
Ontology	Mind and matter real, distinct entities neither reducible to the other	All is matter. Mind: emergent epiphenomenon, or nonexistent (materialism seen as truncated dualism with mind lopped off)
Epistemology	Objectivist/realist: Findings true; meaning repeatable, verifiable, quantifiable. Knowledge accumulates over time, approaching Truth.	
Methodology	Objectivity: separates subject and object; experimental, manipulative	
Axiology	Propositional knowledge about the world—an end in itself, intrinsically valuable. Knowledge is value free.	
Positives	If mind and matter ontologically separate, how can they interface at all?	How can subjectivity, conscious mind emerge from nonsentient matter?
Negatives	Hugely powerful for understanding and manipulating the macroscopic world. Danger: a worldview that brings about disenchantment and a dead world	

Table 1b. Mind and Spirit Worldview (based on Reason and Bradbury, 2001)

	Idealism	Social constructivism
Ontology	All ultimately pure consciousness or spirit. Natural world: either an illusion or reducible to mind	Reality: social construction mediated by language and shaped by social, political, cultural, economic, ethnic, and gender values crystallized over time. "There is nothing outside the text"
Epistemology	Universal or Absolute Mind, knows all things directly. Lesser minds know through participation in Absolute Mind	Knowledge: transactional, subjectivist, politically determined. Deconstruction of grand narratives
Methodology	Intuition, revelation, mysticism, mindfulness disciplines, esoteric	Various forms of dialogical, transactional qualitative linguistic inquiry. Inquiry recognized as partial, politically determined
Axiology	Primary values spirit and mind; contemplation, unity, dissolution of ego—overcomes the illusion of a separate world	Propositional, transactional knowledge instrumentally valuable as a means to social emancipation
Positives	If all is consciousness or social construction, how do we account for universal pragmatic common sense supposition of reality?	
Negatives	Draws attention to contribution of consciousness, social relations power and politics, gender and race in constructing our world. Draws attention to limits of knowledge of the world. Danger: *real* sensuous, embodied, and more than human world disappears in a welter of social construction	

from within the self, from others in the same situation, or from the environment. The mindful practitioner also knows that the process within the domain of disorder has a flow of its own. Listening to or noticing the direction and speed of the flow, any swarming or clustering activities, or any barriers that appear unexpectedly is essential. Noticing the changes and the rate of response required and accepting emergent activities that change the direction or speed of the flow are also skills required in the domain of disorder. Honoring and accepting intuitive whole solutions that appear without logical steps is required as being able to integrate the flow of knowing without fixating on final solutions. Entering into the domain of disorder from a single fixed viewpoint or a single Cynefin quadrant (Figure 2) may be a recipe for further chaos and eventual collapse of an organizational solution.

Differing mindfulness qualities are required during the process of reducing the domain of disorder (Figure 3). On entering, the mindful practitioner knows that patience is required, that the initial situation will appear chaotic, and that solutions cannot be rushed. As the process progresses, further individual mindful qualities of meta-aware-ness, presencing, immersion, focusing and refocusing are required. When the social situation within the domain of disorder is considered, humaneness, understanding of multiple worldviews, and spiritual awareness are required. As awareness grows of the nature of disorder, the mindful practitioner allows appropriate changes to emerge and accepts the rich knowing in holistic solutions.

Table 1c. Mind-Matter Integration (based on Reason and Bradbury, 2001)

	Pan-psychic	Participatory
Ontology	Consciousness and matter arise together and are inseparable. Reality self-organizing, emergent, complex, evolutionary, systemic	Subjective-objective: human self both autonomous and embedded in participatory relationship with the given primordial reality in which the mind/body actively participates
Epistemology	Knowing resides not only in human minds but in wider ecology of mind	Knowing through active participation. We know our world as we act within it with critical subjectivity. Extended epistemology
Methodology	Sympathetic and compassionate inquiry, awareness of subtle sensitivities, holistic approaches	Cooperative forms of action inquiry; community of inquiry within community of practice
Axiology	Universal sympathy and compassion for all beings. All things have intrinsic value, right to existence, and full self-realization. Ecological awareness. Cosmos as sanctuary.	Practical knowing how to foster human ecological flourishing is the primary value, supported by propositional, experiential, and other forms of knowing
Positives	Fundamentally opposed to dominant mechanistic (dualist or materialist) perspective and, as such, appears both mystical and functionally irrelevant. Must struggle for acceptability. Distinguished philosophical lineage unacknowledged and unrecognized	
Negatives	Provides for re-enchantment of the world and an honoring of the rights of more than humans. Challenges us to discover a new form of knowing and methodologies that honor the integration of mind-matter and politics with epistemology. Dangers lie in the huge demands of such methods	

Figure 2. Cynefin Domains (Kurtz & Snowden, 2003)

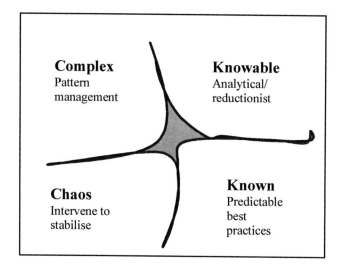

Figure 3. Disorder and Mindfulness Qualities

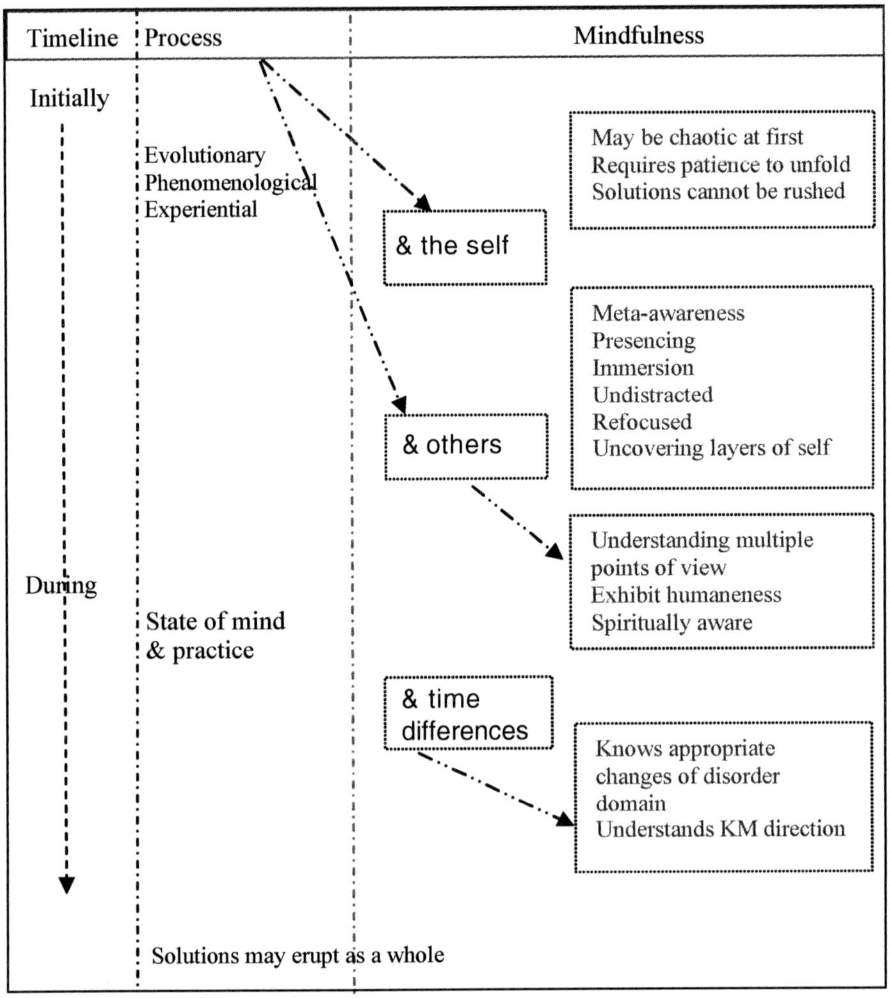

In the third age of knowing (Kurtz & Snowden, 2003), mindfulness is an essential quality of integrated wisdom. Without integrated wisdom, the richness of knowledge as both process and product that is both knowledge domain and context dependent is unlikely to be discovered. Training KM engineers, managers, and leaders as mindful practitioners should be part of all degree programs in KM. Experiential learning, social awareness, and spiritual practice are all required for integrated wisdom.

Disordered Solutions

Who is the self - in a world of disorder
Immersed – as it were in what is not known

Sinking into the chaos - initially at least
No rules to be found, no patterns to see

Going within - divine guidance, maybe
Noticing, dismissing those thoughts from the past

Mind stilled now at last
Now honoring self

.

.

.

Bursting forth whole, ways forward to see
Taking the time to respect and revere

Now sharing and talking - momentum is building
Why couldn't we see, why didn't we know

Phase shifting, shape changing
Boundaries now blurring
Rapid consensus for knowing afresh

Fielden (2003)

Wisdom Defined

When geometric diagrams and digits
Are no longer the keys to living things,
When people who go about singing or kissing
Know deeper things than the great scholars,
When society is returned once more
To unimprisoned life, and to the universe,
And when light and darkness mate
Once more and make something entirely transparent,
And people see in poems and fairy tales
The true history of the world,
Then our entire twisted nature will turn
And run when a single secret word is spoken.
Novalis (translated by Robert Bly)

The *Concise Oxford Dictionary* defines wisdom as "Experience and knowledge together with the power of applying them critically or practically." Microsoft Word Thesaurus lists "common sense, intelligence, prudence, sagacity, sense, understanding, discretion, insight, tact and diplomacy" as multiple meanings for wisdom. Ackoff (1999) stated that "wisdom is the ability to perceive and evaluate the long-run consequences of behavior" (p. 15). In tracing the historical roots of wisdom as a concept, Anderson, Reardon, and Sanzogni (2001) suggest that "wisdom was thought to be an acquired quality or special kind of knowing about life's meaning applicable to the successful living of daily life and attainable by those who seek it be patient reflection" (p. 2059). They also state that wisdom implies the ability and desire to choose from among ethical behaviors.

Wisdom in Inquiring Systems

A wise approach by those within inquiring systems implies, therefore, that a moral and ethical stance will be adopted and that knowledge workers within inquiring systems will return to first principles to unearth underlying principles. Haynes (2001) makes the distinction between tacit knowing, practical knowing, and intuition in defining knowledge and wisdom.

Mindfulness and the Philosophical Foundations of Inquiring Systems

Beachboard (2002) suggests that "multiple methods [of research] informed by differing ontological and epistemological perspectives are not desirable but necessary in achieving research rigor and relevance within the IS community" (p. 1662). Even in situating this discussion in a holistic participative framework within the domain of disorder (Figure 2), it appears that multiple research methods are required. Many more are required if we consider the many points of view represented in Tables 1a-c.

Butler (2001) argues for a constructivist viewpoint in making sense of knowledge: one that considers knowledge as being both "situated and distributed" in "contexts of practice" (p. 1464). He also argues that knowledge "originates in the minds of knowers." Butler's argument appears to be situated in a socially constructed domain, and this is outside the scope of this chapter.

Courtney, Croasdell, and Paradice (1998) suggest that a deconstruction of different views of inquiring systems and their relationships to types of learning organizations provides some insight into the multitude of ways in which knowledge is managed according to the learning status of the organization. Courtney et al. suggest that 'to be successful the modern organization must be capable of continuous learning. And

'Churchman's inquiring system models provide a basis for a new perspective on learning organizations.' Learning system approaches are assumed as given in exploring mindfulness in this discussion.

Integrated Wisdom

Integrated wisdom does not happen over night, nor can it be acquired in a two-day training program for knowledge engineers trained in the scientific method. Integrated wisdom evolves in organizational communities that free themselves from traditional working patterns. Integrated wisdom appears when individuals are respected, honored, and revered for their individual and collective efforts within organizations. Integrated wisdom happens when creative acts of knowing mean as much as stored company information, policies, and procedures. Integrated wisdom happens as businesses experience shifts from and between varying degrees of order, unorder, and disorder. Integrated wisdom happens as mindful practices are accepted and incorporated as everyday working guidelines for everyone involved. Integrated wisdom happens as self-responsibility for all is practiced as the norm.

Integrated Wisdom

Is it mountain top leaping
Or forest floor plodding

Does it happen alone
Or with the minds of the many

Do we feel with our heads
And think with our hearts

Do we stand back in our minds
For the orchestra to play
Fielden (2003)

Integrated wisdom happens as meta-awareness of which layer of mindful social interactions occur (Figure 4). Integrated wisdom is more likely to happen within communities of practice within inquiring organizations. The evolutionary learning process for all involves the knowledge that everyone learns and practices mindfulness in their own way.

Figure 4. Multi-Layered Conceptualization of Mindfulness

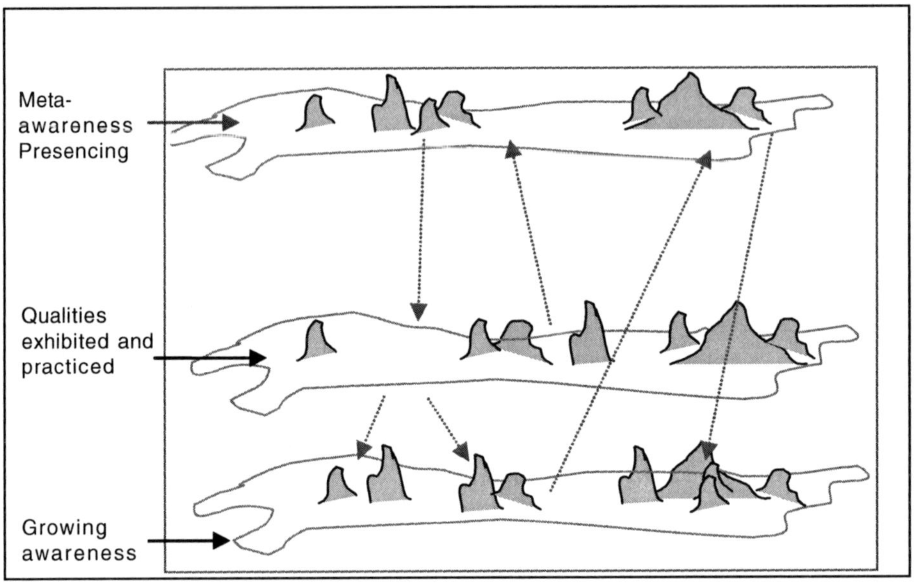

Link Between Mindfulness and Integrated Wisdom

Mindfulness is a necessary precursor as well as a continuous present state for KM practitioners. Mindfulness with its multi-layeredness (Figure 4) is the mental state required for integrated wisdom to appear, to emerge, to govern, and to lead communities of practice (Hildreth & Kimble, 2002) within inquiring organizations. Without a mindful approach, the diverse approaches needed for third generation KM are unlikely to happen. Mindful managers are aware of boundaries as they shift and of appropriate human qualities required in transition. Flood (1999) suggests that operating in conscious recognition of paradoxes in managing organizations includes "knowing of the unknowable" (p. 192).

A Mindfulness Plan

A plan for developing mindfulness both within organizations and for external consultants/academic researchers is described (Table 2). This plan includes consideration of multi-layered development on all learning dimensions—intellectual, emotional, psychological, and spiritual—and the rich interplay and connections between these layers both on an individual and an organizational level. Complexities abound when the maturity levels on these layers become widely disparate. Integrated wisdom can only be achieved when we move toward alignment on all levels. The most difficult situation to resolve is when intellectual development races ahead of learning and development in other dimensions. Also, in any organization in any human activity system, there will be people with greatly varying mixes of intellectual, psychological, emotional, and spiritual development, and within each dimension, there will be greater maturity with some elements within each dimension than others. Integrated wisdom allows for this complex mix, is aware of the appropriate level and type of communication and or interaction required, and acts accordingly without prejudice or judgment.

The first step in establishing mindfulness in integrated wisdom is to increase awareness of the essential nature of mindfulness so that integrated wisdom is applied in KM. Changed practices, education and training, and an awareness of multiple worldviews are required to raise awareness of the essential nature of mindfulness.

Step 2 is to introduce mindfulness practices into both undergraduate and postgraduate curriculum—listening, reflection and reflexivity, cooperation, collaboration, ethics, and integrity—from peripheral issues to be addressed in a philosophy of KM topics to core practices in educating KM professionals. Case studies that incorporate uncertainty, not knowing, role playing, and experiential learning (in the Cynefin framework, for instance) should be included.

Table 2. Mindfulness Plan

Step	Action
1	Increase awareness of mindfulness Introduce into KM curriculum Train academics and industry trainers in mindful practices
2	Teach new curriculum with mindful practices – meditation, visualization, narrative skills, group problem solving, dealing with uncertainty, self responsibility, respect for others, alternate conflict resolution
3	Teach awareness and acceptance of multiple world views, systems thinking, complexity theory, philosophy, chaos theory
4	KM researchers and consultants practice dynamic action research mindfully in organizations
5	KM leaders apply integrated wisdom consensually in own organizations
6	Organizations operate as consensual, mindful communities for effective 3rd generation KM
7	KM communities develop own sense-making models for dealing with all degrees of order, unorder and disorder

Step 3 is to educate undergraduates and postgraduates in multiple worldviews. For instance, presenting multiple worldviews within an undergraduate curriculum in KM exposes students early to complex situations. All KM curriculum topics should be situated on a worldview philosophical landscape to raise awareness of the predominance of mechanistic views in KM.

Step 4 is for KM researchers and consultants to conduct dynamic action research within organizations with integrated wisdom, awareness and integrity, and honoring all stakeholders in the research process. Awareness of degrees of order, unorder, and disorder is required for effective research within complex organizations.

In Step 5, KM leaders within organizations apply integrated wisdom consensually within their own organizations.

In the sixth step whole organizations operate as consensual mindful communities for effective third generation KM.

The final step involves KM communities developing their own conceptual models for dealing with all degrees of order, unorder, and disorder.

Mindfulness for the Future

Mindfulness for the future is largely unexplored territory. There seems to be more questions than answers. Some questions that come to mind are:

- What are the diverse ways in which conceptual leaps between and among multi-layered and multi-dimensional mindfulness are made?
- How do group interactions affect individual multi-layered mindful skills and vice versa?
- What are the cultural, environmental, organizational, emotional, psychological, and spiritual influences and interactions in a multi-layered multi-dimensional conceptual landscape of mindfulness?
- How do we become the wise facilitators for others to integrate knowledge skills in inquiring organizations?
- Is there a knowledge architecture within organizations that incorporates integrated wisdom?
- What are the technical mechanisms that support integrated wisdom within organizations?
- How do mindful practices become integrated into organizations in acceptable, meaningful, and effective ways?

Conclusion

This discussion has concluded with more questions than answers and that is indicative of the great need for more research and a much deeper level of understanding of how to manage knowledge in complex times.

The main contention explored in this discussion is that third generation approaches to knowledge management require many management skills drawn from multiple scenarios, management *spaces*, and worldviews. No longer can we rely on *knowledge as fact* (whether tacit or explicit) that can be managed, stored, retrieved, manipulated, reported, and acted on.

As we move into the fifth central domain of disorder (Kurtz & Snowden, 2003) (Figure 2), mindful knowledge workers are essential. No longer can knowledge workers rely on the basic assumptions of order, rational choice, and intentional capability. Multiple characteristics of mindfulness incorporated into an integrated whole are required for establishing integrated wisdom in third generation knowledge management.

Sense-making devices in managing complexity in organizations (like the Cynefin framework) allow for the fine distinctions required in managing across unordered, ordered, and disordered domains. It is in the domain of disorder that this discussion on mindfulness has been situated, and it is the knowledge gained about how particular domains of disorder operate effectively that characterizes third generation knowledge management.

References

Anderson, P., Reardon, M., & Sanzogni, I. (2001). Ethical dimensions of knowledge management. In J. DeGross (Ed.), *AMCIS2001*, August, 2058-2062.

Beachboard, J. C. (2000). Rigor, relevance and research paradigms: A journey from practitioner to neophyte researcher. In J. DeGross (Ed.), *AMCIS2002*, August, 1660-1666.

Braud, W., & Anderson, J. (1998). *Transpersonal research methods for the social sciences:Honoring human experience*. Thousand Oaks, CA: Sage.

Butler, T. (2001). Making sense of knowledge: A constructivist viewpoint. In J. DeGross (Ed.), *AMCIS2001*, August, 1462-1466.

Courtney, J. F., Croasdell, D. T., & Paradice, D. B. (1998). Inquiring organizations. *Australian Journal of Information Systems, 6*(1), 75-91.

Csikszentmihalyi, M. (1979). The flow experience. In G. Davidson (Ed.), *Consciousness: Brain and states of awareness and mysticism* (pp. 63-67). New York: Simon & Schuster.

Fielden, K. (2003). *Disordered solutions*. Unpublished.

Flood, R. L. (1999). *Rethinking the fifth discipline: Learning within the unknowable.* New York: Routledge.

Goodenough, U., & Woodruff, P. (2001). Mindful virtue, mindful reverence. *Zygon, 36*(4), 585-595.

Haynes, J. (2001). Inquiring organizations and tacit knowledge. *AMCIS2001*, 1544-1547.

Hildreth, P. M., & Kimble, C. (2002). The duality of knowledge. *Information Research, 8*(1). Retrieved September 26, 2004, from *http://InformationR.net/ir/8-1/paper142.html*

Kurtz, C. F., & Snowden, D. J. (2003). The new dynamics of strategy: Sense-making in a complex-complicated world. *IBM Systems Journal,* Fall, 1-23.

Langer, E. J. (2000). Mindful learning. *Current Issues in Psychological Science, 9*(6), 220-223.

Novalis (n.d.). Poem translated by Robert Bly. Retrieved September 26, 2004, from *http://www.geocities.com/Paris/Pavilion/1467/files/west_novalis.html*

Novalis (1800). When geometric diagrams. In J. Bly (translator) (1980), *Poems of news of the universe: Twofold consciousness*, Sierra Club, p.42.

Reason, P., & Bradbury, H. (Eds.). (2001). *Handbook of action research: Participative inquiry and practice.* Thousand Oaks, CA: Sage.

Scharmer, C. O. (2000). Presencing: Learning from the future as it emerges: On the tacit dimension of learning revolutionary change. Presented at the *Conference on Knowledge and Intuition*, May, Helsinki, Finland.

Snowden, D. J. (2002). Complex acts of knowledge: Paradox and descriptive self-awareness. Special Edition of the *Journal of Knowledge Management, 6*(2), 1-13.

Waddock, S. (2001). Integrity and mindfulness: Foundations of corporate citizenship. In J. Andriof & M. McIntosh (Eds.), *Perspectives on corporate citizenship.* Sheffield, UK: Greenleaf.

Wheatley, M. (2001a). Listening. *Berkana Institute Writings.* Retrieved September 26, 2004, from *http://www.berkana.org/resources/listening.hmtl*

Wheatley, M. (2001b). Partnering with confusion and uncertainty. *Shambala Sun. http://www.margaretwheatley.com/articles/partneringwithconfusion.html*

Zukav, G. (1989). *The seat of the soul.* New York: Simon & Schuster Inc.

Chapter XII

Wise Organizations?

Chauncey Bell
Bell & Associates, Business Design for Innovation (BABDI),
California, USA

Abstract

In seeking wisdom, the first step is silence; the second, listening; the third, remembering; the fourth, practicing; the fifth teaching others. Solomon Ibn Gabirol, Jewish Poet and Philosopher (c. 1021-1058)

"There is no use trying," said Alice; "one can't believe impossible things." "I dare say you haven't had much practice," said the Queen. "When I was your age, I always did it for half an hour a day. Why, sometimes I've believed as many as six impossible things before breakfast." Lewis Carroll, Alice in Wonderland

This chapter explores the ways that wisdom and wise action appear in the work of organizations and asks how systems can be designed to support that. Building on C. West Churchman's thought experiment with five philosophers about how to improve the design of systems, the author asks and brings fresh answers to the questions, "What is wisdom?" and "What is wisdom in organizations?" The author offers a series of six brief reflections about foundations that he believes can make the design of systems that support people in acting wisely far easier to do. The chapter concludes with a case example of a system illustrating many of the chapter's themes and specific recommendations for IT designers about how to think from the chapter's suggestions. The author hopes to build a richer background for IT designers, leading to systems that do a better job of supporting people in the wise exercise of their responsibilities in all kinds of organizations.

Introduction

In this chapter, I want to help put a richer background in place to support the work of IT designers. I hope that an examination of wisdom may inform those who have the ambition, or are charged with, designing and building software systems, and lead to the development of systems that do a better job of supporting people in the wise exercise of their responsibilities in all kinds of organizations. The subject is too big for a chapter in a book, but perhaps with the following I can inspire, suggest some foundations, suggest directions for exploration, and, at the same time, point out some goofy interpretations that may be adjusted or altered.

In his exploration of the idea of designing inquiring systems, C. West Churchman (1968) challenged himself to invent a basis for building systems that support human action more effectively:

"Instead of just asking the traditional questions of how human minds come to learn from experience, [I] asked how one could design a system that would learn from its experience in some 'optimal fashion.' My plan was to translate some of the historical texts in the theory of knowledge into modern systems terminology, by assuming that the authors were discussing the components of a system design...I was struck again [while studying Leibniz] by the fact that in his approach to the inquiring system he was insisting that a concept of the whole system was essential in understanding how each 'part' worked...Now in these days of rather intense study of systems and their management, few seem in the least concerned about...the characteristics of the whole system in any but a very narrow sense. If Leibniz was right, then modern theories of system design and managerial control are sadly lacking in their reasoning." (pp. v-vi)

I am a designer of business habits. I design ways that human beings— in explicit or tacit collaboration with others—do things to shape their futures by adjusting or changing their habits. Mostly, I work in large institutions. In the process of building new working habits in a number of industries over the years, I have designed and led the development of several complex software systems.

We human beings are creatures of habit, and habits are deeply relevant to the question of wisdom. Even before we notice we are doing it, we act out of structures in which we are predisposed to act in particular ways—ways that are shaped by habits of thought, word, and deed. Most of the time, people pay little attention to the way that acting in habitual and unexamined ways shapes our world. I have for many years been interested in ways of thinking and acting that allow me and my clients to look beneath the world's neatly ordered stories about why and how people do the things they do. Further, because the construction of new habits always involves breaking or reshaping old habits, I also study how to intervene in old habits. As the reader will see, these matters are deeply relevant to the subject of designing and building systems that support wise action in organizations.

The chapter is organized into five parts followed by a short conclusion.

1. In *What is Wisdom?* we begin by exploring what we mean by that word and the implications of setting out in pursuit of it.

2. In *What About Wisdom in an Organization?* we do the same with *organizations*, asking questions about what happens to people when they work together in organizations.

3. In *Churchman's Gathering of Philosophers*, I turn to a series of reflections on the philosophical traditions in which C. West Churchman gathered five philosophers to help him in his work and open an exploration of what those traditions tell us that could be important for the job of IT designers.

4. *Preparing the Way for Wisdom in Organizations* offers a set of reflections about underpinnings, or conditions, in which wisdom can be cultivated and exercised in organizational settings.

5. A *Well-Tooled Investment Management Process* sketches a case example of design, implementation, the underlying logic of a set of practices and supporting tools for investment management in large organizations, and makes a series of specific recommendations for systems designers.

What is Wisdom?

For Churchman, *knowledge* bespoke an accumulation of the capacity to act wisely. His interpretation of what would need to be examined in order to develop systems that engender wise action was remarkable. Courtney (2001) tells us that Churchman saw knowledge as at once *collection, activity,* and *potential*:

1. Deeply connected to action, "a vital force, which makes an enormous difference in the world," in the midst of action, or as "potential for action";

2. Dynamic, as one of knowledge is able "to learn as circumstances change";

3. Somehow deeply connected to ethics and morality; and

4. In some way requiring the actor to break with rationalist scientific traditions and become entangled in one's own feelings and thought processes. (p. 22)

In this chapter, we want to interpret wisdom as the substrate of what Churchman was observing—the *base metal* if you will. We will explore the construction of wisdom and its appearance in enterprises so that when it comes time to cultivate or accumulate wise action, we have explored what that is and where it comes from.

Looking in *http://www.dictionary.com*, we find wise defined as "Having the ability to discern or judge what is true, right, or lasting; sagacious: a wise leader."[2] The behavior of organizations,[3] and of people working in organizations, seems at first glance to be a good place to observe everything but wise behaviors. Something about the notion of a wise organization is oxymoronic, like *a deafening silence*. Why are organizations not automatically bastions of wisdom? After all, a whole lot of people should be smarter than any one of us, right? Our experience with the behavior of people in organizations tells us that this logic doesn't work reliably.

Let us first turn our attention more to the question of what we mean when we say *wise* or *wisdom*. Think back to an interaction you had at some moment in your life with someone you consider wise. Think about what happened before, during, and after your saying to yourself, or to another, "That is wise," or the equivalent. Here are three examples of my own, the first personal and the second and third institutional. See how your example is similar to and different from these examples:

1.   During our teens, 20s, and into our 30s, my younger brother and I were not close. He is two and a half years younger and on coming into adulthood, he concluded that I was not interested in listening to him or learning from him. For my part, I carried forward one of those standard older brother irritations with the *too-full-of-himself* younger brother. As a result, when we were together at family affairs, we would be found at opposite ends of the room, and we did not speak between such events. Unbeknownst to me, as he came into his thirties, my brother had shared with our mother his yearning for a relationship with me. In the spring of 1984, my wife suddenly became very ill, lost the child with whom she was nearly at term in her pregnancy, and found herself at death's door. In that moment, my mother called my brother and said to him, "I know that you have wanted a relationship with your brother. He is in trouble and he needs you. If you want that relationship, figure out how to drop everything and go and be beside him immediately, where he is sitting in the hospital praying and waiting to see what will happen with his wife." He followed her suggestion, and, in the ensuing weeks, our relationship transformed.

2.   Perhaps some of you reading this are familiar with the "Iron Ring" that Canadian Engineers wear on the fifth finger of their right hands. The ceremony in which the ring is delivered to a young engineer about to graduate from engineering school, called the "Ritual of the Calling of an Engineer" was invented early in the 1900s by the engineering professors Herbert Haultain and Rudyard Kipling after a railway bridge to link Winnipeg, Manitoba, and Moncton, New Brunswick twice collapsed while under construction, over the course of 10 years, at a human cost of 85 lives and untold other damage. An inquiry revealed that the collapses resulted from errors in judgment by the bridge's engineers. Haultain and Kipling invented the ritual to alter Canadian engineers' sense of their responsibilities and their experience of the realities of their profession. Graduating new engineers are told, "The ring itself symbolizes the pride we have in our profession while, at the same time, reminds us of our humility." The humility is cemented into the memories of those engineers by the fact that the rings were originally crafted from the iron of the bridge that collapsed.[4]

3.   A decade ago, I was working on the management practices at one of the world's largest copper mines, operating more than two miles up, and at the end of one day, a colleague of mine arrived back from the smelter in a terrible mood. A young man he had met and formed a small friendship with had died during the day when a huge oven belched a cloud of toxic gas while he was walking across the top of it. I asked my colleague many questions about the accident, and here is what we pieced together. This had happened before. I don't remember the numbers, but let us say there had been three deaths over the previous four or five years. The conditions in which the belching occurred were understood by the engineers but could not be predicted or stopped in any way that the engineers could figure out. The engineers involved were skillful, well-educated, and dedicated. All of the deaths recorded under these circumstances were of young workers. I suggested to my colleague that he discuss with the responsible engineers and managers the advisability of a new work practice to the effect that young workers would not go onto the top of this oven without being accompanied by an older worker. In the discussion, some older workers acknowledged that they sometimes had a weird sense about when not to be on top of the oven, a sense that they obeyed, although they did not even know how to describe it. The new work practice was instituted immediately and without further discussion.

Using only these few examples as a point of departure, what can we begin to say about wisdom? Here are some of the elements that I think are essential:

1.   When we enter into a conversation about wisdom and wise action, one of our central concerns is to intervene in some set of current behaviors, to bring about possible futures that will not otherwise happen, and to lead people away from other futures that would be better avoided. I am grateful to James Gosling (Sun Microsystems, inventor of Java) for introducing me to the use of the word *goofy* for pointing to situations in which sincere, otherwise intelligent people behave in ways that are wildly inconsistent with their ambitions, declarations, and/or capabilities. A whole lot of behavior in organizations, including much of what we call bureaucratic behavior, is goofy.

2.   Wisdom is born in a concern for action to take care of things that matter to people, and it is fundamentally connected to human bodies and language. Wisdom is something that we ascribe after some actions are taken in response to some set of circumstances that we find in our world. The actions can be of word or deed, but they are not purely cognitive actions.

3.   Some change, or learning, or new adaptation is possible in the moment of such actions. Wise people have their attention on different things than those who are primarily absorbed in everyday activities. Before the actions, there was a continuity of circumstances, but in the moment of action, the whole world changes. Deep caring and solidarity is evidenced in the way that the wise party acts to take care of things that matter to the futures of the other party.

4.   Wisdom happens in the right kinds of conversations and practices and in the right kinds of communities. It is not a solitary occupation. Buddhist monks who spend years or even decades apparently alone and silent are participating in conversations that have been going on for generations.

5.   The wise party in an event of wisdom is using the moment of change to illuminate, emphasize, and expand some human ethical values. Wisdom is about getting the best out of individuals and communities of people and inventing futures and relationships from a new expanded point of departure. To be wise is to be able to observe deep and abiding stabilities and regularities in the world. We are each born unable to care for ourselves; the sun comes up every morning and goes down every night; each of us will die, and we do not know or control the moment of our death. At the same time, to be wise *in action* is more about changes than it is about these regularities that are the foundations of wisdom.

6.   At the moment of the intervention (about which we will subsequently say, "That was wise"), it is not clear that the intended beneficiary of the wisdom actually has the qualities, virtues, or skills that are called forth by the wise action. The wise speaker or actor is, in effect, making a bet that the other parties have those qualities, virtues, or skills as possibilities, is inviting those parties to commit themselves to learn and grow, and is inventing a future out of that invention and invitation.

Now, for a moment, before we go on in our exploration of wisdom and wisdom in organizations, let us consider the alternative. Not all opportunities for wise action produce reinvented relationships, transformed professions, or lives saved. We have all spent countless hours observing and participating in conversations in which people were communicating with each other, but the actions that bring the moment of wise action were missing:

•   Someone declares responsibility for a matter of concern.

•   Someone proposes, offers, or requests new actions.

•   Someone criticizes the results of our historic actions as being below what we are capable of.

What do we observe instead of wisdom? People immobilized in the moment of possible action; people repeating standard actions from the past; people in private conversations of intentions, but not in action.

The moment of a possibility of wisdom is a moment in which people are called to respond to some situation with integrity and authenticity, stepping outside of traditional ways of observing the situation, entering a domain in which they put themselves at risk of being ridiculed or assessed negatively by the community of their peers. In this regard, my colleague Guillermo Wechsler reminds me that this conversation about wisdom is also a conversation about a human tragedy—about the enormous numbers of intelligent caring people who are coupled together in the wrong ways—having organized themselves to continue their lives along paths of behavior that are recurrently unproductive, self-defeating, or, worse, that literally produce damage to the lives involved.

Finally along these lines, a deep look into the question of wisdom will also show us that sometimes it is better to be silent. Sometimes we call someone wise after we see that they have "smelled" a tragedy coming, and then let it happen, thereby bringing hidden emotions to the fore, unfreezing the situation, accepting the consequences, and building out of that with relentless intention. Sometimes it is wiser to be patient and wait, let things happen, and deal with the ensuing mess.

Then we need to conclude that wisdom is paradoxical, contradictory, controversial, and sometimes vexing. It does not follow the kinds of rules under which we build stable recurrent practices or systems. Think about how we understand the roles of managers and leaders in enterprises today. Professor John Kotter[5] (1990), Harvard Business School Professor and expert on leadership, tells us that:

"... the pioneers who invented modern management ... were trying to produce consistent results on key dimensions expected by customers, stockholders, employees, and other organizational constituencies, despite the complexity caused by large size, modern technologies, and geographic dispersion. ... Leadership is very different. It does not produce consistency and order, as the word itself implies. It produces movement. Throughout the ages, individuals who have been seen as leaders have created change, sometimes for the better, and sometimes not." (p. 4)

Building on top of the claim that we should understand wisdom as associated with actions responding to circumstances we encounter, we can add one more distinction at the beginning of this exploration. I propose we distinguish three *levels* or *orders* of wisdom to observe from:

1. *Level One Wisdom* has to do with learning from mistakes, finding ways to eliminate waste, inventing shortcuts, the like. Continuous improvement programs set up the conditions for this level. Finding ways of doing more with less is an example of the kind of result of this level of wisdom.

2. *Level Two Wisdom* is what is needed for producing discontinuous changes. Instead of learning from your mistakes or eliminating waste, you invent circumstances in which particular mistakes or wastes cannot happen. *Poka-yoke* is a Japanese expression that originated in the Toyota Production System that means a way of eliminating mistakes by design. Simple mechanical examples are the throttles on railway trains that stop the train if continuous pressure is not placed on them or switches for dangerous equipment that stop the equipment if the operator's hand leaves the switch before a hand can come into contact with the equipment.

3. *Level Three Wisdom* is where I will speak about philosophical breakthroughs and reinvention of social realities. Such wisdom creates alternative interpretations of what is possible and builds new discourses in which to observe changes. The Toyota Production System, an example, creates a kind of mass production in which each car is customizable as it moves down the production line. It is less expensive

to put quality into a production line than it is to leave it out, the absence of inventories helps, rather than hindering the process of producing, and in which the place to put the final authority for determining when the production line needs to stop for process repairs is in the hands of the lowest employees on the totem pole.

Wisdom is not something that lands on the planet automatically like moonlight; it belongs to the world of intentional human action, not to accident, and it has been the subject of intense attention for millennia.[6] To call someone or something wise is to make an historical *assessment*[7] that we ascribe to particular behaviors within specific traditions and structures at particular moments of time. We cultivate the capacity to make that assessment within the communities that ascribe wisdom to particular behaviors. Human beings live uncertain existences. We live with historical possibilities, facts, courage, and to navigate in our worlds we make judgments and interpretations to underpin our actions. As we invent meaning and actions for ourselves, we invent assessments like *wise* (and standards for judging what we mean by them) when we need them for preparing a space of action. Whom shall we turn to in the moment of a particular difficulty? Why, someone wise in the matters at hand, of course!

What About Wisdom in an Organization?

Now let us turn our attention to wisdom in organizations, per se. The first thing that we will do is to introduce several questions and foundations that we will employ for thinking with you about wisdom, mostly without resolving them.

Do you admire the way that the bank handles your questions, the supermarket manages your experience, the dealer handles the maintenance of your car, or manufacturers of things you buy handle your questions and suggestions? We may admire the wisdom of someone in dealing with his children, spouse, or even colleagues or employees in his company, but a wise organization? Can you remember a real sustained experience with an organization that learns from its mistakes, as Churchman dreamed?

Even those small community and fraternal organizations over which we might think we have the greatest control are often sources of epic frustration. I listen to my neighbor: "You will not *believe* what just happened at the neighborhood association meeting." (Yes, I will.) Does *anyone* admire the way our governments interact with us? Take a deep breath and prepare yourself to stand patiently in line and wait. When, as does occasionally happen, we have the experience of someone in an organization listening carefully and acting with alacrity in response to our request, this is an occasion for a celebration. "A miracle happened!" My wife will begin a report of that rare event: an organization acting wisely.

Some institutions produce disproportionately large numbers of people adjudged *wise* in their communities. Consider, for example, the histories of the great religious institutions of the East and West, the institution of science itself, and the institution of medicine down through the ages. These are not the only examples by any means. Can you think of other examples of your own? Why does this happen? And why are these histories so uneven? Why great wisdom at some moments and behaviors that we would call stupid, self-serving, or even criminal at others?

Churchman (1968) speaks particularly of his admiration for the institution of science and points directly at the revolutionary nature of the life of that institution:

"The inspiration of Singer's story was his account of the history of science, one episode after another in which complacency was shattered, by Copernicus, by Newton, by Einstein, by Heisenberg. One 'ideal' of progress is to create the 'optimal' shatterer of old tablets, a shatterer that does not simultaneously shatter all chance of further progress in the cooperative ideals. Mood plays its part in all this process: The mood of the cooperative ideals is sanguine, phlegmatic, comic; the mood of the shattering ideal is filled with despair and joy, is tragic." (p. 215)

Sometimes organizations exhibit behaviors we call wise, and sometimes they do that over long periods of time. We can find examples of moments in which leaders set organizations on paths that produced luminous results for the people in and served by those organizations. Consider, for a big example, the founding of the United States of America. This country also provides ample examples of goofy behaviors, for example, in a long history of supporting oppressive dictatorships around the world while we have simultaneously kept our borders open to new citizens and espoused freedom, equal opportunity, and governance under the rule of law.

The point of organizations has to do with what we can do together that we cannot do alone. Working in organizations, people can do things the scope and scale of which is not possible for individual people or even for people gathered together in other assembly. It is in what we call *organizations* that we human beings constitute the capacity to deliver products and services of an extraordinary variety on local and global scales. Effective organizations create value for their clients and customers, focus on expanding possibilities for them, and demonstrate commitments to cultivating authentic styles. When those characteristics appear together, we create space for people to be wise in that culture.

Here is one source of confusion in the matter. Organizations are not human unities; they are unities *constituted of and by* human beings. Frequently, we describe the behavior of organizations with analogies, metaphors, and assessments that are more properly applied to human beings. I will do that in this chapter. For example, we can, with validity and to good effect, characterize organizations as existing in or having emotional states or moods.

Nevertheless, I insist that humans and organizations are different kinds of beings. The temptation to anthropomorphize organizations—to speak of them as collective human beings—is not valid and will mislead us in this conversation. Organizations, per se, are not capable of being wise. We need to look to human beings, not the organizations in which they work, for wisdom. The central reason for this is that wisdom comes from a capacity made up of other capacities that are dependent on the existence of human will and intellect, the emotions, and other structures, all of which require the presence of a human body.[8] *People* sometimes are wise; *organizations* are not.

Churchman pursued the question of how an organization could learn from its experience. What does this mean? I propose that it means, for a start, that people in such an organization would continuously adjust the organization to the concerns of client/ constituents and to changes in the world. The organization will be continuously reinvented in ways that encourage people to listen to each other, bring people together to be responsible for things that matter in the world, and so forth.

If we look closely at any moment of organizational reinvention, we will see that one or more people are speaking, guiding the institution into a new future. We may call these phenomena one of the attributes of *wisdom in organizations*. When this happens repeatedly over time, if we look closely, we will see that the institution has organized itself around a set of rules and practices (sometimes set out explicitly in documents of its governance and more often embodied in a common sense shared by those responsible for the organization) that govern its operation by (1) specifying who will occupy certain roles of responsibility in which they promise to take care of the future of the organization and (2) specifying who will declare those roles obsolete over time and see that they are changed. I think that families often are more reliable than traditional business organizations for taking care of these particularly important roles over long periods.

We speak about wisdom in many contexts, especially in ethical and spiritual domains, in spiritual, religious, and community leaders, in the arts and the helping professions, in commerce, and even in politics. We also find people speaking of *wise* executives, salespeople, or even sometimes criminals —people in roles in which the purpose of their actions is the economic, political, or social benefit they derive from their actions. When we ascribe wise behavior to those in such instrumental roles, we have crossed a line. We can ascribe wisdom to players in instrumental roles, but we should be careful when we do so. Is the experienced salesman wise in recommending to us options on a vehicle when he will sell it to us and then take a profit from the sale? Remember that the slang name for members of certain criminal gangs is *wise guys*. Wisdom is deeply connected to ethics; we will explore this more carefully later in the chapter.

I will not deal with the kind of wisdom that is merely synonymous with smart or intelligent. Significantly, organizations that are structured or managed in ways that do not encourage (or permit) relationships among its people that are more than exclusively instrumental (e.g., relationships that are not connected to the purposes of the business) will be unable to produce any but the shallowest kinds of wisdom, or being wise in such organizations will simply not be relevant.

Inevitable Goofiness

Over time, all organizations become rigid, fall out of touch with the worlds they were constituted to serve, and behave in goofy or sometimes even criminal fashions. As time passes, every organization accumulates rigidities and practices that lead, inexorably, to these kinds of behaviors. How does this happen? (If we look closely, we will see that organizations that are successful over long periods are periodically reconstructed, sometimes violently, sometimes quietly.)

One of the central mechanisms for accumulating rigidity has this remarkably simple and apparently benign structure of action:

1. Something goes wrong.
2. Those responsible act to repair the situation.
3. At the same time, those responsible put in place mechanisms to prevent the same error from happening again.
4. They do this with rules, new procedures, changes in roles, and so forth.

Ronald Heifetz (1996) points well to the heart of the matter in *Leadership Without Easy Answers:*

"Living systems seek equilibrium. They respond to stress by working to regain balance. If the human body becomes infected by bacteria, the system responds to fight off the infection and restore health...These responses to disequilibrium are the product of evolutionary adaptations that transformed into routine problems what were once nearly overwhelming threats. Looking backward in time, we marvel at the abundant success of these adaptations and the breadth of exploited opportunities. Yet we tend to notice the successes and innovations more than the failures. By definition, the successes survive while the failures disappear. The roads of evolution are strewn with the bones of creatures that could not thrive in the next environment." (p. 28)

We are saying that organizations accumulate rigidities as a consequence of the same thing that underlies their faculty as a place for generating wise behavior—they are made up of human beings. What happens in an organization is a lot like what happens when a patient of modern Western medicine has a bunch of prescriptions: the remedies begin to interact badly with each other and produce second and third-order side effects. In organizational life, if we look carefully over time, we will see that as time passes the majority of our prescriptions are dealing with the unintentional side effects of other previously applied prescriptions.

The general situation in human organizations is the same as the case of medicine. The behaviors of the people in the organization are habitual. When we install repairs and modifications to avert future occurrences of an error, if we look carefully, we will see that the conditions that led to the error are often preserved so that the difficulty will arise again but next time in new clothing so that we will not recognize it. Over time, the accumulation of a propensity to goofiness in organizations is inevitable, and periodic reconstruction is required.

Organizations and Authentic Ways of Being

One of Churchman's central questions, repeated often in his work, concerned the interplay of the parts of a system and the whole system, understood as a unity. Let me start a new approach to this question. In this chapter, we will come back to this question repeatedly, asking first the question, "who is observing the unity, and on what basis does a person interpret that as a unity?" At this moment, I want to start this process by introducing the notion of authenticity, which I take principally from the philosopher Martin Heidegger.[9] Heidegger was convinced that it is impossible for human beings to make good sense of our lives except in the context of a process of continuous reinterpretation of our entire situatedness in the worlds in which we dwell. I think this is more than analogy to the question that Churchman posed; it is a foundational distinction. The question, as I said a moment ago, is this: who is observing the unity? Those who are considering a system and its relationship to ourselves, our work, and our worlds—that is, ourselves—cannot make sense of who we are as observers and speakers unless we have a very specific kind of understanding ourselves. In the process of constructing that understanding, we must have avoided exactly the same trap that Churchman fears—the decontextualization of ourselves—not at the level of the system but at the level of the individual human beings who are conceiving the system and of the individual human beings who will be the beneficiaries of the system.

We understand ourselves well, Heidegger tells us, *only in the midst of our worlds,* and not abstractly (Dreyfus, 1991, p. 10ff). As we conduct ourselves in our worlds, we are *thrown* (taken, or swept away, by our normal ways of being) to *inauthentic* ways of being. Ironically, those inauthentic ways of being provide us with signals inviting us to construct ourselves authentically.

There are two principal inauthentic ways of being. The first is *falling* into normal everyday busyness—coping with our anxieties and problems by *throwing ourselves into* activities that are familiar to us from our histories and experience, activities that we hope will suppress or tranquilize our anxieties because we remember that they have worked for us in the past. The second is becoming frozen in fearful patterns of conforming to accepted everyday behavioral norms. Can you see that organizations—with all of the kinds of pressures that we tend to find there to follow rules, not rock boats, not offend people, and so forth, are very often effective places for producing inauthentic ways of being? In contrast, authentic being confronts, in a public way, its anxieties and concerns, and invents new ways of being and acting in the midst of the messes of everyday life. You can see examples of this characteristic in each of the wisdom examples I gave at the beginning of this chapter. Can you think of examples from your own life?

Heidegger (1962) characterized humans as having a way of being the central focus of which is *the issue of being*:

"... to work out the question of Being adequately, we must make an entity — the inquirer (sic) — transparent in his own being. The very asking of this question is an entity's mode of Being; and as such it gets its essential character from what is inquired about—

namely, Being. This entity which each of us is himself and which includes inquiring as one of the possibilities of being, we shall denote by the term 'Dasein.'" (p. 27)

Working in modern organizations may not be a healthy practice for building the kind of observer who can help Churchman with his inquiry. Most of us cannot avoid working in organizations of some size; none of us can avoid interacting with organizations. John Kotter (1990) concludes that training as a manager or executive in a (Western) corporation is not good for building wisdom. (He speaks of leadership, but if you listen carefully, you will see that what he calls leadership is a kind of wisdom-on-the-hoof.)

"For the vast majority of people today, including most of those with leadership potential, on-the-job experiences actually seem to undermine the development of attributes needed for leadership. ... managerial careers in many corporations produce individuals who are remarkably narrow in focus and understanding, moderately risk averse, weak in communications skills, and relatively blind to the values of others. They produce people who know little about competitive business strategies, who have limited credibility, and who know more about how to play games with a budget than how to celebrate the real achievements of their people.

Four characteristics of managerial careers seem to be particularly important in producing these [negative] results. First, these careers usually begin in centralized and specialized hierarchies and, as such, in jobs that are narrow in scope and tactical in focus. ... [Second,] promotions in many firms are almost entirely up a narrow, vertical hierarchy. ... [T]he knowledge and relationship base of successful people is often extremely narrow; they understand only one aspect of the business and only one group of people in their corporation. ...[Third,] moving through jobs every twelve to eighteen months, these people rarely have an opportunity to learn anything in depth, and never see the longer-term consequences of their actions   [Fourth, and] perhaps most damaging of all... all too often, people are rewarded almost exclusively for short-term results. As a result, most individuals focus on the process that produces those results-- management. This is especially true for ambitious young people. Because of this, they learn little about leadership. Since developing the leadership potential of others is also not a short-term activity, senior executives are strongly encouraged by such reward systems not to invest time in such an activity. The overall result can be devastating." (p. 119ff)

The question and reflection that I would like to bring to the reader at this moment in the conversation is this. While on the one hand there are obvious reasons that someone could be interested in knowledge or the cultivation of wisdom as Churchman was, on the other hand, the cultivation of wisdom and knowledge is not a mainstream concern in organizational life today. What was it about Churchman's interests that took him in this direction?

Churchman's Gathering of Philosophers

Churchman gathered five philosophers to help him in his work. What was he doing when he did that? What can an exploration of those traditions tell us about what could be important from the work of philosophers for the job of IT designers? Many computer scientists and IT professionals read at least some philosophy; few study it broadly, and few write about it. Churchman put five philosophers into a thought exercise, in which he asked and answered questions—inquired— about how systems might participate in the creation of knowledge.[10]

Here is my next question: *What was Churchman doing with his five philosophers?* Why did he bring them to the conversation? Why these five—Gottfried Wilhelm von Leibniz, John Locke, Immanuel Kant, Georg Wilhelm Friedrich Hegel, and Edgar A. Singer, Jr.— and not others? What did he intend we understand in the conversation? How did he intend to alter us, his readers, and students with this thought experiment of his?

There are various ways that we can interpret what he was doing with his five philosophers. I propose the following interpretations for the reader's consideration. I warn in advance that I am not going to claim that any one is right. The point here is to go beyond the standard conversation about using each as emblematic of a member of taxonomy of organizational types. I invite an exploration in which readers get their own answers.

1.   Perhaps each philosopher is symbolic of a particular *style of inquiry* that we can see was important in that philosopher's work and life. Churchman, the argument goes, saw certain virtues and vices of each of the styles he characterized with the help of the philosophers, and he uses their names to compare and contrast these styles. In this sense, the name of each is iconic, representing that style. Leibniz stands for *analytic deduction*, Locke for *consensual induction*, and so forth.

2.   Perhaps the first four are foils for Singer, Churchman's teacher, whose answers Churchman may have preferred for the questions of how to productively inquire. The role of each of the first four, in this sense, is to help Churchman show dimensions of Singer's propositions that would otherwise be cumbersome to show. In this sense, the name of each of the four stands for an era of incomplete thinking about how to constitute human enterprise, and Singer, though no wiser necessarily than the others, stands on their shoulders, just as Churchman stands on Singers'.

3.   Perhaps, as a trained philosopher himself, Churchman gathered around him a gaggle of philosophers to provide a *space of conversation* through the implicit dialogue, in which certain deep questions could be revealed more richly than they might have been in a straight textual description. In this sense, the entire sensibility of the work of each philosopher is important, and their names point us to the concerns of each in the times in which they worked on those concerns.

4.   Perhaps Churchman used the device of introducing an argument among the five philosophers as a way of inviting his students into a richer investigation of the philosophical literature as a foundation for thinking about the design of systems.

5. Finally, perhaps Churchman—not fully resolved himself about the place of inquiry in the operation of organizations—was using the five philosophers' work to inquire into the nature of inquiry in purposeful social interchange.

Churchman chose five philosophers to bring to the party, introduced them and certain aspects of their work to us, and then, through his writings, invited us to go on in conversation with him and with them for as long as the questions he was asking yielded fruit. He did not invite other philosophers whose work we can guess he knew. Why did he do these things? I propose that insufficient attention has been given to this question and invite conversation about it. I do not find in the literature much in the way of additional exploration along the lines that Churchman was exploring.

Let us ask now about a series of themes we can discern in the work of those philosophers Churchman gathered around him. I think that these same themes appear in his questions about knowledge and systems. In the following, I invite you to explore with me three concerns that all six philosophers (I include Churchman himself) grappled with. I will call these concerns (1) the ambitions of philosophy; (2) the problem of what a thing is, objectivity, and the problem of the observer; and (3) the problems of ethics, morality, and value. Obviously, in the limits of this chapter, I will only touch on these questions, but I do so in the spirit of offering a provocation—an invitation to the reader to consider more deeply what Churchman may have intended with his gathering of philosophers. The reader will notice that in order to do this, I have assembled my own group of philosophers with the help of Anthony Kenny,[11] and that my group includes some new faces.

The Ambitions of Philosophy

Churchman, a trained philosopher, did not attempt to avoid standing in the middle of traditional philosophical ambitions as he worked in his adopted country—the field of computer systems. My impression is that we can appreciate some of Churchman's thinking by looking at the ambitions of the field of philosophy as a whole. Werner Ulrich, a student of Churchman who is now a professor in his own right, quotes his teacher in "An Appreciation of C. West Churchman," talking about Churchman's (1968) concern with the ignorance of the investigator in critical matters, and the centrality of the unity of the system as a whole: "How can we design improvement in large systems without understanding the whole system, and if the answer is that we cannot, how is it possible to understand the whole system?" (p. 3).

Ulrich (1999) explores Churchman's conviction:

"The systems idea, provided we take it seriously, urges us to recognize our constant failure to think and act rationally in a comprehensive sense. Mainstream systems literature somehow always manages to have us forget the fact that a lack of comprehensive rationality is inevitably part of the conditio humana. Most authors seek to demonstrate how and why their systems approaches extend the bounds of rational explanation or

design accepted in their fields. West Churchman never does. To him, the systems idea poses a challenge to critical self-reflection. It compels him to raise fundamental epistemological and ethical issues concerning the systems planner's claim to rationality. He never pretends to have the answers; instead, he asks himself and his readers a lot of thoroughly puzzling questions."

Now we turn to Anthony Kenny (1997), who tells us that this struggle of Churchman's implicitly *belongs to philosophy*:

"The ambition of philosophy is to achieve truth of a kind which transcends what is merely local and temporal; but not even the greatest of philosophers have come near to achieving that goal in any comprehensive manner. There is a constant temptation to minimize the difficulty of philosophy by redefining the subject in such a way that its goal seems more attainable ...even the greatest philosophers of the past propounded doctrines which we can see—through hindsight of the other great philosophers who stand between them and ourselves—to be profoundly mistaken. This should be taken not as reflecting on the genius of our great predecessors, but as an indication of the extreme difficulty of the discipline...But we philosophers must resist [the] temptation [to understate the difficulty]; we should combine unashamed pride in the loftiness of our goal with undeluded modesty about the poverty of our achievement." (p. 368)

Thus, this central question of Churchman's and something important about the form in which he held the question, he shared, in important ways, with philosophy as a tradition. He knew it was a central question to be confronted by any who would dare to think *how to think* in the domain in which he had chosen to work, and he knew that it would not be easily answered.

What is a Thing, Objectivity, and the Observer

Churchman and his five philosophers were profoundly aware of the danger of assuming the validity of prevailing common senses about the nature of things, objectivity, and the role and capacity of any observer to observe objectively. Philosophers' concerns over these questions have never abated over the last two millennia. To speak in a way that transcends the local about the interplay of designers, organizations, and systems of things supporting people working in organizations, philosophy teaches us that we need to stand on good interpretations about what these *things* are—people, things, and gatherings of people. To address the question of how organizations might better learn from experience, Churchman was looking for answers to these questions.

Churchman gave center stage to something he called *inquiring*. What did he mean by this? Who inquires? About what? He was particularly interested in the *how* part of the question. I take it that he was not calling primarily for a process composed of questions and answers, nor for a narrow questioning style, but instead was looking for something

broader—particularly, I suspect, inquiring as a style of openness to different interpretations about the world and the actions we are taking in it. And, he was surfacing the
problem of the observer and objectivity. On the other hand, he was calling for the
invention of processes, rather than questioning the nature and role of the human being
in the center of the puzzle, as we saw Heidegger doing earlier in this chapter. My opinion
is that the absence of this element in his questioning marks a serious weakness in his
overall project of inquiry.

Churchman speaks of constructing effective powers of observation through the application of diversity: "To deal with such connectedness ... Singerian organizations must
deploy UST to go well beyond the bounds of the other four organizational styles, by
bringing in multiple *perspectives* or *worldviews*, and employing a holistic systems
approach in their thinking and decision-making processes" (Courtney, 2001, p. 20).

Courtney goes on to show elements of the richness of what Churchman had in mind—
ethics, spirituality, and aesthetics—and to show Churchman's dissatisfaction with a
strictly scientific orientation:

*"The multiple perspectives approach does not end with the technical, organizational,
and personal perspectives. It also explicitly brings ethics and aesthetics into play.
Many factors in the Industrial Age, the machine metaphor, the desire for "objectivity"
and "rigor" in academic work, modeling social science research on "hard science"
approaches, and the study of "rational man" to the neglect of our "spiritual" being,
have all led to the demise of ethics, morality and aesthetics in decision making today.
As we move into the Information Age, or perhaps the Knowledge Age, we seem to be stuck
with this legacy of neglecting the factors that make us human." (p. 29)*

More than 200 years ago, Kant concluded that the nature of things is inescapably
unknown to us: " 'If we take away the subject space and time disappear; these as
phenomena cannot exist in themselves but only in us.' The nature of things in themselves
is unknown to us" (Kenny, 1997, p. 171).

Arthur Schopenhauer, who followed Kant by a few decades, shifted the place of the
observer in the conversation and put the observer under the microscope in a new
way:

*"The empirical world exists, for the subject, only as representation: 'every object,
whatever its origin, is, as object, already conditioned by the subject, and thus is
essentially only the subject's representation'... The search for the thing-in-itself behind
the representation is futile, so long as we turn our thoughts towards the natural world.
Every argument and every experience leads only to the same final point: the system of
representations, standing like a veil between subject and thing-in-itself. No scientific
investigation can penetrate the veil; and yet it is only a veil, Schopenhauer affirms, a
tissue of illusions which we can, if we choose, penetrate by another means."*

We are not merely the *knowing subject*, but that *we ourselves* are also among those entities we require to know, that *we ourselves are the thing-in-itself*. Consequently, a way *from within* stands open to us to that real inner nature of things to which we cannot penetrate *from without*. [Kenny's emphasis] (Kenny, 1997, p. 212)

At about the same time, others, including Hegel, were moving in the same direction, asking new questions about the observer and how to understand the observer in ways that allow us to responsibly make sense of what he observes.

Churchman, Courtney tells us, puts the Singerian inquirer at a level of extreme abstraction, "above teleological, a grand teleology with an ethical base" (Courtney, 2001, p. 28). We need to give full credit to Churchman for his ambition and the validity of the concerns he brings us, but I am not happy with Churchman's thinking in this regard. Perhaps from his commitment that the observer needs to be looking at systems as a whole, he does something that I regard as a serious mistake and attempts to raise the observer to a lofty position of omniscience. He does not confront the real difficulty at the center of this dilemma.

Singer's better known contemporary Martin Heidegger made important contributions to this discussion that do not appear in Churchman's thought experiment. Following the tradition from Kant, Heidegger distinguished between persons and things and then distinguished further between the ways of being that things are for people when those things are held conceptually and when they are held practically in action. He distinguished between the way of being of things when they are *ready-to-hand*—having a way of being that is experienced in the middle of their use (as in hammering a nail)—and when they are *present-at-hand*—experienced as conceptual or abstract objects *as when knowledge is contained in a database* [my emphasis]. I think this is important when we are considering how to think in regards to building systems.

In Churchman's conversation with his five philosophers, I have the impression that he never escapes the grip of pre-Heideggerian Western analytic philosophy and, under the influence of Singer, moves to ever-more abstract ways of interpreting knowledge, leaving the role of the observer largely unresolved. His worthy ambitions demand more.

The Problem of Ethics, Morality, and Values

Churchman exhorts his readers to put the concerns of ethics, morality, and values in the front rank of their attention, at least alongside rational logic. Courtney (2001) sums up Churchman's understanding of the interplay of knowledge, acting, learning, and moral and ethical values as: "Thus, one might say that knowledge involves the ability to act intelligently and to learn. Wisdom guides knowledgeable actions on the basis of moral and ethical values" (p. 23).

It should be clear from the first and second sections of this chapter that I agree fully with Churchman that the exercise of wisdom and learning are ethical occupations and that architects and designers should put these questions in the center of their concerns. I'll say more about this in the next section of the chapter.

As a provocation, however, I would say that I understand the way that these matters interrelate with each other in a radically different way than does Churchman. Here is how I will put my version of the proposition that Courtney articulates for Churchman just above: People ascribe wisdom and knowledge to actions enacted from embodied structures of ethical behaviors, and learning ensues from repetition of the action together with reflection on those actions and the consequences of the actions.

I will spell out why I say this in the next section of the chapter.

Preparing the Way for Wisdom in Organizations

In this section, I will offer a set of six tiny essays that invite reflection about the construction of the conditions and situations in which wisdom can be cultivated and exercised in organizational settings. The essays are:

- Taking Language and Listening Seriously
- Language-Action and the Constitution of Organizations
- Preparing for Ethical Action
- Learning and Competence
- "Inventing" Waste
- Pain-Free Wisdom?

Taking Language and Listening Seriously

Language, including the misconceptions and confusion that abide in it, underlies everything we understand and know and all our actions. We encounter and invent ourselves in language. What we find desirable and fearsome, our ambitions, doubts, and resignations, the identities in which we make sense of ourselves, those we live and work with, and our worlds, all these live in language. Our problems with things, observers, and ethics all arrive escorted by and clothed in language, and we encounter them only in their clothing, as Schopenhauer pointed out. Heidegger called language "the house of being."

The warp and woof of the tapestry of organizations and the threads that reveal the patterns of that tapestry belong to language. Cars, to take an example, move down assembly lines in the wake of a network of conversations in which an extraordinarily complex set of conversations has set every part of the stage of action, and they move because people are making commitments, to shape, build, sell, and buy. Long before any parts move, design engineers speak instructions telling all concerned how the actors, instruments, and parts will come together into a set of unities that will make sense to all concerned. In operation, production managers lay plans, workers come to work as asked, suppliers deliver materials as promised, and salesmen make offers and customers accept those offers.

All the joys and all the miseries, all the services and all the destruction and waste laid by people working together in organizations begins and is shaped in language. Ethics and values are created, understood or not, passed on, and acted on in language. We speak to each other, and we listen. And, we underestimate, continuously and vastly, the role that language plays in our affairs.

The serious student of wisdom and organizations, I suggest, must put language in the center of his inquiry.

Listening, I propose, is the first prerequisite of wisdom. By the word listening, I point to the biolinguistic process through which we attune ourselves to situations, the concerns of others, our own concerns, and prepare ourselves for action. I distinguish *listening* from hearing. I use the latter word to point to the mechanics of receiving and decoding disturbances in airwaves, signs, and signals in our worlds—receiving data—what most people refer to as listening. The two are related, but the deaf who were not born deaf listen, just as the blind who were not born blind see. What I call to our attention with the term listening is exemplified by what happens to us when we read poetry or attend a great performance and are touched by it. We are altered by the experience of listening. Listening is partially an automatic process that is out of our control, going on continuously in life, while we are awake and asleep, and the process of listening can be affected, as when "we take a walk" "to collect ourselves" before undertaking a difficult conversation to be responsible for the emotional state in which we will be listening to our conversant. Listening happens all the time and not just when we are listening to spoken language. Here is a partial list of situations in which we can observe listening happening:

- Language spoken and written in our native tongues;
- Distinctions in other languages ranging, for example, from moods and music to finance and marketing;
- Gestures and silence, absorbed and interpreted; and
- Brands, icons, images, art, machinery, offices, and other features of our worlds.

To encounter wisdom in a fresh way, that can give grounding for the work of people preparing tools for working in organizations, we need first to prepare ourselves to get closer to language—to observe some things that happen as we speak and listen to each other.

Listen carefully to the following pair of passages by Gemma Corradi Fiumara (1990) in her book *The Other Side of Language*, in which she wrestles with the poverty of listening in our time. Neither she, nor Martin Heidegger, whom she quotes, is easy to read. You may have to read each short passage a few times to catch the heart of what she is saying.

"One is often tempted to maintain that the 'richness' of our inner world possesses a guarantee of existence in itself, and that the 'problem' merely consists in knowing how

to select the words which are best suited to expressing and representing it in a context of consensus. In this way, we may be tempted to believe that words are 'like a grasp that fastens upon the things already in being and held to be in being' (Heidegger, 1971, p. 68)—a grasp which seizes and compresses. In fact, however, the situation is far more complex, demanding and enigmatic than that. The organization of our innerness seems to exist on condition that it is heard, brought out—in effect brought to be born. It is not just a matter of entities lying there waiting to be linguistically seized and organized in the most diversified expressions." (p. 148)

"To pay heed to what the words say is particularly difficult for us moderns, because we find it hard to detach ourselves from the 'at first' of what is common (e.g., from the common sense that strikes us immediately from what is said); and if we succeed for once (in detaching ourselves from the common sense), we relapse all too easily." (p. 130)

Language-Action and the Constitution of Organizations

For the vast majority of the moments of our lives, including in a great proportion of our sleeping hours, we are doing things in language with each other, and language is doing things to us. The opportunity of this topic is that language-action offers a radically improved path to knowing what we are doing as we are speaking. When we speak, we create new interpretations, moods, possibilities, and futures in the bodies and minds of those with whom we are speaking. Therefore, one of the distinctions that will be essential for us is language-action, observing language as communicative *acts*.

The English philosopher John L. Austin (1962) was the first to notice the existence of a class of verbs that he called *performatives* (p. 148)—verbs that, rather than describing actions, perform actions. When someone says "I promise to ...," he is performing the action of promising, not reporting that he will, did, or might promise. It turns out that all human languages contain performatives. For the purpose of designing work in organizations, I distinguish six classes of performatives: *declarations, offers, requests, promises, assessments*, and *assertions*. The most important and interesting thing about these verbs is that, when we look carefully, we can see that it is with these acts that we human beings invent our futures. Very often we don't actually use the words; people make promises all the time without saying "I promise" and make requests even more often without saying "I request" (for example, "The soup needs salt" and "Don't you think that it is cold in here?"). The roles that the major classes of language-acts play in our invention of our futures?

- With *declarations*, we create new distinctions—identities, products, roles, services, companies, names, and so forth—with which to take care of our concerns.
- With *offers*, *requests*, and *promises*, we orchestrate new spaces in which we can take action, and we elicit mutual commitment and coordinated action.
- With assessments, we take stock of our world, evaluate our progress, assure that we are prepared for action, and navigate in our projects and worlds.

- With assertions, we build confidence in our judgments and consistent reliable *coordination*.

Each language action has standard elements which, when recognized, can help guide designers in their specification of systems: speakers, listeners, conditions of satisfaction, time of speaking, time of expected response, time of committed action, and so forth. The implications of Austin's discovery are vast and substantially unrecognized.[12] For example, ask the question, "What makes something be an organization?" Within every culture there are a variety of standard modes of business operation that can be observed (sales activities, billing, and so forth) but underneath all of the variety is a more fundamental core. Whether a business is as simple as an individual sitting on the ground with a pile of fruit for sale or it is a multinational conglomerate, and whether it produces tangible goods in factories, provides janitorial services, or operates entirely "on paper," as in many financial businesses,

"A business is created when a person or group of people declares that they will recurrently make certain classes of offers to some population of customers and that they will satisfy the conditions of those offers (deliver what they promised) in exchange for some offer the customer makes in return, or the fulfillment of some request they may make to the customer."

This definition shows several key aspects of how an enterprise is constructed.

- First, it says that the business is *created by a declaration*. In order to be in business, you have to declare to the appropriate people that you are entering a domain of potential business transactions.
- Second, it says that the business is constituted by *classes of offers*. If you are in the automobile business, you offer to provide automobiles. If you are in the doctor business, you offer to see and treat patients. A single business may have a variety of different classes of offers but without some public declaration of what they are, the business is not defined.
- Third, to be in business, you must be prepared to *satisfy the conditions* of the whole transaction: to make offers, recognize acceptance of those offers by customers, complete the conditions of the offers (by providing goods, services, etc.) and recognize that the customer declares the transaction completed to satisfaction.
- Finally and centrally, a business is distinguished from other kinds of enterprises (e.g., charities and governments) by the fact that there is an explicit *offer in return* from the customer (some form of payment, whether in money or other actions), which is linked to successful completion of the offer made by the business entity.

We can identify these common elements in every business activity we see around the world. Moreover, these structural features of a business belong to how human beings take care of things with each other. The deep structures that we are observing in this conversation have existed since people have been exchanging goods and services, and it is impossible to conceptualize businesses that do not have these underlying structures. In the simplest case, a single individual in verbal communication does them all with customers. In large organizations, each aspect is supported by organizational structures and business processes that have evolved in the ambition to make sure the conditions can be met regularly with a minimum of breakdowns.

Let us take "wise" as an example and look at what it is from the perspective of language-action. Wise, as I said earlier, is an assessment—a judgment or evaluation made by an observer with a particular background, experience, and concerns that shape that judgment. (Examples of assessments: *I am late. The cat is sick. The car is behaving strangely. Your hair is getting long. The project is expensive. The new president is not doing well.*) Assessments are never true or false; they are effective or not. Assessments help us make sense of our worlds, our place and progress in it, and, most important, they prepare us to take action in those worlds. Judgments about the state of affairs in my world or yours invite us to consider actions to take advantage of opportunities or avoid dangers.

To ascribe wisdom to someone or to some action is to make an evaluation, and that evaluation originally comes from the mouth (or fingers, gestures, silence, written words, etc.) of a particular individual.

Not only is wise an assessment, but it is difficult to be wise (perhaps impossible) without skill at distinguishing *assessments* from *assertions*—the class of language action that we call facts—and without the corollary capacity to test assessments by grounding them with facts. (Examples of assertions: *The project is late; 60% of the project deliverables are still incomplete one month before its scheduled end.*) We may make an assessment shared by many others, even in very large populations. However, even if a measured majority of the French people of France think that Americans have no judgment or taste, it is still an assessment and not a fact. People can ground their interpretations by citing facts that defend the judgment. The evaluation—an assessment—and the facts brought forth to *ground* it, which are assertions, are two different kinds of language actions, and they have different purposes.

Assertions—facts that can be observed by a universal witness—are true or false. However, the act of making an assertion—stating a fact—does not invite action, except when for the speaker or a listener, the fact elicits a judgment (assessment) of a shift in the expected future and sets up a condition inviting action. *(Just look at those black clouds! Implied: The clouds are forbidding. It looks like rain is coming. Let's get under cover.)*

Different observers have different assessments about the same phenomena; the source of the difference is that they do not have the same concerns. *(One man's meat is another man's poison. A flat tire for a driver is business for a garage.)*

Turning to the implications of language-action for the design of systems, Fernando Flores and Terry Winograd (1986) outline a three point theory of management and conversation in their book, *Understanding Computers and Cognition,* that shows well many of the features of how software designs could embody the insights we are exploring here:

1. Organizations exist as networks of directives and commissives.[13] Directives include orders, requests, consultations, and offers; commissives include promises, acceptances, and rejections.

2. Breakdowns will inevitably occur, and the organization needs to be prepared. In coping with breakdowns, further networks of directives and commissives are generated.

3. People in an organization (including, but not limited to managers) issue utterances, by speaking or writing, to develop the conversations required in the organizational network. They participate in the creation and maintenance of a process of communication. At the core of this process is the performance of linguistic acts that bring forth different kinds of commitments. (p. 157)

Flores and Winograd (1986) further claim, and I am convinced that they are right, that the classical idea of decision making is not well supported phenomenologically, and we can usefully substitute a notion of "dealing with irresolution" and supporting people in coming to resolution (p. 144ff).

Preparing for Ethical Action

The concern for action is central to the question of wisdom. Even the extraordinarily rigorous contemplative activities frequently found in the practices of wisdom traditions, when carefully examined, will be found to have to do with *getting prepared for taking action.*

At the same time that wisdom has more to do with action and less to do with dry abstraction than many traditions would have us believe, as I said before, Churchman is right about the relationship of wisdom and ethics. Here is Heifetz (1996), again putting the case beautifully in the context of effective (i.e., wise) leaders:

Understandably, scholars who have studied "leadership" have tended to side with the value-free connotation of the term because it lends itself more easily to analytic reasoning and empirical examination. But this will not do for them any more than it will do for practitioners of leadership who intervene in organizations and communities everyday.

"We have to take sides. When we teach, write about, and model the exercise of leadership, we inevitably support or challenge people's conceptions of themselves, their roles, and most importantly their ideas about how social systems make progress on problems. Leadership is a normative concept because implicit in people's notions of leadership are images of a social contract. Imagine the differences in behavior when

people operate with the idea that 'leadership means influencing the community to follow the leader's vision' versus "leadership means influencing the community to face its problems." (p. 14)

"If a leader personally wants to turn away from the difficulty of problems, and so do his constituents, does he exercise leadership by coming up with a fake remedy? ... socially useful goals not only have to meet the needs of followers, they also should elevate followers to a higher moral level." (p. 21)

Similarly, in *The Reflective Practitioner*, Donald Schon (1983) reported that he found that the most effective professionals' skills are not built on rational structures learned in school but instead result from intuitions and improvisations built through a process of observing themselves in the midst of their practices.[14]

The reader may be tempted to discard aspects of this discussion as *philosophizing* or *a matter of semantics*. I urge you to be patient and follow the thread of this part of the inquiry. This is not a minor theoretical part of the conversation. Recent discoveries in neurophysiology show clearly that the traditional ways of understanding wisdom as a matter of distilling action from abstract conceptions is wrong.

The cognitive scientist Francisco Varela (1999), trained as a neurobiologist, gave a series of three short lectures in 1994 on conclusions about the construction of wisdom in human beings, which he bases on the intersection of recent developments in the science of mind and the teachings of Eastern wisdom traditions. The lectures have been published as a little jewel of a book entitled *Ethical Know-How: Action, Wisdom, and Cognition*. "As a first approximation," he says, "let me say that a wise (or virtuous) person is *one who knows what is good and spontaneously does it*" [Varela's emphasis] (p. 4). Quoting the philosopher Charles Taylor, Varela (1999) says:

"Ethics is closer to wisdom than to reason, closer to understanding what is good than to correctly adjudicating particular situations. ... the focus [of the current examination of these questions] has moved away from meta-ethical issues to a much sharper debate between those who demand a detached, critical morality based on prescriptive principles and those who pursue an active and engaged ethics based on a tradition that identifies the good." (p. 3)

Varela (1999) builds his arguments upon current scientific research regarding the functioning of the brain and the human nervous system. Here are three conclusions that bear on our concerns in this chapter:

1. Truly ethical behavior does not arise from mere habit or from obedience to patterns or rules. Truly expert people act from extended inclinations, not from precepts, and thus transcend the limitations inherent in a repertoire of purely habitual responses. This is why truly ethical behavior[15] may sometimes seem unfathomable to the untrained eye, why it can be what is called in the Vajrayana tradition "crazy wisdom." (p. 31)

2.   We acquire our ethical behavior in much the same way we acquire all other modes of behavior: they become transparent to us as we grow up in society. This is because learning is, as we know, circular: we learn what we are supposed to be in order to be accepted as learners. (p. 24)

3.   Contrary to what seems to be the case from a cursory introspection, cognition does not flow seamlessly from one "state" to another, but rather consists in a punctuated succession of behavioral patterns that arise and subside in measurable time. This insight of recent neuroscience—and of cognitive science in general—is fundamental, for it relieves us from the tyranny of searching for a centralized homuncular quality to account for a cognitive agent's normal behavior. (p. 49)

In a passage that sounds as if Varela were right in the middle of the conversation we are having with Churchman and his five philosophers, Varela (1999) says:

"Were we to entertain the idea that there is no hard and fast distinction between science and philosophy, philosophers such as Descartes, Locke, Leibniz, Hume, Kant, and Husserl would take on a new significance: they could be seen as, among other things, proto-cognitive scientists." (p. 25)

In this background, I propose that in the pursuit of systems that support wise organizational action, architects and designers must take careful note of recent developments in some apparently distant parts of the field of cognitive sciences. Along the way, I propose that some treasured wisdoms of the IT and DSS field should be rethought, including for example, the notions that at the heart of the process is a mental model that decision processes begin with the recognition that problems exist and decisions need to be made.

Learning and Competence

When people set out to increase their competence in some domain, they begin by revealing themselves as having a certain level of competence and also incompetence. Our ability to learn depends first upon our acceptance of our incompetence in the domain in which we will learn. In all great wisdom traditions, there are famous stories about masters laughing at what they do not understand and are incompetent for doing (Dreyfus & Dreyfus, 2000, p. 16).

When we speak of a master, we refer to a person of historical excellence, set apart from peers by participation in the ongoing invention of a domain of practices. A master is not only able to act in that domain; a master can produce important innovations in the standard practices of the domain, revolutionizing the history of the domain. Richard Warren Sears of Sears Roebuck invented catalog sales. Sam Walton of Wal-Mart invented another kind of merchandising. Each changed the face of their industry.

Masters do not differ from the competent or virtuoso practitioners in some domain so much by the character of their performance, as by the concerns they bring to the practice.

While a competent person attends to the business of the day and a virtuoso explores the limits of invention inside the domain, the master lives in a larger conversation about the meaning of the practice and its place in the larger culture. By focusing on *anomalies* (situations in which something appears not quite right or violates the expectations the master has built up from long experience), masters find ways to transform the practice of their skill to take on a different meaning in the culture. While a proficient person or even a virtuoso might pass over an anomaly as an exceptional circumstance, a master may become obsessed with an anomaly. *Accidental* discoveries, such as the discovery of penicillin or the vulcanization of rubber, offer vivid examples of this phenomenon.

"Inventing" Waste

Historic inventions are often built from historic difficulties, and they *always* involve the invention of new distinctions. At the end of the Second World War, the people of Japan were in terrible trouble, their morale, productive capacity, and international relations demolished. An engineer named Taiichi Ohno, in the enterprise today known as Toyota, began the task of building a new capacity for Japanese production on top of Henry Ford's designs with some important additions. Ford incorporated everything into one plant; Ohno designed for operation in a network. The operational heart of Ford's designs were the way the engineers designed the coordination of the work; Ohno's design was centered in processes that built the capacity of each person on the production floor to take responsibility for the quality and coordination of their work. His invention became the foundation of the quality movement that swept the world starting in the 1970s and 1980s.

To keep the workers thinking, Ohno invented a new collection of *wastes* for them to observe and eliminate. Waste, like wisdom, is an assessment, an interpretation. For example, inventories, he said, were waste, as was time that workers spent waiting—for parts, others to complete work, and so forth. By inventing these new interpretations, Ohno was able to trigger important revisions in the way the people of Toyota thought and acted. What we in the West now call *just-in-time logistics* and many other innovations of the last 30 years were born in these inventions.

The organizational wastes with which we have orchestrated our interpretations of work for the last 50 years—wasted movement, wasted time, wasted resources, and so forth— were invented in the traditions of the industrial revolution. I am convinced that they will not be the most important organizational wastes of the next 50 years. Here is my own list of what will be the five most important new waste generators:

1. *Not Listening:* Tolerating working together in conditions in which people cannot effectively listen to each other in the midst of mistrust, resignation, resentment, and simple incompetence.

2. *Bureaucratic Styles:* Interacting with each other as if people were machines doing tasks—sequences of movements and activities—in which our concerns, moods, and emotions show up at best only briefly before and after the work but not during it.

3.   *Worship of Information:* Tolerating the illusion that the essential matters of work can be invented, managed, and sustained through the creation, storage, retrieval, display, and publication of information.

4.   *Suppressing Innovation:* Tolerating ways of working in that which is different, unusual, or new is feared, rejected, or avoided so that it becomes all but impossible to develop flexibility and evolve practices for dealing with a changing world.

5.   *Work as Toil:* Tolerating the interpretation that work consists fundamentally of sequences of *things to do.* In this interpretation, most people appear to be victims trapped by their needs to make a living, prepare for retirement, support families, and so forth. We ignore, diminish, or distort the ways that most work can bring meaning to people's lives and take care of features of the world for which people care.

Pain-Free Wisdom?

Finally, the kind of wisdom that is involved in historic innovations and longstanding successful leadership of organizations and even that which is required for important reconstructions of organizations does not come from mechanical, procedural, or algorithmic structures. Recently, the Harvard Business Review published a letter that colleagues and I wrote to the editors about an article by Gary Hamel and Liisa Välikangas ("The Quest for Resilience," September 2003), in which we strongly criticized the authors' proposal of what we called "a utopian corporate capacity that adapts to strategic failure without the traumatic wake-up calls of lost market share, protracted earnings slumps, the need for wrenching turnarounds" (Bell et al., 2004). We said to the authors:

"A recipe for pain-free learning could work only if learning were solely about developing valuable new ideas."

"The strategically important innovations that give companies resilience do not come from experiments, less still from multiple bet-hedging experiments—and least of all from people whose careers are protected from the consequences of failed experiments. Instead senior managers need to develop the commitment to risking their careers to develop new ideas. The value of new ideas only becomes real in the midst of failed pilots, funding losses, and heartbreaking rejiggerings."

"Likewise, corporate resilience generally does not come from training senior managers to apply resources, like markets, to a hundred different well-hedged futures. Companies learn to spot difficulties early, invent opportunities in the midst of breakdowns, and fundamentally change how they interact with suppliers and customers by taking a single-minded stand on the core customer concerns they serve. Disconnection from these concerns occurs when managers begin to seek pain-free solutions—such as focusing on one well-understood set of products or segments. Resilience requires reigniting managers' passion and commitment to taking chances and working through them, not pain free experimentation." (Bell et al., 2004)

I agree with Churchman (1968) in his ambition to "create the 'optimal' shatterer of old tablets, a shatterer that does not simultaneously shatter all chance of further progress in the cooperative ideals." (p. 215)

Well-Tooled Investment Management Process

The next several pages recount the process of designing, building, and deploying a software-supported system to help a large institution with the integration of its processes for strategic planning, capital expenditures, and a number of important functions adjacent to those. The reader will see many of the concerns and topics we have discussed in this chapter appearing in the way that the design was done. Here are some of those that I think most relevant and graspable from the written story of what we invented:

1. The example illustrates an important aspect of Churchman's concern with the unity of the system we are designing. The design does not merely *integrate many functions*, as some software brochure might tout; it would not be possible to do what it does as a function of *integration*. It is able to do what it does because the design invents a new unity—here called investment management— that did not exist in the language or explicit concerns of the people of the company before we went to work with them.

2. In the example, investment management conversations are managed as interactions among people, paying attention to the interpretations they are making with a system helping keep their attention there, and the articulation of what is handled in the system the investments—is always held in that context.

3. The design assumes that the participants in the process are ethical actors and does not attempt to police their actions. On the other hand, the system makes their actions visible to other actors and prompts them to act in ways that are coherent with the promises for which they are responsible in the organization (for example, at a high level, for directing operations or for advising others as they direct operations). The system also records everyone's actions for auditors, regulators, and posterity, and it does all that in a way that encourages authentic action.

4. The interpretation of the enterprise that underlies the design of the application is that of a network of commitments, constructed in language-actions, and invented, articulated, and enacted by human beings speaking and listening to each other. All *data* in the system gets there in that way—by people speaking and listening—and to the extent that a new future is shaped in the process we designed, it is shaped by the human beings and not the data, formulae, and so forth.

5. The design of the system allows the human beings involved to improvise as they invent ways to define their futures under many different kinds of situations and to design structures of coordination that can be adapted to wildly different circum-

stances that may be encountered. One important effect is to make it possible for new things to emerge rather than only old ones.

6. The way that the system puts a spotlight on the behavior of each participant in the process has the effect of helping the people involved to see their own strengths and weaknesses and thereby encourages and supports learning.

The Situation

During the 1990s, one of my clients was a large and very successful electric utility company (primarily operating coal-fired power plants and a distribution network) that was attempting to shift itself from a style of management suitable to a regulated monopoly in a bounded geographical region to one suited to competition in an open market on a continental or, even eventually, global scale. In the course of several years of work together, we examined and rebuilt many of the company's pivotal processes and ways of working. One of the most important we called their *Investment Management* process.

Like any modern industrial firm, the company had standard ways of doing a whole variety of things to responsibly prepare to take care of the fact that the future coming to them was not exactly the same as the present, including:

1. Strategic planning,
2. Forecasting demand,
3. Proposing and approving capital budgets,
4. Managing the process of committing to capital expenditures,
5. Managing the actual flows of cash to make capital investments,
6. Managing the execution of capital projects,
7. Accounting for capital expenditures, and
8. Measuring overall returns on capital invested.

As is normally the case with most large firms, these eight processes were related to each other because they all involved money. Indicators of each appeared in the company's accounting system. Also as is normally the case, they had no standard practices for tracking particular investments, nor for measuring the return on any one particular investment, unless a special project was set up to do that. New capital investments once implemented and accepted went into the company's general asset accounts, and their returns were measured along with all other assets.

Anyone with experience in the workings of large enterprises has seen examples of similar collections of processes and can follow as I give a quick critique of them.

- They were slow, expensive, bureaucratic, and generated a lot of paper.

- Most importantly, the processes had the effect of diffusing responsibility, authority, and accountability for one of the most important aspects of the management of an organization's future.

- As a result, the management of the conversation about investing in the company's future moved into a set of essentially unmanageable, highly politicized, *back-corridor* conversations.

- When proposal packages moved through the organization with their signature lists on the cover, you would hear executives complain, "If all these other people are approving this, of course I am going to go along," "The approval happens in another conversation; this is irrelevant," "This is <so and so's> pet project, and if I don't approve this he'll go after my projects," and the like.

- The processes actually slowed down the speed at which the company's managers were able to think and design how the company moved into the future and pitted people against each other in political contests in the background.

Diagnosis and Design Criteria

In conversation with the company's executives, I characterized their processes as more or less consistent with the processes that I called *allowance* when dealing with my children. At my request, the children make up stories about what they will need money for in the future, we discuss the stories and arrive at a figure that fits our family finances, fits my wife's and my idea about how much money our children should have access to, and then announce a final number. After that, the children nag us each week for their allowance. We have general anecdotal conversations about what they spend their money on, and at the end of the year when we review the family finances, we discuss how much we spent on allowances.

The difference, as you might guess, was that the allowance process works relatively smoothly, and the collection of eight processes I mentioned above broke, or failed to deliver, the kinds of results that my client's company needed in an agonizingly large proportion of the most important cases. Those processes did not work:

- When the company needed to make a new investment in a hurry.
- When the making of an investment stretched over a long period of time.
- When an unconventional investment was being considered.
- When new ideas were being brought.

In short, they did not work in a lot of the most important investment opportunities.

To cite just one example, in the middle of a scheduled maintenance event, engineers would discover that a turbine blade costing a million dollars needed replacement. The standard processes would all be put aside, as over a period of a few hours a few executives would approve all parts of the purchase, and then people would "fill in the blanks" on the process forms after the fact. The consequence of not acting was far too great to allow action to be constrained by the bureaucratic processes.

In thinking carefully about the diagnosis we would make, I proposed and the client agreed that the support of the intelligence of the people in the company—i.e., wise action—was the critical matter, along with supporting discipline in conversation. We concluded with the client's team that an algorithmic approach (i.e., a fully defined procedure or protocol, possibly supported by mathematical modeling or artificial intelligence tools), which they had been attempting to do for some time, *would actually make the situation worse, no matter how sophisticated an approach was taken.* For an analogy to understand the claim, think about what is involved in managing the conversation between the pilot and the tower during takeoffs and landings at a major airport. This conversation cannot--nay, must not--be automated. On the other hand, the *capacity* to have that conversation can be supported with multiple redundant communications channels to mitigate against interruption with radar that allows both to have second opinions about what they observe with their own eyes (or what they cannot see) and other tools.

I proposed criteria for judging a new design:

1. The process should help them manage a unity called "managing our investment in the future of the company" rather than attempting to manage the components that had previously been considered unities.

2. The process should work across a wide spectrum of investment situations, as for example, spanning from an investment where a commitment had to be made in a hurry to investment conversations stretching over a period of years.

3. The process should be organized so that it reveals to managers and executives things going wrong within it as they occur.

4. The roles of participants in the process should be organized in ways that are consistent with the participants' roles in the organization as a whole. For example, senior strategic, operational, and financial managers should have control over the pacing of the process, and senior technical advisors should be able to force their assessments to be heard by all who should listen to them but should not control the pace of the process.

5. The process should automatically generate all the records that will be needed by regulators as a by-product of the participants' work and not require additional processes to complete.

We designed a new process to span all eight component processes, along with a tool implementing the process. The process defined who speaks at which points in the process, whose commitments move the process forward or slow it down, how records are kept, assures that what is happening in the process is transparently visible to all participants, and makes records of everything that happens in the process accessible to all participants. The process could be followed for an investment conversation that lasts only a few hours or for one that lasts years.

We prototyped and tested the process and tool in the utility company and then implemented it across the company. A year later, we repeated the whole process for the investment management processes of a six billion dollar multinational cement company.

The Design

The process and tool at the center of the design are remarkably simple but also subtle and not intuitive for most system designers. Key elements embodied in the final design are:

1.   Participants in the process are assigned to roles during the first phase of the process. Three *line* roles are defined: *Investor, Proposer* (who must be a line operational manager), and *Manager* (the person who implements the investment). An unlimited number of *staff* roles are defined, covering whatever technical, financial, social, political, or other issues that may need to be topics of conversation for the investment to be properly vetted and designed.

2.   The process as a whole is organized, conducted, and recorded as sets of conversations, each set covering a single investment. Each set begins when a potential investment, indicated by the assessment that something important is missing, broken, or in the way, is proposed by a *proposer* speaking to an *investor*. After the *investor* has agreed to make an investment, a *manager* (who may be the same

Figure 1. Make an Investment

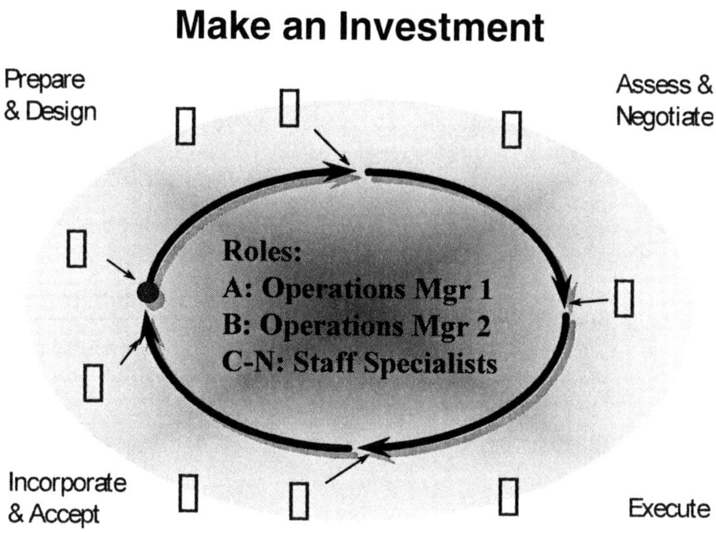

Table 1. Critical Moments

Step	Action
0	An investment process begins when someone notices an anomaly, or something missing, broken, or in the way and declares an investment opportunity (or the necessity of an investment). Individuals or groups are named to three roles for operational managers (*line*) and any number of *staff* roles. A timetable is declared for the conversation, including the moments in which each of the critical actions must be taken.
1	Under the direction of people in the key roles, work begins to prepare an investment offer. Conversations among them are conducted through electronic media in a public space, where people in all roles defined for this particular investment are able to read and observe the conversations.
2	The ***Proposer*** role offers a specific investment to ***Investor*** with ***Manager*** and staff roles observing. Additional staff roles are named at this point for giving assessments in technical, environmental, economic, and other domains as appropriate for the particular investment. In addition, the main operational roles can, at this point, define process elements in which particular staff roles are compelled to make assessments at particular moments in the process.
3	A very flexible and yet also formal choreographed conversation now ensues among the key roles, guided by requests from the operational managers. In the conversation, the participants answer questions about the value that will be contributed by the investment to the organization, its clients, and others, the costs it will produce, and how it will be evaluated once completed. The governing assumptions (assessments) behind the investment are spelled out in this conversation, in context.
4	The ***Investor*** commits the organization to go ahead with the investment. This commitment is understood by all to have these dimensions: the ***Investor*** is committing the organization (a) to make a specified investment, (b) under specified assumptions, (c) to produce a particular result. At any point in the execution of this investment that any of these "get sideways," the parties understand that the commitment as a whole is in trouble, and those responsible at the moment (usually the ***Manager***) must go back to the ***Investor*** and revisit the commitment.
5	The ***Manager*** manages the implementation of the investment, using whatever resources were spelled out in the assumptions at Stage 3 above. The other roles are informed about progress and ask questions during the implementation, and those conversations are preserved as part of the record, along with the records of costs during the implementation.
6	The ***Manager*** reports the successful implementation of the investment to the ***Investor***.
7	Under the direction of the ***Investor***, the participants in the process evaluate the investment's results, including defining future benchmarks of review and evaluation as appropriate along with accounting standards that will be followed for tracking the investment's results.
8	The ***Investor*** declares himself or herself satisfied with the investment on behalf of the organization.

person as the *proposer*), promises to implement the investment, does so, and then comes back to the *investor* to get the latter's declaration of satisfaction. After an investment has been implemented, additional conversations are initiated and managed covering the assessment of its contribution to the enterprise.

3. Every action (transaction) in the process and the system that supports it is structured as a performative. Line roles make requests, offers, promises, and declare investments complete and satisfactory. Staff roles make assessments and recommendations about the investments, including for example, the desirability of a particular investment, conditions for its successful execution, likely costs and returns on investment, assessments of progress, and of the value produced. In this way, each role is being asked to do what "they are paid to do"—line managers for producing results and staff for providing counsel.

4. Each "investment conversation set" is invoked, conducted, and recorded through four phases of the process: *preparation and design*; *assessment and negotiation*; *execution*; and *incorporation and assessment*. This process is diagrammed in the figure below.16 The four arcs headed with arrows correspond to the four phases of the process, and the arrowheads correspond to the four critical language-actions that brace the action when an investment is successfully proposed, constructed, and implemented. In the figure, I have numbered the critical moments in each investment conversation. The table explains these moments.

5. Prospective and completed investments are organized into a hierarchy of portfolios matching the current organization chart, with each manager responsible for a portfolio corresponding to his or her role. The senior executives of the company define which investments will be located in each portfolio. Managers can review the progress and performance of all portfolios located *below* them in the hierarchy through online tools.

6. Schedule objectives are set out at the beginning of each investment process, and requests, offers and promises carry fulfillment dates, which then allow the status of the work in each part of the process to be color-coded.

Table 2. Example of the Display of the Index to an Investment Management Conversation

Date	Who	Act		Subject	
Replace blade 110 in Winn Dixie Turbine A					
20040510	Wiseman	OPEN		Trouble with blade 110, no spare available	
20040510	Blanquette		Assess		Cost of delays will be $650k/day
20040512	Demasio		Assess		Vendor promises to find replacement
20040512	Wiseman	OFFER		Acquire replacement blade by 5/22	
20040512	Demasio		Assess		Vendor wants $12k
20040513	Blanquette		Assess		Bargain! Grab it.
20040513	Demasio		Assess		Committed - in our hands 5/24
20040513	McMaster	COMMIT		Acquisition authorized	
20040526	Wiseman	COMPLET		Blade installed	
20040528	Wiseman		Assess		Tests passed
20040528	McMaster	SATISF		Thanks, Dwight. Well done all.	

7. Displays of the progress of each investment show hierarchies of conversations under each phase of the investment process. These displays show in a transparent way the progress of the investment conversation, arguments and difficulties in the process, and so forth. The next figure illustrates what these look like. Entries in the displays are active; clicking on them brings records of the language actions (communications) to the screen.

8. Files and databases supporting the process are organized by the logic of the sets of conversations and integrated with the organization's standard accounting tools.

We built our first prototype of the supporting system (rapidly) with Lotus Notes and later built with more robust platforms.

Benefits

Here are a few of the results that came out of this invention:

- Radical improvement in the organization's capacity to oversee its capital investments, with consequential improvements in the speed of all processes, reduction in the cost of operating all the processes, reduction in the actual risks of investments, increased rates of success in investments, and many other benefits.

- Capacity to couple strategy, capital budgeting, and capital expenditures in ways never before possible.

- Greatly improved and earlier identification of ineffective investments, investment managers, and early warning of investments in trouble.

- A new capacity to cut cycle times for investment decisions and implementation almost at will.

- The approach is tremendously helpful in training young managers and detecting opportunities to improve the skills of senior managers.

Conclusion

Having come to the end of this brief inquiry into a question to which some of the best minds in the history of humankind have devoted much, or sometimes all of their adult working lives, what shall we say?

First, I conclude that to care about wisdom, to ask what it is and how to cultivate it, is, itself, to take an ethical stand. To set the possibility of wise action as a standard for judging the way that we develop management and leadership practices in organizations and as a standard for the design of systems to support action in enterprises, is, itself, to take an ethical stand. To set out to produce the capacity for wisdom is no less than to commit to act in a way that is designed to bring out, make available, the very best that people have to offer. In big and little circumstances that call for wise action, where someone who is in a position to act has not before that moment been prepared to address what is happening, wisdom is possible. In that moment, someone prepared to act with wisdom does not flee or turn away from those circumstances. Instead, they themselves take an ethical stand and use the moment to discover something heretofore undiscovered about themselves, others, and/or the circumstances, as the foundation for building something new. And then they act in a way that is not merely following the rules or repeating what others before them have done.

Then, as a last question, let us ask, "Where, after all, does wisdom come from?" I propose that whatever we may conclude are the essential structures of wisdom, we may be clear that when we say someone is wise, or say that some action was wise, that what we observed is rooted in *at least* these four places:

1. In the fact that human beings are historical beings, able to remember and continuously reinterpret our experiences, and possessed of practices that allow us to record, read about, and interpret the experience of others.

2. In our capacity to *learn* from our interactions in our worlds.

3. In our capacity to *speak and act* from that background.

4. In the biology that gives us the wherewithal for all of the above--cognition, memory, intellect, and language itself, as well as our emotional reactions and predispositions with which we orient ourselves to each other, our experience, and our worlds.

Curiously, in each of these areas, a great deal of new current research is yielding remarkable new insights into what it is that human beings do. I propose these give us a good point of departure and can give us a whole series of places in which to continue Churchman's inquiry and to draw inspiration and ideas for improving the quality of our work on the design and construction of organizational practices and systems to support them.

References

Austin, J. L. (1962). *How to do things with words.* Cambridge, MA: Harvard University Press.

Bell, C. (2000). Re-membering the future: Organizational change, technology, and the role of the archivist. *Journal of the Midwest Archives Conference, 25*(1/2), 11-31. [Additional citations to electronic versions of original talks may be found at *http://www.chaunceybell.com*]

Bell, C., et al. (2004, February). *Harvard Business Review.*

Bell, C., & Bell, S. (2003). *Reflections on listening and anxiety in designing a life.* Unpublished manuscript, available from the author.

Churchman, C. W. (1968). *Challenge to reason.* New York: McGraw-Hill.

Courtney, J. F. (2001). Decision making and knowledge management in inquiring organizations: Toward a new decision-making model paradigm for DSS. *Decision Support Systems, 31*(1), 17-38.

Damasio, A. (1999). *The feeling of what happens: Body and emotion in the making of consciousness.* San Diego: Harcourt.

Dreyfus, H. L. (1991). *Being-in-the-world: A commentary on Heidegger's* Being and Time, *division I.* Cambridge, MA: MIT Press.

Dreyfus, H. L., & Dreyfus, S. E. (2000). *Mind over machine.* New York: Simon & Schuster.

Fiumara, G. C. (1990). *The other side of language: A philosophy of listening.* London: Routledge.

Flores, F., & Winograd, T. (1986). *Understanding computers and cognition: A new foundation for design.* Norwood, NJ: Ablex.

Goleman, D. (2003). *Destructive emotions: How can we overcome them? ... A scientific dialogue with the Dalai Lama.* New York: Bantam Dell.

Heidegger, M. (1962). *Being and time* (J. Macquarrie & E.Robinson, Trans.). New York: Harper and Row.

Heidegger, M. (1971). *On the way to language.* San Francisco: Harper.

Heifetz, R. A. (1996). Leadership without easy answers. Cambridge, MA: Harvard University Press.

Kenny, A. (1992). *The metaphysics of mind.* Oxford: Oxford University Press.

Kenny, A. (1997). *The Oxford illustrated history of Western philosophy.* Oxford: Oxford University Press.

Kotter, J. P. (1990). *A force for change: How leadership differs from management* (p.119ff). New York: The Free Press: A Division of Macmillan, Inc.

Lown, B. (1996, 1999). *The lost art of healing: Practicing compassion in medicine.* New York: Ballantine Books.

Maturana, H., & Varela, F. J. (1998). *The tree of knowledge.* Boston & London: Shambhala.

Schein, E. H. (1992). *Organizational culture and leadership* (2nd ed.). San Francisco: Jossey-Bass.

Schon, D. A. (1983). *The reflective practitioner: How professionals think in action.* New York: Basic Books.

Spinosa, C., Flores, F., & Dreyfus, H. (1997). *Disclosing new worlds: Entrepreneurship, democratic action, and the cultivation of solidarity.* Cambridge, MA: MIT Press.

Ulrich, W. (1999). An aprreciation of C. West Churchman. Retrieved September 26, 2004, from *http://www.geocities.com/postfach1/cwc_appreciation.html*

Varela, F. J. (1999). *Ethical know-how: Action, wisdom, and cognition.* Stanford, CA: Stanford University Press.

Williamson, O. E. (1996). *The mechanisms of governance.* New York, Oxford: Oxford University Press.

Endnotes

[1]   Chauncey Bell is managing partner of Bell & Associates, Business Design for Innovation, and CEO of the design community (sm), *a worldwide conversation generating social and business innovation.* For more than two decades, he has worked with senior executives to transform the skills, processes, and cultural characteristics of large firms in North America, Latin America, and Europe. More about the author may be found at www.babdi.com and www.chaunceybell.com

[2]   *http://www.dictionary.com offers the following contributions:*

wise:

Having the ability to discern or judge what is true, right, or lasting; sagacious: a wise leader.

Exhibiting common sense; prudent: a wise decision.

Shrewd; crafty.

Having great learning; erudite.

Provided with information; informed. Used with to: was wise to the politics of the department.

Source: The American Heritage® Dictionary of the English Language, Fourth Edition. Copyright © 2000 by Houghton Mifflin Company. Published by Houghton Mifflin Company. All rights reserved.

wise

\Wise\, a. [Compar. Wiser; superl. Wisest.] [OE. wis, AS. w[=i]s; akin to OS. & OFries. w[=i]s, D. wijs, G. weise, OHG. w[=i]s, w[=i]si, Icel. v[=i]ss, Sw. vis, Dan. viis, Goth. weis; akin to wit, v. i. See Wit, v., and cf. Righteous, Wisdom.]

1. Having knowledge; knowing; enlightened; of extensive information; erudite; learned.

They are wise to do evil, but to do good they have no knowledge. --Jer. iv. 22.

2. Hence, especially, making due use of knowledge; discerning and judging soundly concerning what is true or false, proper or improper; choosing the best ends and the best means for accomplishing them; sagacious.

When clouds appear, wise men put their cloaks. --Shak.

From a child thou hast known the holy scriptures, which are able to make thee wise unto salvation. --2 Tim. iii. 15.

3. Versed in art or science; skillful; dexterous; specifically, skilled in divination.

Fal. There was, mine host, an old fat woman even now with me; but she's gone. Sim. Pray you, sir, was't not the wise woman of Brentford? — Shak.

4. Hence, prudent; calculating; shrewd; wary; subtle; crafty. [R.] "Thou art . . . no novice, but a governor wily and wise." --Chaucer.

Nor, on the other side, Will I be penuriously wise As to make money, that's my slave, my idol. --Beau. & Fl.

Lords do not care for me: I am too wise to die yet. --Ford.

5. Dictated or guided by wisdom; containing or exhibiting wisdom; well adapted to produce good effects; judicious; discreet; as, a wise saying; a wise scheme or plan; wise conduct or management; a wise determination. "Eminent in wise deport." --Milton.

To make it wise, to make it a matter of deliberation. [Obs.] " We thought it was not worth to make it wise."--Chaucer.

Wise in years, old enough to be wise; wise from age and experience; hence, aged; old. [Obs.]

A very grave, state bachelor, my dainty one; He's wise in years, and of a temperate warmth. --Ford.

You are too wise in years, too full of counsel, For my green experience. --Ford.

Source: Webster's Revised Unabridged Dictionary, © 1996, 1998 MICRA, Inc.

wise

\Wise\, a. [OE. wise, AS. w[=i]se; akin to OS. w[=i]sa, OFries. w[=i]s, D. wijs, wijze, OHG. w[=i]sa, G. weise, Sw. vis, Dan. viis, Icel. ["o]?ruv[=i]s otherwise; from the root of E. wit; hence, originally, knowledge, skill. See Wit, v., and cf. Guise.] Way   of being or acting; manner; mode; fashion. ``All armed in complete wise.'' --Spenser.

To love her in my beste wyse. --Chaucer.

This song she sings in most commanding wise. --Sir P. Sidney.

Let not these blessings then, sent from above, Abused be, or spilt in profane wise. --Fairfax.

Note: This word is nearly obsolete, except in such phrases as in any wise, in no wise, on this wise, etc. " Fret not thyself in any wise to do evil."--Ps. xxxvii. 8. "He shall in no wise lose his reward." --Matt. x. 42. " On this wise ye shall bless the children of Israel." --Num. vi. 23.

Note: Wise is often used as a suffix in composition, as in likewise, nowise, lengthwise, etc., in which words -ways is often substituted with the same sense; as, noways, lengthways, etc.

Source: Webster's Revised Unabridged Dictionary, © 1996, 1998 MICRA, Inc.

wise

adj 1: having or prompted by wisdom or discernment; "a wise leader"; "a wise and perceptive comment" [ant: foolish] 2: marked by the exercise of good judgment or common sense in practical matters; "judicious use of one's money"; "a sensible manager"; "a wise deci sion" [syn: judicious, sensible] 3: evidencing the possession of inside information [syn: knowing, wise(p), wise to(p)] 4: able to take a broad view of negotiations between states [syn: diplomatic] 5: carefully considered; "a considered opinion" [syn: considered] n : a way of doing or being: "in no wise"; "in this wise" [syn: method]

Source: WordNet ® 1.6, © 1997 Princeton University

3   I understand *organizations* as a broad range of human enterprise, including what we construct within the institutions of families, communities, societies, governments, as well as businesses of all sizes and types.

4   *http://traditions.skule.ca/articles/ironring/ironringinfo/ironringinfo.html*

5   In October 2001, *Business Week* magazine rated Kotter the #1 "leadership guru" in America based on a survey they conducted of 504 enterprises.

6   The development of wisdom has been a central theme in a number of ancient traditions for millennia. I am thinking of traditions that come to us principally from India, China, Japan, Asian countries, and from Judaism, Christianity, and Islam. These traditions share principles about wisdom, "paths to enlightenment," and styles of learning. I cite a few below. They are relevant to our ambition for improving systems, but beyond our grasp in such a short work. The names that I give in the following are not universally accepted labels but rather the nomenclature I have given to a short list of topics that can be found in the great books of many traditions.

Transcendence: the principle that meaning, satisfaction, and the organizing principles in life are rarely found first in the phenomenal world of things.

Transformation: the principle that life is far more mutable than any of us is given to suspect in the day-to-day living of it. Our understanding of our lives, our situations, and what we are doing are subject to change rather suddenly. Through our behavior, we can influence how that happens.

Tension: the principle that in life many important things are born in the middle of tensions and that tension, as a result, sometimes needs to be cultivated in order to support invention.

Temporal Structures: the principle that calls for close attention to the temporal horizons in which we conceive and understand life. "Be here now," living in the present, planning and envisioning the future, and care with the processes of recording and accounting for the past are part of this.

The Unity of Existence: John Donne pointed to the center of the question with his Meditation XVII: "All mankind is of one author, and is one volume; when one man dies, one chapter is not torn out of the book, but translated into a better language; and every chapter must be so translated...As therefore the bell that rings to a sermon, calls not upon the preacher only, but upon the congregation to come: so this bell calls us all: but how much more me, who am brought so near the door by this sickness....No man is an island, entire of itself... any man's death diminishes me, because I am involved in mankind; and therefore never send to know for whom the bell tolls; it tolls for thee."

7   I'll say more formally later about assessments. For this moment, take the word in its conventional sense of an interpretation or a judgment.

8   See for example the following from Anthony Kenny, (1992). *The Metaphysics of Mind*, Oxford: Oxford University Press, p. 17ff, 20.

"To say that I have an intellect is to say that I have the capacity to acquire and exercise intellectual abilities of various kinds, such as the mastery of language and the possession of objective information. To say that I have a will is to say that I have the capacity for the free pursuit of goals formulated by the intellect. My intellect and my will are in essence capacities. What are they capacities *of*? Of the living human being, the body you would see if you were here in the room where I write.

"The most important intellectual skill is the mastery of language. Others, such as the knowledge of mathematics, are acquired by human beings through the languages they have mastered. So the study of the acquisition and exercise of language is the way *par excellence* to study the nature of the human mind. To study knowledge of language you have to consider what the exercise of linguistic knowledge is... for instance, reciting a poem to myself in my head imperceptibly will count as an instance of linguistic behavior."

9   I build a substantial portion of my interpretations about the behaviors of humans and organizations on the work of Kierkegaard, Heidegger, Wittgenstein, and Anthony Kenny. Heidegger is particularly difficult. I use Hubert Dreyfus' *Being-in-the-World* (see next footnote) as my guide to the Heidegger of *Being and Time*. I have found Lawrence Vogel's *The Fragile "We": Ethical Implications of Heidegger's "Being and Time"* particularly useful in picking my way through the ethical thicket presented by Heidegger's interactions with National Socialism during the time of Hitler. This controversial 20th century philosopher is rapidly becoming, by the measures philosophers use to assess each other's importance, the most important philosopher of all time.

10   The creation of knowledge as *a capacity for taking action* - I normally speak of it as different kinds of capital that enable one to act skillfully, act in ways that convoke action on the parts of others, and produce satisfaction to those served--is a central issue in my interpretation of what we do with each other in organizations. On the other hand, most speaking in the IT, DSS, and adjacent traditions give the central role in the activities of those leading and managing organizations to what is called decision making. I do not. I think it is important that I note that I have an alternative view of how people in an organization conclude that new actions are possible or

called for, come to resolution about how to take those actions, and then put themselves into action. I do not address this difference in this chapter.

[11]   Anthony Kenny is Warden of Rhodes House, Oxford, and Chairman of the British Library. Until recently, he was Master of Balliol College, Oxford, and President of the British Academy. In *The Oxford Illustrated History of Western Philosophy* he brought together essays by a series of philosophers covering the epochs of the five Churchman philosophers.

[12]   Dr. Fernando Flores Labra, currently a Senator in the Chilean government and candidate for President of his country, was the first to point out the importance of performatives for understanding and shaping the behaviors of people in organizations as an underpinning of design in organizations. Flores originally assembled the traditions and many of the thinkers on which I rely in this chapter.

[13]   *Directives* and *commissives* refer to a different categorization of performative verbs than the one I employ in my own work.

[14]   Donald A. Schon, (1983). *The Reflective Practitioner: How Professionals Think in Action.* New York: Basic Books.

[15]   … or, I would say, wise behavior.

[16]   The ellipse shown is based upon representations of *The Conversation for Action* copyright by Business Design Associates, Inc., and Action Technologies, Inc. The author of this chapter was the original author of these representations.

Chapter XIII

Phenomenon of Duality:
A Key to Facilitate the Transition From Knowledge Mangement to Wisdom for Inquiring Organizations

Nilmini Wickramasinghe
Cleveland State University, USA

Abstract

"Wisdom is what you learn after you think you know it all" - unknown

In today's knowledge-based economy, sustainable strategic advantages are gained more from an organization's knowledge assets than from its more traditional types of assets, namely, land, labor, and capital. Knowledge, however, is a compound construct, exhibiting many manifestations of the phenomenon of duality such as subjectivity and objectivity as well as having tacit and explicit forms. Overlooking this phenomenon of duality in the knowledge construct has not only led many knowledge management initiatives to stumble but has also resulted in the discussion of the apparent contradictions associated with knowledge management in the IS literature as well as numerous discussions and debates regarding the "nonsense of knowledge management." It is the thesis of this chapter that a full appreciation of the phenomenon of duality is indeed necessary to enable inquiring organizations to reach the state of wisdom and enlightenment.

Introduction

Throughout the ages, the nature of knowledge has been central to many debates between philosophers, scientists, academics, and practitioners. In fact, it was the forbidden fruit from the Tree of Knowledge of Good and Evil that caused Adam and Eve to be dismissed from the Garden of Eden; in addition, interestingly enough, the understanding of Good and Evil, a duality, was to lead Adam and Eve to wisdom. A key underlying and recurring theme in some shape or form with respect to knowledge in all these discussions is the phenomenon of duality as it relates to the knowledge construct and its management. Duality, or the principle of duality, refers to the existence of two irreducible aspects or perspectives that tend to complement each other, as in the example of Adam and Eve, the Tree had knowledge of good and evil. The key to the understanding of duality is that given the existence of duality, one must take a holistic perspective and realize that there is a harmonious balance between these duals. In contrast, taking a singular or one-dimensional perspective will lead to an incomplete understanding and consequently decisions and/or judgments based on such an incomplete view will then be suboptimal or less sound.

Webster's Dictionary defines wisdom as accumulated learning that provides knowledge, the ability to discern inner qualities and relationships, that is, insight and leads to sound judgment. Succinctly stated then, wisdom requires knowledge and is concerned with understanding principles and then being able to make sound decisions and/or judgments based on such an understanding. Knowledge is not a homogenous construct, rather it is a compound complex construct. One of the reasons knowledge is compound in nature is because it exhibits numerous duals at many levels. This chapter contends that by understanding the phenomenon of duality and how it relates to the knowledge construct, not only will inquiring organizations firstly be able to better understand the compound knowledge construct and its management, but also this will facilitate their moving from knowledge management to wisdom.

In this chapter, many specific manifestations of the duality phenomenon as it relates to knowledge and its management are highlighted, such as the subjective and objective perspectives, the consensus versus disensus perspective, the Lockean/Leibnizian aspects of knowledge versus the Hegelian/Kantian aspects, and the people versus technology dimensions. Throughout the chapter, no one perspective is singled out as correct or incorrect, rather the emphasis is on the fact that these respective duals not only underscore the duality phenomenon at different levels but are all useful, necessary, and important for an inquiring organization to fully appreciate the compound quality exhibited by the knowledge construct and thereby embrace superior knowledge management strategies, techniques, tools, and processes. In addition, a sound understanding of the duality phenomenon as it relates to knowledge will not only facilitate a better understanding of how to embrace knowledge management, an important strategy in today's knowledge economy (Drucker, 1993), but also address key needs such as identified by Nonaka that "few managers grasp the true nature of knowledge creating companies--let alone how to manage it" (Holsapple & Joshi, 2002, p. 47) and Ann Stuart that "[m]any managers would be hard pressed to explain precisely and concisely, what this evolving business trend (knowledge management) means" (Holsapple & Joshi, 2002, p. 47). The following then, serves to address this duality phenomenon with respect to the knowledge construct and thereby highlight that a true appreciation of this duality phenomenon with respect to knowledge and knowledge management, more specifically, should enable "the getting of wisdom" for inquiring organizations.

The chapter is structured as follows: first a background section which gives a brief description of key terms required for an inquiring organization to move from knowledge management to wisdom is presented as well as a brief synopsis of inquiring organizations and the integral role of knowledge and its management for these organizations. In addition, this section discusses the compound nature of knowledge and why knowledge as opposed to its related cousins, data, and information, exhibits this duality phenomenon. Then, a discussion of knowledge management, the knowledge construct as well as the major philosophical perspectives for understanding knowledge management is presented.   This is followed by a discussion of the key perspectives of knowledge creation. Next, some specific dualities are highlighted and discussed in turn. Finally, conclusions are drawn and avenues for future research highlighted.

Background

This sections serves to define knowledge and why it is a compound construct. In so doing, it also discusses other relevant terms, including data, information, wisdom, and understanding. The section will also summarize the integral nature of knowledge and knowledge management for inquiring organizations.

From Data to Wisdom

In today's knowledge economy, data can be viewed as an abundant, vital, and necessary resource. It is then possible to tap into this reservoir and by utilizing new ways to channel raw data into meaningful or processed data to form information. This information, in turn, can then become knowledge that ultimately with further understanding leads to wisdom (Alberthal, 1995). Thus data, information, knowledge, and ultimately wisdom are not just connected, but it is also possible to generate knowledge from data, thereby making data and information valuable raw materials in the knowledge economy.

Data can be defined as a series of discrete events, observations, measurements, or facts in the form of numbers, words, sounds, and/or images. In organizations, much of the useful data is in the form of transaction records, stored in data bases and generated through various business processes and activities. Today organizations generate large amounts of various types of data. Given its discrete form, data is not very useful as it is and needs to be processed. When this data is processed and organized into a context, it becomes information. In transforming data into information, five important Cs have taken place as noted by Davenport and Prusak (1998), as follow:

1. Contextualized: the purpose surrounding the data collection/gathering is known.
2. Categorized: the key units of analysis and key factors relating to this data are known.
3. Calculated: mathematical and/or statistical analyses have been performed on this data.
4 . Corrected: errors in this data have been corrected or accounted for.
5. Condensed: the data has been summarized and distilled.

There exist many plausible definitions of knowledge. For the purposes of this chapter, the definition of knowledge given by Davenport and Prusak (1998) will be used because it is not only broad and thus serves to capture the breadth of the construct but also and, perhaps more importantly for this discussion, it serves to underscore that knowledge is not a simple homogeneous construct, rather a compound construct:

Figure 1 Data to Wisdom

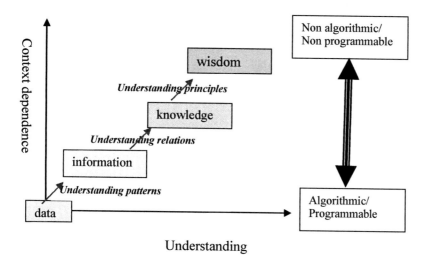

"Knowledge is a fluid mix of framed experiences, values, contextual information, and expert insights that provides a framework for evaluating and incorporating new experiences and information. It originates and is applied in the minds of knowers. In organizations, it is often embedded not only in documents or repositories but also in organizational routine, processes, practices and norms." (p. 5)

In transforming information to knowledge, the role of people is integral. Furthermore, such transformations take place with four key C activities identified by Davenport and Prusak (1998), including:

1.   Comparison: information in one scenario is compared and contrasted with another.

2.   Consequences: what implications does the information have for decision making?

3.   Connections: how does this bit of information and/or knowledge relate to another?

4.   Conversation: what do people think of this information?

What is important to note about these four C activities is that they require human cognitive processes to take place, which are all concerned, to a greater or lesser degree, to the understanding of relations and tend to be subjective in nature, unlike the five C activities associated with information which require more mechanistic or objective functions of understanding patterns. Herein lies the reason for why knowledge as opposed to its cousins of data and information can exhibit the phenomenon of duality, while the more simplistic constructs of data and information do not.

Understanding is an interpolative and probabilistic process where one can take knowledge and synthesize new knowledge from the previously held knowledge. The difference between understanding and knowledge is the difference between learning and memorizing (Wickramasinghe & Sharma, in press). Finally, wisdom is an extrapolative and nondeterministic, nonprobabilistic process (Wickramasinghe & Sharma, in press). It calls on all the previous levels of consciousness, and specifically on special types of human programming (moral, ethical codes, etc.). Given this explanation of wisdom coupled with Webster's definition of wisdom presented in the introduction, what becomes apparent is that to obtain wisdom in addition to knowledge, the understanding of principles is required, and a holistic rather than a singular inquiry system is necessary but not sufficient to the achievement of such a state. Furthermore, such a state of wisdom will lead to sound decision making and judgments.

From Figure 1, several aspects are important to note with respect to the progression from data to wisdom. First, as we move from left to right in the figure, or as we move from data to wisdom, we also move from constructs that are algorithmic and programmable to constructs that are nonalgorithmic and nonprogrammable. This means that while data is highly programmable and algorithmic, wisdom is almost nonprogrammable and nonalgorithmic. Further, we can see from Figure 1 that data is highly context independent while wisdom is highly context dependent. Therefore, the specific context becomes an integral component in the managing of wisdom, and while it is possible to generate a precise prescription for managing data, it is very difficult to generate a similar prescription for facilitating an organization to manage wisdom. The key then to achieving wisdom lies in the understanding and consequent application of principles, that is, making sound judgments and decisions based on a solid understanding of key underlying principles. One such principle is the principle of duality as it relates to the knowledge construct and knowledge management.

Synopsis of Knowledge and Its Management for Inquiring Organizations

In trying to understand knowledge, knowledge management, and related concepts, such as organizational learning and organizational memory, numerous researchers have employed the structure of an inquiring organization (Churchman, 1971; Courtney, 2001; Courtney, Croasdell & Paradice, 1998; Hall, Guo & Davis, 2003; Malhotra, 1997). By doing so, they are able to view knowledge creation and thereby examine knowledge, its management, as well as organizational learning and organizational memory through a systems lens. Since inquiring organizations employ inquiring systems consisting of interrelated processes, procedures, and other measures for producing knowledge on a problem or issues of significance (Courtney, Chae & Hall, 2000; Mitroff & Linstone, 1993), knowledge and its management then become integral to all major activities of inquiring organizations. To be successful today, the modern organization must be a learning organization (Senge, 1990). By viewing such a learning organization as an inquiring system and thus an inquiring organization, it is not only possible but useful to do so in order to identify knowledge creation, in particular, *valid* knowledge produced (Courtney et al., 1998; Courtney, 2001; Hall, Paradice, & Coutrney, 2003; Malhotra, 1997).

These inquiring organizations have typically been discussed as different types, corresponding to the different types of inquiring systems first identified by Churchman (Courtney et al., 2000) where Churchman's Leibnizian inquirer has led to the Leibnizian inquiring organization, his Lockean inquirer has led to the Lockean inquiring organization, his Hegelian inquirer has led to the Hegelian inquiring organization, his Kantian inquirer has led to the Kantian inquiring organization, and his Singerian inquirer has led to the Singerian inquiring organization, respectively. Such a singular perspective, however, appears limiting given the compound nature of knowledge itself. In this way, knowledge as a construct is set apart from related constructs of data or information because, unlike its distant cousins, it does in fact display instantiations of the phenomenon of duality. Hence, this chapter proposes an embracing of the phenomenon of duality into such inquiring systems and corresponding inquiring organizations as a necessary step to the acquiring of wisdom. Duality with respect to the knowledge construct and some of its manifestations will now be presented.

Knowledge Management

Knowledge management is a key approach currently being embraced by many organizations, irrespective of their industry to solve problems, such as competitiveness and the need to innovate, which are key challenges faced by businesses today. The premise for the need for knowledge management is based on a paradigm shift in the business environment where knowledge is central to organizational performance (Swan, Scarbrough & Preston, 1999). This macro-level paradigm shift also has significant implications on the micro-level processes of assimilation and implementation of knowledge management concepts and techniques (Wickramasinghe & Mills, 2001), that is, the Knowledge Management Systems (KMS) that are in place. In essence then, knowledge management not only involves the production of information but also the capture of data at the source, the transmission and analysis of this data as well as the communication of information based on or derived from the data to those who can act on it (Davenport & Prusak, 1998). Hence, knowledge management consists of four key steps (create/generate, represent/ store, access/use/reuse, and disseminate/transfer) as depicted in Figure 2.

From Figure 2, it is important to notice that these steps are all interrelated, continuous, and impact each other and the knowledge itself throughout the organization. Furthermore, a full appreciation of the knowledge construct, the central component in Figure 2, has far reaching implications on the well functioning of all four steps and the sustainability of sound knowledge management practices. In order to better understand this knowledge construct, it is first important to identify the types of knowledge that exist. Given that the inquiring systems within inquiring organizations result in knowledge creation (Courtney et al., 1998), knowledge management becomes a necessity for inquiring organizations while a fuller understanding of the knowledge construct itself becomes a vital pursuit, and such a fuller understanding should incorporate an understanding of

Figure 2. Four Key Steps of Knowledge Management

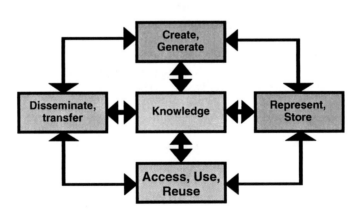

the various dualities that exist and the need for achieving a harmonious balance of these duals in all their manifestations.

Types of Knowledge

In trying to understand the knowledge construct, it is necessary first to recognize the binary nature of knowledge, namely, its objective and subjective components (Wickramasinghe & Mills, 2001; Alavi & Leidner, 2001; Schultze & Leidner, 2002; WIckramasinghe & Lamb, 2002). Knowledge can exist as an object, in essentially two forms: explicit or factual knowledge and tacit or know-how (Haynes, 1999, 2000; Polyani, 1958, 1966). It is well established that while both types of knowledge are important, tacit knowledge is more difficult to identify and thus manage (Nonaka, 1994; Nonaka & Nishiguchi, 2001). Of equal importance, though perhaps less well defined, knowledge also has a subjective component and can be viewed as an ongoing phenomenon being shaped by social practices of communities (Boland & Tenkasi, 1995). The objective elements of knowledge can be thought of as primarily having an impact on process while the subjective elements typically impact innovation. Both effective and efficient processes as well as the functions of supporting and fostering innovation are key concerns of knowledge management. Thus, we have an interesting duality in knowledge management that some have called a contradiction (Schultze, 1998) and others describe as the *loose-tight* nature of knowledge management (Malhotra, 2000).

The *loose-tight* nature of knowledge management comes to being because of the need to recognize and draw upon some distinct philosophical perspectives, namely, the Lockean/Leibnizian stream and the Hegelian/Kantian stream. Models of convergence and compliance representing the *tight* side are grounded in a Lockean/Leibnizian tradition. These models are essential to provide the information processing aspects of knowledge management, most notably by enabling efficiencies of scale and scope and thus supporting the objective view of knowledge management. In contrast, the *loose* side provides agility and flexibility in the tradition of a Hegelian/Kantian perspective. Such models recognize the importance of divergence of meaning which is essential to support the *sense-making* subjective view of knowledge management. Figure 3 depicts the Yin-Yang model of knowledge management (Wickramasinghe & Mills, 2001). The principle of Yin-Yang is at the very roots of Chinese thinking and is centered around the notion of polarity or duality not to be confused with the ideas of opposition or conflict (Watts, 1992). By incorporating this Yin-Yang concept of duality and the need to have or recognize the existence of both components present, yet not necessarily in equal amounts, is appropriate for describing knowledge management from a holistic perspective. Further, by recognizing the manifestations of duality that exist with the knowledge construct as identified in Figure 3 and thereby taking such a holistic perspective, not only are both sides of these duals recognized (i.e., the loose and tight perspectives, subjective/objective, consensus/disensus, Lockean/Lebnizian vs. Hegelian/Kantian) but also, and more importantly, both are required (at least to some extent) in order for knowledge management to truly flourish.

Specifically, Figure 3 shows that given a radical change to an environment or given a highly competitive environment, an organization needs knowledge to survive; implicit in this model is the fact that the organizations that are being described are in fact inquiring organizations in today's competitive business environment. From the Yin-Yang depiction of knowledge management, we see that knowledge is required for the organization to be effective and efficient, but new knowledge and knowledge renewal is also necessary, thereby making both forms of knowledge (i.e., both sides of the duality) important for an organization to capture in order to truly benefit from knowledge management. The knowledge spiral represents the transformations that take place in knowledge creation (Nonaka, 1994; Nonaka & Nishiguchi, 2001) as well as a dynamic equilibrium between key dualities.

Such a holistic perspective then strongly suggests that focusing on only one component or having a singular perspective of an inquiring system without any regard for the other side of any given dual is limiting and likely to lead to a less complete picture of knowledge creation, hence, the need to recognize the duality phenomenon for inquiring organizations. The importance for inquiring organizations then, becomes twofold: (a) to recognize and understand this underlying principle of duality and (b) to utilize it by, in essence,

Figure 3. Yin-Yang Model of Knowledge Management (adapted from Wickramasinghe & Mills, 2001)

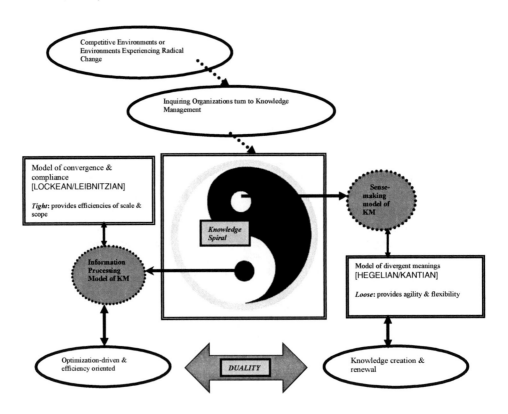

finding the *right mix* of the duality or harmonious balance between these duals for the specific context, given the context-dependent nature of wisdom. Thus, the Lockean inquiring organization grounded in a Lockean inquiring system should not totally ignore aspects of a Hegelian or Kantian inquiry system in order to create a fuller picture of *valid* knowledge. It is important to note here, however, that unlike the case with data, this *right mix* is neither programmable nor algorithmic and thus requires a deep understanding of the duality principle as well as the organization's specific context and what is key in that specific context; in this way, *valid* knowledge should be resultant and hence a state of wisdom achieved.

The Knowledge Spiral

Knowledge is not static; rather it changes and evolves during the life of an organization. What is more, it is possible to change the form of knowledge, that is, turn tacit knowledge into explicit and explicit knowledge into tacit or to turn the subjective form of knowledge into the objective form of knowledge (Wickramasinghe & Mills, 2001). This process of changing the form of knowledge is known as the knowledge spiral (Nonaka, 1994; Nonaka & Nishiguchi, 2001). Integral to this changing of knowledge through the knowledge spiral is that new knowledge is created (Nonaka, 1994), and this can bring many benefits to organizations. In the case of transferring tacit knowledge to explicit knowledge, for example, an organization is able to capture the expertise of particular individuals; hence, this adds not only to the organizational memory but also enables single-loop and double-loop organizational learning to take place (Huber, 1984). Implicit in this is the underlying dualities and a dynamic equilibrium or *right mix* between dualities that is determined by context. In the process of creating *valid* knowledge, inquiring organizations are in fact enacting these transformations and thus experiencing these dualities; however, it is unconscious and, to a great extent, much of the knowledge that potentially could be acquired is never captured by ignoring the underlying dualities and taking a singular focus, such as only a Lockean inquiring system as the lens to view knowledge creation.

Knowledge Creation

The processes of creating and capturing knowledge, irrespective of the specific philosophical orientation (i.e., Lockean/Leibnizian versus Hegelian/Kantian), has been approached from two major perspectives, namely, a people-oriented perspective and a technology-oriented perspective, another duality.

People-Oriented Perspective to Knowledge Creation

This section briefly describes three well known people-oriented knowledge creation frameworks: namely, Nonaka's Knowledge Spiral, Spender's and Blackler's respective frameworks.

According to Nonaka (1994): (1) Tacit to tacit knowledge transformation usually occurs through apprenticeship type relations where the teacher or master passes on the skill to the apprentice. (2) Explicit to explicit knowledge transformation usually occurs via formal learning of facts. (3) Tacit to explicit knowledge transformation usually occurs when there is an articulation of nuances; for example, as in healthcare if a renowned surgeon is questioned as to why he does a particular procedure in a certain manner, by his articulation of the steps, the tacit knowledge becomes explicit. (4) Explicit to tacit knowledge transformation usually occurs as new explicit knowledge is internalized; it can then be used to broaden, reframe, and extend one's tacit knowledge. These transformations are often referred to as the modes of socialization, combination, externalization, and internalization, respectively (Nonaka & Nishiguchi, 2001).

Spender draws a distinction between individual knowledge and social knowledge (yet another duality), each of which he claims can be implicit or explicit (Newell et al., 2002). From this framework, we can see that Spender's definition of implicit knowledge corresponds to Nonaka's tacit knowledge. However, unlike Spender, Nonaka doesn't differentiate between individual and social dimensions of knowledge; rather he just focuses on the nature and types of the knowledge itself. In contrast, Blackler (Newell et al., 2002) views knowledge creation from an organizational perspective, noting that knowledge can exist as encoded, embedded, embodied, encultured, and/or embrained. In addition, Blackler emphasized that for different organizational types, different types of knowledge predominate, and highlights the connection between knowledge and organizational processes (Newell et al., 2002). Blackler's types of knowledge can be thought of in terms of spanning a continuum of tacit (implicit) through to explicit with embrained being predominantly tacit (implicit) and encoded being predominantly explicit while embedded, embodied, and encultured types of knowledge exhibit varying degrees of a tacit (implicit)/explicit combination. Figure 4 depicts an integrated view of all the three frameworks.

Specifically, from Figure 4 we can see that Spender's and Blackler's perspectives complement Nonaka's conceptualization of knowledge creation and, more importantly, do not contradict his thesis of the knowledge spiral wherein the extant knowledge base is continually being expanded to a new knowledge base, be it tacit/explicit (in Nonaka's terminology), implicit/explicit (in Spender's terminology), or embrained/encultured/embodied/embedded/encoded (in Blackler's terminology). What is important to underscore here is that these three frameworks take a primarily people-oriented perspective of knowledge creation. In particular, Nonaka's framework, the most general of the three frameworks, describes knowledge creation in terms of knowledge transformations as discussed above that are all initiated by human cognitive activities as well as the enacting of at least one of the four Cs relating to knowledge discussed earlier. Needless to say that both Spender and Blackler's respective frameworks also view knowledge creation through a primarily people-oriented perspective. Typically, Hegelian and Kantian inquiring systems would incorporate knowledge creation that is consistent with these people-oriented perspectives (Malhotra, 1997).

Figure 4. Integrative Framework of the Main People-Oriented Perspectives

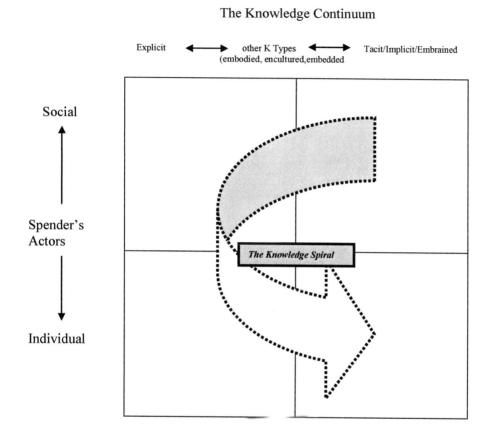

The Knowledge Continuum

Explicit ⟷ other K Types ⟷ Tacit/Implicit/Embrained
(embodied, encultured,embedded

Social

Spender's
Actors

Individual

The Knowledge Spiral

Technology-Oriented Perspective to Knowledge Creation

In contrast to the above primarily people-oriented perspectives pertaining to knowledge creation, knowledge discovery in databases (KDD) (and, more specifically, data mining), approaches knowledge creation from a primarily technology-oriented perspective. In particular, the KDD process focuses on how data is transformed into knowledge by identifying valid, novel, potentially useful, and ultimately understandable patterns in data (Fayyad, Piatetsky-Shapiro & Smyth, 1996). KDD is primarily used on data sets for creating knowledge through model building or by finding patterns and relationships in data. How to manage such newly discovered knowledge and other organizational knowledge is at the core of knowledge management. Figure 5 summarizes the key steps within the KDD process; while it is beyond the scope of this chapter to describe in detail all the steps which constitute the KDD process, an important duality to highlight here is that between exploratory and predictive data mining. Typically, Lockean and Leibnizian inquiring systems would subscribe to a technology-oriented perspective for knowledge creation (Malhotra, 1997).

The preceding discussions then have highlighted some key aspects of knowledge creation from both a people-oriented perspective as well as a technology-oriented perspective. Irrespective of which knowledge creation perspective the concept of duality is reflected in, the knowledge creation process both between the people-oriented and technology-oriented perspectives as well as within each respective perspective; for example, within the people-oriented perspective we have the dualities of social versus individual and tacit versus explicit, while in the technology-oriented perspective we have the duality of exploratory versus predictive data mining. Unlike the dualities identified in the Yin-Yang model of knowledge management though, these dualities represent instantiations of the duality principle at the micro-level. So it is possible then to have the manifestations of dualities with respect to the knowledge construct at both the macro- and micro-levels, yet another reason why the knowledge construct is compound in nature. The following section elaborates on these dualities at both the macro- and micro-levels with respect to the knowledge construct and the impact they have on knowledge management.

Figure 5. Integrative Framework of the Technology-Oriented Perspectives

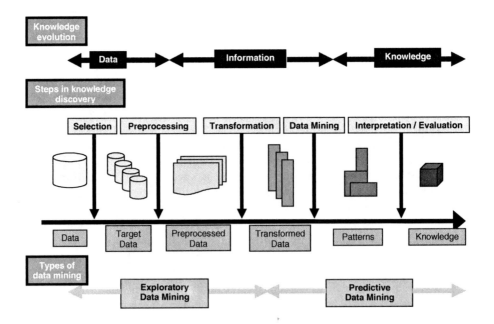

Dualities in the Knowledge Construct

The previous section highlighted several dualities with respect to the knowledge construct and knowledge creation at both a macro- and micro-level. In so doing, we can see that in fact many dualities manifest themselves when we begin to understand the knowledge construct and its management. It would make sense then that our inquiring systems, which are creating knowledge through their activities, should also be viewed in such a light and embrace such a perspective. Before discussing the benefits of embracing such a perspective, it is first useful to summarize the key dualities discussed and their benefits to knowledge management. Table 1 highlights these key dualities and why each side of the duality has importance with respect to knowledge management.

As noted in the introduction, any duality represents the existence of two irreducible aspects or perspectives. By recognizing both sides of a specific dual then, be it tacit/ explicit, individual/social, Lockean/Leibnizian versus Hegelian/Kantian, subjective/ objective, consensus/disensus, loose/tight or people/technology, a more complete and richer picture of knowledge is created and hence the impact to knowledge management, be it in terms of sharing knowledge, creating knowledge or enhancing the knowledge context, in turn is superior. On the other hand, taking a one-dimensional view, which is more often than not what too many organizations tend to do with respect to their knowledge management initiatives, for example, only recognizing the technology side of knowledge creation (and not being cognizant of the people side of knowledge creation, i.e., the Lockean and/or Leibnizian inquiring organization) or disregarding the existence of explicit knowledge (and only recognizing the existence of tacit knowledge; i.e., the Hegelian and/or Kantian inquiring organization), in a knowledge creation will lead to a much narrower and limited resultant body of knowledge as well as an inferior and most likely less useful or appropriate knowledge management initiative. Hence, we should not be surprised by the many discussions prevalent in the literature regarding the "nonsense of knowledge management" (Wilson, 2002).

Two key characteristics of inquiring organizations are (1) accuracy of the system basis and (2) continual review of the stored knowledge for accuracy in changing environments (Hall et al., 2003). Surely, a partial picture of knowledge would never be able to provide a similar level of accuracy as a fuller richer picture, hence, the benefit to inquiring organizations of understanding the duality principle and incorporating the many mani-festations of these duals both macro and micro with respect to the compound knowledge construct.

Understanding the duality principle necessitates an understanding of the *right mix* or dynamic equilibrium for the given context. Given this connection with the context and the nonprogrammable nature of the knowledge construct, such an understanding becomes a necessary albeit not sufficient step for transforming inquiring organizations from knowledge to wisdom.

Table 1. Key Knowledge Management Dualities

Duality	Impact on KM	Benefits of Recognizing the Dual
Tacit/Explicit	Knowledge creation	From Nonaka's knowledge spiral both tacit and explicit knowledge as well as the transformations of tacit to explicit and vice versa are important to KM. Only focusing on tacit (or only focusing on explicit) provides an incomplete picture with respect to knowledge creation.
Individual/Social	Knowledge sharing	Spender and Blackler, in particular, highlight the significance of both sides of this duality. Only focusing on individually constructed knowledge limits us to a much narrower domain of knowledge creation. Especially given the gregarious nature of humans socially, constructed knowledge should also form an important part of the total knowledge created.
Lockean/Leibnizian vs. Hegelian/Kantian	Knowledge context	These fundamental philosophical perspectives all highlight important facets of the knowledge context (a key dimension of wisdom) and thus, when taken together, facilitate the understanding of the full spectrum for knowledge management.
Subjective/Objective	Knowledge capture	The sides of this duality highlight both the complexities of knowledge capture relative to the knowledge type being captured as well as the importance of capturing all types of knowledge.
Consensus/Disensus	Knowledge sharing/dissemination	While the consensus side of this duality emphasizes convergence of thought, the disensus side emphasizes the need for divergence; however, both are reflections of group dynamics that are important for knowledge sharing/dissemination.
Loose/Tight	Knowledge context	This duality also highlights the need for considering both internal and external organizational context in the framing of KM issues for supporting activities that lead to optimization as well as activities that lead to knowledge creation and renewal.
People/Technology	**Knowledge creation**	This duality underscores the need for a sociotechnical approach to knowledge creation because it highlights that knowledge can be created by technologies and people as well as it also being embedded in processes.

Conclusion

This chapter has served to highlight several instances of the duality principle as it relates to knowledge and its management. These instances represented dualities at both the macro- and micro-levels. By so doing, the pervasive nature of the duality principle to knowledge as well as to knowledge management was emphasized. In presenting the duality principle as it relates to knowledge and its management, it is important to recognize its macro and micro aspects because these aspects are characteristics of any organizational setting. Furthermore, an appropriate mix of these dualities is determined by the specific organizational, environmental, technological, and situational context and is necessary but not sufficient in the formulation of an appropriate knowledge management strategy; while the understanding of the underlying principles is important for the achievement of wisdom.

Integral to inquiring organizations is the creation of knowledge; however, as discussed in this chapter, these inquiring systems have tended to focus on a singular line of inquiry, be it Lockean, Leibnizian, Hegelian, Kantian, or Singerian and thus do not recognize or explicitly capture the dualities as connected with knowledge and its management.

Underlying the Yin-Yang model of knowledge management is the recognition of the need to take a holistic view, and thus a fuller richer perspective to knowledge and its management is achieved by understanding the duality principle. Given the importance of knowledge and its management to inquiring organizations, such an understanding would then appear to be essential. Wisdom was defined as the understanding of principles which in turn lead to the making of sound decisions and judgments. Thus, the understanding of the duality principle, in its many manifestations as it relates to knowledge and its management, represents a transition to wisdom or, at the very least, a key step for inquiring organizations trying to attain a state of wisdom. This chapter has severed to create the awareness and appreciation of the existence of the duality principle with respect to knowledge and its management for inquiring organizations; future research will focus on identifying the *right mix* or equilibrium point for specific inquiring organizations to reach the harmonious balance with respect to these many duals.

References

Alavi, M., & Leidner, D. (2001). Review: Knowledge management and knowledge management Systems: Conceptual foundations and research issues. *MIS Quarterly, 25*(1), 107-136.

Alberthal, L. (1995, October 23). Remarks to the Financial Executives Institute. Dallas, TX.

Boland, R., & Tenkasi, R. (1995). Perspective making, perspective taking. *Organizational Science, 6,* 350-372.

Churchman, C. W. (1971). *The design of inquiring systems: Basic concepts of systems and organizations.* New York: Basic Books.

Courtney, J. F. (2001). Decision making and knowledge management in inquiring organizations: Toward a new decision-making paradigm for DSS. *Decision Support Systems, 31*(1), 17-38.

Courtney, J. F., Chae, B., & Hall, D. (2000). Developing inquiring organizations. *Knowledge and Innovation, 1*(1), 132-145.

Courtney, J. F., Croasdell, D. T., & Paradice, D. B. (1998). Inquiring organizations. *Australian Journal of Information Systems, 6*(1), 3-15.

Davenport, T. H., & Prusak, L. (1998). *Working knowledge: How organizations manage what they know*. Boston: Harvard Business School Press.

Drucker, P. (1993). *Post-capitalist society*. New York: Harper Collins.

Fayyad, U. M., Piatetsky-Shapiro, G., Smyth, P., & Uthurusamy, R. (1996). From data mining to knowledge discovery: An overview. In U. M. Fayyad, G. Piatetsky-Shapiro, P. Smyth, & R. Uthurusamy (Eds.), *Advances in knowledge discovery and data mining* (pp. 249–271), Menlo Park, CA: AAAI Press/MIT Press.

Hall, D., Guo, Y., & Davis R. (2003, January 6-9). *Developing a value-based decision-making model for inquiring organizations*. Proceedings of the 36th Hawaii International Conference on System Sciences.

Hall, D. J., Paradice, D. B., & Courtney, J. F. (2003). Building a theoretical foundation for a learning-oriented knowledge management system. *Journal of Information Technology Theory and Application (JITTA), 5*(2), 63-89.

Haynes, J. D. (1999). Practical thinking and tacit knowing as a foundation for information systems. *Australian Journal of Information Systems, 6*(2), 57-64.

Haynes, J. D. (2000, August 9-12). *Inquiring organizations and tacit knowing*. Proceedings of the AMCIS (pp. 1544–1547), California.

Holsapple, C., & Joshi, K. (2002). Knowledge management: A threefold framework. *The Information Society, 18,* 47-64.

Huber, G. (1984). The nature and design of postindustrial organizations. *Management Science, 30*(8), 928-951.

Malhotra, Y. (1997, August 15-17). *Knowledge management in inquiring organizations*. Proceedings of the 3rd Americas Conference on Information Systems (Philosophy of Information Systems Minitrack)(pp. 293-295), Indianapolis, IN.

Malhotra, Y. (2000). Knowledge management and new organizational form. In Y. Malhotra (Ed.), *Knowledge management and virtual organizations* (pp. 000-000) Hershey, PA: Idea Group.

Mitroff, I., & Linstone, H. A. (1993). *The unbounded mind: Breaking the chains of traditional business thinking*. New York: Oxford University Press.

Newell, S., Robertson, M., Scarbrough, H., & Swan, J. (2002). *Managing knowledge work*. Palgrave, New York.

Nonaka, I. (1994). A dynamic theory of organizational knowledge creation. *Organizational Science, 5,* 14-37.

Nonaka, I., & Nishiguchi, T. (2001). *Knowledge emergence*. Oxford: Oxford University Press.

Polyani, M. (1958). *Personal knowledge: Towards a post-critical philosophy*. Chicago: University of Chicago Press.

Polyani, M. (1966). *The tacit dimension*. London: Routledge & Kegan Paul.

Schultze, U. (1998). Investigating the contradictions in knowledge management. Presentation at IFIP Dec. Helsinki, Finland.

Schultze, U., & Leidner, D. (2002). Studying knowledge management in information systems research: Discourses and theoretical assumptions. *MIS Quarterly, 26*(3), 212-242.

Senge, P. M. (1992). *The fifth discipline: The art and practice of the learning organization.* New York: Doubleday.

Swan, J., Scarbrough, H., & Preston, J. (1999, June). *Knowledge management: The next fad to forget people?* Proceedings of the 7th European Conference on Information Systems.

Watts, A. (1992). *Tao the watercourse way.* London: Arkana.

Wickramasinghe, N., & Lamb, R. (2002). Enterprise-wide systems enabling physicians to manage care. *International Journal Healthcare Technology and Management, 4*(3/4), 288-302.

Wickramasinghe, N., & Mills, G. (2001). MARS: The electronic medical record system the core of the Kaiser Galaxy. *International Journal Healthcare Technology Management, 3*(5/6), 406-423

Wickramasinghe, N., & Sharma, S. (in press). *The fundamentals of knowledge-based organizations.* Upper Saddle River, NJ: Prentice Hall.

Wilson, T. (2002). The nonsense of knowledge management. *Information Systems Research, 8*(1), 1-41.

Endnotes

[1]   The author wishes to acknowledge the input from Adam Fadlalla on earlier versions of this chapter and extends sincere thanks to the two anonymous reviewers and Jim Courtney who provided her with great insights to refining the work and crystallizing her ideas.

Section IV:

Hermeneutics, Transformations, and Abstractions

Chapter XIV

Understanding Organizational Philosophies of Inquiry Through Hermeneutic Analysis of Organizational Texts

Michael H. Dickey
Florida State University, USA

David B. Paradice
Florida State University, USA

Abstract

This chapter introduces cultural hermeneutics as a lens for understanding philosophies of inquiry in distributed work groups. The authors suggest that philosophies of inquiry can be ascertained through hermeneutic analysis of written texts created by distributed workers using computer-mediated communication systems. Using this approach, elements of context in written artifacts that should be evident for each of Churchman's inquiring models (Leibnizian, Lockean, Kantian, Hegelian, and Singerian) are delineated, which should help identify the underlying philosophies of inquiry being used by a particular group. Sample texts for each inquiring model are also presented. Understanding philosophies of inquiry can both guide the design and implementation of computer-mediated communication systems used to create knowledge and illuminate best practices for their use.

Introduction

In today's competitive environment, computer-mediated communication (CMC) systems play a crucial role in managing and transferring knowledge in organizations. As work continues to be conducted by individuals who are spatially and/or temporally distant from each other (Burn & Barnett, 1999; Jarvenpaa & Leidner, 1999; Kirkman et al., 2002), reliance on collaborative communication technologies increases (DeSanctis & Monge, 1999; El-Shinnawy, 1999; Kraut et al., 1999).

The increasing prevalence of distributed work also expands the role that written texts play in knowledge creation in organizations. In distributed work environments, it is through written communication that workers create, affirm, or change shared meaning and culture (Turkle, 1995). When distributed workers write, they write about themselves, other workers, and events that make up their work environment. When we read the writings of workers, we learn their stories and may come to understand their experiences. To the extent that distributed workers create and/or maintain knowledge, we argue that philosophical assumptions underpinning those knowledge activities are also inscribed within the written texts. Thus, these texts provide a window for understanding organizational philosophies of inquiry or, in other words, philosophies of how knowledge is created (Churchman, 1971).

Understanding organizational philosophies of inquiry is important because certain knowledge philosophies may provide better paradigmatic support for different organizational processes. For example, Leibnizian assumptions of closed systems appear to hold for the process of producing payroll checks with its strict rules for calculation and pre-existing inputs. On the other hand, a group problem-solving process may be more Lockean in nature with an emphasis on the development of consensus among various stakeholders (Churchman, 1971).

Since the effectiveness of information systems depends on good task-technology fit (Zigurs & Buckland, 1998), philosophic assumptions about knowledge may guide information systems design. To extend our example from above, the designer of a payroll system knows that certain facts—pay rates, tax rates, benefit choices—are needed to generate a paycheck. So the system can be designed to capture or derive a set of given inputs and then calculate net pay. However, the designer of a system to support group problem solving may need to be much more focused on providing a way for a solution to be derived with few clear-cut inputs (Churchman 1971). For CMC environments focused on knowledge creation, providing appropriate task and process support for communications may hinge on underlying philosophic assumptions as well.

Philosophic assumptions about knowledge may also guide information systems use in CMC environments. If an optimal inquiring philosophy exists for a given task, it will be important to manage communications in distributed work environments such that an evolution toward an inquiring model that best suits the task occurs.

In this chapter, we suggest a framework for identifying underlying organizational philosophies of inquiry through hermeneutic analysis of written texts. Identification of underlying philosophies will illuminate features and/or flaws in CMC systems that facilitate or hinder knowledge creation, ultimately assisting in CMC design efforts. It will also shed light on best practices for the use of CMC systems for knowledge creation.

Conceptual Foundation

Hermeneutics and philology provide a foundation for our work. Hermeneutics is "the study of interpretation, especially the process of coming to understand text" (Boland, 1991, p. 439). Written documents are not sufficient to deduce meaning because readers interpret them from their own unique perspectives. Hence, understanding text requires uncovering values and norms embedded in the text or, in other words, understanding the context in which the text was written.

Philology provides a useful approach for explaining the relationship between text and its context (Becker, 1979). This approach assumes that individuals bring their biases to their readings of text, which in turn, affect interpretations. Detailed descriptions of context are necessary so that readers may ascribe meaning more accurately (Becker, 1979; Geertz, 1983). To develop descriptions of context, hermeneutics and philology suggest that we study the relationships that text has with the context in which it is written. Four relevant contextual relations, according to Becker (1979), are:

- *Coherence:* the relations of textual units to each other within the text. Sources of coherence include underlying sets of rules or grammars for a text that enable its readers to make sense of it.

- *Invention:* the relations of textual units to other texts. Texts are all related to previous texts within a culture. Textual units "speak the past" when they express old texts or ideas. They "speak the present" when they express new ideas.

- *Intention:* the relations of textual units to the intention of the creators of the text.

- *Reference:* the relations of textual units to nonliterary events which occur independently of the text.

Identifying these elements of context in written organizational artifacts—such as e-mail and discussion forum postings—provides clues for the design and implementation of appropriate knowledge management systems for particular knowledge creation processes. In situations where systems are already in place, these contextual cues provide a means of verifying process/system fit. The following paragraphs discuss how these characteristics will be demonstrated in the textual artifacts of the organization.

We will examine each of Churchman's (1971) inquiring models: Leibnizian, Lockean, Kantian, Hegelian, and Singerian. For each, we will delineate elements of context (including underlying premises and assumptions) that should be evident in texts that exist in the inquiring system. Churchman discusses these models separately, but it is clear that the type of inquiry possible grows more complex with each successive inquirer. In a sense, successive inquirers build on their predecessors.

One can think of the following discussion as describing a set of tools. Each tool has a specific capability for which it is particularly well suited, and the bulk of the discussion will be focused on that specific use. For example, a screwdriver is particularly good for driving a screw into a board. A hammer is particularly good for driving a nail into a board. When a board is made of particularly hard wood, however, one may need a hammer to get the screw started. So, while the hammer may be described as useful for driving nails (with no mention of screws), it can be used with screws to solve a more complex problem. Having both a screwdriver and a hammer does not imply that both tools should always be used on all occasions.

Similarly, we discuss each inquirer separately, but by the end of the discussion we will have presented characteristics shared by inquirers as well as unique to inquirers (see also Hall et al., 2003). Ideally, an organization would have a full range of inquiring capability available and would be able to use these tools individually or in combinations to analyze and understand text.

Leibnizian Inquirer

Churchman (1971) delineates several essential characteristics of a Leibnizian inquirer. A Leibnizian inquirer is a closed system; all ideas and/or symbols are innate. This inquirer is capable of producing strings of symbols that can be decomposed into smaller recognizable units. Furthermore, a Leibnizian inquirer is capable of determining whether any unit is true or false, based upon existing combinations of symbols. The inquirer can form nets of units, or fact nets, using relational operators and can then rank these nets by some prescribed criteria. The process of classifying symbols, building fact nets, and ranking them will lead to derivation of or convergence to an optimal net.

Sources of Leibnizian Text

Leibnizian text is going to be found readily in the descriptions of programmed processes, in codified "standard operating procedures," in descriptions of business (or diplomatic) protocols, and in documents containing descriptions of logical arguments. For example, the process of approving loan applications is a programmed process that lends itself to Leibnizian inquiry. Approval scores are used throughout the lending industry to determine credit worthiness. These scores are calculated from responses to questions, where specific responses are scored, and an applicant is approved for a loan when a specified threshold score is achieved. Similarly, standard operating procedures contain programmed responses to situations. It would be a relatively straightforward exercise to construct a fact net of situations and responses in a Leibnizian fashion. Leibnizian texts will also be found in the descriptions of protocols. Business (or diplomatic) protocols dictate specific entreaties and responses by participants. Finally, where logic is used to draw a conclusion, Leibnizian inquiry will be applicable.

Leibnizian Text Example

Consider the following text from an online chat discussion:

Pat:	*We need to come up with a better solution to the network capacity issue in the TalBank installation. Any ideas?*
Kris:	*Why? Isn't twisted-pair going to be good enough?*
Pat:	*Not enough capacity.*
Kris:	*So you need something faster than electrical signals on TP, huh?*
Kris:	*Let me think...*
Kris:	*Well, if you were using fiber-optic cable, you could use light waves.*
Pat:	*Even that might not be enough. They really need a lot.*
Kris:	*Wow. What about multiplexing on the TP? That would expand capacity.*
Pat:	*Already looked at the numbers. Still not enough.*
Kris:	*You're not helping.*
Kris:	*Hey — what about multiplexing light on fiber?*
Kris:	*I think I saw an article or something about that the other day.*
Pat:	*That would be great.*
Kris:	*I remember... my friend at NetCo told me they recently installed wavelength division multiplexers on his fiber-optic circuits with great success.*
Pat:	*Sounds good. I'll see what I can find out. ttyl*

Coherence

For a Leibnizian inquirer, the underlying rules and grammars of texts will be exhibited in certain form and content characteristics. Leibnizian communication genres for creating knowledge will use pre-existing symbols and logical operators to construct arguments for the expansion, production, or refutation of fact nets. The consistent use of symbols, logical operators, and practices for the articulation of arguments are all sources of coherence in the text.

Consider first how symbols and logical operators will be used. Since all symbols pre-exist, and all logic is given, arguments for the expansion or production of fact nets will be stated in terms of those pre-existing symbols and logical operators. For example:

- We know what the symbols *twisted-pair, fiber-optic*, and *multiplexing* represent.
- We know that the statement, "transmission efficiency on fiber-optic is greater than on twisted-pair," is true.
- We know that the statement, "multiplexing increases circuit capacity," is true.
- So then we can derive another set of true statements, such as "transmission efficiency on twisted-pair is less than on fiber-optic." We can also evaluate the statement, "multiplexing decreases circuit capacity," as false.

For English language speakers versed in telecommunications, the words *twisted-pair, fiber-optic,* and *multiplexing* are known symbols that provide coherence in the written text. As a logical operator, *is greater than* also provides coherence. Conversely, written text would not be understood if the argument were expressed with symbols or logical operators that were not known:

- $\Psi\beta 1$

Furthermore, the form of the argument will be consistent. A Leibnizian inquirer will express arguments thus:

- This is what I know. ("Twisted-pair isn't fast enough.")
- I compare a candidate for the fact net to what I know. ("Would fiber-optic be fast enough?")
- I derive (or falsify) a new statement, or in other words, I incorporate (or not) the new statement into the fact net. ("No, it would not.")

Invention

Since Leibnizian inquirers are closed systems, the degree of invention—or the degree to which a text *speaks the past* or *speaks the present*—will depend on how the innate ideas are combined. Texts that speak the past will articulate innate ideas in pure form or combinations of innate ideas that have been previously articulated. Texts that speak the present will express new combinations of innate ideas.

Assume that we are trying to create knowledge about how to increase network capacity due to the explosive growth of the Internet and that the following ideas are known:

- Fiber-optic cable can transmit light that carries information.
- Twisted-pair wires can transmit electrical signals that carry information.
- Frequency division multiplexing (FDM) of electrical signals can be used to increase network capacity on twisted-pair circuits.

A text can build an argument using innate ideas and existing combinations of ideas to come up with a new combination. In this case, knowledge of FDM and data transmission using fiber-optics and twisted-pairs is combined to derive the notion that we can increase circuit capacity by splitting light frequencies the same way we split electrical signals through multiplexing (e.g., wavelength division multiplexing). The text is speaking the past when it expresses the old knowledge and is speaking the present when it expresses the new combination.

Intention

In Leibnizian texts, three intentions will appear. First, participants in knowledge creation will seek to classify a string of symbols (or textual units) as true or false. Second, participants will attempt to combine symbols (or textual units) with relational operators to produce alternatives. Third, participants will rank possible alternatives. Let us extend the telecommunications example to demonstrate intention:

- "We know that electrical signals can be transmitted on twisted-pair (TP) wires."
    Logical expression: Pure innate idea
    Intention: classify as a true statement
- "We know that light waves can be transmitted on fiber-optic (FO) cable."
    Logical expression: Pure innate idea
    Intention: classify as a true statement
- "We know that electrical signals can be multiplexed on twisted-pair wires to expand network capacity."
    Logical expression: TP + FDM = expansion in network capacity
    Intention: classify as a true statement
- "We know that light waves can be transmitted on fiber-optics faster than electrical signals on twisted-pair."
    Logical expression: FO speed > TP speed
    Intention: classify as a true statement
- "Why not multiplex light waves on fiber-optic circuits the same way as we do on twisted-pair circuits?"
    Logical expression: FO + FDM = expansion in network capacity
    Intention: combine symbols to produce an alternative

- "I think that sounds like a great idea . . . much cheaper than laying additional fiber-optic cable."

> Logical expression: FO + FDM cost < n(FO)

> Intention: rank alternatives

Reference

In Leibnizian texts, reference will be made to events from the nonliterary world that either support or refute fact nets or arguments constructed. For instance:

- "My friend at XYZ Company recently installed wavelength division multiplexers on his fiber-optic circuits with great success."

Implications for Systems Design

Leibnizian processes can be supported by rule-based systems. CMC systems with an underlying Leibnizian philosophy may benefit from inclusion of support for the following:

- Discussion (synchronous or asynchronous).
- A repository of rules.
- Representation of existing fact nets.
- Validation processes for new combinations of innate ideas.

Lockean Inquirer

Churchman (1971) outlines several essential characteristics of a Lockean inquirer. A Lockean inquirer is an open system; no ideas and/or symbols are innate. Whereas the primary task of the Leibnizian inquirer, a closed system, is to assess tautology, the function of the Lockean inquirer is recognize and label inputs. Inputs combined with logical operators result in outputs, which are evaluated by a *community of minds*. This community then develops a consensus about the outputs. In other words, outputs that the group agrees on are regarded as true.

Sources of Lockean Text

Lockean text will be found in informal documents of agreement. For example, meeting notes that outline action items agreed to by a group would be one form of Lockean text. Project management documentation in which agreements were reached regarding requested changes would be another example. Similarly, an assignment of responsibilities in a project or other type of work environment would be Lockean. Documents of correspondence among trading partners might exhibit Lockean characteristics if the documents outline agreements between the partners or if the documents describe market conditions that the partners agree to be true. In a similar vein, one could argue that documents that provide evidence of collusion would be Lockean and that correspondence between cartels could be Lockean as well.

Lockean Text Example

Consider the following text from an online chat discussion:

Pat:	*I just got reprimanded again...*
Kris:	*What now?*
Pat:	*Can't believe we still have to distribute paper copies of our syllabi*
Kris:	*I know I know — but it's a rule.*
Pat:	*But we're putting EVERYTHING on the college server now! That's what the Provost wants, isn't it? So why turn around and PRINT the syllabus?*
Kris:	*It's a rule.*
Pat:	*But WHY is it a RULE?*
Kris:	*It's in the University Handbook.*
Pat:	*But it isn't the real POLICY anymore!*
Kris:	*Rules are rules.*
Pat:	*Yeah yeah. I'm off to waste some paper... ttyl.*

Coherence

The manner in which a Lockean inquirer recognizes and labels inputs and then develops a communal consensus depends on how the community of minds and its communication system is organized (Churchman, 1971). This dependence implies that, in a Lockean inquirer, strong communication genres will exist both for recognizing and labeling inputs and for the way that the labels are negotiated among community members.

Churchman (1971) suggests that negotiation of labels will occur in the form:

- "Why is X labeled P?"

In our example, the question is:

- "Why are printed syllabi necessary?"

Assuming an underlying Lockean philosophy, communication genres must exist for recognizing that X is a *requirement* (or policy) and for negotiating that requirement (or policy) X is *necessary* or *expendable*. In other words, is X an input, and if so, how shall we label it? Thus, in a Lockean inquirer, communication genres will exist that support a communal recognition of inputs and negotiation of labels.

Our example text demonstrates that in a Lockean computer-mediated communication (CMC) environment, content can be structured such that consensus can be built. The final consensus in our text is that printed syllabi are necessary to adhere to university policy. This particular communication genre supported dyadic discussion, but other consensus building processes, such as polling and voting, may also be present in a Lockean inquirer.

Invention

In a Lockean inquirer, the degree of invention will depend upon the degree of change in community agreement. Texts that speak the past will re-enact previous community agreements. Texts that speak the present will articulate new community agreements on the labeling of an input or will attempt to label an input in a new way.

Continuing our example from above, a representative Lockean text that speaks the past would be:

- "Distribution of printed syllabi is a rule—it's in the University Handbook."

A text that speaks the present is:

- "But it isn't the real POLICY anymore."

Intention

The overriding intention in Lockean communities is to seek consensus, but consensus can be built based on previous community agreement or new negotiated agreements. So three types of intentions will appear in Lockean texts. First, participants in knowledge creation will seek *to apply an existing label* (of a property) to candidate knowledge inputs. Failing that, the second intention will be *to classify the new candidate knowledge input according to existing labels*. That is, an attempt will be made to place the candidate in the existing set of properties as a variant of an existing label. If that process fails, the third intention that will be exhibited is *to create a new label* (property) for the input. This process may involve the creation of compound properties using the logical primitives *and*, *or*, and *not*.

In our example text, Pat attempts to label "distribution of paper syllabi" as "not a valid rule." Kris, on the other hand, reclassifies the input as "a rule." Pat attempts to create a new label of "not the real policy," but is unsuccessful.

Reference

Reference will be reflected in texts that compare the Lockean inquirer's classification to nontext outcomes produced by other Lockean inquirers. Nontext outcomes can support or refute existing community agreement and may be embodied in text to substantiate or renegotiate consensus about knowledge.

In addition, texts will also refer to the larger system(s) in which the inquirer is embedded. In our example, the Lockean inquirer is a community of two individuals which is embedded in the larger college system and in the still larger university system. Organizational rules—distribution of printed syllabi, for instance—that affect the two individuals are not defined by the inquirer and are not subject to negotiation by the group, even though Pat tries to renegotiate the labels. Any text that is written about the larger organization is *referring* to a nontext world that is part of the context of the inquirer. Specific references in our sample text are to the college server and to university policy

Implications for Systems Design

Lockean processes involve communal consensus building. So in addition to features outlined for CMCs with underlying Leibnizian philosophies, support for the following may be useful:

- Synchronous discussion.
- Ranking of alternatives.
- Voting.

Kantian Inquirer

Churchman's (1971) description of the Kantian inquirer emphasizes the relevance of an *a priori* science for guiding data collection related to inputs to the knowledge creation process. While still focusing on knowledge creation, the Kantian inquirer also examines the question, "How do you know what data to collect?" Consider two similar organizations that are upgrading communication networks. The data collected in order to design an appropriate strategy will be dependent on *a priori* assumptions about anticipated network traffic, staffing requirements, application use, strategic alliances, and so forth. Even if the two organizations are alike today, they will collect dissimilar data that will result in divergent network designs if their *a priori* assumptions about the future differ.

While the *a priori* is essential, the Kantian inquirer also recognizes that multiple models (in essence, multiple *a priori* sciences) are possible. So the Kantian inquirer blends Leibnizian and Lockean inquirer characteristics. The Kantian inquirer develops Leibnizian fact nets but also develops Lockean community agreement about which *a priori* science works best for solving any given problem.

In addition, the Kantian inquirer depends on time-space measurement, relying on a clock (i.e., some time-keeping instrument) to order events so as to determine causality. It also needs to be able to place events in space.

Sources of Kantian Text

Kantian text will be found in documents that examine multiple models (perspectives) of a situation and assess which has the best fit with what is known about the environment being analyzed. Comparative studies and summaries of scenario analyses are Kantian in nature. Descriptions of rigorously defined experimental studies are also Kantian because one can consider the control and treatment groups as different models.

Kantian Text Example

Consider the following e-mail message:

Hi everyone:

We need to meet to discuss the upcoming Internet-based information system that will be available to our clients. I'm scheduling the meeting for tomorrow at 2:00.

As you all know, the Internet is where our customers expect us and where we need to be. We're well established as the premier payroll processing service provider, but that reputation is based on decades of working in a mainframe environment using extremely stable software and development environments.

This project will be our first one delivered on the Internet. While we will still be interfacing with our usual database technologies, this will be our first application developed using Internet technologies. We have several employees that have finished their training sessions with these new tools and we have a couple of new hires (Shaun and Jocelyn) who have these skills.

That said, we need to scope out this project and determine a schedule. We've got our past experiences developing other systems that we can use as a template, but we need to recognize that this is a new development environment. Come ready to work!

Joe

Coherence

In a Kantian inquirer, underlying rules and grammars for text will be exhibited in the same fashion as for Leibnizian inquirers. Communication genres for creating knowledge will use pre-existing symbols and logical operators to construct arguments for the expansion, production, or refutation of fact nets. The difference is that since multiple *a priori* models are possible, the *a priori* itself will affect how texts are organized and how ideas are communicated. This being the case, an individual that assumes an alternative *a priori* model from the other individuals in a distributed knowledge creation environment may have difficulty communicating. In our sample text, possible *a priori* models for development environments are mentioned—the mainframe and the Internet. Discussions of Java objects and classes with developers who design mainframe COBOL systems using structured techniques would not make sense. Thus, the language of the *a priori* science is a source of coherence. So in a Kantian inquirer, one would expect to see some texts devoted to ensuring that all participants are speaking the same language (i.e., using the same *a priori* model).

Other sources of coherence in a Kantian inquirer will be time-space measurement and sensory inputs. With regard to time-space measurement, artifacts such as time stamps for texts and/or some sort of spatial mapping of texts help readers organize texts linearly. Inputs that do not originate in the senses will not be coherent to the Kantian inquirer. It relies on data that can be sensed, so textual artifacts must deal with only data that is sensory in nature.

Invention

Invention can be viewed with respect to the notion of *fit* with the *a priori* science. Text that speaks the past will have a high degree of fit with the *a priori*; conversely, text that speaks the present will have a low degree of fit with the *a priori*.

To illustrate, consider the firm in our sample text that is well-versed in the provision of payroll services in the mainframe environment (the familiar technology). The firm is considering undertaking the development of similar services in an Internet environment. Texts that embody familiar processes and methods for developing yet another payroll application (e.g., "we will still be interfacing with our usual database technologies") exhibit a low degree of invention. In a Kantian inquirer, these texts will identify aspects of the new system that fit with familiar development approaches. In other words, attempts to place the new development within the firm's *a priori* knowledge of building payroll systems are examples of speaking the past.

Kantian inquirers, however, recognize that the existing *a priori* science doesn't always provide the best (or even an adequate) basis for action. So texts that recognize the limitations of the mainframe model and branch out to form a new *a priori* science for providing payroll services exhibit a high degree of invention and thus speak the present. An example from our sample text is "we need to recognize that this is a new development environment."

Intention

Intention in the Kantian inquirer will be seen in the guidance of the *a priori* to data collection and assessment of the data's fit within the *a priori*. Recognizing that a particular *a priori* may not be adequate, the Kantian inquirer accepts the notion of redefinition of an *a priori* science into another one. In our example, provision of payroll services using mainframe software environments had historically been an acceptable *a priori* science, but changes in customer expectations necessitate moving to the new Internet environment. Texts that recognize the need to redefine the *a priori* in use and that move toward that redefinition reflect an intention of the Kantian inquirer.

Reference

Reference in the Kantian inquirer will be reflected in texts that refer to the *a priori* science(s), particularly those that embody concrete examples of the *a priori* at work. For instance, in the sample text, a reference is made to the firm's reputation built on "decades of working in a mainframe environment using extremely stable software and development environments." Kantian philosophy also relies on *pure sensuous intuition*, or inputs that come from the senses. So texts will also refer to events or actions sensed by the participants. In other words, texts will embody experience, such as the experience of several employees that have finished training sessions with new development tools.

Implications for Systems Design

Kantian processes require systems capable of supporting multiple problem definitions and being able to translate one problem definition into another. Additional system features useful in supporting Kantian knowledge creation include:

- Expanded repository capabilities to support multiple perspectives.

- System support for forcing delineation of *a priori* assumptions.

- System support to facilitate user awareness of the existence of multiple perspectives (and languages).

- Representation and evolution of multiple models.

Hegelian Inquirer

Churchman's (1971) description of the Hegelian inquirer raises a new issue: how does one deal with disagreement? Where the Lockean inquirer recognized the advantages of many minds, and the Kantian inquirer recognized that the many minds may have different perspectives, the Hegelian inquirer considers the situation of many minds with opposing perspectives. The Lockean inquirer reflects consensual communities of agreement. The Kantian inquirer reflects agreement on the *a priori* science that underlies the data collection of the inquiring system but accommodates the idea that different perspectives may have some aspects of difference. The Hegelian inquirer enters new territory by recognizing the conflict that occurs when inquiring systems disagree on fundamental assumptions in play.

The essence of the Hegelian inquirer is a dialectic process involving a thesis and its deadly enemy which occurs in the form of an antithesis. Each has a worldview, or *Weltanshauung*, that defines its perspective. The dialectic involves a mapping of facts (i.e., data) into each worldview with each mapping defining an information function. The *better* worldview is the one capable of accommodating the greatest number of facts. An objective over-observer watches the dialectic process and creates new knowledge through a process of synthesis of the best of the thesis and the antithesis.

Sources of Hegelian Text

Transcriptions of courtroom proceedings are a classic example of Hegelian text, and all related legal artifacts, such as affidavits and depositions, would be Hegelian. However, not all Hegelian text will occur in a legal environment. Transcriptions of negotiations, for example, would be Hegelian in nature. Another example would be a transcript from a press conference. In practice, it may be that the Hegelian dialectic must be constructed from multiple source documents when the dialectic occurs outside of a courtroom setting. This is because many documents will present only one side of the dialectic. For example, a news article that is critical of a business policy without also responding to criticisms of the position taken in the article presents only one side of the dialectic. Thus, any document that is critical in the sense of challenging assumptions will contribute to the construction of an Hegelian dialectic, but other documents may be necessary to create the entire dialectic process.

Hegelian Text Example

Consider the following hypothetical excerpt from a transcript of a video conference:

CIO: *We are requesting $500,000,000 in additional funds to upgrade our technology capabilities.*

CFO: *Say what? The sluggish economy is eating our lunch . . . how can we afford such a large expenditure now?*

CIO: *We have always been a technology leader in our industry. These investments are required to maintain our competitive advantage.*

VP: *I think those funds would be better spent developing our overseas markets.*

CFO: *Besides, technology is changing so rapidly ... shouldn't we wait and see what happens instead of plunging ahead with new technologies?*

CIO: *We too are committed to developing our overseas markets. But technology is not just an operational expense. Take for example, our efforts last year. We've done more to support new product development with technology. And we've completely revamped the way we work with suppliers, which will increase customer demand for our products.*

CEO: *Yes, I agree. We must continue to be a leader in technology innovations to sustain our competitive advantage, so I'll approve the additional expenditures. It is understood that these expenditures will support our overseas expansion efforts as well.*

Coherence

The Hegelian dialectic process in a text-based environment will require that certain types of textual units be presented. Texts with an underlying Hegelian philosophy can be expected to appear in one of five forms: thesis statement, antithesis statement, thesis argument, antithesis argument, and synthesis. Just as in a Kantian inquirer where the language of the *a priori* science provides coherence, in a Hegelian inquirer, the language of the writer's worldview will be a source of coherence. So we will expect to see mechanisms that inform the reader of the writer's worldview.

In the sample text, statements and supporting arguments of both the thesis and antithesis are made:

Thesis: Commitment of large expenditures for technology upgrades are necessary.

- *Argument:* There are benefits to being a technology leader.
- *Argument:* Technological changes in areas, such as the way we work with suppliers, will increase customer demand.
- *Argument:* Our current competitive advantage in technology must be sustained.

Antithesis: Large expenditures for technology upgrades are not necessary.

- *Argument:* The economy is sluggish, decreasing customer demand.
- *Argument:* The existing technology base is adequate to meet customer demand.
- *Argument:* Our resources would be better utilized developing our overseas markets.
- *Argument:* The rapid rate of technological change is better met with a "wait and see" attitude.

The synthesis is provided in the CEO's statement where the expenditure is approved.

Invention

A Hegelian inquirer attempts to assimilate multiple perspectives to create knowledge, while accommodating conflict. Since multiple perspectives exist, in a sense, each text should both speak the present (or be new) to someone in the group and speak the past (or reconfirm existing knowledge) for someone. In addition, the degree of invention in a text may vary by individual writer. At one end of the spectrum, a writer who writes about his/her own perspective or assumptions speaks the past. At the other end, a writer who writes about his/her understanding of someone else's perspective speaks the present. For the independent observer of the dialectic, all texts will speak the present. Knowledge creation will occur as the observer synthesizes both perspectives.

Consider two sides of the debate regarding technology expenditures in our example. The CIO is the proponent of the thesis, who wants additional funding for upgrades. The CFO and the VP of Marketing are proponents of the antithesis; they do not want to approve the spending request, but want to keep the legacy system. The arguments for the thesis are not inventive for the CIO, but they may be for the proponents of the antithesis. Likewise, the reverse is true for texts supporting the antithesis.

Intention

Intention in a Hegelian inquirer will be dependent on the role of the writer. Participants in the discussion can be either (a) proponents of a perspective or (b) the objective observer. Proponents of the thesis or the antithesis will pose arguments that support a position or challenge the position of the opposing thesis, or both. Extending our example from above, statements made by the CIO support the thesis. Statements made by the CFO and the VP of Marketing support the antithesis or challenge the thesis. In this way, the worldviews of the participants become fully articulated. The objective observer will synthesize the two perspectives and eventually, through the text, identify a larger worldview. The objective observer intends to map information into each worldview and evaluate the results. To solve the expenditure issue, the objective CEO approves the expenditure but instructs the CIO to make sure that the upgrades will support overseas expansion, thereby blending the importance of both technological innovation and the overseas markets.

Reference

There must be some shared aspect in a Hegelian dialectic. In the most extreme situation, the thesis and the antithesis will disagree over the definition of the problem at hand. But even in this fundamental disagreement, an objective observer sees two (perhaps extremely different) perspectives of a problem. Reference in Hegelian inquiring systems will be reflected in some aspect of shared context. Paradoxically, the shared context may be disagreement over the context itself!

In stating arguments, the Hegelian writer will use whatever support is available for constructing logical arguments. So texts should refer to events and experience that provide empirical evidence for a writer's position. For instance, "revamping the way in which we do business with suppliers" is an event referenced in the sample text above.

Implications for Systems Design

Hegelian processes require systems capable of supporting critical argument. All Kantian-based features could be incorporated here as well. However, since conflict is introduced here, it may be useful to incorporate support for anonymous contribution. In addition, the existence of an objective observer will also require support for facilitation of the discussion to allow for synthesis of the two worldviews.

Singerian Inquirer

The Singerian inquirer is based in metrology: the science of measurement. For this inquirer, the process that produces accurate measurements is the fundamental focus. The Singerian inquirer thrives on refining measurements, so disagreements regarding measurements are catalysts for Singerian inquiry. In fact, the Singerian inquiry will introduce disagreement in order to seek refinement by *sweeping in* concepts, ideas, and information related to the subject at hand. Because the new information could have any epistemological basis, the Singerian inquirer may draw on all other modes of inquiry in seeking refined measurement capability. Finally, the Singerian inquirer seeks *exoteric knowledge*. This is knowledge useful to everyone.

Sources of Singerian Text

Documents that emphasize measurement, such as assessments (employee or process), financial statements, annual reports, or market analyses, are Singerian in nature. However, because the Singerian inquirer thrives on disagreement, documents that question measurements are prime candidates for Singerian inquiry. In the context of sweeping in new information, Singerian text will be found in any document that integrates information from different disciplines. In a nonbusiness setting, almanacs are fine examples of Singerian text as they not only provide numerous tables of measurement but also integrate these measurements with other information that is useful in many areas of life.

Singerian Text Example

Consider the following letter sent to stockholders of a company and management's response:

Dear Stockholder:

In response to your request for an independent audit of Singerco, Inc. we find the following irregularity.

Last year, Singerco reported committing $500,000,000 to upgrading technology capabilities. We find that their analysis included price discounts that ultimately were not realized. The latest market data indicates the technology base in place prior to last year's technology budget increase was more than adequate to meet the demands of customers. Our own analysis of market trends for other industries, such as the oil and gas industry, clearly predicted additional technology expenditures would realize little in terms of increasing market share. Simultaneously, the value of overseas markets for

Singerco products was clearly overstated as evidenced by the recent collapse of the Singerco business in Malaysia. A better understanding of the Malaysian legal environment could have prevented this loss. Extracting this market value alone reduces the overall value of the stock by almost 25%.

We feel that changing the Singerco analysis to more accurately reflect the price paid for new technology and the loss of the Malaysian market provides a financial assessment of Singerco that is consistent with Generally Accepted Accounting Principles.

Sincerely,

Jamie Associates, CPA

Dear Stockholders:

We have received a copy of Jamie Associates audit. While we do not challenge the adjustments recommended, we would still like to provide you with our accounting for our prior estimates.

We feel it is imperative that Singerco remain a leader in technology innovation in the water purification industry. While we appreciate the expertise of Jamie Associates in the oil and gas industry, we feel their analyses there are not applicable to our industry and would not have predicted the downturn in demand that we ultimately experienced. Simply put, water purification plants and the water purification industry cannot be modeled using oil and gas industry parameters.

Additionally, we were in no position to predict the loss of the Malaysian market. All of our past analyses of international markets have been quite accurate and there was no reason to doubt the one used last year. We disagree that any misunderstanding of international law caused this loss. It was the entry of China's low-cost alternative into our market that had the greatest impact. We are, however, always looking to improve our analysis capabilities and will revise our models to incorporate more variables related to international market competition.

We remain committed to bringing the most value to our stockholders.

Sincerely,

Katie Hebert, CEO

Coherence

Coherence in the Singerian inquirer must be with respect to the system of measurement. There will be two fundamental aspects: the unit and the standard. While the unit is arbitrary, the standard is not. Anything can be selected as a unit of measurement. However, a standard requires some type of agreement to be of any value. That a buyer can measure an area using a ruler and then purchase something that *fits* in that area based on the measurements of a vendor of that thing requires that both the buyer and the supplier use some standard of measurement which, within an acceptable tolerance for the purposes of the exchange, has reliable properties.

In the sample text, Jamie Associates applied a system of measurement that, while applicable to the oil and gas industry, was not applicable to Singerco's industry, water purification. Readers of the text who were familiar with the water purification's industry system of measurement may not have understood the arguments made by the CPA or may have misinterpreted them due to a lack of coherence with respect to the system of measurement.

Invention

When a Singerian inquirer speaks the past, it speaks of agreement. For the Singerian inquirer, measurements that are in agreement are indicative of past decisions or, more precisely, past realities. If the measuring system ever fails to replicate a measurement, or if two measurers produce different measurements, then *reality* is not being accurately modeled, and the system must not be working *properly*. Consequently, when the Singerian inquirer speaks the present, it speaks of disagreement.

The extent of the disagreement may be reflected in any of the inventions described thus far. One may see a Leibnizian disagreement over a candidate for a fact net. Or, at the other extreme, one may see diametrically opposing views embedded in a Hegelian dialectic, such as in our sample text.

Intention

Disagreement is not necessarily a bad situation. The Singerian inquirer enjoys disagreement, for that is where learning occurs. When disagreement exists, the Singerian inquirer invokes a property that is fundamental to it: a sweeping in process of new variables and laws. New variables and laws add new dimensions and explanations, one or more of which may explain the discrepancy leading to the disagreement. When an explanation is found, learning occurs.

The Singerian inquirer enjoys disagreement so much that it actively seeks it. For example, if measurements agree in two decimal places, then more refined measurements are sought in three, four, or more decimal places. Ultimately, the precision of the measuring instruments fails and disagreement occurs. The Singerian inquirer's philosophy is that resolving this disagreement elevates the overall system to a higher level of understanding. Another approach taken by the Singerian inquirer is partitioning complex objects into smaller components. When there is agreement, the Singerian inquirer partitions the object of agreement into components of increasingly fine measurement in an attempt to identify some point of disagreement. This *rock the boat* philosophy is fundamental to the Singerian inquirer.

In our sample text, a Singerian philosophy is evident in management's response. Although there is a difference of opinion about whether or not Singerco management could have prevented the loss of business in Malaysia, management is receptive to sweeping in information about new variables and revising its estimation models with respect to international markets.

Reference

Reference in Singerian texts must be to the system of measurement. The texts will contain references to the standard and the unit of measurement. Variables that form the system of measurement will be referenced. In situations where disagreement occurs, the text will contain references to new variables that are used in other systems.

For instance, the auditor's letter references "Generally Accepted Accounting Principles" as well as analysis of market trends employed in the oil and gas industry. Management's response references degree of technology innovation as a standard of measurement in the water purification industry and past analyses of international markets as a benchmark for the current year analysis.

Implications for Systems Design

Singerian processes require all possible system capabilities as they sweep in any variables that may lead to refinement of existing measurements. Broader more flexible support may be necessary for all facets of knowledge creation, including discussion, repositories of existing models, statistical support, and system support for the refinement of measurement models.

Summary

We believe that examining texts in light of the contextual cues expected in each inquiring environment will provide better support for different organizational processes. Processes that are Leibnizian in nature will suffer from micro-management when required to be Lockean in their processing. Conversely, Lockean processes that are handled as if Leibnizian will be perceived as dictatorial. When Hegelian processes are handled in Leibnizian, Lockean, or even Kantian ways, there is a risk that the full implications of the

Table 1. Texts in Contexts with Various Underlying Organizational Philosophies of Inquiry

Inquirer	Coherence	Invention	Intention	Reference
Leibnizian	Pre-existing symbols and logical operators; Consistent form of argument construction	Speaking the past: articulation of innate ideas in pure form Speaking the present: expression of new combinations of innate ideas	Classify statements as true or false; combine symbols to produce alternatives; rank alternatives	Events that support or refute fact nets or new arguments
Lockean	Communication genre for recognizing and labeling inputs	Speaking the past: re-enactment of previous community agreement Speaking the present: articulation of new community agreement	Seek consensus; apply existing label to candidate knowledge; classify new candidate knowledge according to existing labels; create a new label	Outcomes produced by other Lockean inquirers; larger system(s) in which the inquirer is embedded
Kantian	Language of the *a priori*; time stamps; knowledge of the senses	Speaking the past: texts with a high degree of fit with the *a priori* Speaking the present: texts with a low degree of fit with the *a priori* (e.g., texts that create a new *a priori* science)	Seek fit with *a priori*; redefine an existing *a priori*; develop a new *a priori*	Concrete examples of the *a priori*; sensory experience
Hegelian	Linearity in presentation of arguments; language of each of the worldviews	Most texts will speak both the past and the present, interpreted differently depending on whether the reader is a proponent or an opponent of the thesis	Support the thesis; refute the antithesis; support the antithesis, refute the thesis; synthesize	Shared context; nonliterary events; experience
Singerian	Language of the measurement system - Unit - Standard	Speaking the past: agreement about the measurement system Speaking the present: disagreement about the measurement system	Seek disagreement; resolve disagreement	System of measurement; other systems of measurement

situation are not recognized, and, consequently, a long-lasting solution to the problem will be unlikely. All processes that are allowed to go unexamined will benefit from an occasional *rocking the boat* that is characteristic of a Singerian inquiring environment.

What are the implications of this analysis for information systems design? Our suggestions, which are summarized in Table 1, have included:

- Leibnizian processes can be supported by rule-based systems.

- Lockean processes need support for consensus building and should support ranking and voting processes.

- Kantian processes will require systems capable of supporting multiple problem definitions and able to translate one problem definition into another.

- Hegelian processes require systems capable of supporting critical argument.

- Singerian processes will require the most flexible and broadest type of system capabilities as they sweep in any variables that may lead to refinement of the existing measurements.

In an age where ever increasing amounts of all business transactions are digital, an ability to examine textual artifacts (still a large percentage of all business artifacts) for the cues identified in this chapter will be necessary to automate processes that manage knowledge creation. Leibnizian processes will need to automatically incorporate changes in standard operating procedures. Lockean processes will need to automatically detect when consensus is waning, and new categories of knowledge may be required. Kantian systems will need to automatically recognize new models relevant to existing situations and begin the process of translation from existing models into the new one. Hegelian processes will need to automatically recognize challenges to existing assumptions (i.e., worldviews) and begin structuring an appropriate debate. And Singerian processes will need to recognize all of these situations, invoking the appropriate one in order to refine its internal view of the world.

The reader may have noticed that there could be much confusion in determining an appropriate inquirer. If one does not consider (or overlooks) the consensual nature of the Lockean community, questions regarding the appropriate labels to apply in knowledge creation processes strongly resemble candidates for knowledge in Leibnizian fact nets. Similarly, as soon as any consensual community emerges in a Leibnizian setting, one must consider applying a Lockean inquiring approach. One may reasonably ask, "How different must perspectives be to move us from a Kantian inquiring environment to a Hegelian one?" and "How long should we go before we take a Singerian view of the world and begin to question our processes?"

We suspect that as problems move from new and novel to mundane and routine, they will move from being characteristic of Singerian processes to become more characteristic of Leibnizian processes. This may be where the similarities in the inquiring philosophies can be leveraged. As new variables (Singerian) are accepted into the existing system, there may be debate (Hegelian) from time to time about some of them, but eventually large parts of the measurement system become accepted. Occasionally, there may be multiple models (Kantian), such as Windows and Linux, that are accepted by the community (Lockean) and coexist. Agreement is reached on what it means to work within the various models (Leibnizian).

References

Becker, A. L. (1979). Text-building, epistemology, and aesthetics in Javanese shadow theatre. In A. A. Yengoyan (Ed.), *The imagination of reality: Essays in southeast Asian coherence systems* (pp. 211-243). Norwood, NJ: Ablex.

Boland, R. J. J. (1991). Information system use as a hermeneutic process. In R. Hirschheim (Ed.), *Information systems research: Contemporary approaches and emergent traditions*. North Holland: Elsevier Science.

Burn, J., & Barnett, M. (1999). Communicating for advantage in the virtual organization. *IEEE Transactions on Professional Communication, 42*(4), 215-222.

Churchman, C. W. (1971). *The design of inquiring systems: Basic concepts of systems and organization.* New York: Basic Books.

DeSanctis, G., & Monge, P. (1999). Communication processes for virtual organizations. *Organization Science, 10*(6), 693-703.

El-Shinnawy, M. (1999). Introduction to the special issue: Communication in virtual organizations. *IEEE Transactions on Professional Communication, 42*(4), 213.

Geertz, C. (1983). *Local knowledge: Further essays in interpretive anthropology.* New York: Basic Books.

Hall, D. J., Paradice, D. B., & Courtney, J. F. (2003). Building a theoretical foundation for a learning-oriented knowledge management system. *Journal of Information Technology Theory and Applications, 5*(2), 63-89.

Jarvenpaa, S. L., & Leidner, D. E. (1999). Communication and trust in global virtual teams. *Organization Science, 10*(6), 791-815.

Kirkman, B. L., Rosen, B., Gibson, C. B., Tesluk, P. E., & McPherson, S. O. (2002). Five challenges to virtual team success: Lessons from Sabre, Inc. *Academy of Management Executive, 16*(3), 67-79.

Kraut, R., Steinfield, C., Chan, A. P., Butler, B., & Hoag, A. (1999). Coordination and virtualization: The role of electronic networks and personal relationships. *Organization Science, 10*(6), 722-740.

Turkle, S. (1995). *Life on the screen: Identity in the age of the Internet.* New York: Touchstone.

Zigurs, I., & Buckland, B. K. (1998). A theory of task/technology fit and group support systems effectiveness. *MIS Quarterly, 22*(3), 313-335.

Chapter XV

Transforming Organizational Culture to the Ideal Inquiring Organization:
Hopes and Hurdles

Leoni Warne
Defence Science and Technology Organization, Australia

Helen Hasan
University of Wollongong, Australia

Irena Ali
Defence Science and Technology Organization, Australia

Abstract

This chapter reports on the finding of the research into social learning at the Australian Defence Organization (ADO). The research aim was to identify factors that enable knowledge generation and transfer in organizations and contribute to creation of organizational culture that supports continuous learning. These factors are described in this chapter and include common identity, morale, problem solving, team building, performance management, workplace design, organizational culture, records keeping, information exchange, IT infrastructure, professional training, and induction and enculturation. The chapter concludes with description and suggested application of the Cynefin model which offers a pragmatic and conceptual alternative to the orthodoxy of scientific management.

Introduction

It has been suggested that an inquiring systems approach in organizations can be implemented quickly and easily to leverage knowledge assets and to successfully bring about organizational change (Kienholz, 1999). Furthermore, if organizations integrate their business objectives and intellectual capital and embed them in moral and ethical standards, then inquiring organizations that achieve this will meet business objectives, provide a safe, satisfying and enriching workplace for employees, and have a positive impact on their environment and society in general. While an inquiring system approach can be implemented quickly, the cultural change underlying organizational transformation is notoriously slow.

It is the authors' contention, based on several years research in this area, that ideally, an inquiring organization that aspires to wisdom should have an organizational culture that:

- is ever mindful of its ethical and social obligations;
- is attuned to its customers' requirements;
- is constantly looking for ways of improving its services;
- is network centric in philosophy and structure;
- practices unbounded systems thinking;
- values and trusts its employees and maintains a family friendly and flexible workplace;
- supports employees with sufficient resources, the latest in technology and collaborative work systems; and
- encourages reflection and innovation, allows employees to learn from their own mistakes and celebrates achievements.

While some organizations may be close to this ethos, for many more, the transformation pathway is unclear. Much of the research discussed in this chapter addresses this dilemma, and the Cynefin model is introduced as a possible transformation pathway. However, this chapter also poses another question: What is a realistic expectation for the near future and what are the hopes and hurdles that currently face inquiring organizations in a less than ideal environment?

The Hopes

What are the aspects of the ideal culture that are so appealing? The organization is likely to have realistic and well-articulated business objectives that are socially and environmentally responsible and that are clearly being met. Employees enjoy a friendly and supportive workplace where morale and productivity is likely to be high, and the work is facilitated by the increasing efficiencies and speed of information technology. The organization has the flexibility and adaptability to deal with the complexity dictated by a changing political and economic climate. Such organizations are likely to provide capabilities and systems that facilitate learning from experience, continuous learning, and innovation in learning and an environment where the genuine needs of the customer are uppermost in the minds of employees.

To gain a competitive advantage and to operate effectively in a climate of uncertainty, organizations require flatter hierarchies; decentralized decision-making; a greater capacity for the tolerance of ambiguity; permeable internal and external boundaries; empowerment of employees; the capacity for renewal; self-organizing units; and self-integrating coordination mechanisms (Daft & Lewin, 1993). In such organizations, knowledge is the most strategically important resource, and organizational capabilities are the product of distinctive competencies in integrating and applying this knowledge. Thus, communication is the pervasive underlying force responsible for maintenance and dissemination of strategic capabilities based in knowledge. Tucker and Meyer (1996) point out that strategic capabilities result from new knowledge creation accomplished through a combination of individuals' tacit and objective knowledge, yet this collection of knowledge must somehow be aggregated and communicated at a collective level.

Reflection is an enabler because it allows individuals to remove themselves from the actual performance of the activity. Reflection provides individuals (or teams, if necessary) with the space and distance they need to better understand the activity they are engaged in. Reflection is also a motivator, as it allows personnel to learn from their engagement in the activity with the intention of instigating some form of improvement of the activity. This level of control is empowering.

Working collaboratively is essential to organizational success and for successful problem solving. Very few people work by themselves or achieve results by themselves. So the people who interact together and yet have different tasks and responsibilities need to understand what each of them are trying to do, why they are doing it, how they are doing it, and what results to expect. In this relationship of interdependencies, communication and trust play vital roles (Drucker, 1999). It is useful to understand the difference between the terms team and teamwork and to recognize that the concepts captured by both terms are prerequisites for productive collaborative work. Teamwork means an individual is accountable, it means sharing information, and working better together. On the other hand, in a team everybody holds themselves and each other accountable, and performance is measured against collective output (Drucker, 1999). Teamwork is a skill, and the lack of it can be a barrier to effective performance.

Bowman and Pierce (2003) conducted research aimed to delineate and better understand the cultural barriers to teamwork. They identified several cultural barriers to teamwork, cognitive and organizational. They found that culture influenced cognitive fundamentals of teamwork, such as communication, coordination, and decision making. Culture also influenced the organizational barriers through rules and procedures for training and personnel selection. The implications of that research are that it is important to understand how the cultural and organizational dimensions affect teamwork in order to be able to develop training tools to help leaders and teams to overcome these possible barriers. It is easy to misinterpret the actions of another team member, based on an incomplete or incorrect understanding of that person's cognitive style. Also, learning that some individuals prefer more or less detail in a task or more or less group interaction or are more or less willing to approach a higher-ranking officer could be a simple and cost-effective way of improving team dynamics. Therefore, an understanding of simple psychological profiles of personal working preferences can be enlightening, productive, and constructive in team building.

Another important factor in teamwork is trust in information and knowledge sharing. Effective and efficient exchange of information underpins the success of organizational activities. Without such exchange, the collective action and cooperation necessary for the accomplishment of organizational goals is impossible. However, effective information exchange is often more difficult than it first appears. Factors can emerge which obstruct an individual's willingness to volunteer information or to provide it to others on request, particularly when the information of concern is highly sensitive and when the potential recipient is largely unknown. Concerns over how others might use valuable information often restrict one's readiness to part with it (Erickson, 1979).

A large amount of research has demonstrated that the extent to which an individual trusts another has a significant impact on their willingness to exchange valuable information with others (see, for example, Erickson, 1979; Fine & Holyfield, 1996). Despite this extensive empirical attention, however, consensus on a definition of trust has not been forthcoming (Barber, 1983; Kramer, 1999). For present purposes, trust can be defined as the subjective expectation of positive treatment under conditions of vulnerability. In other words, we trust another to the extent that we believe they will act beneficially (or at least not detrimentally) towards us if we choose to engage them in some form of cooperation and when cooperating involves some degree of risk (Gambetta, 1988). Thus, trust is especially relevant when there is uncertainty or ignorance as to the motives and actions of others. When these can be predicted with absolute certainty, trust is not required. When they cannot, as in most real-world circumstances, a degree of trust is necessary to make human action and interaction possible.

In terms of systems to facilitate learning, there are a number of learning styles that must be considered within an ideal inquiring organization. Leibnizian inquirers are seen primarily as the instrumentalists, placing a great deal of importance on what they already know. Lockean inquirers are known as the consensus builders, typically asking others to generate ideas and focusing on agreement. Kantians are viewed as searchers who combine ideas from diverse sources and unusual associations. Hegelians are known as debaters, arguing internally with themselves to develop ideas. Finally, Singerians are considered as the most flexible inquirers, comfortable with and employing all systems of inquiry (Handzic & Chin, 2003). Despite the current predominance of the Kantian approach to discovering knowledge, for effective idea generation, all of these different approaches to learning and innovation need to be facilitated. To achieve this, informational, technological, and organizational frameworks must support and accommodate all these modes of thinking and learning.

The ADO Study

Researchers from the Defence Science and Technology Organization in Australia conducted a four-year study investigating the procedures that facilitate social learning and knowledge management in a number of different settings in the Australian Defence Organisation (ADO) (Ali et al., 2001, 2002; Warne et al., 2001, 2002). The term *social learning* has been used to reflect that organizations, organizational units, and work groups are social clusters and that learning therefore occurs in a social context.

In the workplace, socially-based learning occurs frequently. Lave and Wenger (1991) refer to the interactions between people and the environment as situated experience or situated learning. It is through learning that we see ourselves in a different context, and this transformation of oneself through learning is particularly important if one is to contribute to the dynamic changes required in inquiring organizations. For the purpose of this study, social learning is defined as learning that occurs within or by a group, an organization, or any cultural cluster, and it includes:

- the procedures by which knowledge and practice are transmitted across different work situations and across time; and
- the procedures that facilitate generative learning that enhances the enterprise's ability to adjust to dynamic and unexpected situations and to react creatively to them.

Social learning represents important processes that contribute to individuals' ability to understand information, create knowledge from that information, and share what they know. Social learning is therefore intrinsic to knowledge management.

The immediate aim of this research was to understand the issues inherent in building learning, adaptive, and sustainable organizations. A long-term objective, however, was to develop architectures that will support the development of information systems which guide and enhance organizational learning and facilitate knowledge management.

Methodology

The importance of the context, the need to understand the social process of learning, and the exploratory nature of the research, particularly in the case of the first study, led to the use of ethnographic techniques in the form of fieldwork as the primary form of data gathering. This entailed observing the work taking place in different settings and, where possible, using directed questioning to clarify issues. In addition to observation, the research team undertook extensive semi-structured interviews with a sample of personnel from the different settings studied. A stratified sampling technique was used to ensure that an adequate representation was achieved. The main advantage of this type of sampling was that it ensured that the relevant variables were represented. Quantitative surveys were also used in all settings, although in some cases a survey was only used at the follow-up visit (Since the research was conducted over a four year period, those settings that were studies in the early years were revisited in the later years to ensure findings were valid over time.) In all cases, response rates were well over 70%, with the response rate for one survey an extraordinary 97%. All research data, therefore, was triangulated by methods of data collection by researcher (a multidisciplinary team) and by each setting's functional role.

These research results, which have been reported widely (see, for example, Ali et al., 2000, 2001, 2002; Warne, 2000; Warne et al., 2001, 2002, 2003), identified a number of motivators and enablers of successful inquiring organizations. If these motivators and enablers are not privileged, the journey to the ideal organization is likely to be blocked by cultural barriers. These constructs then become hurdles on the pathway to the ideal inquiring organization.

The Hurdles

The constructs identified in the research outlined above include:

Common Identity

A common identity implies a similar way of describing and making sense of the world, of determining what is significant and important, and of how to use resources in the environment (Jordan, 1993). In turn, having this common view of the workplace and one's role in it enables effective communication and the development of shared understanding as well as acting to expedite learning and work processes. This common identity is influenced by issues around goal alignment, cultural and social identity, language, morale, and workplace policies. Similarly, systems thinking is tightly coupled with effective knowledge mobilization and contributes to the development of common identity. Systems thinking, according to Senge (1992) requires a shift of mind—from seeing ourselves as separate to seeing ourselves as connected to and part of the world (or part of any other system such as an organization or organizational subunit). The presence of this type of thinking is accompanied by generally higher levels of interaction between staff and by high higher levels of information sharing.

Workplaces that encourage competition between functional groups do not allow all levels in the organization to input into decisions on work processes, make decisions affecting personnel behind closed doors, discourage diversity, and do not encourage a whole-of-organization ethos are placing barriers along the way to success.

Morale

The research studies found evidence of low morale being coupled with higher levels of alienation towards senior management (Ali et al., 2001; Warne, 2001). Such alienation has obvious implications for the successful progression of organizations to an ideal standard.

Perception of low morale has frequently been coupled with comments about not understanding the motivation or agenda of more senior staff. This lack of understanding not only affects morale but also has an impact on trust, organizational cohesiveness, goal alignment and common identity, and, consequently, on opportunities and motivation for learning and innovation. A comment from one interviewee exemplifies this:

"When you're sitting in a meeting and someone says something that you know would not be kosher with your chain, then you can stand up and say, No...you can't do things that way because you know how the people think...You would know what your boss thinks, whether he would approve or disapprove of that particular activity, conflict, whatever. I think that's important for you to have that kind of interaction to actually know what your peers, your chain [of command] thinks."

Problem Solving

For knowledge workers in any organization, problem solving is a core activity. Importantly, the *process* of problem solving fosters knowledge generation and thus learning and innovation. For instance, routine tasks often need to be done slightly differently in different circumstances and, in doing so, involve an element of problem solving that requires generative learning (Lave & Wenger, 1991). An individual's network is one of their most important resources, as personal and social networks are an important means of acquiring, propagating, and sharing knowledge. The individuals who comprise the network can make available their own knowledge, expertise, and experience. In this way, the knowledge resources available to any one person, in their work and when problem solving, can be greatly increased.

Personal networks can also play a pivotal role in the propagation of knowledge. A few members of staff in the settings studied were seen to be systematic in passing on relevant knowledge to colleagues, and many others told the research team that, time permitting, they would pass information onto colleagues. As Davenport and Prusack (1998) claim, when those who are in a position of know-how share their expertise, they contribute to problem solving. Hence, personal networks were seen to function as channels supporting both *information pull* and *information push*. A good deal of effort can go into generating, maintaining, and obtaining value from these networks.

Apart from satisfying social needs, informal networks also play a pivotal role in knowledge propagation. New knowledge often begins with the individual, and making personal knowledge available to others is the central activity of knowledge creating organizations. Through conversations, people discover what they know, what others know, and in the process of sharing, new knowledge is created. Technology, such as e-mails, faxes, and telephones, are invaluable aids in the process of knowledge sharing, but they are only supporting tools. Knowledge sharing depends on the quality of conversations, formal or informal, that people have. Webber (1993) aptly describes it as follows: "Conversations—not rank, title, or the trappings of power—determine who is literally and figuratively 'in the loop' and who is not" (p. 28).

Individual and shared perceptions of the organization and how they operate provide an essential backdrop to problem solving within an organizational context. These perceptions may consist of deeply ingrained assumptions, generalizations, or even pictures or images that influence how people within an organization understand their organizational world and how they should act within it (Senge, 1992). Furthermore, in order to effectively solve problems and innovate, time for inquiry and reflection must be factored into the workplace. Staff is generally more motivated to do so if they know that inquiry and reflection is recognized as a valid and valuable use of their time.

The importance of these perceptions cannot be stressed enough because they directly influence the construction of individuals' knowledge and understandings that they draw on in their day-to-day activities. One general example is appreciating the ways in which an organization's formal rules and processes can be bent to achieve a desired outcome. This class of knowledge can empower people to solve problems by expanding the range of solutions which may be available and by giving them confidence to improvise or innovate. Conversely, a lack of knowledge or incorrect perceptions will constrain the types of solutions that can be found.

Organizations that frown on workers taking time to reflect or chat during the working day and mandate organizational rules and prescriptive work procedures are often placing barriers in the path of innovative problem solving.

Team Building

As stated earlier, very few people work by themselves and achieve results by themselves. During some of the studies undertaken, poor team-based morale was evident where there was a lack of cultural cohesion and team spirit (Pascoe, Ali & Warne, 2002; Warne, 2002). These indications were sometimes explicit, and at other times, they were implicit and were particularly an issue with staff who are either of low rank or remotely located. The attitude of *them and us* as well as a feeling of being undervalued was clearly prevalent. These individuals did not identify themselves as team members of a unit they belonged to but more as members of an organization where they were physically located. Moreover, some felt they were not encouraged to operate in a coordinated way to support organizational goals. This was because they did not see the significance of their particular tasks to the overall goals of the organization. This was a serious demotivator, and these staff members were not anxious to learn or share their knowledge with other team members. They became barriers to successful innovation and successful transformation of the organization.

Constructive Performance Management

Assessment, reporting, and performance management form a significant part of the overall management of personnel throughout their careers; however, if not handled constructively, it may have adverse impacts on team spirit and thus knowledge generation. The prevailing strong emphasis on individual performance management may be divisive as it may influence a proportion of individuals to focus on achieving their individual goals at the expense of assisting their team achieve its goals. Team-based performance management systems have yet to gain wide acceptance.

The Somerset Maugham statement: "people ask you for criticism but they only want praise" (Morgan, 1989) captures the problem endemic to performance appraisal systems. Performance appraisals are supposed to meet the needs of both the organization and the individual. The aim of a performance appraisal is to introduce management practices where merit is recognized and rewarded in a systematic way. Furthermore, a well-planned performance appraisal system should help to make equitable and unbiased decisions regarding staff selection, placement, development, and training (Wood, 1989). The criteria and standards used in a performance appraisal provide a focus for performance measurement and therefore must be clearly related to the individual's job. Many problems associated with performance appraisals stem from the fact that these criteria are not valid, and there is a lack of clear communication about performance expectations.

While constructive performance management enables innovation, in many organizations, performance appraisal is so poorly managed it acts as a barrier to innovation and organizational growth.

One way of valuing skills and increasing morale is to publicly acknowledge outstanding work. Making employees feel appreciated, focusing attention on their good ideas, inviting them to extend themselves and saying, "Thank you, we know that you are a good employee, we value you and your work," is a big factor in motivation (Mitchell, 2000). Many personnel told the research team that a written or verbal word of praise or a pat on the back often means more, for example, than a pay raise—"praise is better than money"—and praise is needed at all levels. This form of reward and incentive should ideally be used in conjunction with constructive performance management.

Effective Workplace Design

Workplace design was seen to have many negative impacts on learning, innovation, and morale. Staff located at small isolated outposts are at risk of feeling isolated and do not identify strongly with the parent organization. As stated elsewhere, outposted staff identified more with the workplace with which they were based than their branch where they administratively belonged.

The issue of workplace design and its impact on team and network building, and on accessing information necessary to getting one's job done, arose repeatedly during the studies. Numerous interviewees were aware that physical location and proximity to each other had the potential to promote the transfer of pertinent knowledge. Indeed, the point was even made that, in addition to more quickly obtaining answers to questions about particular tasks, an open plan workplace enabled one to tap into pertinent knowledge by overhearing others' conversations. Hutchins (1996) uses the term horizon of observation to describe the area of the task environment which can be seen and is therefore available as a context for learning by team members.

However, as Davenport and Prusack (1998) point out, colocation in itself does not guarantee the sharing of knowledge; a common training or experience, or at least a common language, is essential. Unless individuals are prepared to ask and answer questions of one another or to even just chat with each other, the knowledge advantage provided by open plan workplaces will be lost. An example of this was brought to the research team's attention when told that two workers in two different teams had been colocated for three months before they realized that they were both working on the same project.

Many staff members consider the open plan arrangement noisy and an inhibitor of effective communication, as the following comment illustrates:

"If the environment was such that a group of people who worked together were located together and had some form of privacy to do their work as a group, that would be fine but when you're all lumped together and everybody can hear what everybody is saying and everybody's saying a hundred things at the same time, sometimes it can be an absolute nightmare."

An organizational culture that recognizes the value of knowledge and its exchange is a crucial element in whether knowledge work is successfully carried out or not. Such a culture provides the opportunity for personal contact so that tacit knowledge, which cannot effectively be captured in procedures or represented in documents and databases, can be transferred. Webber (1993) claims that "Conversations are the way knowledge workers discover what they know, share it with their colleagues, and in the process create new knowledge for the organization" (p. 36). In a culture that values knowledge, managers recognize not just that knowledge generation is important for business success but also that it can be nurtured with time and space (Davenport & Prusack, 1998).

An organization that does not plan its workplace for diverse purposes and for optimizing knowledge development is installing its own barriers.

Good Records Keeping

The research team observed that general familiarity with records keeping procedures in the settings studied was quite poor, and adherence to formal process was almost nonexistent in some settings. Records management and access to information contained in paper records pose a problem. Some people have developed their own personal records keeping systems, but there is little uniformity in these and no adherence to file naming conventions and standards. Consequently, there seems to be little faith in the integrity of organizational records. Those areas where there was good local practice in records management were seen to be very much the exception. As two informants stated:

"I believe that physical files in the...are no longer managed well because their management has been farmed out to outside bodies. With the file clerks there was consistency of procedures but the file clerks are no longer part of the procedure."

Furthermore, the preference for accessing and transferring information electronically seems to be growing, and the use of electronic tools for communication and decision making is prevalent at all levels. The issue of electronic records, particularly e-mail messages containing evidence of business transactions, posed problems. Research reported in the professional literature on records management (Enneking, 1998; Henricks, 1999; Robles & Langemo, 1999) suggest that the capture of e-mail messages into a records management system offers the best solution to this problem. If this issue is not addressed, access to corporate information is limited, and workers are frustrated by the convoluted procedures required to find information.

Effective Information Exchange

Many meetings at the settings studied were held with the stated aim of propagating and exchanging information. Information transfer is generally considered to be an uni-directional process, while information exchange is a two-way or multi-directional process. The concept of information exchange is further delineated by some theorists (Senge, 1992) into discussion and dialogue, where *dialogue* requires members of a team to suspend assumptions and enter into a genuine *thinking together*. Genuine dialogue is not a heaving of ideas back and forth in a winner-takes-all competition. Instead, it is a free flowing of meaning through a group, allowing the group to discover insights not attainable individually (Senge, 1992) and an extremely effective way of ensuring involvement at all levels of the organization and strengthening communication and cohesiveness.

In one of the settings studies, a survey respondent stated that:

"Whilst at a social level members of...interact well, there is very poor group cohesiveness in the work environment. I believe that this is in part due to the failure to conduct regular progress/section meetings at lower levels and the failure to clearly identify who is doing what."

A number of staff told the research team that a lack of active listening seems to be an endemic problem and examples were given where managers either avoided questions put forth at meetings or terminated meetings prematurely if questioning got too uncomfortable. These staff would have preferred frank openness and to be told "I do not know what the answer is" or "I need to investigate this more" or "At this stage, this has low priority," and so on rather than being brushed off. These managers were creating barriers to organizational success.

While it is sometimes necessary to have meetings for information transfer only, it is more effective when there is an open information exchange and dialogue at meetings and where questions can be asked, views expressed, and problems raised without fear of blame or shame.

IT Infrastructure

The research team observed that information access due to failings in the IT infrastructure inhibited access to information within many of the settings studied. It was especially a problem for those individuals who were not colocated in the central headquarters. They lacked access to classified networks and to the main information resources stored on shared hardware drives; similarly, those staff located within the central headquarters had difficulty accessing some shared information resources of outposted staff. Another issue that was often brought to the team's attention was the difficulty in finding information on the shared drive. Since there was no specific person responsible for maintaining information on the shared drive and no known protocol for naming folders, storage was left to the discretion of individual document originators. The research team observed that in some sections people were more precise in giving explicit names to documents and folders, but this practice was not uniform across the whole of the organization.

Without reliable systems, properly promulgated and understood protocols, and effective training, technology becomes a hurdle and a hinderer, rather than an enabling tool.

Professional Training

Appropriate professional training is a significant component of the development of individual expertise and, therefore, again a fundamental enabler for generating new knowledge. Training courses are also important to furthering individuals' careers, as well as for forming the personal networks that subsequently develop. However, in times of budgetary constraints, training money is often the first to go with damaging consequences for the organization's ability to learn and manage their knowledge.

Numerous researchers, for example, McCauley and Kuhnert (1992) and Argyris (1973), have found that a general trust in management is associated with professional development opportunities at work. The implication is that an employee's sense of trust is promoted when the supervisor provides career growth opportunities because it authenticates the supervisor's commitment to that employee's professional development. This is important to learning and innovation because trust plays a key role in collaboration and teamwork.

Induction and Enculturation

A substantial majority of the knowledge that individuals and groups hold is tacit and, therefore, cannot be taught formally. Many of the sorts of knowledge required for a particular job or role, being tacit, tends to be invisible in that most people are generally not conscious that they have this knowledge. Learning to be a member of an organization, for example, also entails learning what is acceptable behavior and how conflicts are resolved. Induction and enculturation, which has been defined as the process by which humans acquire the culturally constructed meanings attached to various actions in a particular society or subculture (Merten, 1999), are two processes by which staff can learn both explicit and tacit knowledge.

Reports in the literature suggest that orientation of new employees is one of the most overlooked aspects of employee training (Cooke, 1998; Ganzel, 1998; Tyler, 1998). Like appropriate career trajectories and professional currency, effective induction and enculturation programs facilitate social learning by providing a foundation of knowledge on which the individual can become fully productive more quickly, and as a consequence, they are more likely to generate new knowledge.

Good induction, however, is more that just an introduction to new job and workmates; it is a way of helping people find their feet. Attitudes and expectations are shaped during the early days of new employment, and the issue of work satisfaction cannot be considered without examining more basic issues of work orientation (Dunford, 1992; George & Cole, 1992). There are numerous advantages that come from good induction programs. These include morale building, minimization of misunderstanding (because rules and regulations have been clearly explained), establishment of good working relationships, reduction of anxiety, and reduction of inefficiency. An organization without an effective induction program is creating hurdles for its employees and a giant barrier to success for itself.

Since the Australian Defence Organisation still has many hurdles to negotiate on the path to an ideal inquiring organization, the researchers next undertook to find an organizational model that could facilitate this transformation, and the Cynefin model proved to be just such a model.

Cynefin Framework

A culture of trust, with time and place for reflection, confidence in teamwork, hands-off management approaches, flexible technologies, and appropriate reward structures; these are the hoped for attributes of our future inquiring organizations. However, as described above, research has identified a substantial list of hurdles that must be conquered before many organizations can make progress in that direction. In reality, most organizations are a confused mixture of positive, forward-looking strategies amidst ones that constrain and inhibit the way they operate and manage their knowledge. To begin to make sense of the different ways in which organizations can view the future, it is useful

Figure 1. Sense-Making and Decision-Making Cynefin Frameworks

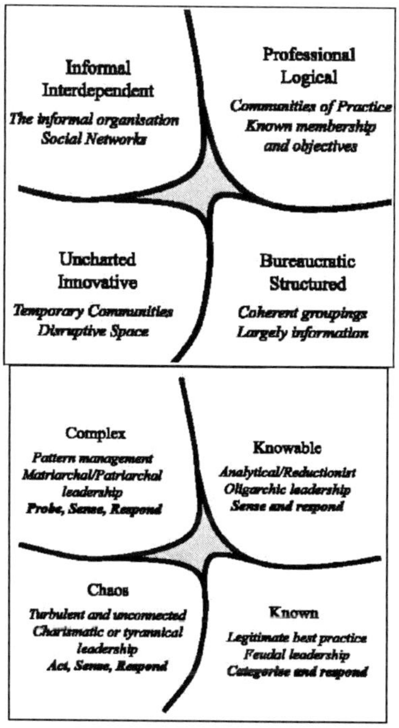

to refer to the model from the Cynefin group at IBM that is influencing current thinking in the field of knowledge management.

This model introduced by Snowden (2002) uses complex adaptive systems theory to create a sense-making model of collective knowledge creation, disruption, and utilization that allows a pragmatic and conceptual alternative to the orthodoxy of scientific management. As shown in Figure 1 the Cynefin model is a knowledge space with five domains which set the context for collective decision making. Four of the domains are named, and then there is a fifth central area, which is the domain of Disorder. The right-hand domains are those of Order, and the left-hand domains those of Unorder. None of the domains is more desirable than any other; there are no implied value axes. Instead, the framework is used primarily to consider the *dynamics* of situations, decisions, perspectives, conflicts, and changes and to recognize in which quadrant a given situation resides and in order to make decision about whether or not transformation to another quadrant would be more desirable for the given situation. There are two domains of order, the Known and the Knowable, the domain of Complexity, the domain of Chaos. Each has a different mode of community behavior, and each implies a different form of management and a different leadership style with the adoption of different tools, practices, and conceptual understanding. Using the Cynefin model, one is able to see how organizations can be part mechanistic and part organic. Snowden (2002) makes a point of strongly resisting the existence of a single or idealized model, but rather the key to survival and growth comes from the ability to adapt to change through diversity. This

Figure 2. Connection Strengths of Cynefin Domains (Kurtz & Snowden, 2003)

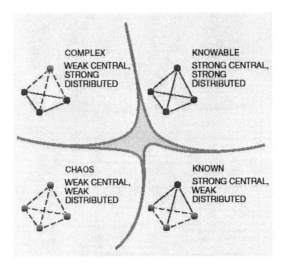

involves an awareness and understanding of the borders between different domains and the acquisition of tools and techniques to enable border transitions when needed.

Kurtz and Snowden (2003) look at the Cynefin framework from the perspective of the types of component connections as shown in Figure 2. In both ordered domains, there are strong connections between a central, usually hierarchical, director (leader, manager, or management group) and the remaining organizational constituents. In the Complex domain, these are weak so that attempts at control through hierarchical organizational structures often fail. On the other hand, connections among constituent components are strong and stable group patterns and can emerge and resist change through repeated interaction, mutual goals, and experiences. This is the domain where organizations should aim to be if they seek innovation through self-adapting teams in a network-centric organizational arrangement.

It would appear that managing organizations would be much simpler and cost effective if it was recognized that we no longer live in an age where it is necessary to act as if all systems are ordered or at least capable of being ordered. As stated on the Cynefin Centre's homepage (Cynefin, 2003): "Learning to recognize and appreciate the domain of un-order is liberating as it allows a new focus on effectiveness in which we stimulate the interactions of employees, customers and markets to enable beneficial patterns of behaviour to emerge." They further say that the Cynefin Centre's work in unordered systems, known as contextual complexity, provides "both capability for the people aspects of the on-demand age, in which we no longer need to sacrifice effectiveness on the altar of efficiency." This may be frightening and even unintelligible to those educated and accustomed to working in the ordered domains where there is an unquestioned assumption of order and control.

If organizations are to take this on board there must be a greater understanding of how productive work takes place in network-centric organizations, in the Complex domain, where loosely coupled autonomous teams behave as self-organizing organic communities, as they would in the ideal inquiring organization, and the Chaotic domain, where innovation takes place.

Using the Cynefin Model to Get Over the Hurdles

Snowden (2002) identifies three generations of knowledge management. The first generation clearly associated with increased ICT (Information and Communication Technologies) capabilities focused on timely information provision for decision support. The second generation, triggered by the SECI model of Nonaka, focused on the tacit-explicit knowledge conversion as the one process of knowledge creation in organizations. The emphasis now is on knowledge rather than information with an implicit assumption that we now know how to manage information. The emerging third generation is associated with Snowden's work at the Cynefin Centre described above. The Cynefin model utilizes the self-organizing capabilities of informal communities to understand how to manage knowledge, both as an entity and as a flow. Rather than implying that chaos is the natural outcome of the self-organizing capabilities of informal communities, Snowden has faith in the human capability to create order and predictability through collective and individual acts of freewill.

The usefulness of the Cynefin model lies in its ability to raise awareness of the dynamics of an organization, which is essential in any deliberate attempt to effect change. The Cynefin framework is created anew each time it is used with distinctions meaningful to that context. To some extent, it does not even exist devoid of context but is always used to enable sense making in a particular setting. It renders itself useful by whole organizations, divisions, or small teams to gain understanding of their present situation and to show the pathways for change.

Many decision makers in conservative hierarchical organizations, common in the military tradition but also elsewhere, are only comfortable in the Known quadrant. Members of inquiring organization are at ease in the Knowable quadrant, as decision makers have the skills and motivation to go beyond what is already known. However, in this quadrant, there is an assumption of order where all relevant information is potentially knowable, and hence, there is one right or best decision in any particular circumstance. Members of the ideal inquiring organization thrive in the environment of the Complex quadrant where patterns of knowledge and practice emerge from an unordered world. Here people are empowered and supported by flexible organizational sociotechnical systems that encourage employees to make their own decisions in self-organizing teams in a people-oriented technology enabled workspace. The ideal inquiring organization operates primarily in the Complex domain but is comfortable in the other domains and in moving between them as required.

Applying the Cynefin Model to the ADO Research

At the macro-level, the Australian Defence Organization would currently appear to reside in the Known domain, which is characterized by strong central hierarchical command and control channels. However, given the political and economic uncertainties of the current global environment, organizations in general, and military organizations in particular, are becoming aware that they should be moving toward a more responsive, flexible, and dynamic network-centric form of structure. Many managers, who have only ever operated in the Known domain, have peered over the boundary of the domain of Chaos and recoiled in horror. There are other staff members, even in the ADO, who have already experienced life in the Complex domain for at least some of their work activities. Air crews and special services units are examples of self-directed teams who are trained and entrusted to work in unordered circumstances. There are therefore precedents in the ADO where characteristics of the unordered domains are understood and valued.

Clearly, more of the ADO should be residing in the Complex domain but venturing into the other domains as required. This would be a dramatic cultural shift for many in the organization, but once the context and change imperatives are fully understood, the Cynefin framework can be used to justify and understand the need for change and to guide the organization, or parts of it, through the process. The Cynefin framework facilitates contextualization of possible issues in relation to each other. The value of the contextualization is that those participating often see patterns, sometimes for the first time, that overturn their entrained beliefs about the issue they are considering and about their purpose, goals, changing dynamics, and identity. The possible benefits of using this framework for the ADO include:

- understanding cultural pull and push forces and learning to use them appropriately;
- allowing for reflection and understanding of what the inhibitors and enablers are and how they interact;
- providing an intellectual vehicle for understanding common intent which could drive the organizational mission/doctrine changes;
- enabling the development of strategies to deal with untested situations and appreciating the need to take and manage risks without the threat of punishment;
- understanding the *chaotic space* which would facilitate faster decision making, that is, quick responses to chaotic situations;
- allowing for rehearsal of possible emergent scenarios and then trusting participants to perform well in real situations; and
- providing *requisite variety* for training purposes and understanding of organizational vision.

Furthermore, the framework can be used at a higher level to guide the transition of the human and organizational dimensions along many paths through the space, in particular one that goes from the Known quadrant through Chaos to the Complex.

Conclusion

Why is it that so many knowledge management initiatives do not reach their full potential? Technological tools of ever increasing sophistication are available for use in achieving the dissemination and sharing of data, information, and knowledge across the organization. However, despite the existence and capability of these tools, knowledge management in many organizations all too often does not deliver the benefits sought from it, and the ideal inquiring organization is still a rarity. The research described in this chapter suggests that organizational, human-related, and cultural issues play a pivotal role in the success of knowledge management initiatives and the journey to wisdom.

Operating effectively as an ideal inquiring organization in times of change and uncertainty requires flatter organizational structures, a suitable technological infrastructure, relationships based on trust, and the many other cultural constructs outlined in this chapter. The Cynefin framework has been introduced as a possible tool that can be used to explore and test the fit of alternative approaches and illuminate a possible transformation pathway for organizations. However, further research and additional case studies are required to validate the use of the model for this purpose.

References

Ali, I. M., Pascoe, C., & Warne, L. (2002, September 16-20). Yet another role for team building and work motivation: Enabler of knowledge creation and knowledge sharing. *Proceedings of the 7th International Command and Control Research and Technology Symposium*, Québec City, Quebec. Retrieved September 27, 2004, from *http://www.dodccrp.org/Activities/Symposia/7th ICCRTS/*

Ali, I. M., Pascoe, C., Warne, L., Gori, R., & Agostino, K. (2000, October 24-26). *Enabling learning: A progress report on the Enterprise Social Learning Architecture Team*. Proceedings of the 5th International Command and Control Research and Technology Symposium, Canberra, Australia.

Ali, I. M., Warne, L., et al. (2001, August 15-17). *The impact of organisational culture, information sharing and collaboration on organisational learning: Reflections from the study by the Enterprise Social Learning Architectures Team*. Proceedings of the Defence Human Factors Special Interest Group Meeting, Adelaide, Australia.

Ali, I. M., Warne, L., Agostino, K., & Pascoe, C. (2001, June 19-22). *Working and learning together: Social learning in the Australian Defence Organisation*. Proceedings of the Informing Science Conference IS2001: Bridging Diverse Disciplines Proceedings, Krakow, Poland, June.

Argyris, C. (1973). *On organizations of the future*. Beverley Hills, CA: Sage.

Barber, B. (1983). The logic and limits of trust. New Brunswick, NJ: Rutgers University Press.

Bowman, E. K., & Pierce, L. G. (2003). Cultural barriers to teamwork. In *A multinational coalition environment*, Army Research Laboratory, Human Research and Engineering Directorate Aberdeen Proving Ground, MD. Retrieved September 27, 2004, from **http://www.asc2002.com/summaries/i/IP-06.pdf**

Cooke, R. (1998). Welcome aboard. *Credit Union Management, 21*(7), 46-47.

Cynefin (2003). IBM's Cynefin Centre for Organisational Complexity. Retrieved September 27, 2004, from *http://www-1.ibm.com/services/cynefin/*

Daft, R. L., & Lewin, A. Y. (1993). Where are the theories for the "new" organizational forms? An editorial essay. *Organization Science, 4*(i-vi), 000-000.

Davenport, T. H., & Prusack, L. (1998). *Working knowledge: How organizations manage what they know.* Boston, MA: Harvard Business School Press.

Drucker, P. F. (1999, October). Beyond the information revolution. *The Atlantic Monthly, 428*(4), 47-57.

Dunford, R. W. (1992). *Organisational behaviour: An organisational analysis perspective.* Sydney, Australia: Addison-Wesley.

Enneking, N. E. (1998). Managing email: Working toward an effective solution. Records *Management Quarterly, 32*(3), 24-43.

Erickson, P. E. (1979). The role of secrecy in complex organizations: From norms of rationality to norms of distrust. *Cornell Journal of Social Relation, 14*(2), 121-138.

Fine, G. A., & Holyfield, L. (1996). Secrecy, trust, and dangerous leisure: Generating group cohesion in voluntary organisations. *Social Psychology Quarterly, 59*(1), 22-38.

Gambetta, D. (1988). *Can we trust? Trust: making and breaking cooperative relationships.* Oxford: Blackwell.

Ganzel, R. (1998). Elements of a great orientation. *Training, 35*(3), 56.

George, C. S., & Cole, K. (1992). *Supervision in action: The art of managing.* Sydney, Australia: Prentice Hall.

Handzic, M., & Lin, C. Y. (2003, November 26-28). *K-space and learning.* Proceedings of the 14th Australian Conference on Information Systems.

Henricks, M. (1999). Sorting out electronic filing. *Office Systems, 16*(2), 30-34.

Hutchins, E. (1996). *Cognition in the wild.* Cambridge, MA: MIT Press.

Jordan, B. (1993). *Ethnographic workplace studies and computer supported cooperative work.* Proceedings of the Interdisciplinary Workshop on Informatics and Psychology, Scharding, Austria.

Kienholz, A. (1999). Systems Rethinking: An inquiring systems approach to the art and practice of the learning organization: Foundations of information systems. Retrieved September 27, 2004, from *http://www.mis.fsu.edu/philosophy/pfis/fisart.htm*

Kramer, R. M. (1999). Trust and distrust in organizations: Emerging perspectives, enduring questions. *Annual Review of Psychology, 50,* 569-598.

Kurtz, C. F., & Snowden, D. J. (2003). The new dynamics of strategy: Sense-making in a complex-complicated world. *IBM Systems Journal, Fall, 47*(3), 462-483.

Lave, J., & Wenger, E. (1991). *Situated learning: Legitimate peripheral participation.* Cambridge University Press.

McCauley, D. P., & Kuhnert, K. W. (1992). *The professional manager.* New York: McGraw-Hill.

Merten, D. E. (1999). Enculturation into secrecy among junior high school girls. *Contemporary Ethnography, 28*(2), 107-137.

Mitchell, S. (2000). Be bold and discover the power of praise. East Roseville: Simon & Schuster.

Morgan, T. (1989). Performance management: The missing link in strategic management and planning. In D. C. Corbett (Ed.), *Public sector policies for the 1990's* (pp. 243-250). Melbourne, Australia: Monash University, Public Sector Management Institute, Faculty of Economics and Politics.

Pascoe, C. Ali, I. M., & Warne, L. (2002). Collaborative knowledge development, dialogue, and team building: Findings from research into social learning in the Australian Defence Organisation. In F. Burstein & H. Linger (Eds.), *Knowledge management in context* (pp. 158-171): Melbourne, Australia.

Robles, M., & Langemo, M. (1999). The fundamentals of record management. *Office Systems, 16*(1), 30-36.

Senge, P. M. (1992). *The fifth discipline: The art and practice of the learning organization.* Sydney, Australia: Random House.

Snowden, D. (2002). Complex acts of knowing: Paradox and descriptive self-awareness. *Journal of Knowledge Management, 6*(2), 1-14.

Tucker, M. L., & Meyer, G. D. (1996). Organizational communication: Development of internal strategic competitive advantage. *Journal of Business Communication, 33*(1), 51-69.

Tyler, K (1998). Take new employee orientation off the back burner. *HR Magazine, 43*(6), 49-57.

Warne, L. (2000). A sociotechnical approach to social learning analysis in the Australian Defence Force. In E. Coakes, R. Lloyd-Jones, & D. Willis (Eds.), The new sociotech: graffiti on the long wall (pp. 219-228). London: Springer-Verlag.

Warne, L. (2001, December 4-5). Knowledge management and social learning in knowledge management for information communities. *Proceedings of the Australian Conference of Knowledge Management and Intelligent Decision Support,* Melbourne, Australia.

Warne, L. (2002). Conflict and politics and information systems failure. In S. Clarke (Ed.), *A challenge for information systems professionals and researchers in sociotechnical and human cognition elements of information systems* (pp. 104-135). Hershey, PA: Idea Group.

Warne, L., Agostino, K., Ali, I. M., Pascoe, C., Bopping, D. (2002). The knowledge edge: knowledge management and social learning in military settings in knowledge and information technology management. In A.G. O. Khalil & S. M. Rahman (Eds.), *Human and social perspectives* (pp. 324-353). Hershey, PA: Idea Group.

Warne, L., Ali, I. M., Linger, H. (2003, December 9-10). Representing social learning in the context of knowledge management: An architectural perspective, the role of quality in knowledge management. *Proceedings of the Australian Conference of Knowledge Management and Intelligent Decision Support*, Melbourne, Australia.

Warne, L., Ali, I. M., Pascoe, C., & Agostino, K. (2001, December). A holistic approach to knowledge management and social learning: Lessons learnt from military headquarters. *Australian Journal of Information Systems, Special Issue on Knowledge Management*, 127-142.

Webber, A. M. (1993, January-February). What's so new about the new economy? *Harvard Business Review*, 24-42.

Wood, R. (1989). Performance appraisal in the reform of public sector management practices. In D. C. Corbett (Ed.), *Public sector policies for the 1990's* (pp. 225-242). Melbourne, Australia: Monash University, Public Sector Management Institute, Faculty of Economics and Politics.

Chapter XVI

Exploiting Reusable Abstractions in Organizational Inquiry: Why Reinvent Square Wheels?

Haim Kilov
Independent Consultant, and Stevens Institute of Technology, USA

Ira Sack
Stevens Institute of Technology, USA

Abstract

This chapter shows how crucial aspects of organizational knowledge and organizational inquiry can be exactified using a relatively small number of abstract concepts common to various areas of human endeavor, such as (exact) philosophy, business management, science, and technology. Abstraction and exactification are essential for taming complexity in general and complexity of the modern-day organization in particular. Exactification is achieved, first and foremost, by creating and using ontologies— business and organizational domain models with precisely defined semantics. An ontology clearly demonstrates the fundamental concepts of a domain and relationships between them. The semantics of generic concepts used in effective modeling is based on mathematics and philosophy, while in too many cases a multitude of concepts invented in buzzword-compliant IT methods has no clear semantics and therefore cannot be reasonably used. Organizational learning and organizational inquiry can be understood and accomplished substantially better in the well-defined contexts of the domain ontologies that provide a foundation of organizational knowledge.

Searching for Knowledge

Aristotle's (2004) *Metaphysics* begins with the sentence: "All men by nature desire to know." More recently, Mario Bunge (2003) noted that inquiry is search for knowledge and that it is the trademark of science and the humanities. Similarly, inquiring organizations may be viewed as inquiring systems, that is, systems whose actions result in the creation of knowledge (Courtney, Croasdell & Paradice, 1998). Bunge observes that inquiry is a particular kind of cognitive process: it starts with some problem found in a given fund of knowledge, employs definite means, and aims at finding something or idea that may solve the problem. As noted by Bunge (1983a),

"Every human inquiry process involves some explicit or tacit epistemological principles. Some of these are regulative, i.e. they guide (or misguide) the planning and execution of inquiry by inspiring problems, methods, hypotheses, or inferences—as well as by suggesting the doubting or rejecting of alternatives, and searching for new principles." (p. 267)

A fair number of descriptive and regulative principles of inquiry is described in Bunge (1983a, pp. 264-270). Thus, inquiry is the composite in a composition[1] of at least six items elucidated by Bunge: a set of inquirers, an incomplete fund of knowledge, a set of problems (gaps in that fund), a set of research tools (conceptual or material), a set of epistemological principles, and a set of goals (cognitive or practical); the emergent properties of this composite include knowledge creation and organizational learning. This applies to any inquiries—be they in *pure* science, *applied* science, or technology. Moreover, the practice of critical rationality, free from any institutional affiliations "assumes a metalanguage in which truth claims can be rationally judged by all" (Deary, 2003). We are adopting these points of view in this chapter.

Although many in the fields of technology and management misperceive philosophy as antipractice, negative, irrelevant, and so forth, in reality, "all factual sciences, whether natural, social, or mixed, share a number of philosophical concepts...and a number of philosophical principles" (Bunge, 2001a, p. 45). This was recognized in the curricula of (at least) the early universities. Moreover, technologists (and technology managers!) who work on general theories of systems, control theory, optimization theory, the design of algorithms or simulation are applied philosophers of sorts, since they use philosophical concepts, such as those of event and system, and philosophical principles, such as those of the existence and lawfulness of the external world. (Bunge, 2001b, p. 360).

Of course, both business analysts as generalists who work on analyzing systems and (information) system designers belong to this esteemed class of people. In the same manner as, according to Aristotle, man reaches wisdom by asking the question *Why?*—

the root of all philosophy, a strategist (including a good business analyst) discovers the prevailing, often unstated, assumptions of different stakeholders and challenges them by asking various kinds of the same question, *Why*? Similarly, the best approaches to information management exemplified by the Reference Model of Open Distributed Processing (RM-ODP)—that have also been described in detail and used in information modeling contexts (Kilov & Ross, 1994) as well as in business modeling (Kilov, 1999, 2002; Kilov & Baclawski, 2003)—are firmly and explicitly based on a philosophical (and mathematical) foundation.

Abstraction and Modeling

In order to understand any given fund of knowledge and the gaps in it, first and foremost, we ought to *abstract*, that is, to separate the essential (knowledge) from the accidental (data). This especially applies to understanding an organization or any of its core domains (including technology) since otherwise we may (or do) get lost in the enormous amount of detail, especially in modern-day organizations and their environments. We follow the description of domain provided by Dines Bjørner (2000a): "By a domain we understand some area of human concern—an infrastructure component, an enterprise or other—for which computing support may be warranted…We shall refer to a generally non-software related universe of discourse as the domain" (pp. 8, 11). As an example, it may be instructive to compare an elegant and complete less-than-100-page description of the banking domain from Charles F. Dunbar's (1901) text published more than a century ago with much longer substantially less elegant and incomplete descriptions published in many modern texts. To accomplish such a separation of knowledge from data, we need to know what we are talking about (that is, the concepts and constructs that we use) and to communicate this knowledge so that it would be understood by its various recipients—participants in the inquiry process—in the same manner as by ourselves.

As Friedrich Hayek (1937) observed in *Economics and Knowledge*, "from time to time it is probably necessary to detach one's self from the technicalities of the argument and to ask quite naively what it is all about" (p. 51). Thus, we need to start with an *abstract model* of an organizational domain—that is, with the *ontology* of that domain. Such models are essential both in analysis (understanding of the stable state of affairs of an organization in its context) and in design (planning and accomplishing changes perceived as providing competitive advantage that may or may not be realized using computer-based information systems). Understanding of a domain comes before understanding a problem, which, in turn, comes before a solution. In the information management context, this approach successfully has been used in information and business modeling (Kilov, 1999, 2002; Kilov & Baclawski, 2003; Kilov & Ross, 1994), as well as in domain engineering work (Bjørner, 2000a, 2000b, 2003) and elsewhere.

Modeling is not trivial: as Mario Bunge (1998) observed in his *Philosophy of Science*, a model "involves a substantial deliberate simplification of empirical knowledge, as well as original constructs not found in experience" (p. 522). In other words, modeling requires abstraction—suppression of irrelevant detail to enhance understanding. Since we can reason about a simplified model of a complex situation much more easily than we can reason about the situation itself, *models help us to manage complexity* and, therefore, to make *substantiated* decisions based on the well-understood and explicitly formulated essentials of the modeled situation. Thus, models are essential for inquiries of any kind. In addition, only abstraction can put decision makers (e.g., management) in control. Observe that managing an organization may be viewed as a continuous cycle of inquiry, decision making, and action based on the results of the inquiry which in turn leads to further inquiry.

When we use abstraction, we can discover and clearly demonstrate deep semantic analogies—in fact, commonalities—between seemingly (very) different systems or their fragments. Clearly, this approach makes our inquiries substantially easier because it provides enormous help in understanding and therefore in decision making: common (basic and more specific) concepts need not be rediscovered and reformulated each and every time we encounter a new system or even a new situation—such as new requirements—within an existing system. Some of these common concepts and structures (such as invariant or composition) are encountered in all systems while some others (such as contract or trade) are more specialized.

Common Basic Concepts and Importance of Mathematics

Several philosophical approaches that may be used in the context of inquiring organizations were presented by Churchman (1971, see excellent overviews in Courtney et al., 1998; Courtney, 2001). These approaches introduce such principles—essential for successful inquiries—as usage of formal logic, usage of empirical information[2], openness and alternative models of the world, conflicting ideas, and so forth. However, certain philosophical approaches, including a few modern ones based on mental acrobatics use ideas that cannot be exactified and therefore are inappropriate for successful inquiries in technology and science. "Because the cult of fuzziness condemns lucidity, it hampers the task of working efficiently on any problem, whether cognitive or practical. This is so because, although exactness does not guarantee truth, system or efficiency, it facilitates the search for all three by enhancing intelligibility" (Bunge, 1991, p. 598). More detailed discussions were provided in, for example, Bunge (2001b, 2003). As an example, consider Christopher Alexander's (1979) observations about the significance of precisely specified invariants in architecture:

"... a pattern defines an invariant field which captures all the possible solutions to the problem given, in the stated range of contexts...the task of finding, or discovering, such an invariant field is immensely hard...anyone who takes the trouble to consider it carefully can understand it...these statements can be challenged because they are precise." (p.261 ff)

We will see how business patterns based on invariants are used to define the ontology of any domain, architectural or not.

Similarly, and more generally, the basic concepts of exact philosophy, business management, and information technology are the same or very similar, although they may be named differently in different contexts. In some cases, concepts used in philosophy or business management ought to be exactified, but this exactification has been successfully accomplished and can be reused. Exactification in any area of human endeavor is both possible and essential for understanding: as Wittgenstein (1933) observed, "everything that can be thought at all can be thought clearly. Everything that can be said can be said clearly" (4.116, p. 77); and contrariwise, "the silent adjustments to understand colloquial language are enormously complicated" (4.002, p. 63). Bunge (2001a) described exactification as "replacing vagueness with precision. This goal is attained by using, wherever necessary, the exact and rich languages of logic and mathematics instead of ordinary language, which is necessarily fuzzy and poor because it must serve to communicate people of widely different backgrounds and interests" (p. 65). And similarly, Yuri Lotman, one of the founding fathers of modern semiotics, noted that mathematics is "a method of scientific thought, and a methodological basis for the discovery of the most general regularities of life." (Lotman, 1964) Exactification also makes it possible to locate key concepts to be elucidated later (Bunge, 2001a): as a relatively simple example, consider the location and elucidation of the financial concept of a composite trade (and its components) in derivative trading (this was induced by the usage of the same term, *trade*, by different stakeholders to denote quite different concepts).

It is well-known—but not always acknowledged—that mathematics and logic provide a solid foundation also, and especially, for information technology. Dijkstra (1996), one of the founding fathers of programming, observed—in a manner similar to Bunge, Russell and Wittgenstein—that the:

"So-called 'natural language' is wonderful for the purposes it was created for, such as to be rude in, to tell jokes in, to cheat or to make love in (and Theorists of Literary Criticism can even be context-free in it), but it is hopelessly inadequate when we have to deal unambiguously with situations of great intricacy, situations which unavoidably arise in such activities as legislation, arbitration, mathematics or programming... The majority of people— even in mathematics and computing!— prefer the comfort of a fuzzy language in which cruel precision is impossible."

At the same time, exactification does not necessarily imply usage of formulas: for example, definitions of the Reference Model of Open Distributed Processing and of the semantics of Algol60, as well as most legislative acts, were written in very stylized and carefully constructed English.

"Needless to say, exactification is not identical with quantitation: there are numerous qualitative mathematical disciplines, such as logic, abstract algebra, and topology. Neither is exactification restricted to the natural sciences: there is a vigorous exactification movement in the social sciences and the humanities, not excluding philosophy" (Bunge, 1983b, p. 185).

The same is true about exactification used by enlightened management! And although exactification "does not replace the original invention of an initially imprecise idea, it helps to develop it" (Bunge, 1983b). Thus, initially imprecise ideas and intuition leading to new concepts, as well as new (or improved) products, services, and the production of radical novelties, must be followed by effective routinization which requires exactification. For example, Adam Smith (1904) observed that joint stock companies could be successful only by means of effective routinization:

> "[t]he only trades which it seems possible for a joint stock company to carry on successfully without an exclusive privilege are those of which all the operations are capable of being reduced to what is called a routine, or to such a uniformity of method as admits of little or no variation. Of this kind is, first, the banking trade; secondly, the trade of insurance from fire, and from sea risk and capture in time of war; thirdly, the trade of making and maintaining a navigable cut or canal; and, fourthly, the similar trade of bringing water for the supply of a great city." (p. 246)

Observe that *precise* is not the same as *detailed*: being overly detailed may lead to excessive complexity or to pursuing accidental exactness at the expense of essential substance. Detailed plans in complex environments are impossible and useless, as noted, for example, in Hayek (1964). However general, strategic planning, prediction of patterns, is not only possible but also essential. The same kind of observations in the context of *hard* and *soft* models were made by V. Arnol'd, one of the most distinguished modern-day mathematicians. In some cases, such as in (justification of) human decision making, it is not necessary to exactify everything: some (political, social, or other) reasons for making a specific decision in a specific context may well remain unspecified (together with some properties of the context relevant for making that human decision). Nevertheless, exactification of certain properties of the decision-making context may help enormously, even if it includes politically unpleasant surprises: demonstrably justified decisions made with open eyes lead to best results. Indeed, as observed by many authors, organizational inquiry has both soft and hard architectural elements. The hard architecture must be precise to enable the implementation of the soft architecture. Personal and organizational perspectives described in Mitroff and Linstone (1993) may be mostly concerned with the soft architecture and its integration with the hard architecture.

There is no need to reinvent the basic concepts and structures used in (organizational) domain modeling, although pretty often some information technologists (and others) try to do just that. The reinventing attempts are—more often than not—dismal failures composed of overly complex but buzzword-compliant artifacts, or (this is not an exclusive *or*) semantic-free constructs. When we discover, formulate, and reuse the basic modeling concepts, we again follow the lead of the classics: in the same manner as Adam Smith's *Wealth of Nations* was preceded by his *Theory of Moral Sentiments* (also by Hutcheson's *System of Moral Philosophy*), the foundations of modeling are in philosophy. As noted above, mathematics—the "art and science of effective reasoning" (Dijkstra, 1986, p. 2)— is essential for concept exactification. Although *explicit* specification of certain basic concepts and structures used in domain modeling may have happened relatively recently, these concepts and structures—as well as the basics of most business domains!—have been around for centuries and perhaps millennia and have been described with varying degrees of explicitness and precision for quite a while. The essential structures of various domains, including business and organizational ones, have been described in an abstract and precise manner, using (often explicitly) such basic concepts as viewpoint, relationship, invariant, composition, subtyping, and so forth. Rigorous and often formal definitions of these basic concepts have been provided more recently. For example, in economics (a science of complex phenomena, according to Hayek, 1964), specifications and discussions of the essential structures may be found in classical works by Adam Smith and Francis Hutcheson and in more recent works by Bagehot, von Mises, Hayek[3], and others. All these structures are abstractions; that is, they have been obtained by suppressing irrelevant details. Thinking in terms of these abstractions helps a lot in finding and formulating a problem to solve. In a business context, finding a problem may lead to finding an opportunity for a possible competitive advantage which is often more substantial than that achieved by virtue of solving a well-recognized problem. Here, effectiveness is more important than efficiency: to quote Tom DeMarco (2001), "an organization that can only accelerate is like a car that can speed but not steer. In the short run, it makes a lot of progress in whatever direction it happened to be going, but in the long run, it's just another road wreck" (p. xii). The same considerations about the relative importance of problem finding and problem solving apply to a scientific context (Bunge, 1998).

Creating a model of a situation (or a system) often requires introducing concepts and constructs that were not clearly discernible in that situation when we considered it in isolation but that become clear when we consider the commonalities between that situation and other more or less similar situations (or systems). In most cases, good judgment and inventiveness of a "well-appointed brain" (Bunge, 2001a) are essential to discover the appropriate—simple and elegant—abstract concepts and to formulate them in a precise and explicit manner. These concepts, also known as business patterns, provide essential guidance to analysts and designers of systems (including organizations) different from those from which they were distilled. The discovery process cannot be formalized. It needs time in which the discoverer—the abstractor—can think, that is, can be undistracted and open to ideas. It is also known as *pondering* or *modeling,* and its descriptions in scientific and mathematical literature often have been suppressed, resulting in too many rabbits taken out of various magic hats. Notable exceptions exist in the work of such authors as Polya, Dijkstra, Hoare, Arnol'd, and some others. Both the discovery process and its result—many *abstract* concepts and constructs—are often inspired by proper, that is, elegant, philosophical works!

Reusing Composition to Exactify Concepts

Let us exactify (to some extent) the concepts of organizational knowledge and organizational inquiry. In doing so, we will use composition as a very important form of abstraction. Indeed, we may consider the description of a composite with its properties—determined by those of its components and by the way they are combined (Bunge, 2003; ISO, 1995b; Kilov & Ross, 1994)—as an abstract and therefore mode general, more essential, more understandable, and less accidental description than that of its components. In other words, describing a composite may and often does introduce a higher abstraction level. (Of course, we may also need to concentrate separately on the appropriately chosen details at the lower levels.) For a familiar example, we start planning a car trip by considering a high-level road map and only then pick and choose more detailed less abstract road maps that show the specifics of the chosen path to our destination.

In order to avoid anthropomorphism and strive for precision, it is reasonable to follow the proposal by Mario Bunge (1990a) that a purpose (as well as, let us add, knowledge and inquiry) can be ascribed only to humans ("highly evolved brains") or sets of humans. Specifically, instead of reasoning about the knowledge and inquiry of an organization, we reason about the knowledge and inquiry of various people—stakeholders of the organization, such as its creators (entrepreneurs), investors, shareholders, directors and managers, workers (both employees and consultants), especially knowledge workers (in von Mises's terms, *technicians*), customers, regulators, and so on. Most of these stakeholders were clearly described in von Mises (1949).

After these introductory remarks, we recall that the knowledge (and the corresponding possible inquiries) of different individuals is clearly different. "Knowledge involves the ability to act intelligently and to learn. Wisdom guides knowledgeable actions on the basis of moral and ethical values" (Courtney, 2001, p. 23). Clearly, only humans have these abilities and values. Moreover, "each sees a problem differently and thus generates a different perspective on it" (Mitroff & Linstone, 1993). The organizational knowledge may be defined as the composite knowledge of all the relevant stakeholders. As usual, the emergent properties of this composite are determined not only by its components but also by the way the components are combined, for example, by the ways of sharing of individuals' tacit and explicit knowledge (these ways may include not only explicit contributions of individuals, but also lobbying, marketing, becoming indispensable, influencing the formal or informal practices, and so on (Kilov, 2002)), the ways of creating and updating a corporate knowledge base (Courtney et al., 1998), the schema of that knowledge base, the relative importance of various individuals in contributing to the knowledge base, and so forth. It would be preferable to consider these ways of combining more explicitly, as explicit components in the composition that define the organizational knowledge. The top management of the organization and, ultimately, its owners will have to balance the conflicting ways various stakeholders contribute to organizational knowledge. To do that, it would be necessary to make the conflicts explicit and thus explicitly to determine, in accordance with the definition of a composition, the emergent properties of the composite (the result of the balance) from the properties of its various components and the way these components are combined. As an important example, it will be necessary to determine the role of an individual expert—both in whether to rely on tacit knowledge of a guru (or, worse, on unspecified common knowledge) as opposed to explicit knowledge to be made available in the knowledge base and in whether to be as independent as possible from the competence (mostly the ability to inquire) of an individual employee (Dijkstra, 1980).

Similarly, it is possible to consider organizational learning as a composite in the composition of individual learnings. The way the components are combined includes sharing individuals' associations, cognitive systems, and memories, as noted in (Courtney et al., 1998). This composition also includes organizational structure and culture—both formal and informal—as its components because they substantially influence the way the individual learnings are combined. And this composition allows us to transfer four levels of professional development (Courtney et al., 1998)—an apprentice, a specialist, a generalist, and a renowned—to the context of organizational learning. Of course, this is a very high-level overview since, for example, there exist different specific kinds of personal and organizational learning, and a person renowned in one area may well be an apprentice in another (Adam Smith described division of labor a long time ago). It is important to observe that learning of a profession differs substantially from learning a trade. Understanding and use of abstraction and precision are the core competencies of a successful professional, and, as Dijkstra noted, in a trade, rather than in a profession, the apprentice had to spend "seven meagre years" to observe and absorb by osmosis the unformulated magic done by the Master. The professional's scientific knowledge is distinct from magic because it is objective or invariant with respect to the knowing subject (Bunge, 2001b), and therefore it can be explicitly formulated and taught.

In this context, it is also interesting to consider how to validate knowledge for inquiring organizations. Clearly, actions of inquiring persons and organizations should be based on valid knowledge (Courtney et al., 1998), but it would probably be insufficient to rely only on imprecise Lockean intra-organizational consensus for such validation. As noted by Courtney, organizational members "must have a common language and mindset, which permits effective communication" (Courtney, 2001, p. 26). This mindset requires an ontology shared by all participants in the inquiry, and such an ontology ought to be made explicit since otherwise it will be unclear whether the mindset is common or not. Different classes of stakeholders may prefer different languages convenient for them to represent the same ontology: after all, as Goguen and Burstall (1992) stated, "truth is invariant under change of notation" (p. 101). The composition that determines the organizational knowledge provides a way to exactify both the components and the emergent properties of the composite in this composition, and such exactification leads to either achieving a consensus or to a clear demonstration that such a consensus is impossible. As a rather well-known example, business decision makers made serious mistakes when they promoted dot-com companies based on business plans presented as a few beautiful graphics (Lovelace, 2001, p. 74). Although a perception of consensus had been achieved in most of these situations, different stakeholders (organizational members) interpreted the same beautiful graphics differently—in ways they considered preferable in their current contexts, and these interpretations were possible because the semantics of the graphics were never exactified. For another example, in the IT context of aspect-oriented programming, it has been discovered and recognized that a joint ontology is essential for communication between modular units of specification (or aspects) (Wand, 2003).

Finally, it is possible to use composition in order to synthesize the five types of approaches to inquiring systems described by Churchman (1971) in the contexts of organizational inquiry and learning (Courtney et al., 1998; Courtney, 2001). The resulting synthesis of different approaches is, of course, a composite approach, the emergent properties of which will be defined by the relevant properties of the component approaches and by the way they are combined. Such a synthesis of properly selected ideas was described in a letter by Leibniz written in 1714 and quoted in Mercer (2002):

"I have tried to uncover and unite the truth buried and scattered under the opinions of all the different Philosophical Sects, and I believe that I have added something of my own which takes a few steps forward. I flatter myself to have penetrated into the Harmony of these different realms."

Similarly, Bunge presented *systemism* as a synthesis of seven philosophical approaches such that we can learn something from each of them (Bunge, 2001a, p. 40)—in the same manner as we can learn something from each of the five (Courtney et al., 1998) philosophical approaches to inquiring systems (so there is no need to choose the single best approach out of these five). And as a similar kind of composition, "a synthesis of broad worldviews" can be developed rather than "adopting the limited view of a single perspective" (Courtney, 2001, p. 29). Of course, not everything ought to be included in the emergent properties of the composite. For example, the Hegelian concept of two diametrically opposing viewpoints (Courtney et al., 1998) is in many contexts deficient, firstly because the number of different viewpoints may be (and often is) greater than two and, secondly, because it may be difficult or impossible to exactify the concept of diametrically opposing viewpoints. (In contract negotiation presented as an example application in a Hegelian environment, it is unclear whether a price of $300, or of $555, for a product is diametrically opposed to $600.) For another example, the Singerian concept of "what is good for the society" can be exactified only in accordance with well-defined explicit and viewpoint-dependent criteria, while holders of different viewpoints may have quite different (but not necessarily diametrically opposing) criteria of goodness that would have to be composed in some (to be specified) manner.

It is very instructive to observe that Bunge's systemism is very close to the approaches used by the professional analysts and designers in information management and described, for example, in RM-ODP. The elucidation of the concept of a system presented by Bunge (2001a) uses semantically the same concepts as those used in RM-ODP: composition, structure, environment, and mechanism. More generally, the concepts of abstraction and precision are essential both for Bunge's systemism and for RM-ODP. Various viewpoints described in RM-ODP are explicitly based on a precisely defined joint ontology—a set of concepts and constructs used in all viewpoints, while each viewpoint brings additional viewpoint-specific concepts and constructs. Similarly, all the factual sciences, whether natural, social, or mixed, share a number of philosophical concepts, use a single logic and the same basic method, and use mathematics (Bunge, 2001a). These approaches are very close to the one described by a modern-day mathematician, Joseph Goguen (1998), when he discussed engineering in general: "the most general concepts of engineering might be system, behavior, and interconnection, formalized in such a way as to include hierarchical whole-part relationships" (p. 98).

Bridging the Business-IT Gap: Reuse Instead of Reinvention

As discussed above, the fundamental concepts and constructs of very different areas of human endeavor are the same. Indeed, as Bunge (2003) noted, the more abstract constructs are "more portable from one discipline to another" (p. 8). As an example, consider Leibnizian inquiring organizations which, as stated in Courtney et al. (1998), "rely heavily on standard operating procedures and formal instruction mechanisms." Clearly, IT support, using an explicitly stated set of reasoning rules, may drastically increase the efficiency of such an organization, a clear description of which was provided, for example, in von Mises (1944, 1949). Using the terminology of RM-ODP, we may say that von Mises provided not only an information viewpoint specification (that is, of stakeholders, actions, and relationships between them) but also an enterprise viewpoint specification (that is, of purpose, scope, policies, communities, environments, etc.). In a similar manner, the description of Kantian organizations in which "middle managers use the resources at their disposal to determine how best to fit tasks into the ongoing operations of the organization" (Courtney et al., 1998) successfully has been exactified by Dines Bjørner (2000) in his distinction between three precisely (and then formally) defined abstraction levels—strategic, tactical, and operational resource management concerns within an enterprise. Similarly and more generally, RM-ODP concepts and constructs perceived by some as usable only in the specific IT context of open distributed processing in fact can be, and have been, used in a wide variety of other disciplines, including those that are far from computer-based information processing. As an example, both the fundamentals and essential specifics of banking as presented in a banking textbook published more than a century ago (Dunbar, 1901) have been described in RM-ODP terms without any problems. Moreover, this exactified description (Kilov, 1999) demonstrated that the underlying concepts of modern day banking (and finance) are precisely those that had been well-known—and elucidated in a textbook—more than a century ago. In this manner, it becomes very easy to bridge the proverbial gap between business and IT experts—just use the same system of concepts!

Current business and organizational modeling literature has often introduced new buzzword-compliant concepts in vogue by some IT experts. Although good IT modeling concepts are well-defined, technology-neutral, and (also) based on mathematics and philosophy4, in quite a few cases, IT-based organizational models have been formulated using only such concepts and constructs that could be easily implemented using currently fashionable technologies. In these models, which often are not understandable to business stakeholders, the semantics of "what an organization is" and "what an organization does" is often lost, leading to appalling failures of IT systems apparently created to help an organization. As a simple (but very unfortunate) example, the concept of a *composition*—well-known in philosophy and defined using (emergent) property determination—too often has been misunderstood in IT just because property determination cannot be implemented by computer-based IT systems in an automatic manner. As discussed above, composition is essential to define the semantics of most, if not all, organizational structures and of systems in general: an emergent property of a system (for example, Bunge, "being alive" or "social structure") if it is determined by its components and by the way they are combined. Similarly, the concept of a *contract* was clearly defined by outstanding philosophers, economists, and software engineers and incorrectly reinvented by too many innovators. Finally, many fashionable IT-based modeling and design approaches are based on examples (including prototypes and *stories*) rather than on the Aristotelian approach to specifications: in example-based approaches, it is often not possible to determine whether a fact corresponds to an example-based specification.

Needless to say, not all IT-based modeling approaches are deficient. Some of them are based on mathematics and philosophy and use the same underlying concepts and constructs as those essential for understanding any systems including organizational ones. These approaches have been described in various sources, including those of information modeling, as well as in international standards based on the Reference Model of Open Distributed Processing (RM-ODP) (ISO, 1995b). RM-ODP is terse (18-pages-long), simple, and elegant and includes, among other things, proper definitions of concepts referred to above, such as a composition and a contract and of many other concepts used in understanding and modeling of systems. It is instructive to observe that RM-ODP has been written in a very carefully constructed stylized English (comparable to understandable legalese) and that the definitions of many basic modeling and specification concepts and constructs from this standard successfully have been interpreted and formalized using a formal specification language Z based on mathematics and logic. This exactification process was applied to an already semi-formal (rigorous) text of the standard and led to feedback that improved its consistency (ISO, 1998). This IT-based modeling approach has been described in detail in Kilov and Ross (1994) and Kilov 1999, 2002) and effectively has been used in business and organizational modeling (Kilov & Baclawski, 2003; Morabito, Sack & Bhate, 1999) for many and varied application areas including finance, insurance, telecommunications, document management, and so forth.

It is not sufficient to discover, formulate, and use (fundamental, basic, and more specific) concepts and structures essential for a good model. We ought to communicate these discoveries, both for understanding of that model and for their usage in other, often apparently very different, models. But in order to transmit a message from one person to another without loss of meaning, the author and recipients of the message have to use the same ontology and the same notation. Using the same natural (colloquial) language, as a notation is not sufficient, since in order to preserve meaning, we need also the same context, the same language experience, language norms, cultural tradition, and so on (Lotman, 1990), and these properties of different people are often implicit and (very) different. At the same time, a restrictive artificial language that does not have contexts, cultural traditions, and so on, can guarantee an adequate transmission of a message's *semantics* provided, of course, that this message can be adequately represented in that language. As a somewhat crude approximation of such a restrictive language, we may consider legalese in which, for example, laws (providing "the same context") and contracts are written. In the modeling context, a concise and elegant system of basic concepts described in RM-ODP (or by Bunge) provides a foundation for such a language. Sometimes the *specifics* of this language or, more often, its fragments ought to be created (collectively, by the modelers together with the subject matter experts) for successful communication of a model's semantics. Models formulated in such a manner (of course, based on concepts and structures common to many if not most systems) establish a common background used by all stakeholders of an organization and its relevant environment (e.g., clients and subcontractors) in understanding and business decision making.

Start with the Domain Knowledge: Ontologies

Inquiries accomplished by humans or organizations—compositions of humans—ought to happen within a very clearly defined context. To quote Mario Bunge (1990b), "every novelty in knowledge is assessed in the light of some background knowledge that is not being questioned during the evaluation process" (p. 631).[5] Similarly, Hayek (1964) observed that "until we have definite questions to ask, we cannot employ our intellect; and questions presuppose that we have formed some provisional hypothesis or theory about the events" (p. 332). This background (perhaps provisional) knowledge is usually that of the business domain—be it specific or more generic—within which the inquiries are happening and various stories are told, and therefore we need to start with the basics, the ontology of the business domain, in order to succeed in our inquiries, to understand the stories, and to avoid reinventions of (often square) wheels. Exactification without a clearly specified context is quite dangerous: "the danger is taking an exact idea and transforming it by abusing or decontexualizing of the exact idea which is in turn transformed into the wrong idea" (Bunge, 1983a). It takes time and nontrivial intellectual effort to create an ontology, especially one understandable to a variety of stakeholders. Ontologies created from scratch may well be excessively complex because they may be too specific. However, by using abstraction, it is possible to determine and formulate the essential characteristics common to several different domains, thus drastically simplifying the ontologies. These common characteristics can and should be reused as the foundation in dealing with specific domains.

The knowledge of a domain includes various perspectives (viewpoints). Specifically, in addition to the technical perspective, "also broad organizational and personal perspectives, and ethical and aesthetic issues as well" (Courtney, 2001, p.18) may need to be considered, especially for decision support systems. On the one hand, exactification is essential in order to make explicit reasoning about these perspectives possible. As noted in Courtney (2001), each camp of stakeholders in the decision-making process "tends to base its position on unstated assumptions which, if left uncovered, often lead to circular debate that goes nowhere" (p. 29). Thus, the ontologies used by each camp's stakeholders ought to be exactified. Of course, stakeholders within the same camp also may use substantially or somewhat different assumptions and therefore ontologies. On the other hand, viewpoints—"forms of abstraction achieved using a selected set of architectural concepts and structuring rules, in order to focus on particular concerns within a system" (ISO, 1995, 3.2.7, p. 6)—are essential for human understanding since otherwise the enormous amount of information, the "too much stuff," will make any reasonable decision making impossible. Thus, when a composition, or various compositions, of viewpoints is being accomplished6 (such as when a single ontology is being created), it is very important to use abstraction in order to include in the composite only those properties that are essential for a general overview of the domain. Such an abstract overview may, of course, also be viewpoint dependent, and it will determine "what data and what perspectives we examine in a world of overabundant data sources and a plethora of ways of viewing that data" (Courtney, 2001, p. 31).

As a result of inquiries, the background knowledge may be updated, and thus our model of the (business) domain, our ontology, may be enhanced. This has happened in science, technology, and other areas of human endeavor. But in order to succeed, a representation of the knowledge ought to be understandable to the interested parties. Since these parties may have quite different backgrounds, the language chosen for the representation ought to use only such constructs that are absolutely essential for understanding and reasoning about knowledge semantics. In other words, the description of the language constructs ought to fit on the proverbial back of an envelope—otherwise the complexity of the domain knowledge would be made intolerable by the addition of avoidable complexity of a poorly chosen notation. At the same time, the language ought to be rich enough in order to support the preservation of essential semantics of the knowledge existing in a person's mind when this knowledge is mapped from the mind to the language-based representation (Goguen, 1999).

Here again, we do not need to reinvent. The basic modeling concepts have been described, for example, by Bunge and in RM-ODP, and there are not too many of them. Specifically, the *structure of a domain* is described by means of (mostly nonbinary) relationships of three kinds—composition, subtyping, and reference; the semantics of each of them is defined using property determination (ISO, 1995a; Kilov, 2002) and fits on the back of a (business-sized) envelope. We have already demonstrated how composition can be used to distill, elucidate, and exactify some important concepts of organizational modeling. Thus, it becomes possible to describe relationship semantics in a precise and explicit manner, rather than, as it had often happened in IT-based modeling, say that "this line between these two boxes formally defines the relationship between the customer and the supplier." And in the context of a Singerian inquirer, which "views the world as a holistic system, in which everything is connected to everything else" (Courtney, 2001, p. 28), or in the context of Bunge's critique of radical holism in Bunge (2003), it becomes possible to determine which of these connections are relationships with clearly defined semantics and which are not (and therefore may need to be redefined or dropped from consideration). In doing so, we use abstraction in order to separate the relevant relationships from the irrelevant ones. Of course, different (kinds of) relationships are relevant for different viewpoints, and, as properly noted in Courtney (2001) referring to Linstone (1984), "multiple perspectives or worldviews" have to be brought in for a "holistic, systems approach [to]... thinking and decision-making processes" (p. 29).

Observe that in an ontology (and in modeling and reasoning in general) it would be a very serious error to rely on "meaningful names" since names are arbitrary tags (Bunge, 2003) and contexts are essential for using names (ISO, 1995b; Wittgenstein, 1933). Usage of a particular name by itself does not mean understanding of the semantics of an individual denoted by that name. William Kent (1979) presents an excellent discussion of this topic with numerous convincing examples. Different naming contexts may evoke different connotations for the same name by different readers, and the name writer cannot control this (van Gasteren, 1990). Substantially different connotations are relatively easy to determine. However, somewhat different connotations are notoriously difficult to discover, and such discoveries require exactification that include a clear and explicit specification of contexts. For these reasons, provisioning of keywords, indexing, or other such activities are of very limited value for understanding the semantics of knowledge. Actual understanding becomes possible only if the structure of this knowledge—the collection of relationships among its elements and also among these and environmental items (Bunge, 2001a)—is made explicit (this structure also makes explicit the necessary contexts for using names).

The role of ontologies is even more important in the context of the inevitable change, especially change in organizations. "Organizational knowledge is in a constant state of flux as new experiences are evaluated and shared" (Courtney, 2001, p. 24). This makes a stable foundation imperative for understanding and reasoning about this change. And such a stable foundation is provided by the model of the appropriate domain—an abstract model is the invariant that remains true no matter what changes (will) appear in the organization and its knowledge (and what are, or will be, the requirements for these changes). This invariant includes the composition of the domain, its structure, environment, and mechanism (Bunge, 2001a). (Of course, the invariant itself may change, but these changes happen much less frequently and usually more slowly than other changes in organization.)

Summing up, we may say that *abstraction and precision* (exactification) are essential for modeling—creating and reasoning about ontologies—and for using ontologies in all kinds of knowledge management (including organizational inquiries) in any areas of human endeavor.

Science, (Information) Technology, and Tinkering

Reading elegant philosophical works—even when we disagree with some statements made by their authors—provides us with fresh air needed to make our thinking more lucid, more explicit, and more expressive. These works introduce and use abstract concepts needed by us to understand the semantics of deep commonalities between apparently very different organizational domains or systems. And the joy of understanding, the *Aha!*, is often based on discovering and using such abstract concepts. In many cases, these concepts have been discovered as a result of contemplation. This was noted by Aristotle (Metaphysics, Book I, Part I):

"Hence when all such inventions were already established, the sciences which do not aim at giving pleasure or at the necessities of life were discovered, and first in the places where men first began to have leisure. This is why the mathematical arts were founded in Egypt; for there the priestly caste was allowed to be at leisure."

This Aristotelian observation leads to a clear distinction between technological innovations—qualitative novelties firmly and explicitly based on (pure and applied) science and neither a result of tinkering nor market-driven but rather generating a new market (Bunge, 2001)—and *technics* based on tinkering[7] (Bunge, 2001). Clearly, technology does not need reinvention of wheels (much less of square ones), while technics is full of such reinventions.

As a very important example, the survival (or otherwise) of information technology as we know it may be determined by its usage of a firm scientific basis, specifically from computing science and mathematics. As Dijkstra (1985) emphasized,

"Back to our original question: Can computing science save the computer industry? My answer is 'If the computer industry can be saved, only computing science can do it.' But it may take a long time before the computer industry—in particular the well-established companies—will share this view. It will almost certainly take longer than the limited period over which they plan their futures. In the mean time, the academic world—which traditionally plans much further ahead—has no choice. It has to refine and to teach to the best of its abilities how computing should be done; would it ever yield to the pressure to propagate the malpractice of today, it had better fold up." (pp. 6-7)

The situation in IT since then appears to have substantially worsened: in addition to numerous serious failures described, for example, in Peter Neumann's comp.risks newsgroup and column in *Software Engineering Notes*, consider such well-known symptoms as massive outsourcing of IT work, unemployment among IT experts, and well thought-out articles with titles like "IT doesn't matter" published in prestigious journals. This happens because the products and services of information technology, like of any technology, should either satisfy the existing business requirements or provide new market opportunities. With respect to the former, all too often what was wanted by the business and what was being proposed by the vendors of "CRM or ERP or SCM or EAI or CYA or whatever…were as different and detached as reality TV shows are from reality" (Evans, 2003, p.106). With respect to the latter, all too often information technology has been based on tinkering, which has involved enormous waste of brainpower, rather than on a firm scientific foundation, and tinkering (even glorified ones) usually cannot result in substantially new market opportunities.

Compare, in the context of this IT example, two approaches to technology. One, advocated by Bunge (2001), states that the acquisition of the requisite background knowledge is an essential component of the technological method. Another, quoted in *Information Week* of November 17, 2003, states that "a programmer's three-year-old experience will be like a three-year-old laptop is today: a quarter of capacity, a quarter of speed, and ready for replacement" (Murphy & Chabrow, 2003). The half-life of three (or less) years is a property of most skills acquired by a modern tradesperson as opposed to knowledge acquired by a professional. This example demonstrates that many contemporary enterprises seem to want to market and sell flowers (technology) without giving attention to the root (science) and stem (applied science) necessary to produce desirable flowers. As we all know, flowers detached from plants wither away in a short period.

Business Patterns

Let us conclude on a more optimistic note. In quite a few cases, it has been possible to discover, formulate, and reuse common constructs—business patterns—in various contexts. This has happened for a while: laws of business, as well as laws of nature, have been known and reused for centuries (and some for millennia). Unfortunately, when businesses became more complex, this complexity often overwhelmed both theoreticians and practitioners so that clear, explicit, and precise business models became an exception rather than a rule. Creating good business models (that is, those that describe the essentials of the business and are understandable to all stakeholders) is not trivial and requires using abstraction and exactification. Exact philosophy and software engineering are professions which involve just that. Mastering complexity is the most important aspect of software engineering (see also the works of E. W. Dijkstra, C.A.R. Hoare, and other founding fathers of computing science), and therefore domain engineering, as noted by Dines Bjørner (2000a, 2000b) is an essential component of software engineering the other two components of which are requirements engineering and software design. Although "most practising software engineers do not grasp abstraction" (Bjørner, 2002, p. 3), some do, and these outstanding software engineers usually are, or can become, good domain engineers (business analysts).

Business patterns provide heuristic guidance to business analysts—creators of business models—in their organizational inquiry activities. In the absence of such guidance, fragments of business models which describe analogous constructs in different (organizational) contexts are not reused: they are reinvented, and more often than not, the reinventions are deficient (this is where square wheels appear). Business patterns are a part of the infrastructure used by business model readers and writers, and thus are described once and instantiated, using appropriate parameters, for each particular situation. Of course, in order to reuse a pattern it is necessary to be able to recognize the structure (shape) of a situation in context. When a business analyst suspects that a particular business pattern (for example, a composition or, more specifically, a financial contract or, even more specifically, a trade) may fit a particular situation and wants to confirm or deny this, the analyst asks questions about the situation based on the invariants that define the business pattern (Kilov, 1999). There is no need to reinvent, and this leads to a substantial economy of intellectual effort, and therefore time and money.

A system of rather specific business patterns may describe a business application area such as derivative trading. By instantiating these patterns, that is, actualizing appropriate parameters (many of which are not elementary!), it is possible to create a complete business model of a domain understandable to all relevant stakeholders, such as that of exotic foreign exchange option trading in a particular firm (Garrison, 2001). In this manner, it becomes possible explicitly to separate the generic aspects of a firm which do not provide any competitive advantage and which therefore may be safely subcontracted (if desired) from proprietary aspects which do provide a competitive advantage to the firm and which ought to be carefully considered by the firm's decision makers. In some cases, competitive advantage may be in a novel business pattern or in novel actions applied within an existing business pattern. Some properties of the competitive advantage may or even ought to be marketed.

Where do business patterns come from? They can be classified by their abstraction level into fundamental (e.g., invariants); generic (e.g., composition, composition-assembly, reference); business-generic (e.g., contract, decision, realization, name in context); and more business-specific (e.g., financial contract, life insurance annuities, underwriting, clearing house, reconciliation) (Kilov, 1999). The fundamental and generic business patterns are (relatively) well-known and have been described in literature, including such standards as ISO, (1995a, 1995b) and EDOC (2001), while some of the business-generic and more business-specific patterns have also become explicitly available (Bjørner, 2003; Kilov, 1999, 2002; Kilov & Baclawski, 2003; Morabito et al., 1999, etc.). If a specific business pattern appropriate for a particular situation is not known or not available, then such a pattern may always be created by instantiating more generic business patterns which are always available by combining existing business patterns or by incremental modification of some partially appropriate specific ones. The combination includes applying composition, subtyping, and reference relationships, which themselves are generic business patterns, to the available business patterns.

In addition to providing a foundation for any kind of decision making (including decisions about changing or automating some business processes), a business model based on business patterns may be used for training and mentoring employees and consultants of the organization and for organizational learning in general. All these activities would be demonstrably based on an explicitly available model instead of handwaving, and therefore—if the model is reasonably complete and clear—strategic, tactical, and operational business decision makers would be able to concentrate on justifiable decisions rather than on exactifying (or even discovering, correctly or otherwise) their context because this context will be already well-defined. Thus, business patterns with well-defined semantics help making the organizational knowledge explicit and usable by all stakeholders.

Conclusion

We have shown how a relatively small number of reusable abstract concepts—business patterns—common to various areas of human endeavor such as exact philosophy, business management, science, and technology, including information technology, can and should be used to exactify crucial aspects of organizational inquiry. Abstraction (accomplished, among other things, by using composition, one of the few most important relationships in modeling) and exactification are essential for taming complexity in general and complexity of the modern-day organization in particular. Exactification is achieved, first and foremost, by creating and using ontologies—business and organizational domain models with precisely defined semantics. An ontology clearly demonstrates the semantics of the fundamental concepts of a domain and relationships between them. The generic concepts used in effective (business and IT) modeling have a well-defined semantics based on mathematics and philosophy, while in too many cases a multitude of concepts invented in buzzword-compliant IT methods based on tinkering has no clear semantics and therefore cannot be reasonably used. Therefore the survival (or otherwise) of IT as we know it may be determined by its usage of a firm scientific basis, specifically from computing science and mathematics. More generally, organizational learning and organizational inquiry for all kinds of organizations and their subdivisions can be understood and accomplished substantially better in the well-defined contexts of the domain ontologies that provide a foundation of organizational knowledge.

Acknowledgments

Many thanks go to our colleagues—especially including students!—with whom concepts and ideas presented in this paper have been discussed. Special thanks go to the anonymous reviewers for their helpful suggestions.

References

Alexander, C. (1979). *The timeless way of building*. Oxford, UK: Oxford University Press.

Aristotle (2004). *Metaphysics* (W. D. Ross, Trans.). Retrieved September 27, 2004, from *http://classics.mit.edu/Aristotle/metaphysics.html*

Bjørner, D. (2000a, August 8). *Domain engineering. Elements of a software engineering methodology: Towards principles, techniques and tools — A Study in Methodology*. Technical University of Denmark (DK-2800), Lyngby, Denmark.

Bjørner, D. (2000b, August 28). *"What is a method?" An essay on some aspects of software engineering*. Technical University of Denmark (DK-2800), Lyngby, Denmark.

Bjørner, D. (2002). Preface [to *The SE Book* - Lecture Notes on Software Engineering]. © Dines Bjørner, Fredsvej 11, DK-2840, Holte, Denmark, 2001-2002. January 2002. See *http://www.imm.dtu.dk/~db/TheSEBook*

Bjørner, D. (2003). Domain models of "The Market"—In preparation of ε-transaction systems. In H. Kilov & K. Baclawski (Eds.), *Practical foundations of business system specifications* (pp. 111-144). Dordrecht/Boston/London: Kluwer Academic.

Bunge, M. (1983a). *Treatise on basic philosophy. Vol. 6. Understanding the world*. Dordrecht: D. Reidel.

Bunge, M. (1983b). *Treatise on basic philosophy. Vol. 5. Exploring the world*. Dordrecht: D. Reidel.

Bunge, M. (1990a). Reply to *Mattessich on the Foundations of the Management and Information Sciences*. In P. Weingartner & G. J. W. Dorn (Eds.), *Studies on Mario Bunge's* Treatise. Amsterdam/Atlanta: Rodopi.

Bunge, M. (1990b). Reply to *Kanitscheider on the Tense Relations between Science and Philosophy*. In P. Weingartner & G. J. W. Dorn (Eds.), *Studies on Mario Bunge's* Treatise. Amsterdam/Atlanta: Rodopi.

Bunge, M. (1991). Why we cherish exactness. In G. Schurz & G. J. W. Dorn (Eds.), *Advances in scientific philosophy. Essays in honor of Paul Weingartner on the occasion of the 60th anniversary of his birthday* (pp. 591-598). Amsterdam/ Atlanta: Rodopi.

Bunge, M. (1998). *Philosophy of science.* New Brunswick/London: Transaction Publishers.

Bunge, M. (2001a). *Philosophy in crisis. The need for reconstruction.* Amherst, NY: Prometheus Books.

Bunge, M. (2001b). *Scientific realism.* Amherst, NY: Prometheus Books.

Bunge, M. (2003). *Philosophical dictionary.* Amherst, NY: Prometheus Books.

Churchman, C. W. (1971). *The design of inquiring systems: Basic concepts of systems and organizations.* New York: Basic Books.

Courtney, J. F. (2001). Decision making and knowledge management in inquiring organizations: Toward a new decision-making paradigm for DSS. *Decision Support Systems, 31,* 17-38.

Courtney, J. F., Croasdell, D. T., & Paradice, D. B. (1998). Inquiring organizations. *Australian Journal of Information Systems, 6*(1), 3-15.

Deary, V. (2003, November 7). Great white males still at large. *The Times Literary Supplement.*

DeMarco, T. (2001). *Slack.* New York, NY: Broadway Books.

Dijkstra, E. W. (1980, September 13). *American programming's plight.* University of Texas at Austin (EWD 750).

Dijkstra, E.W. (1985, May 1). *Can computing science save the computer industry?* University of Texas at Austin (EWD 920).

Dijkstra, E.W. (1986, June 14). *Management and Mathematics.* University of Texas at Austin (EWD 966).

Dijkstra, E. W. (1996, May 12). *Foreword.* University of Texas at Austin (EWD 1238).

Dunbar, C. F. (1901). *Chapters on the theory and history of banking* (2nd ed.). New York/ London: G. P. Putnam's Sons.

EDOC. (2001, June 18). *A UML profile for enterprise distributed object computing. Joint final submission part I* (OMG Doc. No. ad/2001-06-09). Needham, MA.

Evans, B. (2003, November 17). There hangs the tale, or two questions. *Information Week,* 106.

Garrison, J. S. (2001). Business specifications: Using UML to specify the trading of foreign exchange options. *Proceedings of the 10th OOPSLA Workshop on Behavioral Semantics (Back to Basics)* (pp. 79-84). Boston: Northeastern University.

Goguen, J. (1998). Tossing algebraic flowers down the Great Divide. In C. S. Calude (Ed.), *People and ideas in theoretical computer science* (pp. 93-129). New York: Springer Verlag.

Goguen, J. (1999). An introduction to algebraic semiotics, with application to user interface design. In C. Hehaniv, *Computation for metaphor, analogy and agents* (pp. 242-291). New York: Springer Verlag.

Goguen, J.A., Burnstall, R. (1992) Institutions: Abstract model theory for specification and programming. Journal of the ACM, 39 (1): 95-146.

Hayek, F. A. (1937). Economics and knowledge. *Economica, IV,* 33-54.

Hayek, F. A. (1964). The theory of complex phenomena. In M. Bunge (Ed.), *The critical approach to science and technology (In honor of Karl R. Popper)* (pp. 332-349). London: Free Press of Glencoe.

ISO. (1995a). ISO/IEC JTC1/SC21. Information Technology. Open Systems Interconnection - Management Information Services - Structure of Management Information - Part 7: General Relationship Model. ISO/IEC 10165- 7.

ISO. (1995b). ISO/IEC JTC1/SC21. Open Distributed Processing - Reference Model: Part 2: Foundations (ITU-T Recommendation X.902 | ISO/IEC 10746-2).

ISO. (1998). ISO/IEC JTC1/SC21, Open Distributed Processing - Reference Model: Part 4: Architectural Semantics (IS 10746-4 / ITU-T Recommendation X.904).

Kent, W. (1979). *Data and reality.* Amsterdam: North-Holland.

Kilov, H. (1999). *Business specifications.* Englewood Cliffs, NJ: Prentice Hall.

Kilov, H. (2002). *Business models.* Upper Saddle River, NJ: Prentice Hall.

Kilov, H., & Baclawski, K. (Eds.). (2003). *Practical foundations of business system specifications.* Dordrecht/Boston/London: Kluwer Academic.

Kilov, H., & Ross, J. (1994). *Information modeling.* Prentice Hall.

Linstone, H. A. (1984). *Multiple perspectives for decision making: Bridging the gap between analysis and action.* Amsterdam: North-Holland.

Lotman, Y.M. (1964). *Lectures on Structural Poetics (in Russian).* Sign Systems Studies, Vol. I. Tartu, Estonia.

Lotman, Y. M. (1990). *Universe of the mind: A semiotic theory of culture* (A. Shukman, Trans.) London/New York: I.B.Tauris.

Louth, A. (2003, May 30). The unholy market kills divine life of the mind. *The Times Higher Educational Supplement.*

Lovelace, H. W. (2001, July 16). The medium is more than the message. *Information Week,* 74.

Mercer, C. (2002, October 18). A flood of light. *The Times Literary Supplement.*

Minogue, K. (2000, January 14).The escape from serfdom. Giants Refreshed - II. Friedrich von Hayek and the restoration of liberty. *The Times Literary Supplement.*

Mitroff, I. I., & Linstone, H. A. (1993). *The unbounded mind: Breaking the crisis of traditional business thinking.* Oxford: Oxford University Press.

Morabito, J., Sack, I., & Bhate, A. (1999). *Organization modeling: Innovative architectures for the 21st century.* Upper Saddle River, New Jersey: Prentice Hall (PTR).

Murphy, C. & Chabrow, E. (2003) The programmer's future. *Information Week,* November 17. *http://www.informationweek.com/story/showArticle.jhtml?articleID= 16100697*

Parsons, J., & Wand, Y. (1997). Using objects for systems analysis. *Communications of the ACM, 40*(11), 104-110.

Smith, A. (1904). *An inquiry into the nature and causes of the wealth of nations*. New York: G. P. Putnam's Sons.

van Gasteren, A. J. M. (1990). *On the shape of mathematical arguments. Lecture Notes in Computer Science, Vol. 445*. New York: Springer-Verlag.

von Mises, L. (1944). *Bureaucracy*. New Haven, CT: Yale University Press.

von Mises, L. (1949). *Human action: A treatise on economics*. New Haven, CT: Yale University Press.

Wand, M. (2003). *Understanding aspects*. Proceedings of the 2003 ACM SIGPLAN International Conference on Functional Programming (pp. 299-300). Upsala, Sweeden: 25-29 August 2003.

Wittgenstein, L. (1933). *Tractatus logico-philosophicus*. New York: Harcourt Brace.

Endnotes

[1]   *Composition* is a technical term denoting a relationship between a composite and its components such that some (emergent) properties of the composite are not possessed by any of its components and are determined by properties of the components and by the way they are combined (Bunge, 2003; ISO, 1995a, 1995b; Kilov & Ross, 1994).

[2]   As Mario Bunge (2001) observed, Leibniz distinguished *propositions de raison*—which "are proved or refuted by purely conceptual means, namely argument (deduction and criticism) or counterexample"—from *propositions de fait*—which "refer at least partly to real (concrete) entities and … are confirmed or infirmed with the help of direct or indirect empirical observations" (p. 188). Thus, the Leibnizian and Lockean inquirers (Courtney et al., 1998) are perhaps not too far apart.

[3]   Hayek's was "a powerful ancestral voice recalling a straying Western world to the fundamentals that had been so clearly explained by his real contemporaries, the eighteenth-century theorists of commercial society, especially Hume and Adam Smith. …Asked what was the central problem of his intellectual life, he replied: the formation and recognition of complex orders….Competition was a discovery procedure on which progress rested" (Minogue, 2000).

[4]   As noted above, the basic IT modeling concepts and constructs (as defined, for example, in RM-ODP) are the same as the basic business modeling ones. Several sources, for example, Parsons and Wand (1997) and Kilov (2002), demonstrate how Bunge's exact philosophy is directly applicable to modeling in the information management context.

[5]   This often has not been the case in modern information technology.

6   The concept of a viewpoint has been used by Churchman (1971) in the organizational inquiry context: "We also need to design into the inquirer an ability to see the 'same' object from different points of view…. We need to develop the additional idea of an 'object' as a collection of interconnected observations" (p. 149). Exactification of these proposals leads to the need both to create a joint ontology and to compose the viewpoints. Note that the same (exactified!) approach is used in and promoted by RM-ODP.

7   Unfortunately, "the principle of leisure to contemplate is not only not conceded, it is no longer even understood" (Louth, 2003). Karl Marx's quote "the philosophers have only interpreted the world in different ways; the point is to change it," and the Marxist notion of the "intellectual worker" were instrumental in the final defeat of the classical idea of thinking as contemplation (Louth, 2003).

About the Authors

James F. Courtney is professor of management information systems at the University of Central Florida in Orlando, USA. He formerly was Tenneco professor of business administration in the Information and Operations Management Department at Texas A&M University. He received his PhD in business administration (with a major in management science) from the University of Texas at Austin (1974). His papers have appeared in several journals, including *Management Science, MIS Quarterly, Communications of the ACM, IEEE Transactions on Systems, Man and Cybernetics, Decision Sciences, Decision Support Systems, the Journal of Management Information Systems, Database, Interfaces, the Journal of Applied Systems Analysis*, and the *Journal of Experiential Learning and Simulation*. His present research interests are knowledge-based decision support systems, ethical decision making, knowledge management, inquiring (learning) organizations, and sustainable economic systems.

John D. Haynes is currently a visiting professor of management information systems at the University of Central Florida, USA. He was formerly professor and chair in information systems, (information systems and philosophy), Faculty of Humanities and Business at UCOL, Universal College of Learning, Palmerston North, New Zealand. Prior to his UCOL appointment in June 1998, he was at Bond University (Gold Coast, Australia) for just under nine years, where he was foundation head of artificial intelligence (which he inaugurated in 1990). Also, in 1990, he jointly set up the cognitive science course in the School of Humanities and Social Sciences at Bond where he (also) lectured in philosophy of mind (cognitive science). Prior to 1989, he was head of the Department of Computing and Information Systems at the Hunter Institute of Higher Education, Newcastle, NSW, where concurrently, for eight years, he had a private practice as managing director of Mediware Pty Ltd (tailor-made software design, implementation, and programming for the medical profession). He has single authored two books,

Meaning As Perspective: The Contragram and *Perspectival Thinking: For Inquiring Organisations*, both published by ThisOne and Company Pty Ltd, New Zealand, single edited *Internet Management Issues: A Global Perspective*, published by Idea Group Publishing, USA. His papers have appeared in (Australian) *Practice Computing, The Australian and Australasian Journal of Information Systems, IEEE Computer Society Press, Information Systems Frontiers*, and the *International Journal of Business*. He has a (combined) PhD in philosophy and information systems. His research interests are strategic management, e-commerce, the philosophy of information technology, philosophical foundations of information systems, internet management, artificial intelligence, and phenomenology.

David B. Paradice is professor and chairman of the MIS Department at Florida State University, USA. He received his doctor of philosophy in business administration (management information systems) from Texas Tech University. He has worked as a programmer analyst and consultant. Dr. Paradice has published numerous articles focusing on the use of computer-based systems in support of managerial problem formulation and on the influence of computer-based systems on ethical decision-making processes. His publications appear in *Journal of MIS, IEEE Transactions on Systems, Man & Cybernetics, Decision Sciences, Communications of the ACM, Decision Support Systems, Annals of Operations Research, Journal of Business Ethics*, and other journals.

*   *   *

Irena Ali is a defense scientist in DSTO, Australia. Ms. Ali's background is in information management and information seeking. Her work focuses on researching organizational and cultural factors contributing to effective organizational learning and knowledge management. She has published and presented both nationally and internationally in the field of organizational and social learning. In her free time, Irena is pursuing her culinary passion for hot and spicy and enjoys bush walking and snorkeling.

Chauncey Bell is CEO of the design community, a worldwide conversation generating social and business innovation, and managing director of Bell & Associates, Business Design for Innovation (USA). For more than two decades, he has worked with senior executives to transform the skills, processes, and cultural characteristics of large firms in North America, Latin America, and Europe. For more information, visit *http://www.chaunceybell.com*.

Thomas L. Case, PhD, is a professor of information systems in the College of Information Technology at Georgia Southern University, USA. He earned his doctorate in social psychology from the University of Georgia in 1982. His full-time involvement with IS dates from the Basic (1986) and Advanced (1987) AACSB MIS Faculty Development Institutes. His primary graduate and undergraduate teaching responsibilities focus on e-commerce and data communications. In addition to knowledge management and information foraging, his research streams include online shopping and buying patterns, IT evaluation and adoption, human resource information systems, and IS curriculum and pedagogy.

Bongsug Chae is an assistant professor of management information systems at Kansas State University (USA). He holds a PhD in management information systems from Texas A&M University. His current research interests are in the area of large-scale information system and information infrastructure, knowledge management, technology adaptation, decision support systems, and ethics and social theories for IS research. His work also appears in *Decision Support Systems, OMEGA: The international Journal of Management Science, Annals of Cases on Information Technology, Electronic Journal of Information Systems for Developing Countries, Information Resource Management Journal, International Journal of Information Technology and Decision Making*, and *Journal of KMCI*.

David Croasdell is an assistant professor of management information systems in the Department of Accounting and Information Systems at the University of Nevada - Reno (USA). He received his PhD in Information and Operations Management from Texas A&M University. He has also earned an MS in Business Computing Science from Texas A&M University and BS in Zoology from the University of Idaho. Dr. Croasdell's primary areas of research are organizational memory, knowledge management, and inquiring organizations. He serves as the cluster chair for knowledge management, organizational memory, and organizational learning at the Hawaii International Conference on Systems Science.

Margaret Cybulski is a master's student and tutor within the School of Information Systems at Deakin University, Australia. She has over 15 years experience in software systems development and has worked in industry as a developer, business analyst, manager, and consultant. Her professional interests focus on Internet technologies and the business issues associated with the deployment of electronic services. Her current research areas are the human issues affecting the success of knowledge management systems and content management.

Michael H. Dickey is an assistant professor in management information systems in the College of Business at Florida State University, USA. She received her Doctor of Philosophy in business administration (MIS) from Louisiana State University. Prior to receiving her doctorate, Dr. Dickey worked as an information systems professional for 15 years, primarily in the shipping industry but also as a consultant to public and private sector organizations. She has published articles focused on various aspects of distributed work environments and computer-mediated communication in information and management, information systems frontiers, information research, and *Journal of Marketing Channels*.

Kay Fielden holds a PhD and a Postgraduate Diploma in social ecology from the University of Western Sydney, Australia, an MSc in computer science from the University of New South Wales, and a BSc (Hons) from Canterbury University, New Zealand. Currently, she is research coordinator for the School of Computing and Information Technology at UNITEC Institute of Technology, Auckland, New Zealand and is responsible for both staff and postgraduate student research.

Adrian B. Gardiner, PhD, is an assistant professor in the Department of Information Systems at the Georgia Southern University, USA. He earned his doctorate in information systems from the University of New South Wales, Sydney, Australia in 2004. His research interests cover psychological issues in information systems. Some of his current projects include analysts use of online analytical processing, the value of forecast information in decision making, and willingness to participate in online auctions. His primary teaching responsibilities include courses in data management, decision support systems, and systems analysis and design.

Yi Guo (BE, information engineering; MS, management information systems, University of Nebraska at Omaha; PhD, management information systems, Texas A&M University) is currently an assistant professor in University of Michigan – Dearborn, USA. Yi's research interests include e-commerce, online shopping, flow theory, and agent-based systems in knowledge management. Her work has appeared in *Information Resources Management Journal*, *Proceedings of Americas Conference on Information Systems (AMCIS)*, *Proceedings of Annual Hawaii International Conference on System Sciences*, and edited books, *Social and Cognitive Impacts of E-Commerce on Modern Organizations* (M. Khosrow-Pour, ed.) and *Advanced Topics of Information Resources Management Volume 2* (M. Khosrow-Pour, ed.).

Dianne J. Hall is an assistant professor of management information systems at Auburn University, USA. She received her doctorate at Texas A&M University. She has served as an instructor of MIS, computer science, and economics at Texas A&M University in College Station, Corpus Christi, and Kingsville. She has also worked as a consultant. Her work has appeared in books, academic journals, and practitioner publications. Her current research interests include applications of information technologies in support of multiple-perspective and value-based decision-making.

Helen Hasan is IS discipline leader in the School of Economics and Information Systems at the University of Wollongong, Australia. She has a PhD in information systems, is a member of the Australian Standards Committee on Knowledge Management and a member of the board of CTC@Ulladulla. She is director of the Activity Theory Usability Laboratory at the University of Wollongong and director of the cross institutional Socio-Technical Activity Research (STAR) Group on Knowledge Management that is funded, for the next three years, by a Discovery Grant from the Australian Research Council. Helen has published extensively in the areas of human computer interaction, executive information systems and knowledge management and is currently supervising, or cosupervising, 13 research students in these areas.

Alice Kienholz holds a PhD in theoretical and applied psychology from the University of Alberta, Canada, and an MSc in educational psychology from the University of Calgary, Canada. She is founder and principal of Alice Kienholz Associates and has been a certified human resources professional (CHRP) in Alberta for the last 13 years. In the last 20 years, Alice has also been instrumental in the evolution and application of the InQ Educational Materials, where she has worked with their authors in California (USA) to apply them for individual, team, and organizational development and efficacy. Alice has published and presented her work internationally in both psychology and the management of information systems.

Haim Kilov is an independent consultant and an affiliate professor at Stevens Institute of Technology (USA). He has been involved in all stages of information system specification, design, and development. His approach to business and information modeling, widely used in financial, insurance, telecommunications, document management, medical, and other areas, has brought demonstrable clarity and understandability to specifying businesses and systems. It has been described in three of his books published by Prentice Hall in 1994, 1999, and 2002 and in a significant number of other publications. He has also coedited three books on specifications of businesses and systems for Kluwer Academic Publishers. He has been the cochair and proceedings editor for all OOPSLA and ECOOP workshops on behavioral semantics and has been a speaker, tutorial presenter, and program committee member for many international conferences. He substantially contributed to several international standards on open distributed processing and to the work of various OMG working groups and task forces. Haim Kilov is using and extending his approach to specifications in customer engagements and does research and consulting in the areas of business and information modeling. He has been affiliated with Iona Technologies, Bellcore, IBM, and Merrill Lynch.

Sharman Lichtenstein is an associate professor in the School of Information Systems at Deakin University in Melbourne, Australia. Dr Lichtenstein has had a distinguished career in industry, academe, and consulting in computer science and information systems for over thirty years. She first worked as a programmer and systems analyst, moving to academe in the early eighties. She has researched computers in learning, information security management, the influence of the Internet in the workplace, and, most recently, knowledge management in virtual collaborative settings. She is past director of the Deakin Master of Electronic Commerce and currently convenes a research group in knowledge management, which she founded. Dr Lichtenstein has published widely and has presented at many seminars and conferences nationally and abroad.

Martina Sophia Lundin is research assistant at the Department of Informatics, Copenhagen Business School, Denmark. Her research focuses on human communication and interaction within and between organizations. She has written papers dealing with inquiring organizations, one published in IFIP: *Human Choice and Computers – Issues of Choice and Quality of Life in the Information Society* published by Kluwer Academic Publishers.

Ahmed Y. Mahfouz is pursuing his PhD in information and operations management (management information systems track) at Texas A&M University, College Station, Texas, USA. He has an MBA and a BS in management science and information technology from Virginia Polytechnic Institute and State University, Blacksburg, Virginia. His research interests include computer-human interaction (online consumer behavior and Web site design), IT strategy, and interdisciplinary IS research.

Robert M. Mason is professor of MIS and Sprint professor of business at Florida State University, USA. Prior to joining FSU, he served as professor for the practice of technology management at Case Western Reserve University. His background includes being the founding partner of two consulting companies and work experience in industry. His research interests are in knowledge management and the management of technology. He is the past president of the International Association for the Management of Technology and serves as associate editor of Technovation.

John D. Murray, PhD, is an associate professor in the Department of Psychology at Georgia Southern University, USA. He earned his doctorate in psychology from the University of California, Santa Barbara (1989) and did postdoctoral training at the University of Massachusetts at Amherst. His research interests pertain primarily to language and discourse processing, social cognition and categorization, and applications of psychology to information systems. He teaches courses in both the undergraduate and graduate degree programs in psychology. His primary teaching responsibilities include courses in cognitive psychology, research methods, advanced research methods, and introductory psychology.

Craig M. Parker is a senior lecturer within the School of Information Systems at Deakin University, Australia. Dr. Parker was foundation director of the Master of Electronic Commerce at Deakin University and continues to teach postgraduate students in the area of e-commerce. He has spent the last 11 years researching interactive business simulation approaches to teaching university students and business professionals about e-commerce and has published and presented widely in this area at academic venues around the world. He also conducts research and supervises student research projects in the areas of e-commerce strategy, small businesses, and knowledge management.

Ira Sack has been a full-time professor at the Leslie J. Howe School of Technology Management, Stevens Institute of Technology, in Hoboken, New Jersey (USA) for over 20 years where he has taught in executive information management programs at such firms as AT&T, Merck, Solomon Smith Barney, PaineWebber, Prudential, Johnson &

Johnson, and Pearson Education, among others. Prior to his academic career, he was a full-time member of technical staff (MTS) at Bell Laboratories. His current research and publications are centered in organizational modeling, knowledge management, business strategy, organizational ontologies, and diverse areas of information systems. He is a coauthor of the reference text, *Organization Modeling: Innovative Architectures for the 21st Century*, published in June 1999 by Prentice Hall. He served both as principal investigator for two research grants and as a research consultant to the National Agency for Space Administration (NASA) and elsewhere.

Morten Thanning Vendelø, PhD, is associate professor and head of the department at the Department of Informatics, Copenhagen Business School, Denmark. His research interests include IT-entrepreneurship, knowledge networks, organizational learning and adaptation, software-reuse, and the economics and sociology of reputation. He has published his research in books and journals, such as *International Journal of Technology Management* and *International Studies of Management and Organization*. For more information, visit *http://www.cbs.dk/staff/mtv/*.

Leoni Warne is a senior research scientist responsible for leading research in enterprise social learning and knowledge management architectures and the human dimension of decision processes. Dr Warne's research work is primarily focused on the social and organizational aspects of information systems. Her work has been presented in numerous international books, journals, and conferences.

Nilmini Wickramasinghe was born in Sri Lanka. After completing five degrees from The University of Melbourne, Australia, she accepted a full scholarship to undertake PhD studies with Michael Ginzberg at Case Western Reserve University, Ohio, USA. During this time she was involved with many research projects focusing on health care issues. Currently, Dr. Wickramasinghe is an assistant professor in the Computer and Information Science Department at the James J. Nance College of Business Administration at Cleveland State University, Ohio, USA. Here she teaches information systems at the undergraduate and graduate levels in the areas of knowledge management as well as e-commerce and m-commerce, IT for competitive advantage organizational impacts of technology and health care issues. In addition, Dr. Wickramasinghe teaches and presents regularly in many universities in Europe and Australia. She is currently carrying out research and is published in the areas of management of technology, in the field of health care as well as focusing on IS issues. especially as they relate to knowledge work and e-business. Dr. Wickramasinghe is honored to be able to represent the USA for the Health Care Technology Management (HCTM) Association. For more information, visit *http://www.hctm.net/Conferences/2003/Conference_2003.html*.

Index

A

a priori science 302
abstract learning 4
abstract model 339
abstraction 339
abstraction level 344
accountability 259
Ackoff 36
action 200
actionable learning 4
adaptation 233
adhocracy 3
aesthetics 245
agent technology 110
analysis 94, 339
analyst 133, 198
anthropomorphism 344
Aristotelian approach 348
Aristotle 338
arts 238
assertions 249
assessment 236, 249
authenticity 234
authority 94, 236
autopoiesis 7
avoidable complexity 350

B

background knowledge 349
banking domain 339
being 200, 240
being-in-the-world 204
biology 265
Boland 35
brain 250
brain metaphor 13
Buddhist 234
bureaucracies 5
bureaucratic 233
business analysts 338
business patterns 353
business strategy 77
buzzword-compliant concepts 347

C

calculative thinking 204
Canadian Engineers 232
capital expenditures 257
careers 241
change 233, 351
chaotic domains 99
Churchman, C.W. 47, 195, 200, 201,
    230, 340

theme 204, 205
tinkering 352
Toyota 255
Toyota production system 235
tradesperson 352
tragedy 234
traiting 75
transformation pathway 317
trigger 17
triple-loop learning 4
trust 319

U

uncertain environments 28
unconscious level 200
understanding of a domain 339
unity 240
unstated assumptions 349
Upanishads 200
user participation 157

V

Vajrayana tradition 253
values 234
variety 5
Vermont 84
viewpoints 349
virtues 234
virtuoso 254
von Mises 344
vulcanization of rubber 255

W

Wal-Mart 72, 254
waste 247
waste of brainpower 352
well-appointed brain 343
Weltanshauung 305
Werner Ulrich 243
wicked 12, 23
Winograd 253
wisdom 46, 91, 195, 212, 273
wisdom 221
wise guys 238
Wittgenstein 341

workplace design 324
worldview 305

Z

Z based 348

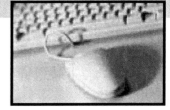